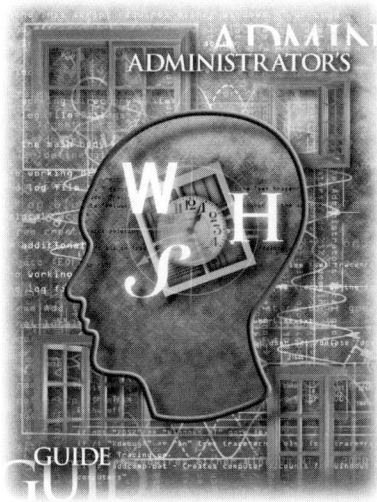

Microsoft®
Windows® Shell
Scripting and WSH
Administrator's
Guide

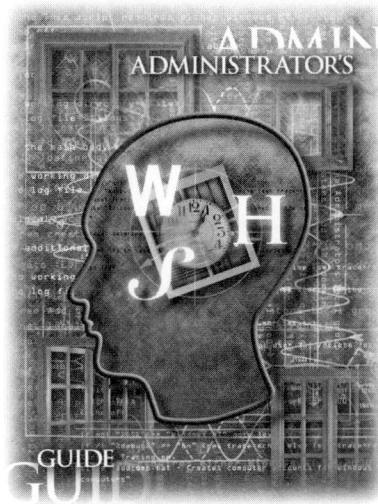

Microsoft®
Windows® Shell
Scripting and WSH
Administrator's
Guide

Jerry Lee Ford, Jr.

Premier

Press

ISBN: 1-931841-26-8

Library of Congress Catalog Card Number: 2001091379

Printed in the United States of America

01 02 03 04 05 HH 10 9 8 7 6 5 4 3 2 1

Publisher:
Stacy L. Hiquet

Marketing Manager:
Heather Buzzingham

Managing Editor:
Sandy Doell

Acquisitions Editor:
Lynette Quinn

Project Editors:
Heather Talbot
Kelly Talbot

Technical Reviewer:
Zac Hester

Copy Editor:
Kezia Endsley

Interior Layout:
LJ Graphics, Susan Honeywell

Cover Design:
Michael Tanamachi

Indexer:
Sharon Hilgenberg

Proofreader:
Jenny Davidson

Dedication

To Mary, Alexander, and William.

Acknowledgments

There are a number of individuals who deserve credit for their work on this book. I especially want to thank Lynette Quinn for her work as acquisitions editor and Kelly Talbot for serving as the book's project editor. I also want to acknowledge the book's copy editor, Kezia Endsley, and its technical editor, Zac Hester. Thanks also goes to everyone else at Premier Press for all their hard work.

About the Author

Jerry Lee Ford, Jr. is an author, educator, and IT professional with over 13 years experience in information technology. Jerry is an MCSE and has earned a Masters in Business Administration from Virginia Commonwealth University in Richmond, Virginia. Jerry is also the author of several other books, including *Learn JavaScript In a Weekend*. Jerry lives in Richmond, Virginia, with his wife, Mary, and their sons William and Alexander.

Contents

Chapter 13 Working with Files and Folders. 289

Introduction

Windows shell scripting and the Windows Script Host, or WSH, are powerful scripting languages that enable users and administrators to automate many mundane and repetitive tasks. Scripting makes you more efficient by enabling you to develop scripts that perform tasks in seconds that otherwise might take hours. Scripts are not only more efficient, but they reduce the possibility of error and ensure a consistent methodology.

Perhaps most importantly, scripts save you valuable time and energy. Once written, a script can be executed as many time as necessary, whereas a manual procedure will have to be performed from start to finish, time and time again. While scripts can be used to develop incredibly complex and detailed processes, you will find that most scripts are usually rather small, sometimes as brief as a few dozen lines. This makes them perfect for developing small, time-saving programs that would take too long to develop and test in other programming languages such as C++ or Visual Basic.

Windows shell scripting and the WSH represent two separate and distinct scripting technologies available for Windows operating systems. Each scripting technology has its strengths and weaknesses. It is the mission of this book to guide you through a detailed examination of both technologies and to show you how you can use them to make your work easier and more enjoyable.

What This Book Is About

This book is about learning to write scripts using the Microsoft Windows shell scripting language and the WSH. The book's primary focus is to show you, step by step, how to develop automated procedures that will assist you in running your computer or administering your local area network.

This book is designed to present you with everything that you need to know from the ground up. In addition to providing instruction on the basics of scripting, it provides complete script language references for Windows Shell scripting and the two default WSH scripting languages, JScript and VBScript. This book explains concepts and reinforces them with examples without assuming that you are already familiar with every little Windows nuance.

By the time that you have finished reading this book, you will have acquired the following knowledge and skills:

◆ An understanding of the Windows command shell and its programming environment.

◆ A knowledge of the Windows operating system and network commands.

◆ An understanding of Windows shell scripting syntax.

◆ An exposure to all the programming statements that comprise the Windows shell scripting language and an understanding of how to use them.

◆ The ability to write shell scripts that automate the creation of user accounts, perform disk drive and printer administration, and a host of other administrative tasks such as managing network sessions, system services, event logs, and so on.

◆ An exposure to all the programming statements that comprise the Windows JScript and VBScript languages and an understanding of how to use them.

◆ The ability to develop WSH scripts using either the JScript or VBScript scripting language.

◆ An understanding of how to combine both JScript and VBScript into Windows Script Files that leverage the strengths of both languages.

◆ Knowledge of how to script the administration of the Windows file system.

◆ The ability to read, write, and append to files and to create logs and reports for your scripts.

◆ An understanding of how to administer various components of the Windows desktop including shortcuts, the start Menu, and the Quick Launch bar.

◆ The ability to develop scripts using either JScript or VBScript that can create user accounts, administer the Windows file system, and perform printer administration and a number of other administrative activities.

◆ An understanding of how to integrate the WSH with the Windows shell.

Who Should Read This Book?

This book is for anyone who needs or wants to start automating tasks on Windows operating systems and local area networks. It provides the background needed by both power users and entry-to-intermediate level system and network administrators.

You will need a basic understanding of computer terminology and concepts. You should know how to perform other user-related procedures such as manually creating shortcuts, configuring the Start menu, and copying, moving, and deleting Windows files and folders. In addition, it would help if you already have knowledge of how to do various Windows administration tasks such as performing disk and printer management, reading events logs, and administering user accounts.

This book provides a review of scripting basics and is designed to provide you with the prerequisite programming knowledge that you will require. However, it would be beneficial if you already have exposure to one other programming language. While knowledge of another computer programming language is not a prerequisite for success, it will make your learning experience a little easier and less stressful. Do not worry if you lack this experience; everybody has to start somewhere, and Windows scripting languages provide an excellent starting point.

What You Need to Begin

If you are working with Windows NT 4, 2000, or XP, you already have everything that you need to begin developing Windows shell scripts. If you plan to work with WSH, you will need to make sure that it is installed on your computer. Windows ME and 2000 ship with WSH 2.0, which is the most current release. Windows 98 supplies WSH 1.0. However, you will want to visit the Microsoft Windows Scripting Technologies Web site at http://msdn.microsoft.com/scripting and download and install WSH 2.0. If you are a Windows 95 or Windows NT 4 user, you will want to download and install WSH 2.0 as well.

You will also need a good text editor. The Windows Notepad will serve this purpose well, although you might prefer to use a more advanced scripting editor. As long as the editor can save files as plain text files, you may use it.

You will need access to a local area network in order to test some of the concepts presented in the book. While certainly beneficial, network access is not a not a requirement, as most concepts can adequately be practiced on a standalone computer.

Finally, if you intend to develop scripts that will run on multiple operating systems, you will want to have access to computers running each operating system that you intend to support.

How This Book Is Organized

The book is organized in four parts. Part I provides an introduction and overview of Windows scripting technologies. Part II focuses on Windows shell scripting. Part III covers the Windows Script Host. In addition, Part IV contains a number of appendices that provide language references for the Windows shell scripting, JScript, and VBScript languages.

The basic outline of the book is presented below:

◆ **Chapter 1, "Getting Started with Windows Scripting."** This chapter introduces the reader to Windows shell scripting and the Windows Script Host. It identifies which operating systems are compatible with which scripting option and provides a list of things that scripts are capable of performing. The chapter also provides a brief history of scripting on Windows operating systems and tells the reader where to find the book's source code and where on the Internet to find additional scripting resources.

◆ **Chapter 2, "Overview of Shell Scripting and WSH."** This chapter provides a basic overview of Microsoft's two scripting options: shell scripting and the Windows Script Host. The first portion of the chapter explains the basic components of the shell environment and how they work together. The rest of the chapter is devoted to the Windows Script Host. It includes an overview of WSH components and explains the reasons for using one component over another. The chapter ends with a discussion of the two default scripting engines supplied with WSH.

◆ **Chapter 3, "Getting Comfortable with the Command Shell Environment."** This chapter begins to delve deeper into the specifics of the shell environment. It shows how to start and configure the shell environment and provides a starter set of shell commands that will be used in scripts in subsequent chapters.

◆ **Chapter 4, "Writing Your First Shell Script."** This chapter begins the instruction on shell programming. This chapter's focus is on explaining basic syntax, case sensitivity, and other basic shell programming concerns. It helps the reader develop the first of many shell scripts. It also introduces the reader to several additional programming statements.

◆ **Chapter 5, "Working with Variables."** This chapter introduces variables and variable manipulation. It explains the rules for working with variables and provides multiple examples. It also discusses the differences between local and global variables and the reasons for using each.

◆ **Chapter 6, "Conditional Logic."** This chapter teaches the use of conditional programming logic using variations of the IF statement. This discussion is combined with a review of comparison operators, which, when combined with conditional programming logic, will enable the reader to write scripts capable of analyzing different options before determining which processes to execute.

◆ **Chapter 7, "Iterative Processing."** This chapter focuses on looping logic and demonstrates how to develop small scripts that are capable of processing large amounts of data. The chapter emphasizes working with files and folders.

◆ **Chapter 8, "Organizing Your Scripts with Subroutines and Procedures."** This chapter introduces the use of procedures and subroutines as a means for better organizing scripts and script execution. Topics include argument passing, the localization of variables, and miscellaneous programming efficiencies.

◆ **Chapter 9, "Putting It All Together."** This chapter finishes the book's coverage of Windows shell scripting with a look at error handling followed by a collection of examples that include user account administration, printer management, managing services, shares, network connections, and event logs. The chapter concludes with a demonstration of how to set up the automatic scheduling of shell scripts.

◆ **Chapter 10, "Introducing the Windows Script Host."** This chapter begins the technical discussion of the Windows Script Host. It provides detailed information regarding the JScript and VBScript engines. It also explains the various file types used in creating WSH scripts.

◆ **Chapter 11, "Writing JScript Scripts."** This chapter provides the book's coverage of basic JScript programming. Programming topics include using variables, operations, expressions, conditional logic, string manipulation, looping, procedures, arrays, and the use of pop-up dialogs.

◆ **Chapter 12, "Writing VBScript Scripts."** This chapter provides the book's coverage of basic VBScript programming. It is structured very similarly to Chapter 11. Programming topics include using variables, operations, expressions, conditional logic, string manipulation, looping, procedures, arrays, and the use of pop-up dialogs.

◆ **Chapter 13, "Working with Files and Folders."** This chapter explains how WSH can be used to work with files and folders and demonstrates each concept with multiple sample scripts. It shows the reader how to programmatically manage their files and folders. It also demonstrates how to read and write to files to create reports and logs.

◆ **Chapter 14, "Managing the Windows Desktop."** This chapter shows the reader how to programmatically manage an assortment of administrative chores using WSH scripts. Examples include creating shortcuts, working with windows applications, working with drives, and managing the Start Menu.

◆ **Chapter 15, "Computer and Network Administration."** This chapter supplements all previous examples, providing a comprehensive collection of WSH examples. These examples focus on both local computer and network administration. Examples include account management, working with local and network drives, Windows services, printers, and event logs.

◆ **Appendix A, "A Windows Command Reference."** This appendix provides a complete reference of Windows commands.

◆ **Appendix B, "JScript Language Reference."** This appendix provides a complete JScript reference that includes all of the following categories: objects, properties, methods, statements, and functions.

◆ **Appendix C, "VBScript Language Reference."** This appendix provides a complete VBScript reference that includes all of the following categories: objects, properties, methods, statements, and functions.

◆ **Glossary.** A list of terms used throughout this book.

Conventions Used in This Book

This book uses a number of conventions to help make it easier for you to work with. These are briefly described below:

NOTE

Notes provide additional helpful or interesting information.

TIP

Tips often suggest techniques and shortcuts to make your life easier.

Italics are used throughout the book to highlight new terms and emphasize key information.

W S H

PART I

Introducing Windows Scripting

Chapter 1

**Getting Started with
Windows Scripting**

Despite its ease of use and intuitive design, many tasks are difficult to perform using the Windows *graphical user interface,* or *GUI.* This is especially true for tasks that involve a large number of steps or that are repetitive. This is where scripting comes into play. *Scripting* is a specialized form of programming that enables users and administrators to quickly develop small utilities and programs that automate complex or mundane procedures with minimum investment of time and energy.

Microsoft provides two scripting solutions, Windows Shell Scripting and the Windows Script Host (WSH). Both of these scripting tools have their own strengths and weaknesses. The purpose of this chapter is to introduce you to each of these scripting options and to help you understand when to choose one over the other.

Topics covered in this chapter include:

◆ Understanding what scripts can and cannot do

◆ Reviewing Microsoft Windows operating systems' support for scripting

◆ Reviewing the history behind Windows scripting languages

◆ Comparing Windows Shell Scripting to the Windows Script Host

◆ Organizing and preparing your own script library

What Is Windows Scripting?

In the dark ages of Windows operating systems, Microsoft provided only limited scripting capabilities in the form of simple *batch files*. Batch files were plain text files into which user, and administrators typed lists of commands. When a batch file was executed, the operating system opened it and read and executed each command line sequentially. Batch files had an extension of `.bat`. Batch files were limited in that they executed only command-line instructions and lacked any integration with the operating system.

Beyond this simple scripting capability, you had three options when working with Microsoft Windows operating systems. You could do one of the following:

- Manually interact with the operating system using the graphical user interface or command prompt
- Purchase a software application that provided the required functionality
- Write your own program using an advanced programming language such as Visual Basic or C++

Each of these options had its drawbacks and often required more time and money than people were willing to invest. Working from the command line was tiresome and prone to error while using the GUI took too long. Purchasing new software was not only expensive but for many tasks there simply were no software applications that filled the need.

Enter Windows Shell Scripting and WSH scripts. These scripts are written as plain ASCII text files and can be created using any text editor, including the Windows Notepad program. No other tools are required.

The great thing about scripting is that once you are familiar with the scripting language that you want to work with, you can usually create most scripts in a matter of minutes. In fact, many scripts are no more than 10 to 20 lines long. The same cannot be said for advanced programming languages.

What Kinds of Things Can You Do with Scripts?

The basic purpose of Windows scripting is to automate the processing of tasks, including:

- **The automation of mundane or repetitive tasks**. Using both Windows Shell Scripting and the WSH, anything that you can do from the command line can be scripted. In addition, many of the tasks that you perform from the GUI can be scripted as well. Scripts are especially good at automating simple yet time-consuming tasks such as creating one hundred new user accounts. Scripts can perform tasks in moments that might otherwise take you hours to complete.
- **The automation of complicated tasks**. Scripts can be developed to automate tasks that are subject to human error, thus eliminating mistakes. Scripts also enable you to develop procedures that you can then delegate to less experienced users or administrators.

◆ **The scheduling of off-hours tasks**. Scripts can be scheduled to run at any time. This allows you to set them up to run at times that are most convenient. For example, a script that backs up a server is probably best executed at night when no one is logged on and using the system.

So what can you do with scripting? The following list provides a partial list of the examples demonstrated in this book:

◆ Create user and group accounts

◆ Automate system backups

◆ Manage Windows NT and Windows 2000 services

◆ Schedule after-hours tasks

◆ Manage file systems

◆ Create shortcuts

◆ Work with other applications

◆ Manage local and network printers

◆ Print reports

◆ Gather system information

◆ Manage network resources such as active sessions or shares

◆ Manage Windows NT and Windows 2000 event logs

A Brief History of Windows Scripting

Microsoft's support for scripting has traditionally been lagging. Although UNIX administrators and users have long been accustomed to working with various UNIX shells such as the Korn or Bash shells, it has not been until the last few years that Microsoft has finally caught up. Between shell scripting and the WSH, scripting on Microsoft operating systems is now every bit as powerful and arguably much easier than doing so on other platforms, including UNIX.

Microsoft's support for batch files goes back to the company's MS-DOS days, when simple .bat files contained small lists of MS-DOS commands. The most important of these batch files was the autoexec.bat file. This file was located in the root directory of the boot disk and executed a sequential list of MS-DOS commands during system initialization. Autoexec.bat also played a major role in Windows 3.1, where it was usually responsible for automatically issuing the command to start Windows and for performing other miscellaneous tasks such as loading software drivers, setting the PATH statement, and loading memory-resident programs.

When Windows for Workgroups or Windows 3.11 arrived, autoexec.bat picked up new the responsibility of starting network drivers. Windows 95 signaled the beginning of the end of autoexec.bat. Microsoft began porting the information stored in individual configuration files and batch scripts to the Registry. Although it was still supported, Windows 95 used autoexec.bat to provide backwards compatibility with older applications. If an autoexec.bat file is present, Windows 95 processes it sequentially until all commands had been processed. Windows 98 and Windows Me continue the same level of support for autoexec.bat.

Unfortunately, Microsoft never got around to adding a real batch programming environment to the MS-DOS, Windows 3.X, and Windows 9.X operating systems. However, ever since the early days of Windows 3.1, third-party developers have worked to fill this void. One such developer was Quercus Systems, which developed an implementation of the REXX scripting language for both DOS and Windows.

NOTE

Quercus Systems still provides support for Personal REXX and has added support for Windows NT and Windows 2000. You can learn more about Personal REXX at http://www.quercus-sys.com.

At the same time that it was working on Windows 3.X operations systems, Microsoft partnered with IBM and co-developed the OS/2 operating system. This operating system supported a fairly sophisticated level of batch processing using the REXX script language. REXX scripts were stored in .cmd files. Eventually the Microsoft/IBM partnership broke up and Microsoft began working on Windows NT.

NOTE

You can learn tons more about REXX from the REXX Language page at http://www2.hursley.ibm.com/rexx.

It was not until Windows NT 4.0 that Windows NT had its own true scripting language, shell scripting. Windows NT 4.0 shell scripts are stored as either `.bat` or `.cmd` files and contain support for variables, looping, conditional logic, and procedures. These scripts can execute any Windows command and also work with Windows utilities that provide command-line support.

Scripting and Operating System Compatibility

Windows Shell Scripting has become a core component of the Windows NT, Windows 2000, and Windows XP line of operating systems. Windows operating systems based on the 9.X kernel—including Windows 95, Windows 98 and Windows Me—do not provide a robust Windows Shell Scripting environment. Their built-in scripting capabilities are limited to old-style batch files and specialized scripting support for logon and dial-up scripting. If you need to write scripts in support of these operating systems, you need to install the WSH.

> **NOTE**
>
> Microsoft provides WSH version 2.0 for free, allowing you to install or upgrade to that version on your Windows 95, Windows 98, or Windows NT system. As of the writing of this book, you can download the latest version of WSH from `http://msdn.microsoft.com/scripting`.

Table 1.1 summarizes the compatibility and availability of both of Microsoft's scripting solutions on its operating systems.

Table 1.1 Comparison of Microsoft Operating System Support for Scripting Solutions

Operating System	Windows Shell Scripting	Windows Script Host
Windows 3.X	No	No
Windows 95	No	Yes*
Windows 98	No	Yes**
Windows Me	No	Yes
Windows NT	Yes	Yes***
Windows 2000	Yes	Yes
Windows XP	Yes	Yes

* Available for download at `http://msdn.microsoft.com/scripting`.

** Ships with WSH 1.0. Upgradeable to WSH 2.0 via download.

*** WSH 1.0 installed with Service Pack 4. Upgradeable to WSH 2.0 via download.

Comparing Windows Shell Scripting to the Windows Script Host (WSH)

Which scripting language you should use depends on many criteria, including your own programming background and the strengths of each scripting language. As a rule of thumb, the more complex the task, the more likely it is that you will need to write your script using the WSH.

Before you begin writing any script, it is important that you understand the steps that need to be performed and the logic flow required to carry them out. Take some time to sketch and design your script. Identify major components and think about the process involved. For example, will the script need to run on different types of operating systems? Will it need to perform a lot of file input and output, or is the task something easily performed at the command prompt? For small scripts, this level of analysis might be overkill, but for medium to large tasks, it's best to follow this more disciplined approach.

Use Windows Shell Scripting when:

♦ You need to support only the Windows NT, Windows 2000, or Windows XP operating systems

♦ The task can be performed via line commands

♦ You need to execute a lengthy sequence of commands

♦ You want to schedule commands for later execution

♦ You have to execute a set of commands repeatedly

♦ You are unfamiliar with JScript or VBScript

♦ You want to automate the execution of utilities with command-line extensions

♦ It is acceptable to communicate with users via the command line

Use the Windows Script Host when:

♦ You need to support multiple operating system platforms including Windows 95, 98, Me, NT, 2000, and XP

♦ The task cannot be completed using line commands and utilities

♦ You need to develop complex tasks requiring the extensive programming environment provided by JScript, VBScript, or another WSH scripting engine

♦ You need to work with Windows applications such as Microsoft Office

♦ You need to perform file and folder administration

♦ You need to communicate with the users via GUI dialog boxes

Windows Shell Scripting

In order to develop shell scripts for the Windows NT line of operating systems, you must become intimately familiar with the Windows shell. Accomplished Windows script programmers are users and administrators with high levels of experience and a strong technical understanding of the Windows shell.

The Windows shell provides an interface between the users and the operating system. You can interact with the Windows shell directly from the command prompt, as depicted in Figure 1.1.

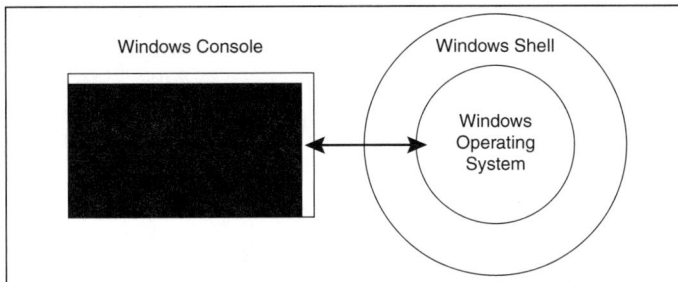

FIGURE 1.1

The Windows console provides an interface to the Windows shell on Windows NT, 2000, and XP operating systems.

The Windows shell provides an interface with the operating system via the Windows command prompt. You access the command prompt from the Windows console, as shown in Figure 1.2. By default, the Windows console is 80 characters wide and 25 lines tall and is highly customizable.

NOTE

For detailed instructions on configuring the Windows console, refer to Chapter 3, "Getting Comfortable with the Command Shell Environment".

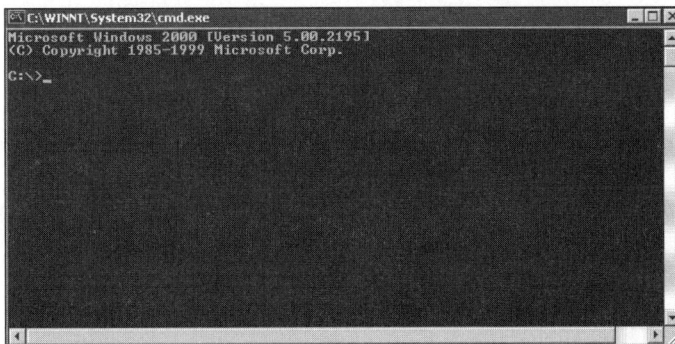

FIGURE 1.2

The command prompt allows you to submit commands for processing by the Windows shell.

The Windows shell translates user commands or script statements into instructions that are then fed to the operation system and executed on behalf of the users or script.

Windows shell scripts are saved as either .bat or .cmd files. The .bat file extension is inherited from earlier Windows operating systems. The .cmd extension has its roots from OS/2. Use of the .bat extension is far more common, but beyond personal preference, there is no technical difference between the two file extensions. (This book uses the more common .bat extension in all its examples.)

After it's created, a shell script runs just like any other application; simply double-click it from Windows Explorer or type its name at the command prompt.

You might also be aware that both Windows NT and Windows 2000 include a 16-bit version of the MS-DOS command shell named COMMAND.COM, as shown in Figure 1.3.

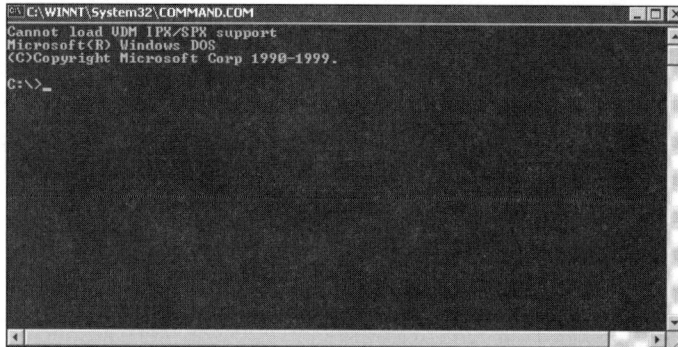

FIGURE 1.3

Windows NT and 2000 also include support for a modified version of the MS-DOS command shell.

CMD.EXE and COMMAND.COM look almost identical. Windows NT and 2000 do not support a true MS-DOS environment, therefore the COMMAND.COM shell has been adapted. When a command is executed in COMMAND.COM, it is actually passed over to CMD.EXE for execution. The results are then passed back after the command has been processed. Unless you have a utility that specifically instructs you to use the COMMAND.COM shell, you should always work with CMD.EXE.

The Windows Script Host

Unlike shell scripts, scripts that work with WSH do not look like the friendly or not-so-friendly commands that you type in the Windows console. Instead, WSH scripts are composed of language statements specific to the scripting engine they are written in. By default, Microsoft includes support for JScript and VBScript. In addition, third-party developers have developed scripting engines for languages such as Perl and Python.

In order to write scripts that work with WSH, you must have a level of knowledge and expertise with at least one WSH compatible scripting language.

WSH also allows you to combine JScript and VBScript into a single Windows script, but this necessitates a working knowledge of both scripting languages. Therefore, unless you have experience with JavaScript or Visual Basic, you have to learn each language before you can leverage the power of Windows scripts. Don't worry, the second half of this book helps you with these issues.

The Windows Script Host is actually a collection of several components, including:

♦ **Core Object Model**. Provided in the form of an ActiveX control named WSH.OCX. This object model provides access to Windows objects that allow you to communicate and control computer and network resources such as local and network disk drivers and printers.

♦ **Execution Environments**. Two execution environments are available: WScript.exe provides the capability to execute scripts from the Windows desktop and to take advantage of graphical pop-up dialog boxes and CSript.exe executes scripts in a command-line mode.

♦ **Scripting Engines**. These are host-independent scripting engines that snap into the WSH and allow you to write scripts using popular programming languages such as VBScript and JScript. Each scripting engine provides its own core set of objects and methods.

NOTE

Third-party scripting engines for languages such as Perl and Python are also available and are discussed in Chapter 10, "Introducing the Windows Script Host."

NOTE

You might be thinking that JScript and VBScript are scripting languages designed for Web page development. You are right. However, Microsoft has greatly extended support for these languages to allow them to function outside the Web browser.

The WScript execution host allows you to develop scripts that can communicate with the users via GUI dialog boxes, as demonstrated in Figure 1.4. With the exception of the WScript's support for GUI dialog boxes, the WScript and CScript execution hosts provide the same functionality and can usually be used interchangeably.

FIGURE 1.4

The WSH WScript execution host supports GUI pop-up dialog boxes and provides an excellent user interface.

Other Scripting Languages

The Windows Shell Scripting language is a core component of Windows NT 4.0, Windows 2000, and Windows XP and is always present on these operating systems. Microsoft supplies JScript and VBScript as default script engines for the Windows Script Host and has designed WSH so that third-party software developers can provide additional scripting engines. This allows the use of other scripting languages such as Perl, Python, and REXX.

NOTE

Perl stands for *Practical Extraction and Reporting Language*. Perl started out as a UNIX language designed to scan text files and extract data and format it into reports. It has since been expanded into a complete scripting language and has been ported over to all major operating system platforms.

Python is a scripting language named after the comedic troupe Monty Python. It is popular among the Linux community.

REXX stands for Restructured Extended Extractor language. REXX has a strong mainframe and OS/2 background and was one of the first scripting languages to be ported over to Windows.

PerlScript

ActivePerl is a complete stand-alone implementation of Perl that runs on the Windows, Linux, and Solaris operating systems. ActivePerl includes PerlScript, which provides a Perl scripting engine for the WSH. The ActivePerl distribution includes comprehensive documentation and instructions for installing ActivePerl.

> **NOTE**
>
> As of the writing of this book, ActivePerl is available as a free download from `http://www.activestate.com/Products/ActivePerl`.

ActivePython

ActivePython is a free distribution of the Python programming language developed by Active State. It runs on the Windows, Linux, and Solaris operating systems. The download also includes comprehensive documentation and instructions for installing ActivePython. This version of Python can function as a stand-alone product or be integrated as a scripting engine with the WSH.

> **NOTE**
>
> As of the writing of this book, ActivePython is a free download and can be obtained at `http://www.activestate.com/Products/ActivePython`.

Object REXX

Object REXX is a stand-alone implementation of the REXX language developed by IBM for the Windows, AIX, Linux, OS/390, and OS/2 operating systems. IBM has extended Object REXX to include integration with the WSH. As of the writing of this book, this support is offered as a beta program.

> **NOTE**
>
> More information on Object REXX can be obtained at `http://www-.ibm.com/software/ad/obj-rexx`. The download for Object REXX's WSH support is available at `http://www-4.ibm.com/software/ad/obj-rexx/download` under the heading of *Object REXX support for OLE/ActiveX automation*.

Each of the preceding scripting language examples integrate with the WSH but are also capable as running in stand-alone mode, which means that they do not require the WSH in order to operate. Personal REXX is another example of a REXX scripting language that supports Windows and OS/2 operating systems. This REXX implementation does not currently integrate with the WSH. However, this does not mean that this scripting language or others like it are not of great value to Windows shell programmers.

NOTE

A trial download of Personal REXX can be obtained at `http://www.quercus-sys.com`.

Building Your Script Library

The best way to learn Windows Shell Scripting or WSH with JScript, VBScript, or one of the other compatible WSH scripting languages is to begin writing your own scripts. Another good way to start your scripting career is to examine other people's scripts and then change them to see what happens.

Building Your Own Scripts Collection

This book's CD contains a Links page that provides links to various Internet sites where tons of example code awaits you. This section highlights a few of these links and provides you with a good starting point for building your own script library. You might even want to submit some of your own scripts to these sites so that you can share them with others.

WIN32 Scripting, shown in Figure 1.5, provides information on shell scripting, VBScript, and JScript. In addition, it provides a lot of information on Perl, Python, and REXX. The site features a script search engine that assists you in locating example scripts. You can then choose between viewing the scripts online or downloading them.

Check WIN32 Scripting out at `http://cwashington.netreach.net`.

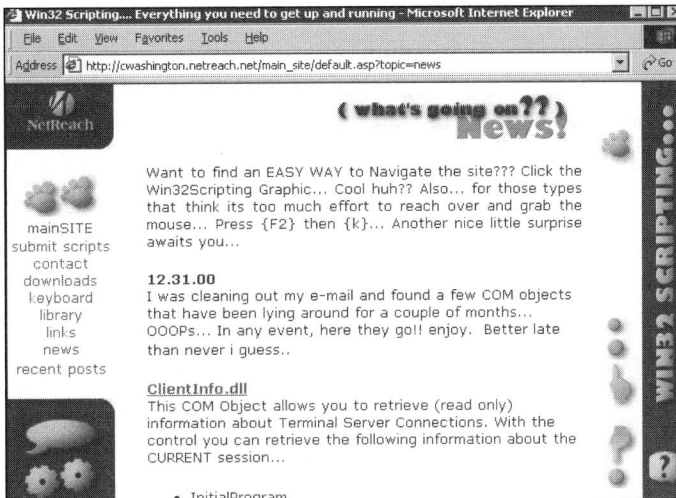

FIGURE 1.5

WIN32 Scripting provides information and examples for all major scripting languages.

Winscripter.com, shown in Figure 1.6, is a good source for WSH information and for obtaining JScript and VBScript examples. It is also a good place to find out about the latest developments. You can find helpful articles and post questions to the site's message board to receive advice from other site visitors.

Check out Winscripter.com at `http://www.winscripter.com`.

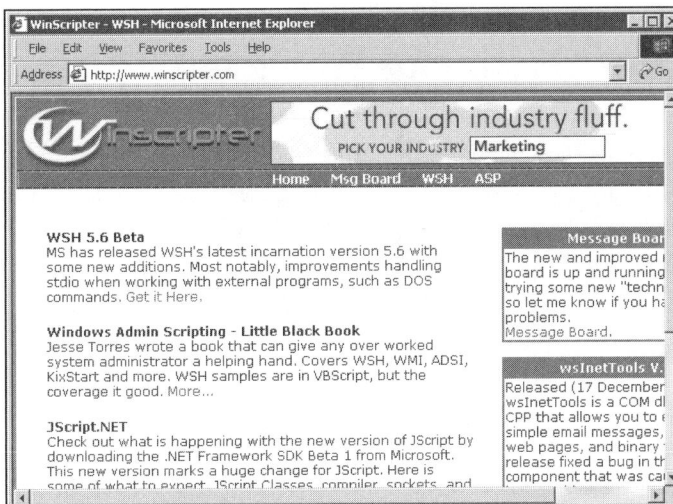

FIGURE 1.6

Winscripter.com features lots of articles and downloadable WSH examples.

Windows Scripting Solutions is a Web site sponsored by *Windows 2000 Magazine Network* (see Figure 1.7). It is a good source for Windows Shell Scripting and WSH examples using VBScript. There is a lot of information on Perl scripting as well. Its main benefit, though, is its abundance of articles. You can also subscribe to the monthly Windows Scripting Solution Newsletter.

Check out Windows Scripting Solutions at `http://www.win32scripting.com`.

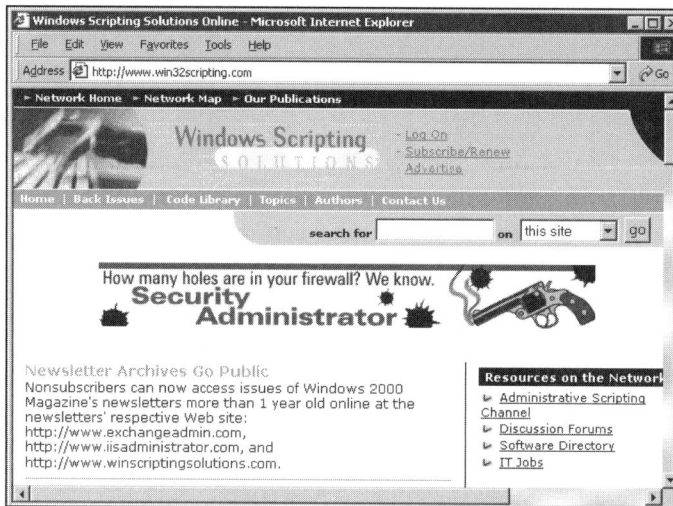

FIGURE 1.7

Windows 2000 Magazine Network *sponsors the Windows Scripting Solutions Web site.*

Microsoft Script Technologies Web Page

The best source for finding more information about the WSH is the Microsoft Windows Script Technologies Web site, as shown in Figure 1.8. As of the writing of this book you can find it at `http://msdn.microsoft.com/scripting`. This site is exclusively dedicated to the WSH. Therefore, you will not find any information about Windows Shell Scripting here.

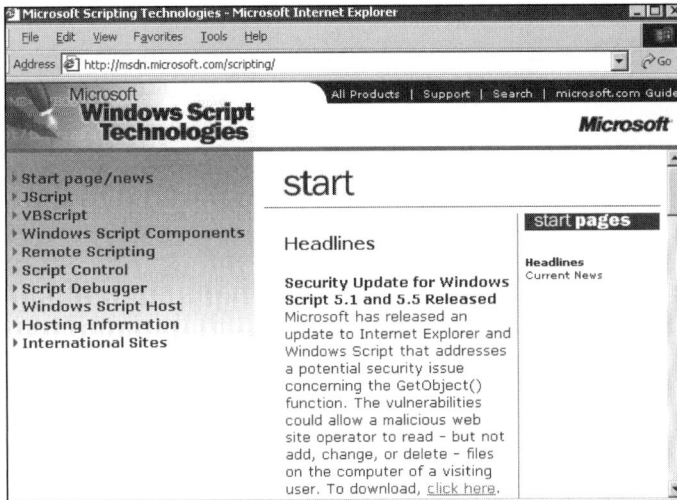

FIGURE 1.8

The Microsoft Windows Script Technologies Web site is Microsoft's headquarters for providing information on WSH.

This site contains an abundance of information about the WSH. Microsoft does an excellent job of keeping this site current with the latest WSH developments. From here you'll find *Current Headlines*, which Microsoft uses as a vehicle for announcing the release of new versions of WSH and scripting engines as well as other major products advances.

The Microsoft Windows Script Technologies Web site is also the place to go when you want to download the most recent version of WSH or one of Microsoft's scripting engines. Other materials include:

◆ JScript and VBScript overviews

◆ JScript and VBScript documentation

◆ Links to other scripting resources

◆ A WSH tutorial

You can also download the latest version of Internet Explorer and the Windows Script Debugger from this site.

NOTE

The Windows Script Debugger is a script-debugging tool that you can use to test and debug your VBScript and JScript scripts.

Microsoft also provides a collection of sample scripts at this site. Most examples are provided in both JScript and VBScript versions. The following list summarizes the kinds of scripts that you find here:

- Sample scripts for adding and deleting user accounts on Windows 2000
- Examples of how to integrate WSH scripts and Microsoft Excel
- Scripts that gather systems information
- Scripts that collect network information about your computer
- An example of mapping a network drive
- An example of how to edit the Windows Registry
- An example of how to create desktop shortcuts

Organizing Your Script Collections

For purposes of administration and organization, consider placing all your scripts into some kind of logical order by grouping them into a collection of directories. Doing so will:

- Make scripts easier to find and manage
- Simplify administration
- Simplify script execution

For example, the scripts provided in this book are stored in a hierarchy similar to the one shown in Figure 1.9.

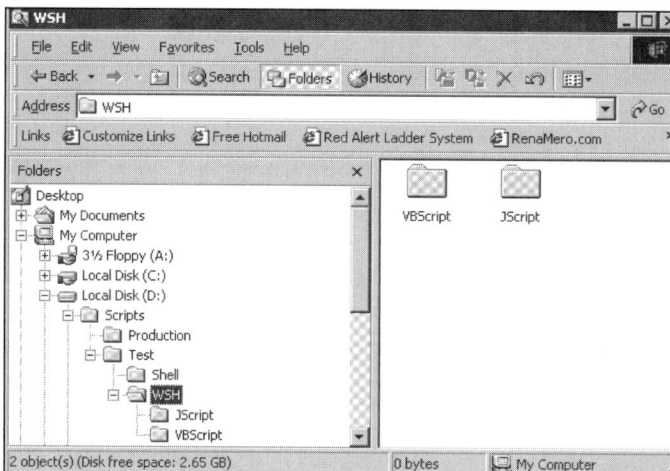

FIGURE 1.9

Consider creating a folder structure that facilitates the management of your script libraries.

As you can see, a folder named Scripts contains other folders that further organize the scripts. The first folder is named Production. This is where copies of all tested scripts are placed when they are ready for production use. The Test folder also contains copies of all scripts, but breaks them down into various categories based on script type and language.

By design, scripts should be written, stored, and tested from these folders and then copied into the Production folder when they are ready for prime time. The Test folder contains two subfolders that further delineate scripts into shell and WSH categories. Finally, all the WSH scripts are stored in subfolders that indicate whether they are written in JScript or VBScript.

TIP

Of course, you need to build this organization structure only on the systems where you create and test your scripts. Other computers, where you distribute copies of these scripts, require only the \Scripts\Production folder.

NOTE

A Windows script is supported by the WSH and allows you to combine Jscript and VBScript into a single script. JScripts have a `.js` file extension, VBScripts have a `.vbs` file extension, and Windows scripts have a `.ws` file extension. The advantage to Windows scripts is that you can develop a script that can incorporate the best of both scripting languages. For more information on the use of Windows scripts files, refer to Chapter 10, "Introducing the Windows Script Host".

Chapter 2

Overview of Shell Scripting and WSH

The first part of this chapter covers topics related to the Windows shell and is specifically targeted at users and administrators who need to write scripts to support the Windows NT, 2000, and XP operating systems. The last part of the chapter provides additional material regarding the Windows Script Host. Users and administrators who work with and support a combination of Microsoft operating systems will want to review this material.

Topics covered in this chapter include:

◆ Stopping and starting the command shell
◆ Understanding command shell processing
◆ Understanding Windows command syntax
◆ Understanding how Windows locates commands
◆ Working with internal and external commands
◆ Examining WSH components

Working with the Windows Shell

The Windows shell is your primary interface for executing Windows commands, Windows shell scripts, and WSH text-based scripts. You interact with the Windows shell using the command prompt in the Windows console. The Windows console is also the default location for all script and command output.

The Windows Shell Scripting language is integrated into the Windows shell and includes a number of internal commands. In addition, the Windows shell can execute external commands, giving it a wide range of automation capabilities.

Starting a Command Shell

The Windows console is encapsulated in a program named CMD.EXE. You'll find CMD.EXE in the `%SystemRoot%\System32` folder. `%SystemRoot%` is an environmental variable that is created during the installation of Windows NT or

Windows 2000. It specifies the location of the operating system. On most computers, %SystemRoot% is the C:\Winnt directory.

There are a number of ways to start a Windows shell session, as follows:

◆ Click Start, Programs, Accessories, and then Command Prompt.

◆ Click Start, Run. Type **CMD** and press Enter.

◆ Double-click a shell script. CMD.EXE will then start, execute the script, and close the Windows console.

◆ Type either **CMD** or **START** in any open Windows console.

NOTE

Starting a new Windows shell from within an existing Windows shell using the CMD command creates a new Windows shell session in the current console window, whereas using the START command opens the Windows shell session in a new Windows console. To test this, open a Windows shell session using any of the previous methods and then type **CMD**. Then type **EXIT** to close the new session and return to the previous session. Next, type **START**. This time, a new Windows shell session is started in an entirely different window. As the following sections show, the default behavior of the CMD and START commands can be changed.

Syntax for Command Shell Commands

Every Windows command has its own syntax. However, all commands follow the same basic set of rules. Windows command syntax consists of a command followed by any number of arguments, as demonstrated in Figure 2.1.

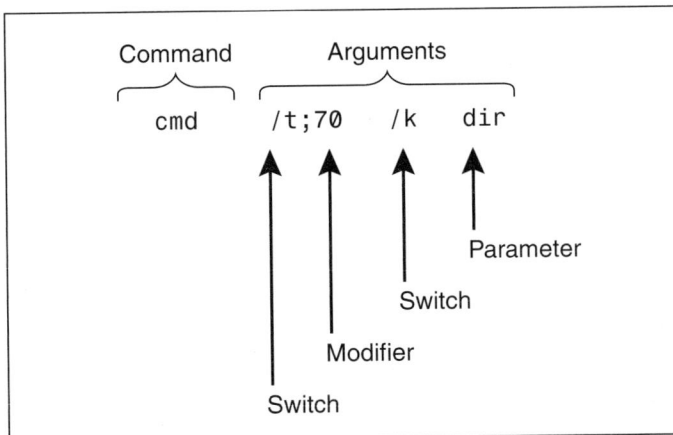

FIGURE 2.1

All Windows commands follow a basic set of syntax rules.

Arguments can include one or more of any of the following:

- ◆ **Parameters**. Arguments that are passed to the command for processing.
- ◆ **Switches**. Arguments that alter the way the command is processed. The format of a switch is a forward slash followed by one or more characters. Each command provides its own set of switches.
- ◆ **Modifiers**. Arguments that modify the behavior of a switch. The format of a modifier is a colon followed by one or more characters. Like switches, modifiers are not universal. Each command supports its own set of switches and modifiers.

The syntax of the CMD command used in the previous example is shown here:

```
cmd [ [/c | /k] [/q] [/a | /u] [/t:fg] [/x | /y] string]
```

The following list of rules further refines Windows command syntax:

- ◆ The command name identifies the command that is to be executed
- ◆ The commands and arguments are separated by spaces
- ◆ Arguments inside brackets are optional
- ◆ Arguments inside brackets but not in italic must be typed exactly as shown
- ◆ Arguments typed in italics are placeholders for values that you are expected to supply
- ◆ Arguments inside brackets but separated by a | sign are *mutually exclusive,* which means that you cannot use both options at the same time
- ◆ Arguments that contain spaces must be wrapped inside double quotes

---

NOTE

Windows commands are not case-sensitive, so you can type any of the following commands and expect the same results:

PROMPT XXX

Prompt XXX

prompt XXX

> **NOTE**
>
> There is no documented maximum length of a command and its arguments. Technically, it is possible to formulate a command that is hundreds or even thousands of characters long.

Microsoft applies a special meaning to some characters. These are called *reserved characters*. These characters include & | ( ) < > ^. In order to use them in a command you can either wrap the argument that contains them in double quotes or escape them. *Escaping* means placing a caret ^ character in front of the reserved character. However, because the caret character is also a reserved word, it must also be escaped in order to be used as a part of an argument. See the following example:

```
C:\>echo This is a caret ^^
This is a caret ^
C:\>echo "This is a caret ^"
"This is a caret ^"
```

Starting a New Shell Session

The CMD command is the most common means of starting a session with the Windows shell. Each new session is independent of any other active session. This means that any changes that you make within the environment of the current session do not impact other sessions. For example, changes made to environmental variables are localized.

If you start a new shell session from an active shell session by typing CMD and pressing Enter at the command prompt, the new shell session loads in the parent shell session's Windows console as a nested session. The new session inherits the current session's environment but any changes made to it are undone when the new session is terminated.

Basically, a copy is made of the current session environment. When the new session terminates, the copy is used to restore the parent session to its previous state. This process holds true no matter how many layers deep you nest Windows shell sessions.

The advantage to nesting Windows shell sessions is that you can make changes without affecting the parent environment, thus localizing changes. When you are done working in the nested shell session, just type **EXIT** and press Enter to terminate the new session and return to the parent session.

The syntax of the CMD command is shown here:

```
cmd [ [/c | /k] [/q] [/a | /u] [/t:fg] [/x | /y] string]
```

CMD accepts a number of switches that alter its execution. The switches are listed in Table 2.1.

Table 2.1 CMD **Switches**

Switch	Description
/c	Executes the command and exits the Windows shell
/k	Executes the command but does not exit the Windows shell
/q	Disables echo
/a	Lists all output in ANSI format
/u	Lists all command output in Unicode format
/t	Sets the background and foreground colors displayed in the Windows console
/x	Enables extensions to the Windows shell required by certain commands (default)*
/y	Disables extensions to the command shell*

*The following commands take advantage of these extensions: `assoc`, `call`, `cd`, `color`, `del`, `endlocal`, `for`, `ftype`, `goto`, `if`, `md`, `popd`, `prompt`, `pushd`, `set`, `setlocal`, `shift`, and `start`.

By default, the command shell opens in interactive mode and displays the command prompt. You can instruct CMD.EXE to execute a command as soon as it starts by typing **CMD** followed by the command, as shown here:

```
cmd /k prompt $d
```

The /k switch is not required because, by default, the CMD command executes the command and leaves the command shell session open. Therefore, the following command produces the same results:

```
cmd prompt $d
```

However, in certain circumstances, you might not want to see the output of a particular command and prefer that the command simply execute and then close the Windows console when it's done. This can be achieved by modifying the command as follows:

```
cmd /c prompt $d
```

The /c and /k switches are mutually exclusive. The /c switch causes the Windows console to terminate as soon as the command is executed.

The following example demonstrates the use of modifiers. In this example, the /t switch, which sets foreground and background Windows console colors, is modified with :70. The colon character identifies the beginning of the modifier:

```
cmd /t:70 /k dir
```

In this case, the second character (7) specifies a background color and the third character (0) specifies a foreground color. This has the effect of changing the Windows console's background color to white and its foreground text to black, as shown in Figure 2.2. Table 2.2 lists the possible range of color values supported by the Windows console.

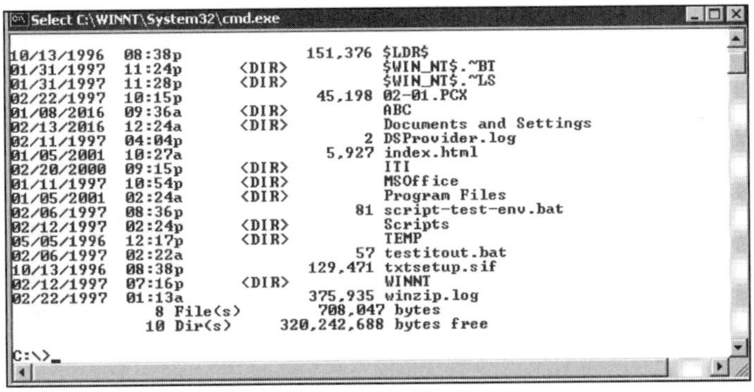

FIGURE 2.2

You can easily configure the command console's properties including foreground and background colors.

NOTE

In most cases you can type command switches in any order. However, this is not always the case and can lead to some confusion. For example, switching the order of the switches in the previous example yields a syntax error when executing the command.

Table 2.2   Colors Supported by the Windows Command Console

Value	Color
0	Black
1	Blue
2	Green
3	Aqua
4	Red
5	Purple
6	Yellow
7	White
8	Gray
9	Light blue
A	Light green
B	Light aqua
C	Light red
D	Light purple
E	Light yellow
F	Bright white

Starting a New Shell Session in a New Console Window

The START command provides another means of starting a command shell. Its benefit over CMD is that it provides additional controls that can be used when starting new Windows shell sessions. Unlike CMD, START always spawns a new Windows console for every command shell session that it opens.

The syntax of the START command is shown here:

```
start ["title"] [/dpath] [/i] [/min] [/max] [/separate| /shared]
[/low|/normal|/high|/realtime] [/wait] [/b] [filename] [parameters]
```

The START command accepts a number of parameters, as outlined in Table 2.3.

Table 2.3 START **Command Parameters**

Parameter	Description
None	Opens a new command console.
"title"	Text to be placed in the Windows console title bar.
/d path	Sets the startup directory.
/I	Passes the command shell startup environment to the new console window.
/min	Minimizes the console window.
/max	Maximizes the console window.
/separate	Starts a 16-bit program in its own memory space.
/shared	Starts a 16-bit program in a shared memory space.
/low	Starts an application using the low priority.
/normal	Starts an application using the normal priority.
/high	Starts an application using the high priority.
/realtime	Starts an application using the realtime priority.
/wait	Starts an application and waits for it to end.
/b	Executes the command without opening a new window.
filename	Specifies the command or program to start.
parameters	Optional parameters to be passed to the command.

The following example starts a new shell session in a new console window, executes the DIR command, and displays a message in the console window's title bar.

```
Start "Welcome!" prompt $d$g
```

The START command supports a number of switches. For example, adding the /min switch to the previous example enables you to open a new Windows shell while keeping the Windows console minimized on the Windows taskbar. Figure 2.3 shows what the Windows console looks like when selected.

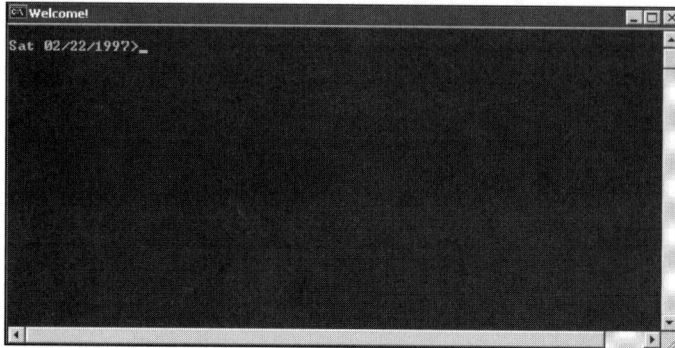

FIGURE 2.3

This example shows the Windows console when it has been restored to normal size.

NOTE

By default, the START command executes a new command shell using the CMD /k command. To change the previous example so that the command shell automatically closes when processing is completed, rewrite the command as follows:

```
Start "Welcome!" cmd /c prompt $d$g
```

Terminating a Command Shell

Regardless of how you start a session, you can always terminate it by typing **EXIT** at the command prompt and pressing Enter. You can also close the command console, thus terminating the shell session, by right-clicking the title bar and selecting Close or by clicking the Close button in the upper-right corner of the Windows console.

Command Shell Modes

By default, the command shell opens in *interactive mode,* as shown here:

```
Microsoft Windows 2000 [Version 5.00.2195]
(C) Copyright 1985-1999 Microsoft Corp.


C:\>_
```

In interactive mode, the command console presents the command prompt and a blinking cursor indicating that it is ready to process any keyboard input. The shell automatically switches to *batch* or *script* mode when a script is started.

Instead of waiting for keyboard input, the command shell begins reading and interpreting each line in the script and executing it as a command until it reaches the end of the script. The command shell automatically switches back to interactive mode when the script ends.

Figure 2.4 depicts the behavior of the command shell in both interactive and batch modes

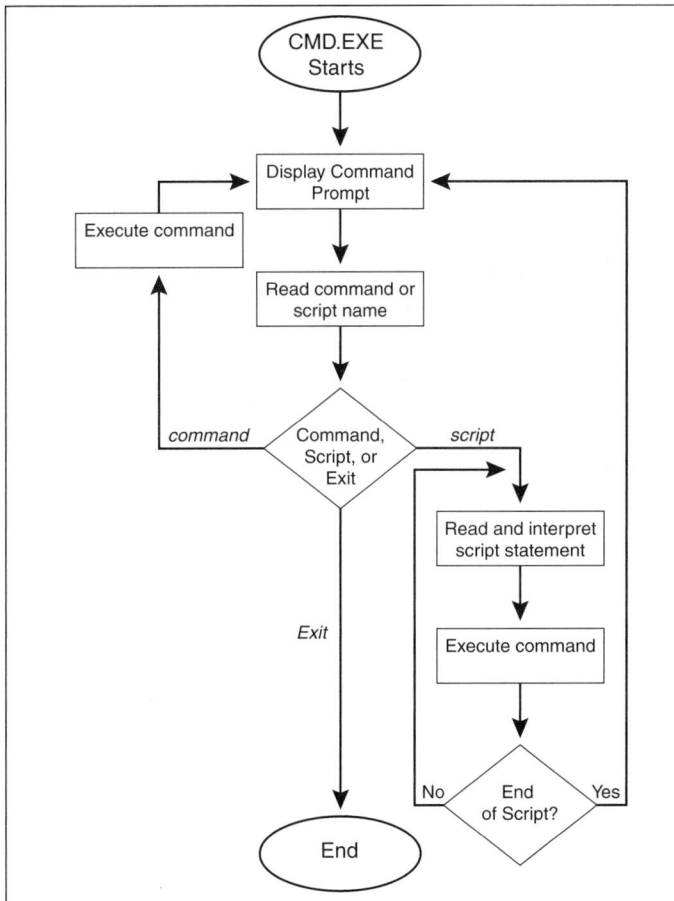

FIGURE 2.4

Shell processing varies depending on whether it is in interactive or script mode.

NOTE

You can pause the Windows console by pressing Ctrl+S and resume it by pressing Ctrl+S again. This is especially useful when you are working with commands that produce a lot of output or when you are executing long running scripts.

The default startup mode for the command shell is the interactive mode as evidenced by the display of the command prompt. At this point the command shell is ready to accept input. For example, try typing **TITLE My command console**. The TITLE command changes the title displayed in the Windows console's title bar, as demonstrated in Figure 2.5.

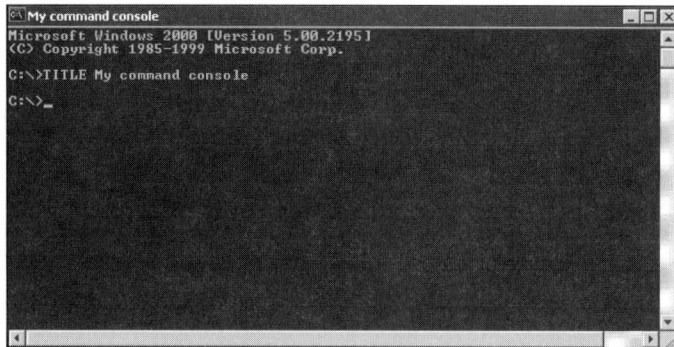

FIGURE 2.5

You can customize the command console title bar with the TITLE *command to display any message that you want.*

The command is interpreted and executed as soon as you press Enter. Once the command has been processed, the command shell displays the command prompt again, which indicates that it is ready to accept new input.

If the command that is entered is the name of a script, the shell switches into batch or script mode. The shell then begins reading and interpreting each line of the script one line at a time and continues until all the lines have been processed. When the script ends, the command prompt is again displayed and the command shell returns to interactive mode.

The Command Prompt

The default command prompt is displayed in the form of a drive letter followed by a colon, a backward slash, and a greater than character. In most cases it will look like C:\>.

You can change this composition of the command prompt using the PROMPT command. The syntax of the PROMPT command is:

PROMPT [*text*]

text can be any characters that you want to include. For example, type **PROMPT Jerry:** and press Enter. This changes the prompt as shown:

C:\>**prompt Jerry:**

Jerry:

Typing **PROMPT** by itself changes the command prompt back to its default setting:

Jerry:**prompt**

C:\>

You can add special characters in the text portion of the PROMPT command to display an assortment of information in the command prompt, as listed in Table 2.4. For example, using the dg special characters, you can change the command prompt to display the current day of the week and time followed by the greater than sign.

C:\>**prompt dg**

Mon 02/17/1997>

Table 2.4 Special Command Prompt Characters

Character	Description
$a	& - Ampersand character
$b	| - Pipe character
$c	(- Left parenthesis character
$d	The Current date
$e	ANSI escape code 27
$f	) - Right parenthesis character
$g	> - Greater-than character (greater-than sign)
$h	Backspace character
$l	< - Less-than character (less-than sign)
$m	The UNC name for the current drive
$n	The current drive name
$p	The current drive and path names
$q	= - Equal character (equal sign)
$s	Blank space
$t	The current system time
$v	The Windows NT or Windows 2000 version number
$_	Inserts a new line
$$	$ - Dollar character (dollar sign)
$+	Displays a + sign representing the depth of the pushd stack.*

* More information is available on pushd in Chapter 8, "Organizing Your Scripts with Subroutines and Procedures."

Windows Commands

The Windows NT 4.0 and Windows 2000 shells support two types of commands: internal and external. *Internal commands* are built into the shell (CMD.EXE). *External commands* exist as executable files somewhere on your computer's hard drive. Typically most commands reside in \Winnt\System32.

For example, `ping`, `netstat`, and `tracert` are all external network-related commands found in this directory.

The syntax for internal and external commands is the same and typically you need not be aware of what type of command you are working with. However, because it is conceivable that someone might delete an external command it is possible that some external commands might not be available to your scripts, whereas the internal commands are always present.

NOTE

If your script fails when attempting to use external commands, it might be that they have been locked down for security reasons. Check the command's security permissions and make sure that you have the appropriate permission to access and execute the command.

To view a complete list of commands for Windows 2000, select Start, Help, and then the Index properties sheet, as shown in Figure 2.6. Then type **Command Reference** and press the Enter key.

NOTE

In Windows NT 4.0, select Start, Help, and select the Contents property sheet. Next double-click the Windows NT Command and select Windows NT Command and click Display.

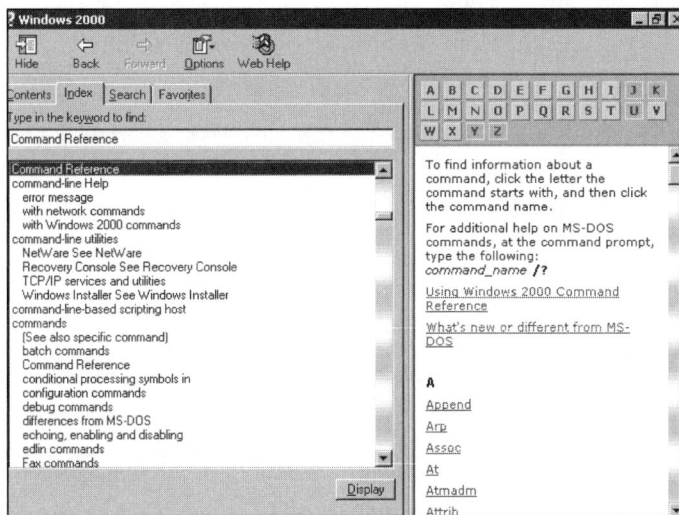

FIGURE 2.6

Windows 2000 provides a command reference to all internal and external commands.

Windows 2000 and Windows NT 4.0 support the same set of internal commands. Table 2.5 provides a brief description of each internal command.

Table 2.5   Internal Windows Shell Commands

Command	Description
Assoc	Displays and changes file name extension associations.
Call	Calls one script from another without stopping the calling script. In Windows 2000, the `call` command also allows calls to labels within a script.
Cd	Changes the current directory.
Chdir	Changes the current directory.
Cls	Clears the screen and displays the command prompt.
Color	Sets the foreground and background colors for the Windows console.
Copy	Copies files from one location to another.
Date	Displays or changes the date.
Del	Deletes one or more files.
Dir	Displays a listing for the specified directory.
Echo	Enables or disables command echoing.
Endlocal	Terminates the localization of changes in a script and restores the variables to their settings before the preceding `setlocal` command was executed.
Erase	Deletes one or more files.
Exit	Terminates the Windows console and closes the command shell.
For	Executes a command for each file in a set of files.
Ftype	Displays and changes file types that are used to associate file name extensions.
Goto	Changes processing flow in a script to a line marked with a label.
If	Performs conditional processing in scripts and alters logic flow based on tested results.
Md	Creates a directory or subdirectory.
Mkdir	Creates a directory or subdirectory.
Move	Moves files from one location to another.
Path	Establishes a search path that Windows uses to locate executable files.
Pause	Suspends script execution until the user presses a key to resume processing.

Table 2.5 Internal Windows Shell Commands

Command	Description
Popd	Changes the current directory to the directory stored by a corresponding pushd command.
Prompt	Changes the Windows command prompt.
Pushd	Changes to a specified directory and stores the previous directory for later reference by the popd command.
Rd	Deletes a specified directory.
Rem	Allows comments to be added to scripts.
Ren	Renames a file or folder.
Rename	Renames a file or folder.
Rmdir	Deletes a specified directory.
Set	Displays, creates, modifies, and deletes variables.
Setlocal	Records the value of environment variables in the Windows shell so that they can later be restored to their previous values by the endlocal command.
Shift	Changes the position of parameters in a script.
Start	Starts a new command shell and executes specified commands.
Time	Sets and displays the time.
Title	Changes the title displayed in the Windows console.
Type	Displays the contents of a text file without opening it.
Ver	Displays the Windows version number.

Refer to Appendix A, "A Windows Command Reference," for more detailed information about all the Windows 2000 and Windows NT 4.0 internal and external commands.

Working with PATH and PATHEXT

To understand how the Windows shell locates commands, you need to be familiar with the PATH and PATHEXT variables. The PATH variable contains a list of directories, called the *search path*, that the shell can search when looking for commands. To see the contents of the PATH variable, type **PATH** at the command prompt and press Enter as demonstrated:

```
C:\>path
PATH=C:\WINNT\system32;C:\WINNT;C:\WINNT\system32\WBEM
```

Here, the PATH variable defines three directories, each of which is separated by a semicolon:

```
C:\Winnnt\system32
C:\Winnt
C:\Winnt\system32\wbem
```

The directories defined in the PATH variable are searched in the order in which they are listed. The PATH variable is created from several sources, including the hardware information that is gathered during system initialization and stored in the Registry in the HKEY_LOCAL_MACHINE key and user information collected during login and stored in the HKEY_LOCAL_USER key. Additional PATH information can also come from the PATH statement in AUTOEXEC.BAT if such a file is present.

You can reference variables in shell scripts by placing variable names in between percent signs. So the PATH variable is referenced inside a script as %path%. Finally, you can also supply path information using the PATH command. For example, to add the C:\scripts\production path to the end of the search list, you type:

```
path %path%;C:\scripts\production
```

Similarly you can put the new PATH statement at the beginning of the search list by typing the following:

```
path C:\scripts\production;%path%
```

Notice that a semicolon separates the PATH commands.

TIP

Always remember to include the word %path% when adding new path statements to the PATH variable. If you forget to add it, you will delete the original search path and be left with only your modifications.

NOTE

Chapter 1 discussed the idea of grouping all your scripts into a common set of folders. Chapter 1 suggested using a \scripts\production folder, in which copies of all completed scripts are found. Modifying the PATH statement via %path%;C:\scripts\production places this folder into the shell search path. This makes it easy for the shell to find your scripts.

The PATHEXT variable lists all the file extensions that Windows associates with executable files. By default, the PATHEXT variable includes the following list of file extensions:

- .com
- .exe
- .bat
- .cmd

You can add to this list using the SET command. For example, if you wanted to add .scr as a new file extension for your shell scripts you would type the following:

```
pathext=%pathext%;.scr
```

NOTE

Additional executable file extensions might be included on your PATHEXT variable as a result of installing other applications. For example, installing the WSH automatically adds the .js, .vbs, .ws, and .wsh extensions. File extensions are substituted and tested in the order in which they are listed in the PATHEXT variable.

How the Command Shell Finds Commands

When you type a command at the command prompt in the Windows console, it is passed to the Windows shell. The Windows shell then proceeds through the following steps until it finds the command or fails:

1. All variables in the command are replaced with their values.
2. If multiple commands were included on the same line (separated by semicolons, of course), they are separated into distinct statements for individual processing.

3. If the command included a path, the command shell searches that path for the command and executes it. If the command shell doesn't find the command, it fails and an error is generated.

4. If the command does not include a path, the Windows shell determines whether the command is an internal command. If there is a match, the command is executed. Otherwise, the Windows shell keeps looking.

5. The Windows shell next checks the current directory and executes the command if found there.

6. Finally, if the command still has not been located, the Windows shell checks each directory listed in the PATH variable in the order in which the directories are listed. The command is executed from the first directory in which it is found. If it is not found, an error is reported.

NOTE

If you type the name of a script without adding its file extension and press Enter, the shell will automatically try to locate a matching file by substituting the file extensions listed in the PATHEXT variable one at a time in the order they are listed.

TIP

User information will not be available for scripts that run when users are not logged in to the computer. You need to keep this in mind when developing scripts that you plan to run during off hours.

NOTE

Each instance of the command shell that you open is isolated from other instances. Therefore, any changes that you make to the PATH or any other variable are local to the particular Windows shell where the changes were made.

Windows Script Host Components

The WSH runs as a 32-bit application on Windows operating systems. It consists of several components, including:

- ◆ **WScript.EXE**. An executable environment that provides GUI controls.

- ◆ **CScript.EXE**. An executable environment that provides support for character-based scripts.
- ◆ **WSH.OCX**. An ActiveX control responsible for providing a core object model for all scripts.

> ## NOTE
>
> The Windows command shell exists only on Windows NT 4.0, Windows 2000, and Windows XP and is not applicable to other Windows operating systems. If you are only interested in scripting Windows 95, Windows 98, or Windows Me operating systems, you might want to skip the rest of this chapter.

These three components work together as demonstrated in Figure 2.7 to provide a robust scripting environment. The core object model is implemented as an ActiveX control. This object model provides access to Windows-specific resources such as shortcuts, printers, the Registry, and files and folders. Each object exposed by WSH.ocx has associated properties and methods, which WSH scripts can then change or execute. Properties are object-specific attributes and methods are object-specific functions that can be used to affect the object.

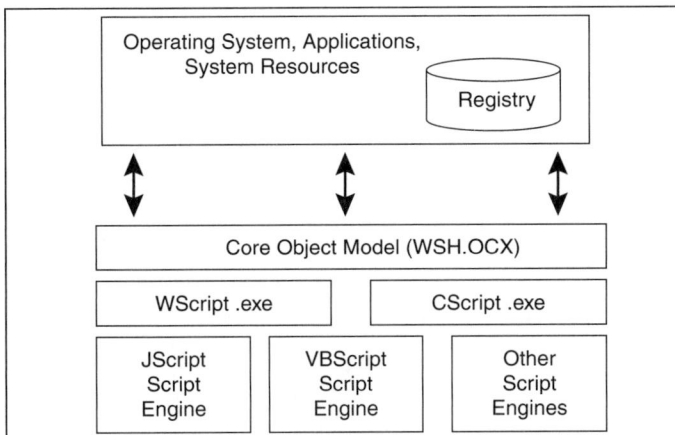

FIGURE 2.7

Overview of the Windows Script Host architecture.

Like Windows Shell Scripting scripts, WSH scripts are text files that can be created using any text editor, including Notepad. Once created and saved with the appropriate file extension (`.js` for JScripts and `.vbs` for VBScripts), WSH scripts can be executed using either the WScript or CScript execution hosts.

Script Host Options

As Figure 2.7 shows, the WSH provides two script execution hosts: WScript and CScript. Both script hosts provide the same basic functionality, allowing many scripts to be executed using either host. WScript's built-in support for GUI dialog boxes makes it the better choice for scripts that must communicate with users, whereas CScript is better suited for scripts that run as scheduled processes or that require no human interaction.

WScript is an executable environment for scripts that display GUI dialog boxes. CScript is an executable environment that provides a character-based interface.

Windows Script Host Engines

Unlike the Windows shell script language, the scripting languages that work with the WSH are syntactically different from normal shell commands. These scripting languages have their own syntax and programming environment with roots more closely related to Web programming than to Windows scripting.

Microsoft reengineered these two languages (JScript and VBScript) to include support for the host-based scripting. This means that WSH scripts written in JScript or VBScript can now access local folders, drives, the Registry, and even network printers and drives.

> **NOTE**
>
> The WSH implementations of JScript and VBScript lack Web browser-specific functionality, such as support for frames or browser objects. These functions are not relevant to non-browser environments.

Instead of embedding JScripts or VBScripts inside Web pages, you now write them as stand-alone components and save them in ASCII text files. These scripts can then be submitted to either the WScript or CScript execution hosts (instead of being processed by a Web browser).

Each of Microsoft's WSH scripting engines provides its own collection of objects and methods and has its own strengths and weaknesses, as outlined in the following sections.

JScript

JScript is Microsoft's implementation of Netscape's JavaScript Web scripting language. The WSH version of JScript is a complete programming language that includes all the control structures that you expect, including flow control, conditional logic, string handling, as well as support for variables, functions, and procedures.

Compared to VBScript, JScript features stronger support for mathematical operations but lacks VBScript's strength when it comes to ability to work with arrays. JScript also has stricter case-sensitivity and syntax rules and, as such, might be considered a little more difficult to learn and use. Of course, JavaScript programmers will probably find that JScript is more intuitive.

JScript files are saved with a `.js` file extension and contain ASCII text with no special formatting requirements.

VBScript

VBScript is a modified implementation of Microsoft's Visual Basic programming language. Besides being the obvious scripting language of choice for Visual Basic programmers, VBScript's syntax structure is somewhat easier to learn than JScript's. Like JScript, it provides a full complement of programming structures. It lags a little behind JScript in its library of mathematical functions, but excels in its support for arrays.

VBScript files are saved with a `.vbs` file extension and contain ASCII text with no special formatting requirements.

The Best of Both Worlds

The WSH also supports Windows script files. Windows script files enable you to combine JScript and VBScript statements into a single script that is saved using a `.ws` file extension. Windows script files use *Extensible Markup Language* (or *XML)* tags to label script elements. This includes identifying one scripting language from another. XML is similar to HTML, which is a markup language made popular by its use on the Internet.

NOTE

Microsoft packages new releases of the JScript and VBScript script engines with each release of Internet Explorer. These engines are automatically installed as part of Internet Explorer's installation process. You can also download the latest version of each scripting engine from `http://msdn/Microsoft.com/scripting`.

WSH

PART II

Writing Shell Scripts

Chapter 3

**Getting Comfortable with the
Command Shell Environment**

efore you begin writing your first shell script, it's a good idea to take a minute or two to familiarize yourself with some of the nuances of working with the Windows shell. A preliminary step to working with shell scripts is to prepare your shell-scripting environment. You will also want to learn how to work with the editing features provided by the shell. In addition to these topics, this chapter also introduces you to several new shell commands and demonstrates their usage.

Topics covered in this chapter include:

◆ Becoming more efficient by using shell editing features
◆ Customizing your environment using the command console's Properties dialog box
◆ Customizing the Windows shell and the command console from the command line

Understanding the Windows Shell Environment

The Windows shell provides a powerful and highly customizable programming environment that includes a full set of editing tools. This section provides a review of the editing features built into the command shell and explains how you can use them to work more efficiently. It also shows you how to create a desktop shortcut that you can then use to create a customized command console.

Working with the Windows Shell

As a shell script programmer, you are going to be spending a lot of time interacting with the Windows shell. To make this experience as constructive and efficient as possible, you need to familiarize yourself with the Windows shell's built-in editing features. It might surprise you to find out that the command shell provides many of the kinds of editing features that you have come to expect from other Windows applications, including cut and paste, command recall, and command history.

Using Basic Shell Editing Features

The Windows shell provides a generous supply of line-editing commands. These include the capability to move the cursor a space or word at a time or to jump to the beginning or the end of a line. In addition to these navigation features, the shell also supplies text-editing capabilities including text insertion, overlay, and deletion. Table 3.1 provides a summary of the Windows shell's editing options.

Table 3.1   **Windows Shell Editing Features**

Editing Feature	Description
Enter	Submits the current command to the shell for execution
Esc	Deletes the command at the command prompt
Backspace	Deletes the character to the left of the cursor
Delete	Deletes the character to the right of the cursor
Insert	Toggles insert mode off and on
Home	Places the cursor at the beginning of the line
End	Places the cursor at the end of the line
Arrow keys	Moves the cursor to the left or right a space at a time
Ctrl + arrow keys	Moves the cursor left or right a word at a time

Recycling Old Commands

Another command shell editing tool is the command history tool. Command history is stored in history buffers, which record every shell command that you type and make them available for later recall. This is especially helpful when you are working with a new command and are trying to format it correctly. Command history allows you to recall, modify, and submit the command as many times as you need until you get it just right.

The size of the history buffer is configured on the Options property sheet on the command console's Properties dialog box. You can also configure the command history dialog box's color scheme from the Color property sheet. These configuration options are reviewed later in this chapter.

The easiest way to access the commands stored in the history buffer is to press the up arrow key. This recalls the previously executed command to the command prompt. Pressing the up arrow repeatedly allows you to scroll through all commands in the history buffer. Press the down arrow key to scroll the other way in the list. Commands stored in the history buffer are copied to the command prompt when displayed in this way but are not executed unless you press the Enter key.

You can also press the F7 key to display the command history dialog box and view the commands stored in the history buffer, as shown in Figure 3.1.

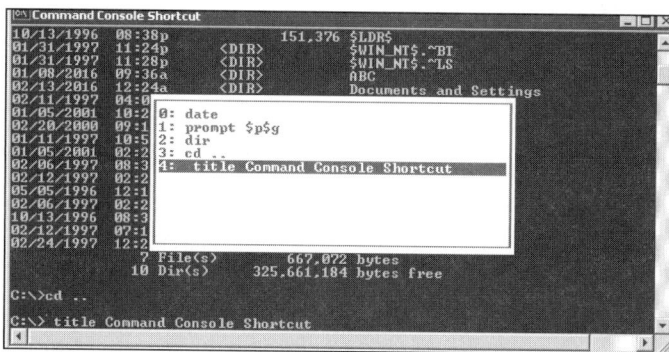

FIGURE 3.1

The command history dialog box provides ready access to previously executed shell commands.

After the command history dialog box is displayed, you can use the up and down arrow keys to navigate up and down the history buffer. You can also use the Page Up and Page Down keys to jump to the top and bottom of the history buffer. To select a command, highlight it and press Enter. The command is copied to the command prompt where you can edit it and then press Enter to execute it. Pressing the Esc key closes the command history dialog box without selecting a command.

There is a number displayed to the left of each command displayed in the command history pop-up dialog box. If you have a good memory and can remember the number associated a previous command, you can press F9 and type the number assigned to the command. The command will be copied to the command prompt where you can edit and run it.

If you have been working for a while and have configured a lengthy history list, finding a command using the previous methods might not be convenient. Another option for recalling previously executed commands from the history buffer is to search the history buffer for the command.

To start a command search, type the first few characters of the command and press F8. The first matching entry in the history buffer is then displayed at the command prompt. If this is not the command that you want, press F8 to continue the search.

Creating a Desktop Shortcut for the Command Console

You can start a new command console on Windows 2000 by clicking Start, Programs, Accessories, and then Command Prompt or by selecting Start, Programs, Command Prompt on Windows NT. However, sometimes having a shortcut on the Windows desktop is more convenient. This provides faster access to a command console and makes customization easier.

The following procedure outlines the steps required to set up a desktop shortcut for the command console.

1. Right-click an open area on the Windows 2000 desktop and select New followed by Shortcut.
2. The Create Shortcut Wizard appears. Type **CMD** in the field shown and click Next.
3. Type a name that identifies the shortcut in the field shown and click Finish. An icon representing the shortcut will appear on the Windows desktop, as shown in Figure 3.2.

FIGURE 3.2

Creating a desktop shortcut is the first step in creating a customized command console.

My Shortcut

To start a new shell session, either double-click the shortcut icon or right-click it and select Open, as demonstrated in Figure 3.3. The command shell opens, displays the command prompt, and is now ready to accept new commands.

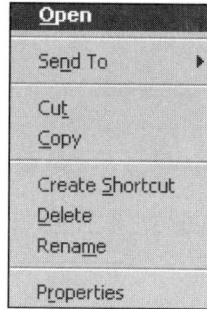

```
Open
Send To          ▶
Cut
Copy
Create Shortcut
Delete
Rename
Properties
```

FIGURE 3.3

Starting a new Windows shell session using your shortcut.

Command Console Customization

The command console is your interface for running and interacting with shell scripts and the Windows shell. The command console emulates a computer terminal and, by default, presents a 25-line by 80-character display that presents white text on a black background. The command console is highly customizable, allowing you to specify colors, fonts, and various behavioral settings.

The command console is customized from its Properties dialog box, which can be accessed in a number of ways, including:

◆ Right-clicking a command console shortcut and selecting properties from the pop-up menu.
◆ Clicking the console icon in the upper-left corner of an open command console and selecting Properties.
◆ Using scripts to execute commands that customize the console.

NOTE

On Windows NT 4.0, you can also configure command console settings from the Console applet located in the Windows control panel.

Saving Command Console Configuration Changes

Making customization changes to a shortcut affects only that shortcut. However, if you modify a command console that you did not open using a shortcut you will be asked how you want the changes to be applied, as shown in Figure 3.4. The first option is to apply the configuration changes only to the current command console, which means that the changes will not be in effect the next time you open a console. The second option is to save the modifications as settings to be implemented the next time you open a command console in the same manner.

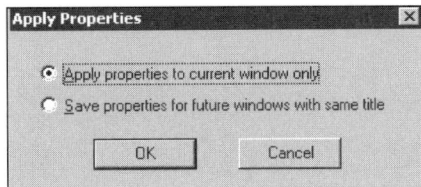

FIGURE 3.4

*Customizations made
to the command console
can be applied locally or
universally.*

Command Console Customization Options

Command console customization is performed using four properties sheets located on the command console Properties dialog box. These four property sheets are listed here:

◆ Options

◆ Font

◆ Layout

◆ Colors

Each property sheet configures a different aspect of the command console; they are outlined in the sections that follow.

Configuring Command Console Options

The Windows 2000 Option property sheet, shown in Figure 3.5, allows you to configure options affecting cursor and window size as well as the history buffer and basic editing options, as outlined:

◆ **Cursor Size**. Changes the size of the cursor.

◆ **Display Options**. Determines whether the command console opens as a window or fills the entire display area.

◆ **Command History**. Configures command history options including the number of commands that can be stored, the total number of buffers, and whether duplicate entries will be stored.

◆ **Edit Options**. Enables or disables the QuickEdit and Insert modes. Enabling QuickEdit mode allows you to cut or copy text and then paste it onto the command line in the Windows console without having to use the Mark command. Insert mode determines whether text is overtyped when editing. Insert mode can also be turned off and on using the Insert keyboard key.

NOTE

The Edit options on the Options property sheet are specific to Windows 2000 and do not apply to Windows NT 4.0.

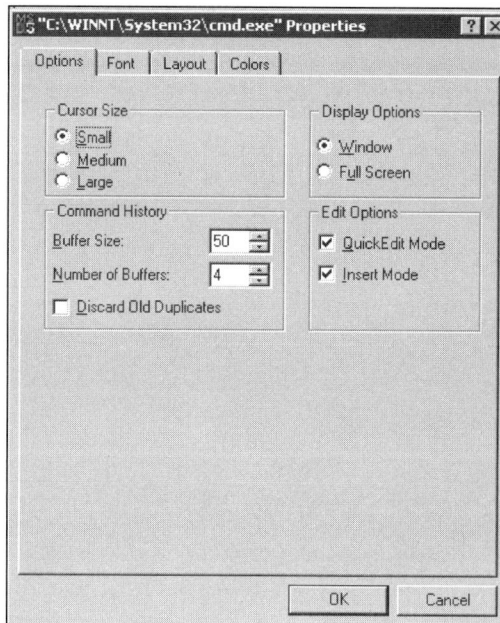

FIGURE 3.5

The Options property sheet allows you to configure the history buffer and basic editing options, as well as specify cursor and window size.

Configuring Command Console Fonts

The Windows 2000 Font property sheet, shown in Figure 3.6, allows you to specify the font size and type displayed in the Windows console. You can configure either of the following options:

◆ **Size**. Allows you to choose from a pre-configured selection of font sizes. This option affects the size of the text displayed in the command console window. In addition, the selected font size also affects the size of the Windows console. A preview of this effect is provided in the Windows Preview field.

◆ **Font**. Displays a list of available fonts from which to select. Depending on the font that is selected, the Bold fonts option might be enabled, thus allowing you to further define the appearance of displayed text. The Selected Font section of the Font property sheet shows how the currently configured settings will appear.

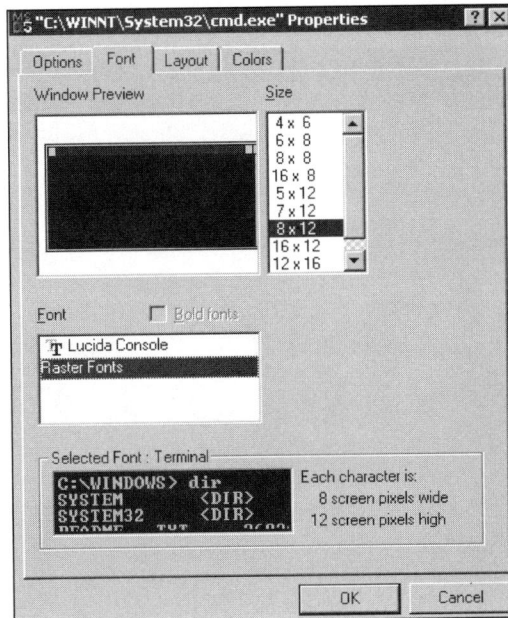

FIGURE 3.6

The Font property sheet allows you to select font type and size and provides a preview of your configuration changes.

Configuring Command Console Layout

The Windows 2000 Layout property sheet, shown in Figure 3.7, allows you to configure the size and location of the Windows console as well as the amount of text that can be displayed and recalled using the following options:

◆ **Screen Buffer Size**. The Width option allows you to specify the number of characters that can be displayed in a single line. The Height option allows you to specify the number of lines of console text that are retained in memory.

◆ **Window Size**. The Width and Height options specify the physical width and height of the command console. The console can later be resized up to the size of the display area or the size of the area established by the screen buffer settings, whichever is smaller.

◆ **Window Position**. Determines the initial location of the command console in the display area as specified in pixels, beginning in the upper-left corner.

◆ **Let System Position Window**. Gives control of the initial console location to the operating system.

TIP

Setting the Screen Buffer Size Height setting larger than the height of the Window Size setting allows you to scroll back and view previous commands or output. This is especially useful when you execute commands that produce a great deal of output. Try changing this setting to at least two or three times the value of the Window Size Height value as a good starting point.

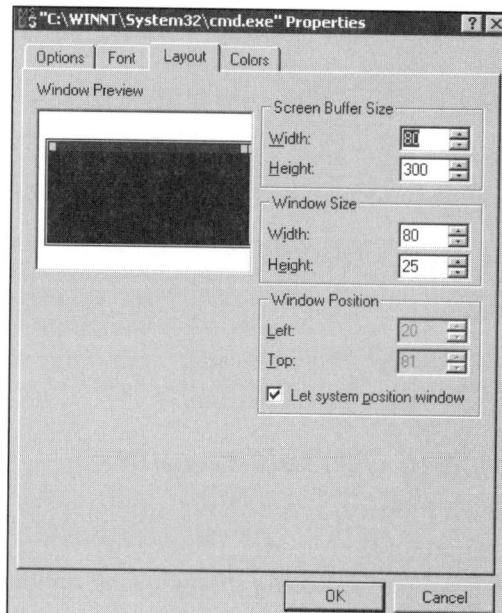

FIGURE 3.7

The Layout property sheet lets you configure logical and physical screen size as well as the initial position of the command console.

Configuring Command Console Color Schemes

The Windows 2000 Colors property sheet, shown in Figure 3.8, allows you to configure the text and background color scheme for the command console and the pop-up window used by the command history feature. The following options are available:

- ◆ **Screen Text**. Allows you to specify the color of the text as it appears in the command console. You can select a color from the color palette in the middle of the property sheet or specify a custom color in the Selected Color Values section.

- ◆ **Screen Background**. Allows you to specify a color for the console window's background. You can select a color from the color palette in the middle of the property sheet or specify a custom color in the Selected Color Values section.

- ◆ **Popup Text**. Allows you to specify the color for text that appears in the command history dialog box. You can select a color from the color palette in the middle of the property sheet or specify a custom color in the Selected Color Values section.

- ◆ **Popup Background**. Allows you to specify the background color displayed in the command history dialog box. You can select a color from the color palette in the middle of the property sheet or specify a custom color in the Selected Color Values section.

- ◆ **Selected Color Values**. Allows you to create custom colors for text and background settings by specifying various levels of red, green, and blue.

The Selected Screen Colors and Selected Popup Colors sections at the bottom of the property sheet preview the selected color schemes.

NOTE

You can also configure the command console's color scheme using the COLOR command, as demonstrated later in this chapter, or by using the /t switch with the CMD command, as discussed in Chapter 2, "Overview of Shell Scripting and WSH."

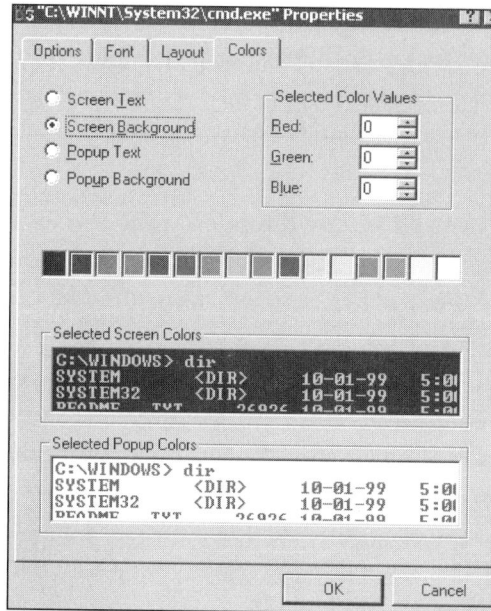

FIGURE 3.8

The Colors property sheet provides control of the color schemes used by the command console and the command history dialog box.

Customizing the Command Console via the Command Line

There are a number of Windows commands that you can use to configure your current shell session. Because each shell session is independent of other shell sessions, changes caused by the command only affect the shell where they are issued. These commands include:

◆ COLOR

◆ TITLE

◆ PROMPT

◆ ECHO

◆ CLS

◆ PATH

The COLOR **Command**

The COLOR command changes the foreground and background colors of the command console. The syntax of the COLOR command is as follows:

Color *bf*

The COLOR command requires two arguments:

◆ b specifies the background color in hexadecimal notation
◆ f specifies the foreground (text) color in hexadecimal notation

Table 3.2 lists the color settings supported by the COLOR command.

Table 3.2 Color Settings

Color	Hexadecimal Value
Black	0
Blue	1
Green	2
Aqua	3
Red	4
Purple	5
Yellow	6
White	7
Gray	8
Light blue	9
Light green	A
Light aqua	B
Light red	C
Light purple	D
Light yellow	E
Bright white	F

For example, the following command changes the command console foreground color to blue and its background color to white (demonstrated in Figure 3.9):

```
color F1
```

> **NOTE**
>
> Windows will not allow you to set the foreground and background to the same colors.

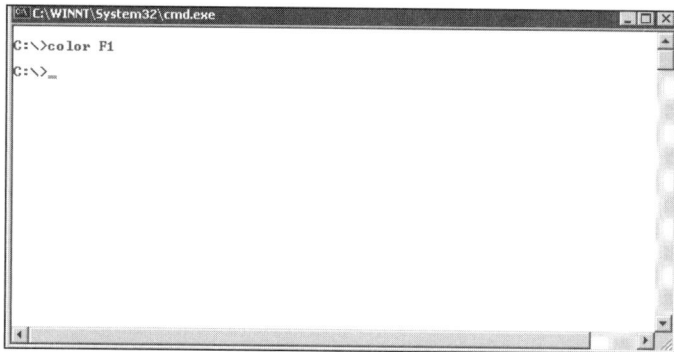

FIGURE 3.9

The COLOR command provides command-line control over the command console's background and foreground colors.

To restore the command console to its default color settings, simply type the COLOR command without any arguments.

> **NOTE**
>
> The default colors for the command console are white text on a black background. However, opening a shell session with the CMD command and the /t switch changes the default colors for the command console. For example, CMD /t:E1 changes the command console's default colors to a light yellow background with blue text.

The TITLE Command

The TITLE command allows you to change the text displayed in the command console title bar. Its syntax is as follows:

```
Title [string]
```

> **NOTE**
>
> The default text displayed in the command console's title bar depends on how you open the session. For example, opening a Windows shell session by typing CMD in the Run menu displays the path and file name of the CMD.EXE executable, whereas clicking Start, Programs, Accessories, Command Prompt displays the words *Command Prompt* in the title bar.

For example, the following command places the words Jerry's Console in the title bar.

```
Title Jerry's Console
```

The PROMPT Command

As you have already seen, the PROMPT command changes the format of the command prompt in the command console. Its syntax is as follows:

```
Prompt [text]
```

text can be any free-form text that you want to display or any of the special characters supported by the PROMPT command. A complete list of the special characters supported by the PROMPT command is provided in Chapter 2.

For example, the following command changes the command prompt to display the current system time:

```
C>prompt $t
17:47:39.82
```

To include a special character in the prompt, precede the character with the escape character (the caret symbol).

```
C:\>prompt $d^>
Tue 02/25/1997>
```

To restore the prompt to its default setting, type **PROMPT** and press Enter.

```
17:47:39.82>prompt
C:\>
```

More information about the PROMPT command is available in Chapter 2.

The ECHO Command

The ECHO command supports two operations. The first operation displays a message. The second operation turns the shell's command echo feature on and off. Normal shell behavior displays the shell command followed by the command output. Turning echo off has little effect when you are working at the command line. However, when used inside scripts, disabling echoing has the effect of suppressing shell commands and only displaying their output, which makes for a much better presentation. You will learn more about incorporating the echo commands into scripts in Chapter 4, "Writing Your First Shell Script."

The syntax of the ECHO command is as follows:

```
Echo [on | off] [message]
```

To view the current echo status, type the ECHO command by itself.

```
C:\>echo
ECHO is on.
```

Use the following command to turn echoing off.

```
C:\>echo off
```

The following command turns echoing back on.

```
C:\>echo on
```

To display message text, type **ECHO** followed by the message and press Enter.

```
C:\>echo Today is a good day to learn shell scripting
Today is a good day to learn shell scripting
```

You can even incorporate variables into your message text, as shown here:

```
C:\>echo Today is %date%
Today is Tue 02/25/1997
```

> **TIP**
>
> The %date% variable is an environmental variable that is automatically created by Windows. More information on variables is provided in Chapter 5, "Working with Variables."

More information about the ECHO command is available in Chapter 2.

The CLS Command

The CLS command clears the current command console display and displays the command prompt and cursor on the first line of the command console window. This allows you to clear a cluttered command console. Its syntax is as follows:

```
Cls
```

The CLS command does not accept any parameters. It clears only displayed console text and does not affect other settings, such as command console color and title bar text.

The PATH Command

You can use the PATH command to view and change the %path% variable. The Windows shell uses this variable to locate commands. Its syntax is as follows:

```
path [[drive:]path[;...]] [%path%]
```

When issued without any arguments, the PATH command displays the current search path:

```
C:\>path
PATH=C:\WINNT\system32;C:\WINNT
```

To add to the current search path, include the %path% variable separated by a semicolon:

```
path %path%;c:\scripts\production
path
```

Then, type **PATH** and press Enter to view the results.

```
PATH=C:\WINNT\system32;C:\WINNT;c:\scripts\production
```

When set to null using the ; character, as shown next, the Windows shell limits its search to the current directory.

```
C:\>path ;
PATH=(null)
```

More information about the PATH command is available in Chapter 2.

Chapter 4

Writing Your First
Shell Script

This chapter shows you how to write your first Windows shell script. In the process, you will get the chance to work with several of the commands that you learned in Chapter 3. The chapter also discusses ways to document your scripts so that it is easy for others who might follow behind you to understand why you did things the way that you did.

Topics covered in this chapter include:

◆ Writing, saving, and executing shell scripts

◆ Customizing your scripting environment

◆ Organizing and documenting your scripts effectively

◆ Controlling script input and output

◆ Creating reports and logs

Creating Your First Script

The first step in creating a new script is to open a text editor. Just about any text editor will do as long as it can save your files in plain ASCII text format. Every script in this book was created using NOTEPAD.EXE, the free text editor included with all versions of Microsoft Windows.

You can start Notepad by clicking Start, Programs, Accessories and then Notepad. You can also start Notepad by clicking Start, Run and typing **Notepad** and then clicking OK.

A script can be as little as one statement. For example, to display a message in the console window, you use the ECHO command. Try typing the following command on the first line in Notepad:

```
echo Today I become a shell script programmer!
```

All that is left to do to create your first script is to save your work as a script. First, click File and then Save. In the File name field type **SCRIPT1.BAT**. Next, locate the folder where you want to store the script. When you're ready, click Save. For example, the shell scripts in this book have been saved to D:\Scripts\Test\Shell. To test your script, start a Windows shell session and type the name of your script, including its drive and path information. For example,

```
D:\Scripts\Test\Shell\Script1.bat
```

To execute the script, press Enter. Figure 4.1 shows the results of running the script.

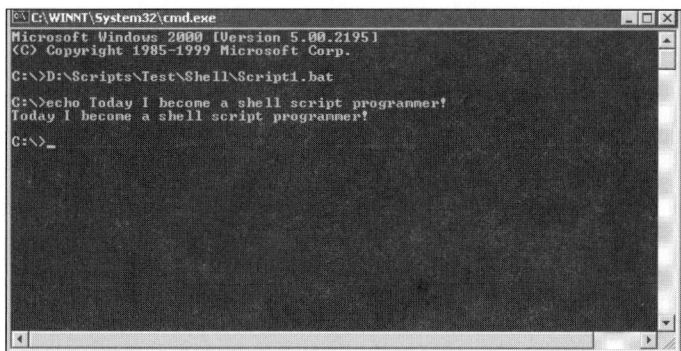

FIGURE 4.1

To execute a script, type its path and name at the command prompt and press Enter.

As Figure 4.1 shows, the shell displayed your command and then executed it, thus displaying the message. Because this script consists of only one line, the shell returns to interactive mode immediately after executing the ECHO command and displays the command prompt.

Now let's add a few more lines of text to the script:

```
echo Today I become a shell script programmer!
echo Mom would be so proud.......
echo And so
echo would my dog
echo Spot!
```

After you add the additional lines, save your script and run it again:

```
C:\>D:\Scripts\Test\Shell\Script1.bat

C:\>echo Today I become a shell script programmer!
Today I become a shell script programmer!
```

```
C:\>echo Mom would be so proud.......
Mom would be so proud.......

C:\>echo And so
And so

C:\>echo would my dog
would my dog

C:\>echo Spot!
Spot!

C:\>
```

As you can see, the script ran as expected, displaying each command and then executing it, and then finally terminating when the last command was processed. The next section improves on this script by showing you how to prevent the display of each command and only show the results.

Refining Message Display

Displaying each command in the script as it executes can make for some pretty unattractive shell scripts. Fortunately, there are commands you can use to clean up its presentation. One option is the @ command. The @ command turns off the display of a command. For example, edit your script by placing the @ sign in front of each statement:

```
@echo Today I become a shell script programmer!
@echo Mom would be so proud.......
@echo And so
@echo would my dog
@echo Spot!
```

Now save and execute the script again. This time you should only see the results of each ECHO command:

```
C:\>D:\Scripts\Test\Shell\Script1.bat
Today I become a shell script programmer!
Mom would be so proud.......
And so
```

```
would my dog
Spot!
```

```
C:\>
```

Adding the @ command to each script statement can get a bit tiresome after a while. Another way to prevent the display of your commands is to place ECHO OFF and ECHO ON statements into your script. For example, remove the @ sign from each statement in your script and insert ECHO OFF as the first line in the script and ECHO ON just above the last line. Then execute the script:

```
C:\>D:\Scripts\Test\Shell\Script1.bat
```

```
C:\>echo off
Today I become a shell script programmer!
Mom would be so proud.......
And so
would my dog
```

```
C:\>echo on
Spot!
```

```
C:\>
```

As you can see, the ECHO OFF statement suppressed the display of all commands, including ECHO commands that follow it until the ECHO ON command is executed. As a result of the ECHO ON command, the last ECHO statement in the script was displayed in addition to its output.

As long as you place ECHO OFF at the top of your scripts, you can suppress the display of other commands. But what about suppressing the ECHO OFF command? This problem is solved by placing the @ command in front of the ECHO OFF command, as demonstrated:

```
@echo off
echo Today I become a shell script programmer!
echo Mom would be so proud.......
echo And so
echo would my dog
echo Spot!
```

As the following output shows, all ECHO commands are now suppressed and it only took one statement to make it happen for the entire script.

```
C:\>D:\Scripts\Test\Shell\Script1.bat
Today I become a shell script programmer!
Mom would be so proud.......
And so
would my dog
Spot!


C:\>
```

Inserting Blank Lines

Programmers often like to add blank lines to their scripts to improve its displayed output. Unfortunately, the Windows shell does not provide support for blank lines in shell scripts. However, there are some alternative ways that you can produce the same effect.

You might think that simply typing the ECHO command on a line by itself would do the trick; however, if you try it, you will see that instead of a blank line, you get a message displaying the current status of ECHO:

```
C:\>echo
ECHO is on.
```

One alternative that you might try is to type an ECHO statement that contains a period, as demonstrated here:

```
@echo off
echo My Name is Jerry Ford
echo .
echo I live in Richmond Virginia
```

The following output shows the results of the previous example.

```
C:\>D:\Scripts\Test\Shell\Script2.bat
My Name is Jerry Ford
.

I live in Richmond Virginia
C:\>
```

Another approach is to type an ECHO statement and insert a number of blank spaces before typing the period character, thus pushing the display of the period to the far right edge of the display where it's less obvious.

Another option is to use a character such as the asterisk, dash, or equals sign to format and organize the script output, as shown here:

```
@echo off
echo *****************************************
echo * Name: Jerry Ford                      *
echo *****************************************
echo *                                        *
echo * Address: Richmond Virginia          *
echo *                                        *
echo *****************************************
```

Adding Comments to Your Scripts

One essential rule of good programming is to always add comments to your scripts. This makes it easier for others who come along behind you to understand why you wrote the script the way you did. It also makes it a lot easier to understand your own scripts a few years later.

The REM statement allows you to place comments into your scripts. A comment is usually a descriptive statement that describes a part of the script. The following example shows how you might use the REM statement to document the ECHO example.

```
@echo off
rem The previous statement turns echoing off

rem display report heading
echo *****************************************
echo * Name: Jerry Ford                      *
echo *****************************************
echo *                                        *
echo * Address: Richmond Virginia          *
echo *                                        *
echo *****************************************

rem The rest of the script goes here
```

Building a Script Template

Now that you know how to add comments to your scripts, it is a good time to think about building a standard documentation shell that you can use as a template for all future scripts.

The first step in creating the template is to type the @ECHO OFF statement on the first line. Next, type a series of REM statements that provides room for the things that you want to document in your scripts, as demonstrated here:

```
@echo off
rem *****************************************
rem * Script Name: template.bat            *
rem * Author:  Jerry Ford                  *
rem * Address: Richmond Virginia           *
rem * Created: 01/06/01                    *
rem *****************************************

rem Script begins here
```

This initial script template might not seem very sophisticated, but it is a good beginning. You will get the opportunity to expand the usefulness of the template in future chapters.

Displaying Status Messages

Often, the most important thing that a script does is communicate effectively with its users and let them know what is happening during execution. One way to accomplish this task is to place ECHO statements throughout the script that describe what the script is doing.

For example, the following script displays three status messages as the script processes. One status message signals the start of the script, one signals the start of the main procedure, and one signals script termination.

```
@echo off
rem ******************************************
rem * Script Name: script3.bat              *
rem * Author:   Jerry Ford                  *
rem * Address: Richmond Virginia            *
rem * Created: 01/06/01                      *
rem ******************************************

rem Script begins here

echo Script starting
rem additional script statements go here

echo Processing the main procedure now
rem more script statements go here

echo Script terminating
rem final script statements go here
```

The following output shows the results of running the previous example. The problem with this type of status reporting is that, if the script is designed to display other output, the status messages can get lost in the rest of the output or can make the output look confusing or unorganized.

```
C:\>D:\Scripts\Test\Shell\script3.bat
Script starting
Processing the main procedure now
Script terminating
C:\>
```

The TITLE command provides an effective alternative because it allows you to display status messages directly in the console window's title bar. The following example replaces the ECHO commands with TITLE commands and provides for a more professional display.

```
@echo off
rem *******************************************
rem * Script Name: script3.bat                 *
rem * Author:   Jerry Ford                      *
rem * Address: Richmond Virginia                *
rem * Created: 01/06/01                         *
rem *******************************************

rem Script begins here

title Script starting
rem Additional script statements go here

title Processing the main procedure now
rem More script statements go here

title Script terminating
rem Final script statements go here
```

Initializing Your Scripting Environment

Over time, you will probably find that there are certain steps that you always seem to go through when beginning to write a script. For example, you might want to change the color scheme of the command console or always use a custom command prompt.

This section shows you how to create a script that you can you use to automatically customize your scripting environment. The first thing that the example does is execute the following command:

```
cls
```

The CLS command clears the display of any existing messages so that you will start with a clean display. Next, the script changes the command prompt as follows:

```
prompt $g
```

In this case, the command prompt has been set up to display as the greater-than sign. Next, the COLOR command is executed. In this case, it sets the console window's background color to bright white and its foreground color to blue.

```
color F1
```

The script then executes the TITLE command, as shown here:

```
title Jerry's Custom Console
```

Next, the PATH command appends the d:\Scripts\Test\shell to the end of the existing path variable, thus ensuring that the Windows shell will not have any trouble locating the folder that contains the shell scripts.

```
path %path%;d:\Scripts\Test\Shell
```

Finally, the last statement in the script executes an ECHO command, which displays a greeting and announces that the scripting environment has been configured:

```
echo "Hello Jerry! Your scripting environment has been set."
```

The complete script follows.

```
@echo off
rem ******************************************
rem * Script Name: startup_env.bat          *
rem * Author:  Jerry Ford                    *
rem * Address: Richmond Virginia             *
rem * Created: 01/06/01                      *
rem ******************************************

rem Initialize the scripting environment
cls
prompt $g
color F1
title Jerry's Custom Console
path %path%;d:\Scripts\Test\Shell
echo "Hello Jerry! Your scripting environment has been set."
```

Figure 4.2 shows the command console when the script is executed. Initializing your scripting environment not only saves you time and effort but also ensures you of a consistent starting point each time you sit down to work. This example can easily be expanded to include other customizations, such as the addition of more paths, the creation of variables, or the execution of various network connectivity commands.

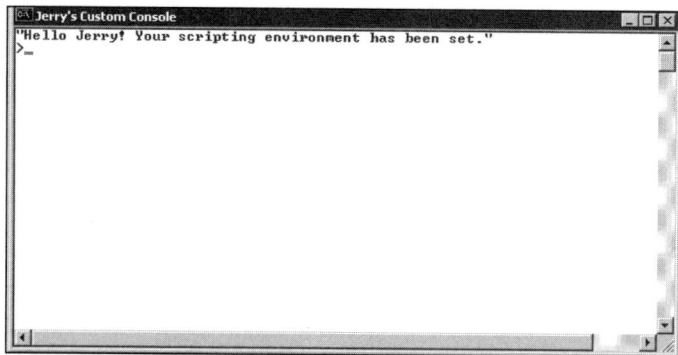

FIGURE 4.2

You can write an initialization script so that you don't have to configure your scripting environment every time you start.

One option for executing the script is to open a command shell by clicking a shell shortcut and then running the script. However, you can save yourself from always having to perform this step. To do so, you have to modify the shortcut so that when you double-click it, the script automatically runs.

The following steps outline the procedure for configuring the automatic execution of the script:

1. Right-click your shell shortcut and select Properties from the pop-up menu that appears.

2. Select the Shortcut tab, shown in Figure 4.3. The text in the Target field should look something like this:

```
%windir%\System32\cmd.exe
```

Change it so that it reads:

```
%windir%\System32\cmd.exe /k
D:\Scripts\Test\Shell\Startup_env.bat
```

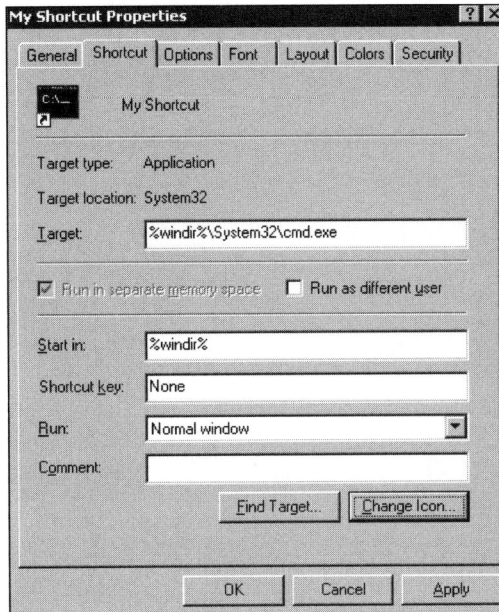

FIGURE 4.3

You can automate the execution of commands and scripts by modifying Windows shell shortcut.

3. Click OK.

4. Double-click your custom shell shortcut to verify that your scripting environment is automatically established.

The default text in the Target field of the Shortcut Properties sheet on the shortcut's properties dialog box is `%windir%\System32\cmd.exe`. `%windir%` is an environment variable and contains the name of the directory where the Windows files have been installed. On most systems, this is set to WINNT. The rest of the command completes the path to CMD.EXE, which is the command that starts a new Windows shell.

The example adds `/k D:\Scripts\Test\Shell\Startup_env.bat` to the end of this text. The `D:\Scripts\Test\Shell\Startup_env.bat` path sets up the execution of the initialization script by specifying its name and location. The `/k` switch keeps the command console from automatically terminating after the initialization script has been executed.

Compound Commands and Command Redirection

So far, every command you have seen in this book has been placed on a line by itself. In addition, all script output has been written to the display and all input has been supplied from the keyboard. The Windows shell provides the capability to combine multiple commands on a single line and to make the execution of these commands dependent upon one another. The Windows shell also allows you to override its default I/O processing. Both of these techniques are outlined in the following sections.

Conditional Command Execution

One way to implement the conditional execution of commands in your shell scripts is to take advantage of compound commands. *Compound commands* allow you to chain together multiple commands on the same line using a collection of reserved characters, known as *compound command characters*. Compound command characters include the following characters: & (ampersand), | (pipe), (, and) (parentheses). The function of each of these characters is outlined in Table 4.1.

Table 4.1 Compound Command Characters

Character	Example(s)	Description
&	Cmd1 & Cmd2	Executes the first command and then executes the second command
&&	Cmd1 && Cmd2	Executes the first command and then executes the second command only when the first command was successful
||	Cmd1 || Cmd2	Executes the first command and then executes the second command only when the first command received an error
( )	(Cmd1 & Cmd2) Cmd1 ||&& Cmd3 (Cmd2 & Cmd3)	Groups commands to ensure their proper sequencing

For example, the & character allows you to chain together two commands:

```
cd \ & dir
```

This command changes the current working directory to the root directory and then displays a directory listing, as shown in Figure 4.4.

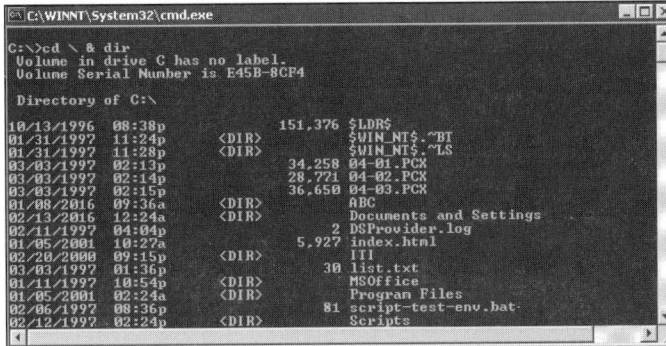

FIGURE 4.4

Compound commands allow you to combine an unlimited number of commands on a single line.

Using && provides a level of conditional control over the execution of the second command by ensuring that it will execute only when the first command is successful. For example, the following command changes the current working directory to c:\temp and then copies all .log files to a folder in the mapped network drive as long as the first command is successful. However, if the first command returns an error, the COPY command is not executed.

```
cd c:\temp && copy *.log z:\logs
```

Use the || command to execute the second command in the event that the first command fails. For example, the following command tries to change the current working directory to a folder named ttemp.

```
cd \ttemp || echo Unable to find folder
```

If the folder exists, the first command executes successfully and the second command is skipped. Otherwise, the ECHO command executes as shown next. You might notice that the system also displays an error message when the command executes. You will learn how to redirect these error messages later in this chapter.

```
C:\>cd \ttemp || echo Unable to find folder
The system cannot find the path specified.
error
```

There is no limit to the number of commands that you can chain together. The following example demonstrates the execution of three commands:

```
hostname & ver & echo No of processors = %NUMBER_OF_PROCESSORS%
```

In this case, every command executes regardless of the success of its predecessor. HOSTNAME displays the name of the current host, which on Windows 2000 is configured from the System Properties dialog box, which you access from the Network Identification property sheet, as shown in Figure 4.5.

NOTE

On Windows NT 4.0, the hostname is configured on the DNS properties sheet of the Microsoft TCP/IP properties dialog box.

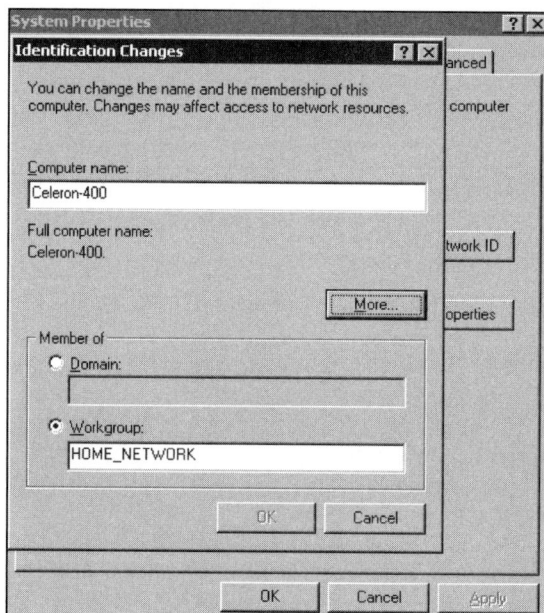

FIGURE 4.5

Configuring a Windows 2000 computer's hostname.

The VER command displays the operating system version. The ECHO statement displays the value of the NUMBER_OF_PROCESSORS environment variable, which tells you the number or processors or CPUs on the system:

```
C:\>Hostname & ver & echo No of processors = %NUMBER_OF_PROCESSORS%
```

p1j1f01-002079

```
Windows NT Version 4.0
No of processors = 1
```

The following example presents another example of compound commands. This example is designed to change the current directory to the \temp folder and then copy all .log files to a mapped network drive. After the COPY operation completes, the .log files are deleted from the \temp directory. In this example, the COPY command executes only if the script can successfully change to the \temp folder. If the COPY command does not execute, neither does the DELETE command.

```
cd \temp && copy *.log z:\logs && del *.log
```

The () compound command allows you to explicitly group commands and dictate the order of execution. In the following example, the two COPY commands both execute only when the directory change to \temp is successful. The DELETE command executes only when both the COPY commands are successful.

```
cd \temp && (copy *.txt z:\logs & copy *.log z:\logs) && del *.*txt
```

Taking Control of Shell I/O

The Windows shell accepts input and output from three sources, known as standard input, standard output, and standard error. A brief description of each source and its default is outlined here:

♦ **Standard Input**. The default input source for all shell commands. By default, this is set to the keyboard.

♦ **Standard Output**. The default location where all shell output is sent. By default, this is set to the display.

♦ **Standard Error**. The default location where all shell error message output is sent. By default, this is set to the display.

Altering the default shell *Input/Output* or *I/O* is known as redirection. *Redirection* is a powerful programming tool. It allows you to create reports by storing script output in files. It also allows you to use information stored in files as input for scripts commands. Also by redirecting standard error, you can easily create error logs.

The shell reserves the following characters as redirection symbols: |, >, and <. Table 4.2 explains the types of redirection supported by the Windows shell.

Table 4.2 Command-Redirection Characters

Character	Example	Description
>	Cmd > File	Redirects output to the specified file or device
<	Cmd < File	Redirects command input from the specified file
>>	Cmd >> File	Appends output to the end of the specified file
2>	Cmd 2> File	Redirects error output to the specified file
2>&1	Cmd 2>&1	Redirects error output to the same location as standard output
|	Cmd1 | Cmd2	Pipes the output of one command to the input of the second command

NOTE

The display, keyboard, and text files are not the only Input/Output options. For example, you can direct output to a parallel printer by using LPT1 or to a serial printer by using PRN and including a serial printer as the output target.

Creating Reports and Logs

Using the > character, you can redirect standard output and create reports and logs. Using >>, you can append information to these reports and logs. For example, the following script executes several commands to create a report that contains TCP/IP configuration information about the computer on which it runs.

```
@echo off
rem *****************************************
rem * Script Name: ipconfig_report.bat      *
rem * Author:   Jerry Ford                  *
rem * Address: Richmond Virginia            *
rem * Created:  01/10/01                     *
rem *****************************************
```

```
rem Display date and host name

echo Date: %date% > C:\temp\TCP_report.txt
echo Host: %hostname% >> C:\temp\TCP_report.txt
echo . >> C:\temp\TCP_report.txt


rem display TCP/IP configuration data

ipconfig /all >> C:\temp\TCP_report.txt


rem Tell the user that the report is complete

echo Report TCP_report.txt has been created in C:\TEMP
```

The script starts by echoing the current date, which is stored in the %date% environmental variable. The results of this command are then redirected into a file called TCP_REPORT.TXT. Next, the name of the host or computer running the script is collected by echoing the %host% environment variable and then appending the results to the end of TCP_REPORT.TXT. If this file exists, it is overridden. If it does not exist, it is automatically created.

The next line appends a new (almost blank) line to the report to improve its readability.

Next, the script executes the IPCONFIG /ALL command, which displays the TCP/IP configuration information for the computer. The last thing that the script does before terminating is display a message to the users stating that TCP_REPORT.TXT has been created and can be found in c:\temp, as shown in Figure 4.6.

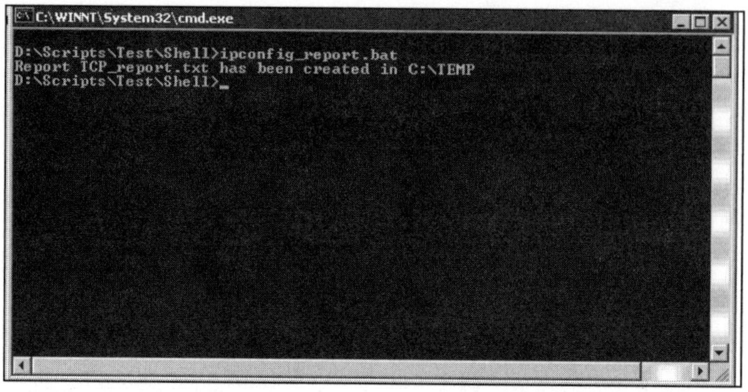

FIGURE 4.6

By taking advantage of the Windows shell's redirection techniques, you can generate custom reports and log files.

Figure 4.7 shows the format of TCP_REPORT.TXT.

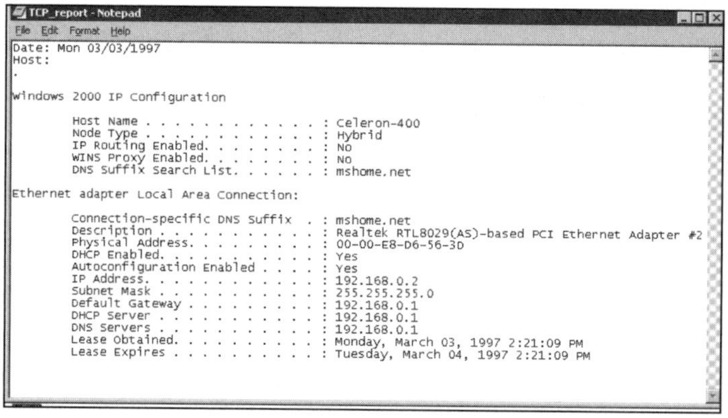

FIGURE 4.7

Viewing a script-generated TCP/IP status report.

NOTE

The preceding example requires that TCP/IP is configured on the computer that executes the script.

Logging Error Messages

The Windows shell allows you to handle standard output separately from standard error. This allows you to write scripts that create error reports. For example, suppose you had a collection of scripts that create .log files in the \temp directory on a daily basis. The absence of any .log files on a given day might mean that your scripts were not executing properly.

You might want to write a script that copies all log files to a network computer at the end of each day and then deletes the log files in preparation for the next day's processing. This would allow you to centralize logging information for critical servers on your network.

Before attempting to copy the .log files, make sure that they are present. The absence of any .log files can be a problem. The following command checks for the .log files and in the event that they are not present, a new error report is generated named ERROR_RPT.TXT.

```
dir *.log 2> C:\TEMP\error_rpt.txt
```

You might then want to send ERROR_RPT.TXT in place of the missing .log files to the network computer where log files are stored. For example, the following command checks for the existence of the .log files. If the .log files are there, nothing happens. If the .log files are not there, the command's standard error output is redirected to a file named ERROR_RPT.TXT. Because the DIR command resulted in an error, the second part of the compound command copies the error file to a network drive.

```
(dir *.log 2> C:\TEMP\error_rpt.txt) || copy C:\TEMP\error_rpt.txt
z:\logs
```

> **TIP**
>
> You can also generate reports that include both standard output and standard error by using the 2>&1 compound command, which redirects errors to the same location where standard output has been set.

Redirecting Command Input

Using the | (pipe-redirection command), you can make the results of one command the input for another. For example, combining | with the MORE command allows you to limit the display of lengthy command output to one page at a time. The following command displays the contents of the current directory. If the results of the command are more than can be displayed in the console window, the shell will only display as much output as fits in the console window. It then displays the - MORE - prompt at the bottom of the screen.

```
dir | more
```

Figure 4.8 demonstrates how the redirection command works. You can press the Enter key to display an additional line of output or press the spacebar to view the remaining output a screen at a time.

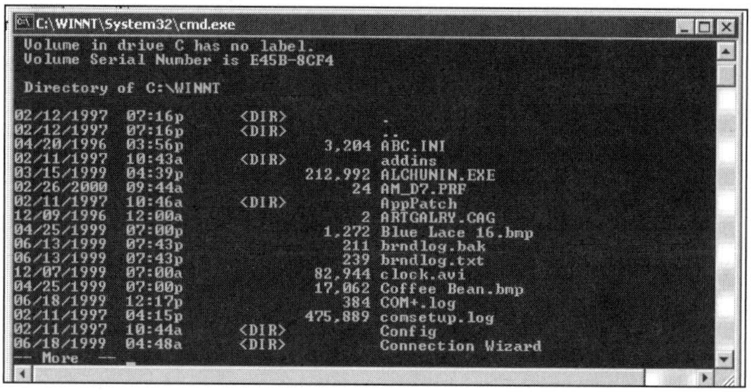

FIGURE 4.8

You can redirect the command output of one command and provide it as the input for another command.

TIP

You can press CTRL+C at any time to interrupt the MORE command and return to the command prompt.

Another example of using one command's output as another command's input is with the use of the SORT command. For example, the following command displays the contents of the current working directory in reverse sorted order.

```
dir | sort /r
```

You can also use a file to provide command input. For example, the following command sorts and displays a list of animals stored in a file named ANIMAL_LIST.TXT.

```
sort < animal_list.txt
```

W

Chapter 5

Working with Variables

You can expand the capabilities of your scripts by taking advantage of environment variables. Environment variables store information about the current shell environment. Your scripts can access and use environment variables. The Windows shell also allows your scripts to create variables of their own. This chapter explains the rules for working with variables and how to incorporate them into your scripts. In addition, this chapter explains how to pass arguments to scripts and process them.

Topics covered in this chapter include:

◆ Processing script arguments

◆ Accessing environment variables

◆ Reviewing the rules for creating new variables

◆ Creating your own variables

◆ Controlling the scope of variables

Working with Script Arguments

So far all the shell script examples that you have seen have executed without the benefit on any input, which means that arguments were not passed to the scripts at the start of execution. An *argument* is an input parameter that the script uses when it executes. Arguments can be passed by typing the name of the script and a space followed by one or more arguments, each of which is separated by a space. The syntax for calling a script and passing it arguments is shown here:

```
Script_name arg1 arg2 arg1 ......
```

NOTE

You can also use commas, tabs, equals signs, and even semicolons to separate arguments.

Scripts can call other scripts. Therefore, scripts can pass and receive arguments from other scripts. Regardless of how a script starts, it processes any arguments by assigning them to parameters, as shown in Table 5.1.

Table 5.1 Script Arguments

Parameter	Description
%*	Contains all arguments passed to the script except for the name of the script
%0	The name of the script
%1	The first argument passed to the script
%2	The second argument passed to the script
%3	The third argument passed to the script
%4	The fourth argument passed to the script
%5	The fifth argument passed to the script
%6	The sixth argument passed to the script
%7	The seventh argument passed to the script
%8	The eighth argument passed to the script
%9	The ninth argument passed to the script

For example, the following script is designed to accept three arguments and then display them using ECHO commands:

```
@echo off
echo Argument 1 = %1
echo Argument 2 = %2
echo Argument 3 = %3
```

The following output is generated if the script is passed the arguments apple, orange, and grape when it is called.

```
Argument 1 = apple
Argument 2 = orange
Argument 3 = grape
```

Unfortunately, the Windows shell does not allow you to directly access parameters beyond nine. Instead you must use the SHIFT command in order to access additional parameters. For example, typing **SHIFT**, as shown next, moves all parameters to the left by one.

```
shift
```

%1 becomes %0 and %2 becomes %1, and so on. In this example, the original %0 is replaced by the value of %1.

You do not have to shift every parameter in order to access additional parameters. For example, SHIFT /5 leaves the value of the parameters %0 through %4 intact, but shifts the values of the rest of the parameters beginning with parameter %6 by changing the value of %6 to %5, %7 to %6, and so on. The previous value of %5 is overwritten. The following example demonstrates the use of SHIFT with a switch of /2:

```
@echo off
echo %*
echo %0 %1 %2 %3 %9
shift /2
echo %0 %1 %2 %3 %9
```

If you save this example as TEST_SCRIPT.BAT and then execute it with the following arguments

```
C:\test_script.bat This is not the beginning of the end but it is per-
haps the end of the beginning
```

you should see the following output.

```
This is not the beginning off the end but it is perhaps the end of the
beginning
test_script.bat This is not but
test_script.bat This not the it
```

> **NOTE**
>
> If you need to pass an argument that contains spaces, you must enclose the argument inside double quotes. For example, the following script deletes a file based on the file name and path that is passed to it as an argument:
>
> ```
> @echo off
>
> del %1
> ```
>
> For example, if you named this script TEST_SCRIPT.BAT and passed it an argument of `"d:\mydocs\records\old_records.txt"`, as shown here
>
> ```
> C:\test_script.bat "d:\mydocs\records\old_records.txt"
> ```
>
> the Windows shell will translate the script's DELETE command as follows before executing it.
>
> ```
> del "d:\mydocs\records\old_records.txt"
> ```

Viewing and Controlling Environmental Variables

Each Windows shell inherits the environment of the process that starts it. All changes made in the shell are local to the shell and do not affect its parent. This localization protects the parent process from any changes made by the new shell process.

Windows stores its configuration information in the Registry. This includes system and user information, some of which is made available in the form of environment variables. Variables come from a variety of sources, including the following:

◆ From hardware and other environment information gathered during system initialization and stored in HKEY_LOCAL_MACHINE

◆ From user information gathered during user logon and stored in HKEY_CURRENT_USER

◆ From within a script using the SET command

> **NOTE**
>
> You will find the terms environmental variable, environment variable, and variable used interchangeably throughout this text.

Hardware and environmental variables are always available to your scripts. Examples of environmental variables include COMSPEC and OS, whose values identify the location of the Windows shell command and the version of Windows being run. However, other types of variables are only available during an active logon session and hence are not available to any scripts that you run using one of the Windows scheduling services.

NOTE

You can schedule your scripts to run on an automated schedule using the scheduling service provided by each version of Windows. Windows 2000 provides the Schedule Task Wizard and the Task Scheduler service and Windows NT provides the Schedule Service. Chapter 10, "Introducing the Windows Script Host," provides detailed information on how to automate your scripts.

Viewing and Changing System Variables

You can view and modify user and system variables in both Windows NT and Windows 2000. When you make changes to these variables, you are actually editing the Windows Registry and not the current environment. In order for changes to system variables to take effect, you have to restart your system. For changes made to user variables to take effect, you need to log off and back on again.

NOTE

Unlike variables that you create in Windows shell scripts, changes made to environment variables from the System Properties dialog box are permanent.

Making Changes to Variables in Windows 2000

Environmental variables can be viewed in Windows 2000 using the System utility. To view and change user and system variables in Windows 2000 click Start, Settings, Control Panel and then the System utility. Next click the Advanced Property sheet, as shown in Figure 5.1.

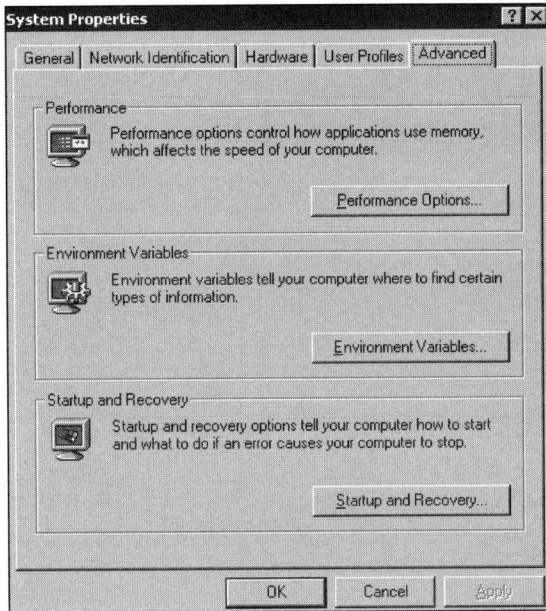

FIGURE 5.1

Windows 2000 environment variables can be found on the Advanced Property sheet of the System Properties dialog box.

To view Windows 2000's environment variables, click Environment Variables. The Environment Variables dialog box appears, as shown in Figure 5.2. The top half of this dialog box displays the User variables for the current user. (In this example, it is the Administrator.) In this example, only two user environment variables are defined, both of which specify where temporary files are stored during the user's login session.

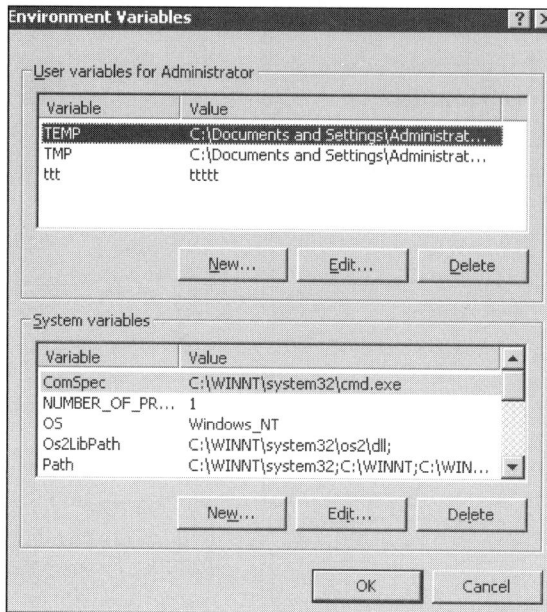

FIGURE 5.2

Windows 2000 allows you to view, modify, and even create new environment variables.

The bottom half of this dialog box displays the system variables. The kinds of variables that you will see here include:

- ◆ **COMSPEC**. Specifies the location of the Windows shell.
- ◆ **OS**. Specifies the name of the operating system.
- ◆ **PATH**. Specifies the current search path.
- ◆ **PATHEXT**. Specifies the current list of executable file extensions.
- ◆ **WINDIR**. Specifies the location of the Windows folder.

You can modify a user or system variable by selecting it and clicking the Edit button for the appropriate variable type. For example, if you select COMSPEC and click Edit, the Edit System Variable dialog box will appear, as shown in Figure 5.3. To modify its value, change the text in the Variable Value field and click OK.

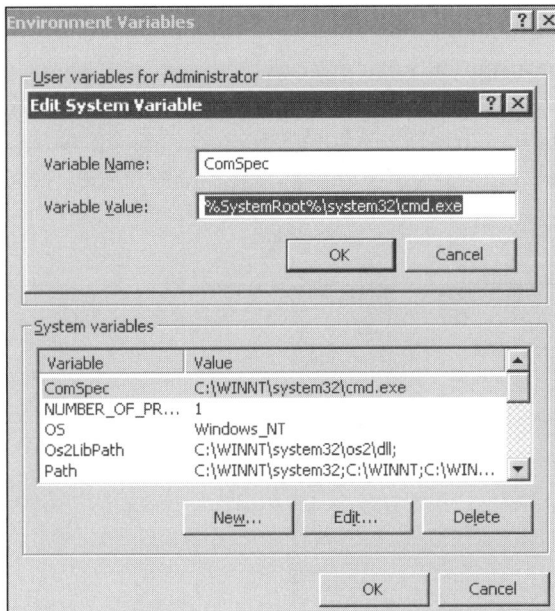

FIGURE 5.3

Environment variables are changed using the Edit System Variable and Edit User Variables dialog boxes.

You can delete an environment variable by selecting it and clicking the appropriate Delete button. To create a new variable, click the New button that represents the type of variable that you want to create. This opens either the New User Variable or New System Variable dialog box, where you can type in the variable's name and value.

NOTE

You must be a member of the Administrator's group to modify environment variables.

TIP

Use the COMSPEC environment variable in place of hard coding the CMD command in your scripts. The COMSPEC environment variable includes both the name of the shell command and its path. Using the COMSPEC variable ensures that you will always start the correct shell (such as %SYSTEMROOT%\System32\cmd.exe). This is not an issue unless you have installed multiple operating systems on your computer, in which case it is possible that the wrong Windows shell version can start. For example, instead of:

```
cmd /k scriptname.bat
```

use:

```
%COMSPEC% /k scriptname.bat
```

Making Changes to Variables in Windows NT 4

Like Windows 2000, environmental variables can be viewed in Windows NT 4 using the System utility. To view and change user and system variables in Windows NT 4, click Start, Settings, and then Control Panel. Next, double-click the System utility and then select the Environment Property sheet, as shown in Figure 5.4.

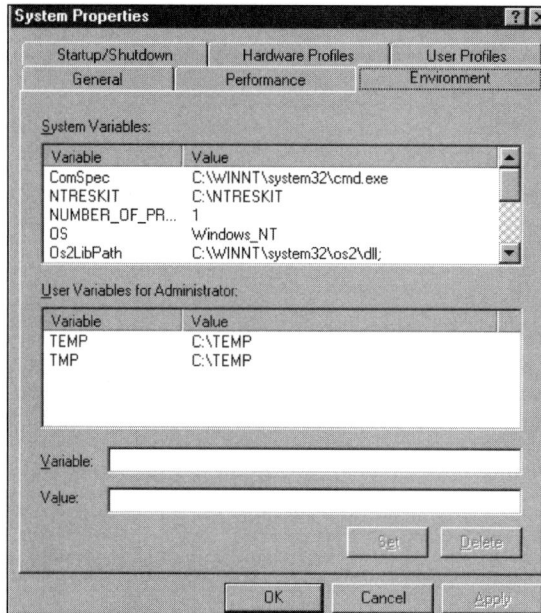

FIGURE 5.4

System and user variables can by viewed and modified from the System Properties dialog box in Windows NT 4.

Adding and modifying variables in Windows NT 4 is a little different than in Windows 2000. The process of adding, changing, and deleting user and system variables in Windows NT is as follows:

◆ **Adding a new variable**. Select a variable of the type that you want to create and then modify its variable name in the Variable field and its value in the Value field and click Set.

◆ **Modifying an existing variable**. Select a variable and then modify the text in the Value field and click Set.

◆ **Deleting a variable**. Select a variable and click Delete.

TIP

Changes made via the Windows 2000 and Windows NT System dialog box do not affect current Windows shell sessions. To ensure that any changes made to system variables are in effect, restart the computer. To make sure that changes to user variables are in effect, log off and back on again.

Viewing Variables from the Command Line

You will find that not every variable is visible from the System utility. For example, any variables created by you during a Windows shell session or by your scripts as they execute are not reflected there. The SET command allows you to view, modify, or delete variables for the current shell session. To view a complete listing of variables available in a shell session, type **SET** and press Enter:

```
C:\>set
ALLUSERSPROFILE=C:\Documents and Settings\All Users
APPDATA=C:\Documents and Settings\Administrator\Application Data
CommonProgramFiles=C:\Program Files\Common Files
COMPUTERNAME=CELERON-400
ComSpec=C:\WINNT\system32\cmd.exe
HOMEDRIVE=C:
HOMEPATH=\
LOGONSERVER=\\CELERON-400
NUMBER_OF_PROCESSORS=1
OS=Windows_NT
Os2LibPath=C:\WINNT\system32\os2\dll;
Path=C:\WINNT\system32;C:\WINNT;C:\WINNT\system32\WBEM;C:\Program
Files\Resource
 Kit\NTRK\;C:\Program Files\Resource Kit\TMC\Shortcut\
PATHEXT=.COM;.EXE;.BAT;.CMD;.VBS;.VBE;.JS;.JSE;.WS;.WSH;.WSF
PROCESSOR_ARCHITECTURE=x86
PROCESSOR_IDENTIFIER=x86 Family 6 Model 6 Stepping 0, GenuineIntel
PROCESSOR_LEVEL=6
PROCESSOR_REVISION=0600
ProgramFiles=C:\Program Files
PROMPT=$P$G
SystemDrive=C:
SystemRoot=C:\WINNT
```

```
TEMP=C:\DOCUME~1\ADMINI~1\LOCALS~1\Temp
TMP=C:\DOCUME~1\ADMINI~1\LOCALS~1\Temp
USERDOMAIN=CELERON-400
USERNAME=Administrator
USERPROFILE=C:\Documents and Settings\Administrator
windir=C:\WINNT
```

You can also use the SET command to view a partial list of matching values by typing **SET**, a space, and the first few characters of a variable's name. For example, typing **SET OS** and pressing Enter lists all the variables whose names begin with the letters OS, as demonstrated here:

```
C:\>set OS
OS=Windows_NT
Os2LibPath=C:\WINNT\system32\os2\dll;
```

You can also display individual variables by typing **SET**, a space, and the variable's complete name:

```
C:\>set USERNAME
USERNAME=Administrator
```

In this example the value of USERNAME, which is the username of the current user, is displayed.

TIP

You can verify whether a variable exists before you try to reference it using the IF DEFINED and IF NOT DEFINED statements. The following example demonstrates how these statements work.

```
@echo off

set default_directory=D:\temp

if defined default_directory echo The default directory is
%default_directory%

set default_directory=

if not defined default_directory echo There is no default direc-
tory
```

When executed, this example produces the following output. Because the default_directory variable exists when the IF DEFINED statement is executed, the first ECHO message is executed. Likewise, the second ECHO message executes because the value has been deleted. Information on how IF statements work is presented in Chapter 6, "Conditional Logic."

```
The default directory is D:\temp

There is no default directory
```

NOTE

If your script attempts to reference a variable that does not exist, the Windows shell will return an empty value, as demonstrated in the following example.

```
set default_directory=

echo The default directory = %default_directory%
```

The default directory =

However, if you use the SET command to display a variable's value, you will receive the following error:

```
set name=bob

echo %name%

set name=

set name
```

Environment variable name not defined

Creating and Deleting Variables

The SET command also allows you to create and delete variables from within your scripts. This command only affects the current shell. To create a new variable, type **SET** followed by an equals sign and then the variable value. The following example creates a variable named working_directory and makes it equal to D:\temp.

```
set working_directory=D:\temp
```

> **NOTE**
>
> Do not place blank spaces before or after the equals sign in a SET command unless you intend for the blank spaces to be a part of the variable's name or value. For example, SET account1=FORD creates a variable name account1 and sets the value equal to FORD. However, if you typed SET account1 = FORD, the name of the variable will include a trailing blank space and the value of the variable will likewise include a preceding blank space.

The SET command also allows you to delete a variable. You can delete a variable by typing **SET** followed by the variable's name and then the equals sign:

```
SET working_directory=
```

Rules for Variable Names

There are a number of rules that govern the creation of new variables. Make sure that all your script variables conform to the following guidelines.

- There is no published limit to the maximum length of variables' names or their values, although variable names larger than 15 to 20 characters are difficult to work with.
- Variable names are not case-sensitive, which means that Working_directory, working_directory, and WORKING_DIRECTORY are all the same as far as the Windows shell is concerned.
- Variable names are case-aware in that, for purposes of presentation, Windows remembers their capitalization.

◆ Reserved shell characters can be used when creating variables only when you place them inside of double quotes or escape them.

◆ If you include a blank space before the equals sign when creating a variable, the space is part of the variable's name.

◆ If you add a blank space after the equals sign when creating a new variable, the space is part of the variable's value.

◆ Placing a variable's value in double quotes also adds the double quotes to the value because everything after the equals sign is part of the variable's value.

Defining a Variable's Scope

A scripts inherits its environment from the process that starts it. Because changes made to its environment are local, any changes made in the shell to its variables are kept local. This type of localization protects the parent from any changes made by the child session. For example, try opening a new Windows shell and typing **SET PROMPT**. This displays the PROMPT variable and its value as inherited from the current system settings. Now, change the value of the PROMPT variable by typing **SET PROMPT=$d**. This changes the Windows shell's command prompt to the current date. Now if you start a new Windows shell session by clicking Start, Programs, Accessories, and then Command Prompt, you will see that this new shell is unaffected by the change.

However, keep in mind that each new instance of the command shell inherits a copy of the environment of its parent. This means that if you start a new Windows shell from within the shell used to modify the command prompt (done by typing **CMD** and pressing Enter), you will see that the new shell session inherits an exact copy of its parent Windows shell's environment, including the modified PROMPT. If you change the value of the PROMPT variable in this child shell session and then exit this session, you will find that the PROMPT variable remains unchanged in the parent Windows shell.

As the previous example demonstrated, a variable's scope is limited to its local environment. The Windows shell allows you to further localize variables and their values by restricting their scope using the SETLOCAL and ENDLOCAL commands.

The following example further demonstrates environment inheritance and the localization of variables. Open a new command shell, type the following command, and press Enter.

```
set my_name="The Boss"
```

Next, create a new script that looks like the following:

```
@echo off
echo my_name = %my_name%
```

Save and execute the script using the new Windows shell session. The results should look like the following:

```
my_name = "The Boss"
```

As you can see, the script has access to the variable and its value. Next, change the script as follows and run it again:

```
@echo off
set my_name=
echo my_name = %my_name%
```

The results should look like the following:

```
my_name =
```

The script has deleted the variable by setting its value to nothing. Now type the following command at the command prompt and press Enter:

```
SET my_name
```

You should see the following output.

```
C:\>set my_name
Environment variable my_name not defined
```

A child shell session inherits the environment of its parent and can make modifications to it without affecting the parent. However, as this example demonstrates, changes made within the shell session, either from the command line or by a script, affect the current session environment.

Global Variables

By default, all variables are global in scope within a script. This means that, after it is established, a variable can be referenced at any point in the script. This is demonstrated in the following example:

```
@echo off
rem Initialize this scripts variables

set working_directory=D:\temp
set log_file=D:\logs

rem the main body of the script goes here

echo working_directory = %working_directory%
echo log_file = %log_file%

rem additional script statement would go here

echo working_directory = %working_directory%
echo log_file = %log_file%
```

As the following output shows, although the variable log_file is created at the beginning of the script, it can be referenced from any location in the script.

```
working_directory = D:\temp
log_file = D:\logs
working_directory = D:\temp
log_file = D:\logs
```

Local Variables

The SETLOCAL command can create a new local scope where all changes are discarded when the scope ends. The scope ends when the ENDLOCAL command is executed. Any changes made to variables within this temporary scope are discarded, as demonstrated in the following example:

```
@echo off
rem Initialize this scripts variables

setlocal
```

```
set working_directory=D:\temp
set log_file=D:\logs

rem the main body of the script goes here

echo working_directory = %working_directory%
echo log_file = %log_file%

endlocal

rem additional script statement would go here

echo working_directory = %working_directory%
echo log_file = %log_file%
```

As the following output shows, the two variables created in the localized environment are discarded when the ENDLOCAL statement executes.

```
C:\>ddd
working_directory = D:\temp
log_file = D:\logs
working_directory =
log_file =
```

> **TIP**
>
> SETLOCAL and ENDLOCAL are especially suited for localizing a variable's values in *procedures*, which are discussed in Chapter 8, "Organizing Your Scripts with Subroutines and Procedures."

Mathematical Variables

The Windows shell supports the creation of variables with numeric values using the SET command and its /a switch. The Windows shell supports a 32-bit numeric range which provides for numbers in the range of −2,147,483,648 to 2,147,483,647. Attempts to reference values outside of this range result in errors. Fortunately, this range is large enough to accommodate just about any value that you might want to assign to a shell variable. For example, you can assign a numeric value to a variable as follows:

```
set /a counter = 2 + 2
```

In the previous example, the value 4 is computed and then assigned to a variable named counter. This is an example of a Windows shell arithmetic operation. The Windows shell also supports the operators listed in Table 5.2.

Table 5.2 Windows Shell Arithmetic Operators

Operator	Name	Description
+	Plus sign	Adds two numeric values
–	Minus sign	Subtracts the second value from the first value
*	Multiplication sign	Multiples two numeric values
/	Division sign	Divides the second value into the first value
%	Modulus sign	Determines the value of the remainder in a division operation

The following example demonstrates the use of these operators. Notice that spaces have been added both before and after the equals signs. When using the /a switch, the Windows shell ignores extra spaces. This allows you to insert spaces for greater readability. Also take note of the %% in the last SET command in this example. This operator is required because otherwise, the Windows shell has to interpret a single percentage as the beginning of a variable and would then expect a closing percentage sign.

```
@echo off
set /a counter = 5
echo %counter%
set /a counter = 5 + 1
echo %counter%
set /a counter = 5 - 1
echo %counter%
set /a counter = 5 / 2
echo %counter%
set /a counter =  5 %% 2
echo %counter%
```

When you run the example, you receive the following output.

```
5
4
3
2
1
```

> **NOTE**
>
> The Windows shell uses a strict set of rules when resolving mathematical equations. First, it resolves all modulus values. Then, it performs all multiplication and division, working from left to right. Finally, it performs addition and subtraction, working from left to right. Unfortunately, you cannot use parentheses to alter the execution of these rules. Therefore, you might have to break complete expressions into multiple statements in order to specify your own order of precedence.

You are not limited to assigning literal values when working with numeric variables. As the following example demonstrates, you can substitute the values of other variables as well.

```
@echo off
set /a a = 1
set /a b = 2
set /a c = a + b
echo %c%
```

When you run the example, you receive the following output.

```
3
```

> **NOTE**
>
> You might also have noticed in the previous example that the final SET statement did not wrap the variables a and b inside percentage signs. The Windows shell allows you to reference numeric values established with the SET command and the /a switch with or without enclosing them inside percentage signs.

You have already seen how the equals sign is used to assign values to variables. The Windows shell provides additional assignment operators, as listed in Table 5.3.

Table 5.3 Windows Shell Assignment Operators

Operator	Description
+=	Add and assign
−=	Subtract and assign
*=	Multiply and assign
/=	Divide and assign
%=	Modulus and assign

For example, SET /a X += 1 is a short way of setting the value of x equal to the current value of x plus 1 and is the equivalent of SET /a X = X + 1. Likewise, SET /a Y *= 3 is the equivalent of SET /a Y = Y * 3. The following example further demonstrates the use of these assignment operators:

```
@echo off
set /a counter = 5
set /a counter +=1
echo %counter%
set /a counter -= 1
echo %counter%
set /a counter *= 2
echo %counter%
set /a counter /= 2
echo %counter%
set /a counter %%=2
echo %counter%
```

When you run the example, you receive the following output.

```
6
5
10
5
1
```

TIP

As the previous example shows, add an additional % character in front of the %= in order to gets the results that you expect as in %%=. Otherwise the Windows shell will give you a `Missing operator` error message.

Error Checking

In Chapter 4, you learned how to use compound commands to make the execution of one command dependent upon the success or failure of the previous command. The Windows shell supports a more robust form of error checking by allowing you to check the error codes of individual commands and perform conditional logic based on the results. Command error code checking is possible because of the ERRORLEVEL variable.

The ERRORLEVEL variable is not visible from either the SET command or the System utilities view of user and system variables. This variable contains the error code of the most recently executed command. An error code of zero indicates a successful command and a non-zero return code indicates an error, as demonstrated:

```
@echo off
cd \
del main_log.txt
echo %ERRORLEVEL%


Could Not Find C:\main_log.txt
1
```

The ERRORLEVEL variable is normally used with the IF statement, which is covered in Chapter 6, to interrogate command results and respond accordingly. You should incorporate the use of exit code checking into your scripts to add logic to handle error conditions. Additional information on how to integrate the ERRORLEVEL variable into your scripts is presented in Chapter 6.

NOTE

Most general errors result in an exit code of 1 whereas command failures usually produce an exit code of 2.

Dissecting Variable Contents

The Windows shell provides two tools for manipulating the value of strings: string substitution and substrings. These techniques allow you to replace string text with new values or to extract a subset of the string value. You can use these techniques when working with the values of both variables and script arguments.

String Substitution

String substitution allows you to substitute a portion of text in a variable or argument's value with new text. String substitution does not alter the variable or argument's value, although it does allow you to pass the substituted value to other commands.

The syntax for string substitution is as follows:

```
%string_name:string_1=string_2%
```

`%variable_name` is the name of the variable or argument to be modified. A colon character follows it. `string_1` specifies the text that is to be substituted and `string_2` specifies the text to be replaced.

For example, using string substitution, you can determine the first name of the person that is stored in the following variable:

```
@echo off
set employee_Name=Bob Jones
echo %employee_Name%
echo %employee_Name:Bob=Robert%
echo %employee_Name%


Bob Jones
Robert Jones
Bob Jones
```

As you can see, the value of `employee_Name` did not change when it was displayed the second time because string substitution does not actually change the value of the variable or argument.

> **TIP**
>
> If you want to retain the new value of substituted text, you can always create a new variable and assign it the substituted value. You can also reassign the substituted value to the original variable.

If you leave the replacement string empty, the Windows shell removes the text in the first string and replaces it with empty spaces, in effect deleting the specified characters, as demonstrated:

```
@echo off
set employee_Name=Bob Jones
echo %employee_Name%
echo %employee_Name:Bob=%
Bob Jones
Jones
```

Substrings

You can extract a portion of string text or *substring* by specifying where the extraction should begin and an optional length that determines where the extraction point ends. This substring technique does not alter the variable value, although it does allow you to pass the substituted value to other commands. As with string substitution, you can assign the substring value to a new value or reassign it to the original variable.

Use the following syntax when extracting substring information from a string:

```
%variable_name:~start_position,length%
```

`Start_position` represents the position of the first character in the substring relative to its index position. The first character in the string has an index value of 0, the second character has an index value of 1, and so on. `Length` is an optional parameter that specifies the end of the substring. If you do not specify the `Length` parameter, all remaining characters after the starting position are extracted.

The following example displays the PATHEXT variable and then extracts the first four characters starting with index 0.

```
@echo off
echo %pathext%
echo %pathext:~0,4%
```

```
.COM;.EXE;.BAT;.CMD
.COM
```

Leaving off the optional *length* value tells the Windows shell to extract all the text beginning at the start_position and continuing to the end of the string, as shown:

```
@echo off
echo %pathext%
echo %pathext:~5%
```

```
.COM;.EXE;.BAT;.CMD
.EXE;.BAT;.CMD
```

Chapter 6

Conditional Logic

Most of the Windows shell scripts that you have seen so far execute sequentially. Each statement is examined and then executed in the order in which it is listed in the script. The one exception to this was the use of compound commands demonstrated in Chapter 4. Compound commands allow scripts to group commands together and then make the execution of one command dependent upon the success or failure of another.

Although certainly helpful, compound commands lack the robustness required to develop complex scripts. This is where the IF statement comes in to play. Like compound commands, the IF statement has provisions for testing command success and failure. In addition, you can use it to alter the logical flow in your scripts by interrogating variable and argument values and making decisions based on those values. You can also use IF statements to test for the existence of variables, files, and even folders before attempting to work with them.

This chapter shows you how to work with the IF statement and provides examples for integrating it into your Windows shell scripts.

Topics covered in this chapter include:

◆ Changing logic flow based on variable values
◆ Verifying that variables exist before working with them
◆ Performing command exit code checking
◆ Nesting multiple IF statements
◆ Working with multiline IF statements

Using Conditional Statements to Alter Script Flow

The Windows shell provides conditional command execution in the form of the IF statement. Both Windows NT and Windows 2000 support many flavors of the IF statement, including the ones listed in Table 6.1.

Table 6.1 Variations of the IF Statement

Type	Description
if	Executes a conditional command
if...else	Provides an alternative execution path
if not	Inverts a conditional test
if defined	Determines whether a variable exists
if not defined	Determines whether a variable does not exist
if errorlevel	Checks the exit code of the previous command
if cmdextension	Verifies the Windows shell's command extension version
if exist	Determines whether a file or folder exists

The *IF* Statement

The IF command tests for a condition and executes a command when the condition is true. In its most common form, the syntax of the IF statement is as follows:

```
if condition == command
```

This version of the IF statement compares the value of a variable. The following example uses an IF statement to check the %SYSTEMROOT% variable and to verify that it has been set to C:\WINNT.

```
if "%SystemRoot%" == "C:\WINNT" echo This server has been set up with a
standard configuration
```

If the %SYSTEMROOT% variable's value is not set to C:\WINNT, the ECHO command will not execute. In this example if %SYSTEMROOT% == "C:\WINNT" is the condition and the ECHO statement is the command that is executed if the condition is true.

NOTE

The default location for the Windows NT and Windows 2000 files is C:\WINNT. The %SYSTEMROOT% variable can be used to locate this folder.

As the previous example demonstrates, both the condition and the command are enclosed inside quotation marks. In addition, blank spaces before and after the double equal signs are permitted.

In the previous example, you compared a variable against a hard-coded value. You can also use the IF statement to compare the value of two variables. In the following example, both x and y have been set to the same value.

```
set x=apple
set y=apple
if %x% == %y% echo The values of x and y are equal
```

> **TIP**
>
> You can use compound commands to execute multiple commands in your IF statements.

The IF statement compares two values. It returns true when the values are identical in text, case, and length. By default, the Windows shell performs a case-sensitive comparison, which means that the value of XXXX and xxxx are different. However, you can perform a case-insensitive comparison using the /i switch, as demonstrated:

```
set x=APPLE
set y=apple
if /i %x% == %y% echo The values of x and y are considered equal
```

Without the /i switch, the comparison will fail.

> **TIP**
>
> There might be times when you do not know whether a variable or argument's value contains spaces. To solve this problem, you can enclose both variables inside quotation marks, as shown:
>
> ```
> If "%x%" == "%y%" echo We have a match!
> ```

The *IF . . . ELSE* Statement

You can use the IF...ELSE statement to specify that a command executes under either true or false conditions. The syntax of this form of the IF statement is as follows:

```
if condition (command) else (command)
```

The first command is executed when the condition proves true and the second is executed when the condition proves false. Both the true and false commands must be placed inside parentheses. If you omit the parentheses, the Windows shell will not recognize the ELSE portion of the statement and will not produce the desired results.

The following example demonstrates the use of the IF...ELSE statement.

```
if "%SystemRoot%" == "C:\WINNT" (echo Server has a standard
  configuration) else (echo Server has a non-standard configuration)
```

In this example, any computer that is not running Windows NT or Windows 2000 or that has changed the name or location of the default Windows folder triggers the ELSE condition.

The *IF NOT* Statement

The IF NOT statement allows you to test for a false condition instead of a true condition. The following example demonstrates the use of the IF NOT statement. In this example, the IF NOT statement tests for the absence of the default Windows NT or Windows 2000 folder.

```
if not "%SystemRoot%" == "C:\WINNT"

   echo This server has not been set up with a standard configuration
```

If the c:\WINNT folder is found, the ECHO command is not executed. Conversely, if it is not found, the ECHO command is executed.

The next example shows a common use of the IF NOT statement. In this case, the script makes sure that the operating system is either Windows NT or Windows 2000 and if this isn't the case, the script executes the GOTO EXIT command.

A message is then displayed explaining that the scripts run only on the Windows NT or Windows 2000 operating systems. A detailed explanation of the GOTO statement is presented in Chapter 8, "Organizing Your Scripts with Subroutines and Procedures." For now, just note that GOTO allows the script to jump to a new location and continue processing.

If the operating system is Windows NT or Windows 2000, the GOTO command is not executed. Instead, the script displays the name of the operating system, the name of the computer, and the name of the user running the script. Then, another GOTO command terminates the execution of the script, thus preventing the execution of the remaining statements.

```
@echo off

if not "%OS%" == "Windows_NT" goto exit

echo Operating System: %OS%
echo Computer Name: %COMPUTERNAME%
echo Username: %USERNAME%

goto :EOF

:exit
echo This script requires either Windows NT or 2000
```

TIP

It is considered good programming practice to have a script check the operating system before processing. Windows Me and 98 do not support a robust shell-scripting environment. Therefore, most shell scripts will not run on either of those operating systems. By incorporating the previous example into your scripts, you can allow them to end gracefully when they determine that they have been started on an unsupported operating system.

If you run the previous example on a Windows NT or 2000 computer, you should see output similar to the following:

```
Operating System: Windows_NT
Computer Name: Database_Server
Username: jford
```

However, if you run the script on a Windows 98 or Window Me computer, you will see the output shown in Figure 6.1.

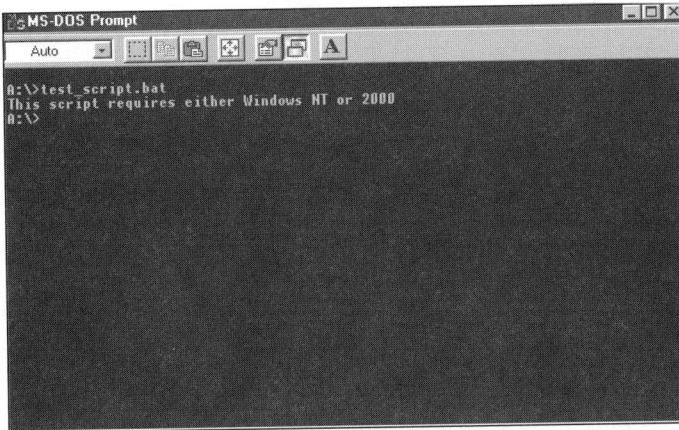

FIGURE 6.1

Windows 98 and Windows Me lack a robust scripting environment and do not support Windows shell scripts.

The *IF DEFINED* Statement

You can add the IF DEFINED statement to your scripts to determine whether a variable exists before trying to reference it.

The syntax for the IF DEFINED statement is shown here:

```
if defined variable command
```

If the specified variable exists, the command executes. Otherwise, the command is skipped.

For example, the following statement checks for the presence of a system variable named os:

```
if defined OS echo This variable is already defined
```

The *IF NOT DEFINED* Statement

The IF NOT DEFINED statement does the opposite of the IF DEFINED statement. It ensures that the variable in question does not exist. You can add the IF NOT DEFINED statement to your scripts to make sure that a variable does not exist before you create it.

The syntax for the IF NOT DEFINED statement is shown here:

```
if not defined variable command
```

If the specified variable does not exist, the command executes. If the variable does exist, the command is skipped. For example, the following statement displays its message only when the variable does not exist. Because OS is a system environment variable and should always be present, the ECHO command will not execute.

```
if not defined OS echo This variable does not exist!
```

The *IF ERRORLEVEL* Statement

The IF ERRORLEVEL statement checks the exit code of the previously executed command. Windows commands supply an exit code upon execution to indicate the success or failure of the command. The Windows shell supports two versions of the IF ERRORLEVEL statement:

The syntax of the first option is as follows:

```
If errorlevel exitcode command
```

ERRORLEVEL specifies an exit code. Commands that complete without error complete with an exit code of 0. Any exit code higher than 0 indicates an error of some type. The IF ERRORLEVEL statement determines whether the previous command's exit code is equal to or greater than the value specified by *exitcode*, in which case the specified command executes.

The following example checks the exit code for the DIR *.xxx command. If there are no files in the current directory with an .xxx file extension, it displays a message.

```
dir *.xxx
if errorlevel 1 echo No files found.
```

The syntax of the second option is as follows:

```
if errorlevel == exitcode
```

In this case, the IF ERRORLEVEL statement checks for a specific exit code. When the exit code matches the value specified by *exitcode*, the specified command executes. For example, the following command checks for an exit code of 2 and executes an ECHO command that displays an error message when there is a match.

```
if "%errorlevel%" == "2" echo Command execution error!
```

> **NOTE**
>
> You can invert the ERRORLEVEL test with the NOT option.

The *IF CMDEXTVERSION* Statement

The IF CMDEXTVERSION statement allows your scripts to check the version of the Windows shell that the script is executing in. Windows NT 4's shell is version 1 and Windows 2000's shell is version 2. Depending on whether Microsoft makes any enhancements to the Windows XP version of the Windows shell, it might have a new version number as well. By interrogating the value of CMDEXTVERSION, your script can alter its behavior accordingly.

Use the IF CMDEXTVERSION statement to test for *compliance* of the indicated shell version number. For example, the version 2 shell will comply with the version 1 shell since the functionality of the version 2 shell is inclusive of functionality of the version 1 shell. In other words, if your script runs on the version 1 shell, it will probably also run on all succeeding shells. However, just because your scripts run with the version 2 shell, it does not mean that they will run on the version 1 shell. You will have to test your scripts by running them on operating systems that have each shell version to see if this is the case.

Although the Windows 2000 and Window NT 4 shells are very similar, there are small differences. For example, Windows 2000 does not support the BACKUP and RESTORE commands used in Windows NT 4. In other cases, Windows 2000 might support new command features that are not available in Windows NT 4. Usually this comes in the form of additional switches or command options. In any case, by determining the value of CMDEXTVERSION, you can build logic into your scripts that allows them to call the appropriate command switches and options for a particular Windows shell version.

The syntax for the IF CMDEXTVERSION statement is shown here:

```
if cmdextversion version command
```

For example, you can use the following example to check the value of CMDEXTVERSION:

```
@echo off
if cmdextversion 1 echo The Windows shell in which this script is exe-
cuting is version 1 or higher.
```

The *IF EXIST* Statement

The IF EXIST statement allows you to check for the existence of files and folders. The syntax for the IF EXIST statement is shown here:

```
if [not] exist file command
```

not is an optional parameter that allows you to invert the test. *File* is the name of the file or folder you want to find and *command* is the command to be executed.

You can use IF EXIST to make sure that a file exists before you try to work with it. Likewise, it makes sense to determine whether a folder exists before you try to create it or add a new file to it. For example, to check for a file named REPORT.LOG in the c:\log folder, you type:

```
if exist C:\log\report.log copy C:\log\report.log \\fileserver\logs
```

This example first verifies that the file exists. If it does exist, the file is copied to a shared folder on a network server. If the file does not exist, there is no point to trying to copy it, so the COPY operation is skipped.

The next example demonstrates how to check for the existence of a folder. In this case, you can check for the name of the folder, but that does not necessarily provide conclusive results because the folder might not exist, yet a file of the same name might. To get around this issue, check for the presence of a file called "." inside the folder. As Figure 6.2 demonstrates, every subfolder in a Windows operating system has this entry.

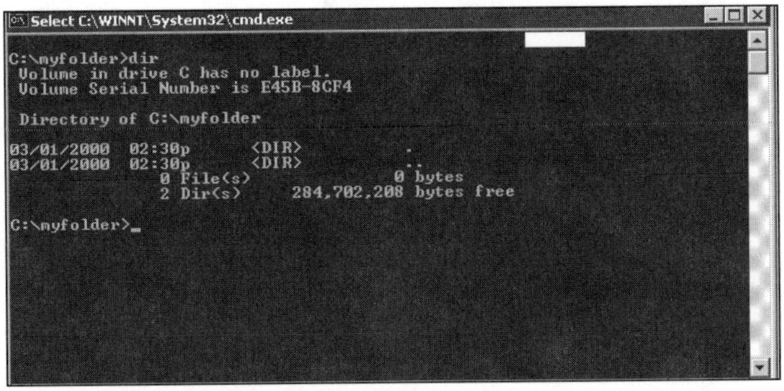

FIGURE 6.2

To verify that an object is a folder and not a file, check for the presence of a "." file inside the folder.

For example, the following statement checks for the existence of a folder called myfolder:

```
if exist C:\myfolder\. Copy C:\report.log C:\myfolder
```

Nested *IF* Statements

The Windows shell also allows you to place IF statements inside other IF statements to create nested IF statements. The primary advantage to nesting IF statements is that it allows you to develop more complicated programming logic in a more efficient manner.

For example, the following script contains a nested set of IF statements. The first IF statement ensures that the script is running on a Windows NT operating system. If this condition proves true, the second IF statement is tested. This IF statement ensures that the script is running on a particular server. If the script is not running on the server in question, the script calls a procedure that displays an error message.

```
@echo off

if "%OS%" == "Windows_NT" if not %COMPUTERNAME% == file-server goto
:exit

goto :EOF

:exit
  echo This script should only be executed on the main file server!
```

The following output shows the results of running the previous example on a Windows NT server that is not named `file-server`:

```
This script should only be executed on the main file server!
```

TIP

The previous example is a little hard to follow. As the following statements show, you can make this example easier to read by applying the syntax of multiline IF statements, as shown here.

```
if "%OS%" == "Windows_NT" (

    if not %COMPUTERNAME% == File-server goto :exit

)
```

Multiline *IF* Statements

You can include multiple statements inside your IF statements by enclosing them inside parentheses using the following syntax:

```
if [not] string1 == string2 command (
  Place multiple statements here.
)
```

Multiline IF statements provide for better script readability and organization. The following example shows a script that includes both nested IF statements and multiline IF statements. The first IF statement verifies that the script is being executed on a Windows NT operating system. If this is not the case, the script skips all the statements included within the IF statement and executes the GOTO :EOF statement to terminate processing.

```
@echo off

if "%OS%" == "Windows_NT" (
  echo Operating system = Windows NT
  if not %COMPUTERNAME% == file-server (
    echo This script should only be executed on the main file server!
    echo This server is %COMPUTERNAME%
```

```
    ) else (
        echo This script Is executing on %COMPUTERNAME%
        rem Add additional statements here
    )
)


goto :EOF
```

If the operating system is Windows NT, the script ensures that the server executing the script is named `file-server`. If this is the case, this multiline `IF` statement executes two `ECHO` statements. If this is not the case, the multiline `ELSE` statement that follows the `IF` statement executes. The following output shows the results of trying to run the script on a server named `PRINT-SERVER`.

```
Operating system = Windows NT
This script should only be executed on the main file server!
This server is PRINT-SERVER
```

Using Comparison Operators

So far, the only comparison operator that you have seen in this chapter is the `==` operator. The Windows shell supports additional comparison operators, as listed in Table 6.2.

Table 6.2   Windows Shell Comparison Operators

Operator	Description
==	Equal to
EQU	Equal to
LSS	Less than
GTR	Greater than
LEQ	Less than or equal to
GEQ	Greater than or equal to
NEQ	Not equal to

Note: In Windows NT 4, you must use uppercase characters for these operators; otherwise, you will receive an error. Windows 2000 supports both upper- and lowercase.

For example, when determining which operating system the script is executing on, you can use the following command:

```
if "%OS%" == "Windows_NT" echo This Is an approved operating system
```

You can also use the following command:

```
if "%OS%" EQU "Windows_NT" echo This Is an approved operating system
```

The comparison operators also apply to numeric data. For example, suppose you have a script that creates the following variables:

```
set /a x=1
set /a y=3
```

You can then compare their values using the following commands:

```
if x LSS y echo x is less than y
if x LEQ y echo x is less than or equal to y
```

Tracing Error and Logic Flow

Unfortunately, the Windows shell does not provide a built-in mechanism for debugging scripts or running traces. However, you can use IF commands to set up your own debugging environment. This is achieved by placing the following statement at the beginning of your script.

```
if /i "%debug%" == "on" (set trace=echo) else (set trace=rem)
```

This statement looks for a variable named %debug% and performs a case-insensitive comparison of its value. If %debug% is set to ON, the value of a variable named trace is set to ECHO; otherwise, it is set to REM. This way, you can control when your script runs in debug mode by toggling the value of the %debug% variable. For example, typing the following command at the command prompt and pressing Enter turns debugging on:

```
set debug=on
```

Likewise, the following command disables debugging:

```
set debug=
```

Now that you know how to set up tracing and turn it off and on, all that remains is to place statements similar to the following throughout your scripts:

```
%trace% Tracing on.
```

This way, either ECHO or REM is substituted for the value of %trace% based on whether the %debug% variable has been set. The following example demonstrates how you might set up debugging logic in your scripts:

```
@echo off

if /i "%debug%" == "on" (set trace=echo) else (set trace=rem)

set /a x = 1
set /a y = 5

%trace% Tracing on.

%trace% The value of x is %x%
%trace% The value of y is %y%

%trace% Main body of script begins here
```

If the %debug% variable has been set, the script will echo the value of the variables as it executes so that you can make sure that they have been set as expected. In addition, other statements have been added to alert you when they execute so that you can follow the execution flow of the script as it executes. If the %debug% variable is not set, the value of %trace% is set to REM and all the %trace% statements become comments.

NOTE

The debugging technique presented in this chapter works because the Windows shell performs variable substitution before attempting to execute any commands. Therefore, assuming that %debug% has been set to ON, a command such as %trace% Tracing is on is resolved to ECHO Tracing is on before the Windows shell tries to execute it.

Updating Your Windows Shell Template

You can now improve your standard script template by incorporating IF statements, which provide the following enhancements:

◆ **Verification of the operation system**. IF statements can verify whether Windows NT or Windows 2000 is executing the script and then terminate its execution if this is not the case.

◆ **Dynamic tracing**. IF statements can enable and disable trace information based on the value of a debugging variable.

The following code shows the updated script template. As you can see, the template ensures that the script will execute only when it's running on Windows NT 4 or Windows 2000. In addition, conditional debugging logic establishes a framework for tracing script errors and processing flow.

```
@echo off
rem ******************************************
rem * Script Name: template.bat             *
rem * Author:   Jerry Ford                   *
rem * Address: Richmond Virginia             *
rem * Created: 03/16/01                      *
rem ******************************************

rem Perform script initialization
if not "%OS%" == "Windows_NT" goto EXIT
if /i "%debug%" == "on" (set trace=echo) else (set trace=rem)
title "Insert script title message here"
cls

%trace% Tracing on.

%trace% Main body of script begins here



goto :EOF

:EXIT
echo This script requires either Windows NT or 2000
```

Chapter 7

Iterative
Processing

One of the most difficult aspects of an NT administrator's job is performing simple but highly repetitive tasks, such as the creation of hundreds of new user accounts. In addition to being time-consuming, repetitive tasks are also prone to human error.

One of the most powerful features of Windows shell scripting is its ability to loop through collections of files, folders, command output, and strings and iteratively perform commands. Looping allows scripts to process large amounts of data and perform actions that would take an intolerably long period of time to perform using the Windows graphical user interface. The Windows shell provides this capability via the FOR command.

Topics covered in this chapter include:

◆ Processing a predetermined range of values
◆ Processing files
◆ Processing folders
◆ Processing file contents
◆ Retrieving and processing lengthy command output

Executing Repetitive Commands and Processes

You can use the FOR loop to repeat the execution of one or more commands. You can use the FOR command to look through any of the following:

◆ Strings
◆ Command output
◆ Text files
◆ Groups of files
◆ Groups of folders

Each of these options has a slightly different syntax and is explained in the sections that follow. However, each FOR loop is based on the following syntax:

```
for /switch %%variable in (set) do command
```

The /switch parameter is used to set up the loop to process different kinds of resources and can be any of the following:

- ◆ /l Loop through a range of values
- ◆ /f Loop through all the elements in a string
- ◆ /d Loop through all the files in a directory
- ◆ /r Loop through and process all subfolders

The %%variable is a special variable type known as an *iterator*. The FOR loop increments the value of %%variable upon each iteration of the loop with the value of the text string in the set. The iterator only exists inside the FOR loop and cannot be referenced either before of after the loop executes. set identifies a list of files, folders, text strings, or a range that is to be iterated through. command specifies the command, compound command, or procedure call to be executed with each execution of the loop.

NOTE

The iterator is a letter in the range of %%A through %%Z. Iterators are case-sensitive, so %%A is not the same as %%a.

TIP

Regardless of which form of the FOR loop you are using, you can execute more than one command by using compound commands or by calling procedures. More information on procedures is provided in Chapter 8, "Organizing Your Scripts with Subroutines and Procedures."

Processing a Range of Values

Windows shell scripts can process a range of values using the FOR loop. This form of the FOR loop allows you to specify a starting and ending range and to execute commands as the range is processed.

The syntax for this form of the FOR loop is as follows:

```
for /l %%variable in (begin,increment,end) do command
```

The increment parameter controls the iterator value. The iterator value is set to the value of BEGIN when the loop starts processing and is incremented by the value of INCREMENT each time the loop executes. The loop continues to iterate until the value of the iterator becomes greater than the value specified by END.

For example, the following statement sets up a loop that executes five times, beginning with 1 and terminating with 5 with an increment of 1. The value of the iterator is displayed with each iteration.

```
for /l %%i in (1,1,5) do echo %%i
```

The previous statement produces the following output:

```
1
2
3
4
5
```

You can use an argument passed to the script or a variable set elsewhere in the program to control loop execution, as demonstrated in the following example.

```
@echo off
set /a no_of_checks = 3
for /l %%i in (1,1,%no_of_checks%) do echo %%i
```

In this example, the END value of the iterator is determined by the value of no_of_checks, which has been set to 3.

NOTE

The /a switch used with the SET statement is required to make the value a numeric setting.

The next example uses the FOR loop and the DIR command to look for a file named ACCOUNTING.XLS. This example assumes that another application is supposed to create this file either before or at approximately the same time that this script executes. The iterator variable is %%i, its initial value is set to 1, and it is incremented by one each time the loop executes, until its value exceeds 10. With each iteration of the loop, the DIR command is executed. If the command is successful, the script immediately terminates. If the ACCOUNT-ING.XLS file is not found, the SLEEP command is executed. In this case, SLEEP causes the script to pause for 60 seconds before resuming. If the file is present when the script first starts, nothing happens and the script terminates. However, if the file is not present and does not appear within 10 minutes, an error message is displayed.

```
@echo off
echo Executing scheduled check for ACCOUNTING.XLS:
for /l %%i in (1,1,10) do ((dir accounting.xls>accounting.log 2>&1 &&
exit) || echo File not found, sleeping... & sleep 60)
echo Time has expired and the accounting spreadsheet file has not been
created!
```

To keep this display clear of command output and error messages that appear when the ACCOUNTING.XLS file is not found, the following parameters were appended to the end of the DIR command:

```
>accounting.log 2>&1
```

>accounting.log has the effect of first sending all command output to a file instead of displaying it on the screen and 2>&1 sends error output to the same location. If you were to remove the logging parameters from the DIR command, you would see output similar to the following every time the FOR loop failed to find the ACCOUNTING.XLS file:

```
C:\>dir accounting.xls
 Volume in drive C has no label.
 Volume Serial Number is E45B-8CF4

 Directory of C:\

File Not Found
```

NOTE

The SLEEP command is a Windows NT and Windows 2000 Resource Kit command that allows you to pause your scripts for a specified period of time.

Figure 7.1 shows how the output of the script will appear when the script is unable to find the file.

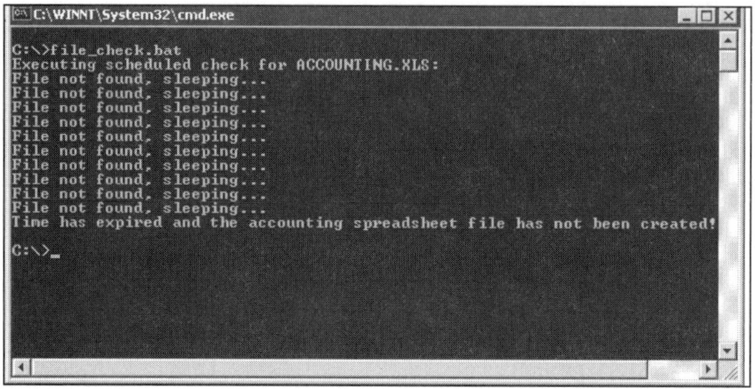

FIGURE 7.1

The Windows NT 4 and Windows 2000 Resource Kit's SLEEP.EXE command provides the capability to put your script into a paused state for a predetermined amount of time.

NOTE

The FOR loop always compares the value specified by BEGIN and END before performing the loop's first iteration. If the value of BEGIN is higher than the value specified by END, the loop never iterates and processing continues with the first statement following the loop.

TIP

You can use a negative number as your INCREMENT value, in which case the value of the iterator is decremented with each iteration and the loop processes as long as the value of the iterator is greater than END.

```
for /l %%i in (5,-1,1) do echo %%i
```

Iteratively Processing String Contents

You can use the following variation of the FOR loop to parse the string contents of a variable string.

```
for /f ["options"] %%variable in ("string") do command
```

This form of the FOR loop supports any of the options specified in Table 7.1.

Table 7.1 Parsing Command Options

Option	Description
delims=xxx	Overrides the default space and tab delimiters with the specified deliminator. A deliminator is a character that serves as a separator between data. For example, in a comma-deliminated file each piece of data in the file is separated by a comma.
eol=c	Identifies an end-of-line comment character.
skip=n	Specifies the number of lines at the top of the file to be skipped.
tokens=a,b,a-c	Specifies the tokens to be used in each iteration. Each element or piece of data in a string is a token. For example, if a string consists of a person's name in the format of last name, first name, and then middle name, it contains three tokens. a,b specifies a list of tokens to be used. a-c specifies a range of tokens to be used. A combination of both token specifications is permitted. By specifying tokens, you can select which pieces of a string you want to process.

This version of the FOR loop breaks the contents of the string into individual elements and assigns each one to a token. Using the TOKENS option, you can specify which tokens are to be processed. For example, the following statements demonstrate how a FOR loop can be set up to process a string that contains a list of file extensions.

```
set fileList=*.log,*.txt,*.bak
 for /f "delims=, tokens=1-3" %%i in ("%fileList%") do (del %%i %%j
%%k)
```

Commas separate each entry in the string. The FOR loop that processes this string specifies the comma as the deliminator character with DELIMS=, and then specifies that the first, second, and third elements in the string are to be processed using TOKENS=1-3. When executed, the FOR statement deletes all files with the specified file extensions in the current folder.

Processing Command Output

The Windows shell lets you issue commands and parse through their output using the following variation of the FOR loop.

```
for /f ["options"] %%variable in ('command') do command
```

The OPTIONS are the same as those listed in Table 7.1. The command to be parsed is placed inside single quotes and parentheses. For example, the following statement executes the command SET USERNAME.

```
for /f "delims== tokens=2" %%i in ('set username') do (echo Currently
logged in user: %%i)
```

If you were to type **SET USERNAME** at the command prompt, you would receive output similar to the following:

```
USERNAME=Administrator
```

However, the FOR loop hides the actual command output so that only the results of the ECHO command are shown. By specifying a deliminator of = and TOKENS=2, the FOR loop captures and assigns the second element in the output string, in this case Administrator, to the iterator variable, which is then displayed as demonstrated:

```
Currently logged in user: jlf04
```

Processing the Contents of Text Files

You can also process the contents of text files with FOR loops. This enables you to process files created by other scripts or applications. By processing files from other scripts, you can build your own applications and management tools. By processing files created by other applications, you can develop ways to provide added value to the data and reports generated by those applications.

The syntax of the FOR loop when parsing file output is as follows:

```
for /f ["options"] %%variable in (filenameset) do command
```

For example, the following script creates a tab-delineated file that contains a list of information about company employees.

```
Filename: hr_file.bat
@echo off
echo =========================================================== >
hr_file.txt
echo Data Security Department user account list >> hr_file.txt
echo =========================================================== >>
hr_file.txt
echo name      user-id  department  ext.  pager >> hr_file.txt
echo Jones     jon01    info_sec    3242  550-8888 #Manager >>
hr_file.txt
echo Davis     dav01    account     3455  550-9999 #Contractor     >>
hr_file.txt
echo Ford      for01    account     7654  550-9876 #SpecialAgent >>
hr_file.txt
echo Benson    ben01    marketing   4543  550-1234 #Salesman       >>
hr_file.txt
echo Clay      cla01    marketing   3453  550-7744 #Trainee >>
hr_file.txt
```

When executed, the script creates a file named HR_FILE.TXT, as shown in Figure 7.2.

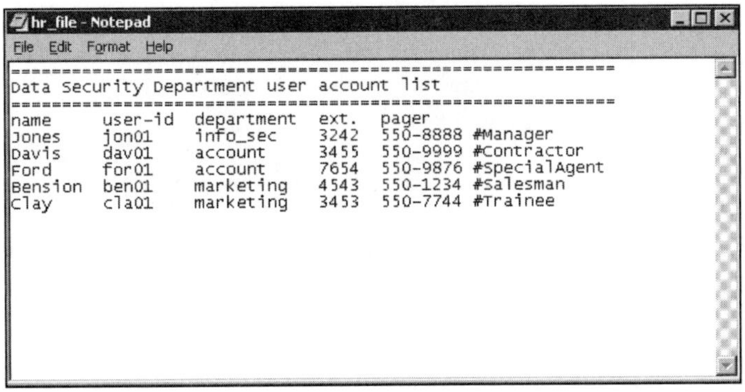


```
===========================================================
Data Security Department user account list
===========================================================
name     user-id  department  ext.  pager
Jones    jon01    info_sec    3242  550-8888 #Manager
Davis    dav01    account     3455  550-9999 #Contractor
Ford     for01    account     7654  550-9876 #SpecialAgent
Bension  ben01    marketing   4543  550-1234 #Salesman
Clay     cla01    marketing   3453  550-7744 #Trainee
```

FIGURE 7.2

A FOR *loop loops through files and processes their contents.*

The first four lines of this file contain header information. Each line after these lines contains records for each employee in a tab-delineated format. At the end of each line is a comment that begins with the # character. The following FOR loop processes the file:

```
for /f %%i in (hr_file.txt) do (echo %%i)
```

This FOR statement demonstrates the simplest form of file parsing. It specifies a deliminator and source file. As the output in Figure 7.3 shows, when no options are specified, the FOR loop processes only the first token in each file.

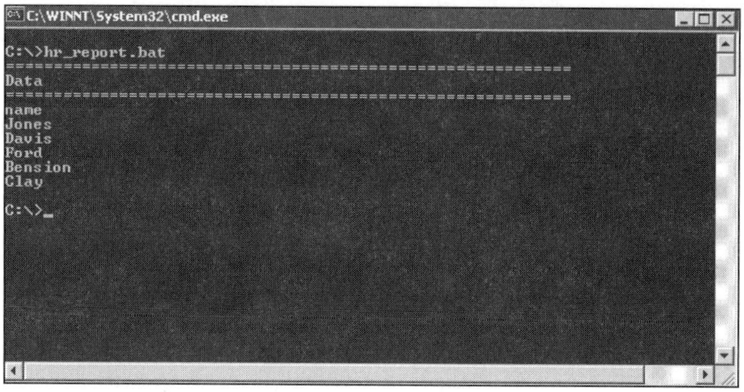

FIGURE 7.3

The default behavior for a FOR loop that processes files is to process only the first token on each line in the file.

TIP

You can process the contents of more than one file at a time by specifying wild-card characters in FILENAMESET or by typing multiple file names separated by spaces.

You can eliminate the first four header lines by adding the SKIP option in the FOR loop. For example, SKIP=4 prevents the display of the first four lines in the file:

```
for /f "skip=4" %%i in (hr_file.txt) do (echo %%i)
```

The following list shows the output of the previous FOR statement:

Jones

Davis

Ford

Benson

Clay

You can modify the FOR statement to process additional fields in the file by adding the TOKENS option and specifying which additional pieces of information should be processed. In the following example, tokens 1, 3, and 4 are specified. This parses the employee's name, department, and phone extension. Tokens 1, 3 and 4 are then associated with %%i, %%j, and %%k, respectively, as shown:

```
for /f "tokens=1,3,4 skip=4" %%i in (hr_file.txt) do (echo NAME: %%i
DEPT: %%j PHONE: %%k)
```

The following list shows the output of the previous FOR statement:

NAME: Jones DEPT: info_sec PHONE: 3242

NAME: Davis DEPT: account PHONE: 3455

NAME: Ford DEPT: account PHONE: 7654

NAME: Benson DEPT: marketing PHONE: 4543

NAME: Clay DEPT: marketing PHONE: 3453

Another way to process the source file is by specifying TOKENS=*. This instructs the FOR loop to assign the contents of each line to the iterator value.

```
for /f "tokens=* skip=4" %%i in (hr_file.txt) do (echo NAME: %%i)
```

The following list shows the output of the previous FOR statement:

NAME: Jones   jon01   info_sec   3242   550-8888 #Manager

NAME: Davis   dav01   account   3455   550-9999 #Contractor

NAME: Ford   for01   account   7654   550-9876 #SpecialAgent

NAME: Benson   ben01   marketing   4543   550-1234 #Salesman

NAME: Clay   cla01   marketing   3453   550-7744 #Trainee

NOTE

You do not need to worry about removing blank lines in source files. The FOR loop will automatically ignore them.

CAUTION

If you need to use a file name that includes spaces, you have to use special syntax to avoid getting an error when parsing text using the FOR loop. In order to work with these files, you must replace (FILENAMESET) with ('type "filename"'). The TYPE command displays the contents of the file specified by *filename* and allows the FOR loop to capture the command results for processing. Make sure that you include both the single quotes and the double quotes exactly as shown.

Processing Groups of Files

Sometimes you might want to process some or all the files in a given folder. The FOR command supports this operation using the following syntax:

```
for %%variable in (set) do command
```

SET specifies the collection of files that you want to process. You can include one or more files in *SET* by using wild-card characters or by including a list of files or file types separated by spaces.

For example, you can list all files with a `.log` file extension in the current directory by specifying the following `*.log` as the SET parameter:

```
for %%i in (*.log) do echo %%i
```

The results of this command should yield output similar to this:

```
account.log
daily.log
report.log
system.log
```

TIP

You can specify drive and path information as part of the SET parameter to process a directory other than the current one.

You can also process more than one file type. For example, the following statement processes all files in the current directory that have either `*.log` or `*.bak` file extensions:

```
for %%i in (*.log *.bak) do echo %%i
```

As you can see, this time the output includes both log and backup files.

```
account.log
daily.log
report.log
system.log
acct_report.bak
mkt_report.bak
```

The following example demonstrates how to use the FOR command to create a report that lists all log and backup files in the current directory.

```
@echo off
echo **************************** > daily.txt
echo  Daily log and backup report >> daily.txt
echo   For date: %date% >> daily.txt
echo **************************** >> daily.txt
for %%i in (*.log *.bak) do echo %%i >> daily.txt
```

Figure 7.4 shows the results of executing the previous script.

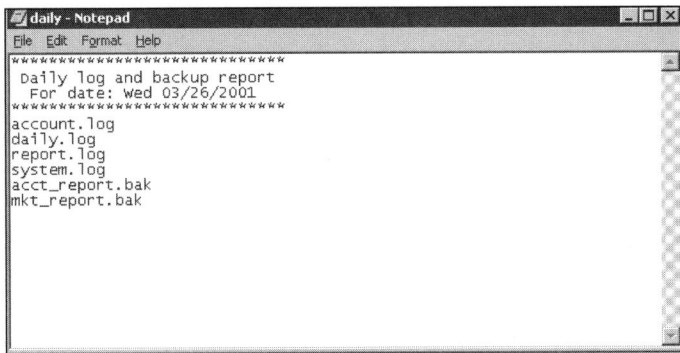

FIGURE 7.4

You can automate the creation of logs, files, and reports using nothing more than Windows shell scripts.

NOTE

The *SET* parameter can contain a single file or a group of files. When specifying the *SET* parameter, you can include wild-card characters, including the * and the ? characters. You can use the ? wild-card character to replace a single character, whereas the * replaces an unlimited number of characters. For example, any of the following are valid *SET* parameters:

```
(*.log)

(*.log *.bak *.txt)

(dec??1999.* dec?2000.* dec??2001.*)

(jan*.log jan*.bak feb*.log feb*.bak)
```

Processing Groups of Folders

In addition to processing files, the FOR loop enables you to process the contents of entire folders. To do this, use the following FOR command syntax:

```
for /d %%variable in (set) do command
```

The /d switch tells the FOR loop to process the current set of subdirectories (folders) instead of files. For example, the following statement allows you to list all the folders located in the root directory:

```
for /d %%i in (c:\) do echo %%i
```

The results should resemble the following:

```
c:\Documents and Settings
c:\MSOffice
c:\Program Files
c:\Scripts
c:\TEMP
c:\WINNT
```

> **NOTE**
>
> The terms *folders* and *directories* are used interchangeably throughout this chapter and in the IT industry.

If you want to check all folders under the current folder, you need to use the following FOR command syntax:

```
for /r [path] %%variable in (set) do command
```

The /r switch tells the Windows shell to process all subfolders, beginning with the currently specified folder. For example, to process every folder under the root directory on the c: drive, execute the following statement.

```
for /r c:\Scripts %%i in (.) do echo %%i
```

Figure 7.5 shows the results of executing the previous statement.

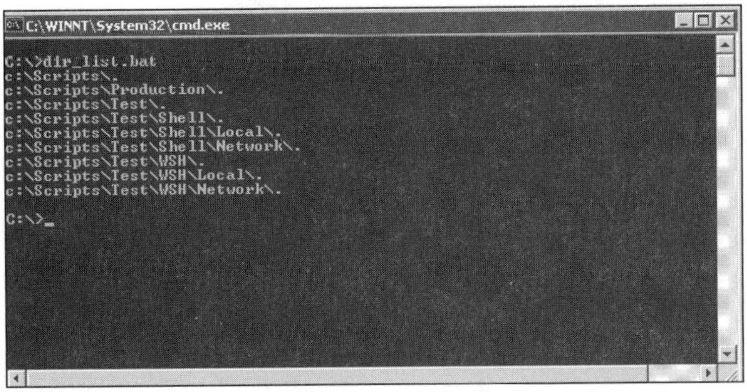

FIGURE 7.5

By using FOR *loops, you can quickly process collections of files and folders or even the contents of entire disk drives.*

Chapter 8

Organizing Your Scripts with Subroutines and Procedures

This chapter introduces you to subroutines and procedures and other forms of script flow control. These programming constructs provide a great deal of flexibility when designing your scripts by allowing you to better organize your scripting logic. Other benefits introduced by these programming techniques include the capability to create loops, to further localize variable values, to execute external and internal procedures, and to create reusable sections of code.

Topics covered in this chapter include:

◆ Calling and executing other scripts

◆ Creating subroutines

◆ Creating internal script procedures

◆ Calling other scripts as external procedures

◆ Localizing procedure variables

◆ Passing script arguments to procedures

Streamlining Your Shell Scripts

By default, Windows shell scripts execute from top to bottom, processing each statement in the order in which it is listed, with script termination occurring at the end of the file. However, this default behavior can easily be changed in a variety of ways.

The Windows shell supports a number of mechanisms that allow scripts to call other scripts or to create and call the following internal subroutines and procedures:

◆ **Chaining**. Occurs when one script executes another script and terminates its own execution.

◆ **Nesting**. Occurs when one script executes another script and then resumes its own execution when the called script terminates.

◆ **Subroutines**. Occurs when a GOTO statement causes the processing flow to jump from one location in a script to another.

◆ **Procedures**. Occurs when a CALL statement executes an internal procedure or external script and then resumes execution when the called procedure or script terminates.

Each of these programming techniques is explained in detail throughout the rest of this chapter.

Chaining Script Execution

Chaining allows you to initiate the execution of one script from another script. When a chaining operation occurs, the Windows shell starts the new script and immediately terminates the calling script, as depicted in Figure 8.1.

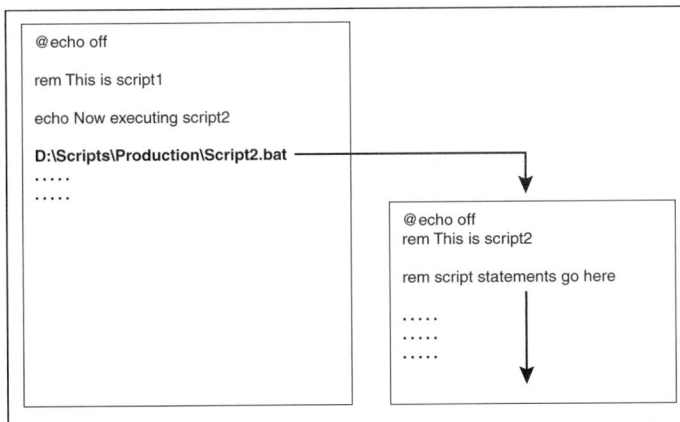

FIGURE 8.1

Chaining allows you to execute one script from within another.

To set up a chaining operation, simply type the name of another script in the calling script:

```
@echo off
rem This is script1
echo Now executing script2
D:\Scripts\Production\script2.bat
```

The new script inherits the current environment. Therefore, it has access to any existing environment variables. However, it does not have access to any of the arguments passed to script1. This is because the chained script expects to receive its own set of arguments. To pass `script1`'s argument to `script2`, you can call `script2` from `script1`, as follows:

`D:\Scripts\Production\Script2.bat %*`

NOTE

You can also set up your scripts to chain back to themselves, thus creating a loop.

Nesting Script Execution

Nesting is a programming technique that provides for the creation of procedures. It is similar to chaining except that instead of being terminated, the parent script waits for the child script to complete and then resumes its own execution. This process is depicted in Figure 8.2.

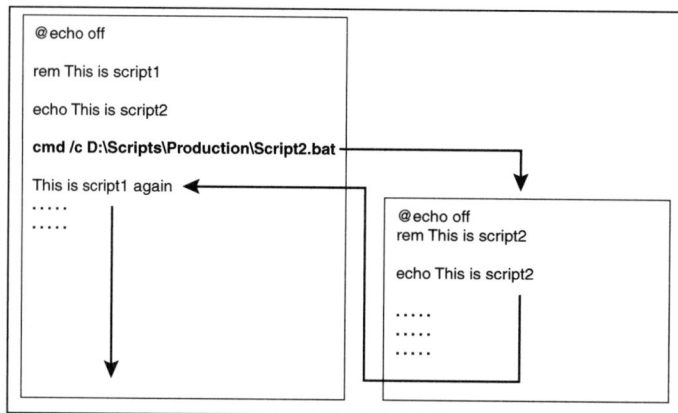

FIGURE 8.2

Nesting allows you to create procedures in the form of external scripts.

To nest another script, you use the CMD command with the `/c` switch. As you do in chaining operations, you must explicitly pass any of the parent script's arguments to the child script. Unlike chaining operations, any changes made by the child script are not retained when the child script terminates.

The following pair of scripts demonstrates how script nesting works. The first script is named SCRIPT1.BAT. When executed, it displays a message and then executes `script2`.

```
@echo off
rem This is script1
echo This is script1
cmd /c D:\Scripts\Production\Script2.bat
echo This is script1 again
```

When `script2` executes, it displays a message and then terminates, passing control back to `script1`, which then displays another message and terminates.

```
@echo off
rem This is script2
echo This is script2
```

The following output demonstrates the results of executing these scripts.

```
C:\>script1.bat
This is script1
This is script2
This is script1 again
```

> **TIP**
>
> Just because the child script's environment is discarded when it completes its execution does not mean that it cannot pass information back to the parent script. The child script can create files and write information in them. These files can then be opened and read by the parent script when it resumes execution. You can also use a technique known as *variable tunneling*, which is described later in this chapter.

> **TIP**
>
> External procedures provide the same basic functionality as nested scripts and are generally considered a more standard and proper way of managing the execution of child scripts. External procedures are explained later in this chapter.

Using Labels

Labels are identifiers or markers placed inside of Windows shell scripts to denote the beginning of a subroutine or procedure. The syntax for a label is the colon character followed by the label name, as shown:

```
:label
```

Label names are not case-sensitive and can consist of alphanumeric characters and the underscore character. The GOTO and CALL statements, discussed in the section that follows, make calls to labels that cause jumps from the current location in the script to the line that immediately follows the label.

Using the *GOTO* Statement

With the GOTO statement, script control jumps to the LABEL specified in the statement. The script then continues its execution from that point, skipping over any commands in between the GOTO statement and the LABEL statement.

The GOTO statement supports two types of operations:

◆ **Looping**. Created by preceding the GOTO statement with the LABEL statement in the script.

◆ **Subroutines**. Created by placing the LABEL statement after the GOTO statement in the script.

Subroutines have complete access to any arguments that have been passed to the script. Any changes made by the subroutines affect the entire script as well.

NOTE

You cannot return from a subroutine and resume processing at the point where the GOTO command was executed. Windows shell scripting provides this functionality in the CALL statement, which is discussed later in this chapter.

Using *GOTO* to Create Loops

You can create a loop inside your script with the GOTO and LABEL statements by placing the LABEL statement before the GOTO statement. Figure 8.3 depicts an example of such a loop. Any statements in between the LABEL and the GOTO statements are repeatedly executed until another command, usually another GOTO statement, executes and breaks the script out of the loop.

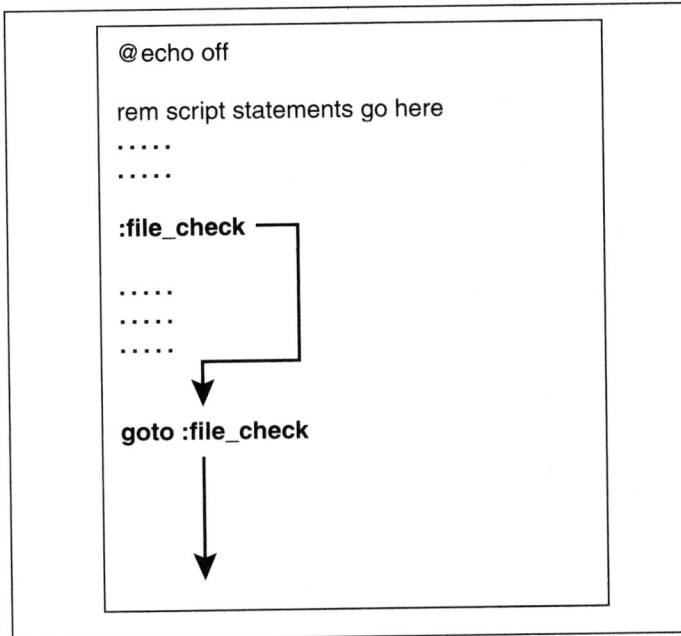

```
@echo off

rem script statements go here
.....
.....

:file_check

.....
.....
.....


goto :file_check
```

FIGURE 8.3

The GOTO *and* LABEL
*statements can be used
to create a loop inside
your scripts.*

The following example demonstrates how to create a loop that is set up to execute five times. The script begins by initializing a controlling variable, x, with a value of 0. Next, the script begins processing the loop. The first time through the loop, the value of x is 0 and the ECHO statement displays this value. Next, the value of x is incremented by 1. Finally, the GOTO statement creates the loop by transferring control back to the first statement after :endless_loop. When the value of x finally exceeds five, the IF statement breaks the loop by issuing a new GOTO statement that jumps to the :exit label. Before the script terminates, a message is displayed.

```
@echo off

echo ***** Script execution beginning *****

set /a x = 0

:endless_loop
  if %x% geq 5 goto :exit
  echo Iteration # %x%
  set /a x = x + 1
  goto :endless_loop
```

```
:exit
  echo *****        Script terminating        *****
```

The following output shows the results of executing the previous example.

```
***** Script execution beginning *****
Iteration # 0
Iteration # 1
Iteration # 2
Iteration # 3
Iteration # 4
*****        Script terminating        *****
```

TIP

A better way to write set /a x = x + 1 in the previous example is set /a x
+= 1.

TIP

If you forget to include a way to break out of the loop, you will create an *endless
loop*. To terminate the script, press CTRL+C and respond with a Y when prompted.
This is demonstrated by the following example:

```
@echo off

echo This script creates an endless loop

:endless_loop

echo Please press CTRL+C to terminate this script!

goto :endless_loop
```

Using *GOTO* to Execute Subroutines

The GOTO statement also supports the creation of subroutines by allowing the
script to transfer control from the current location to the first statement after the
specified LABEL. Figure 8.4 depicts an example of how the GOTO statement can
call a subroutine.

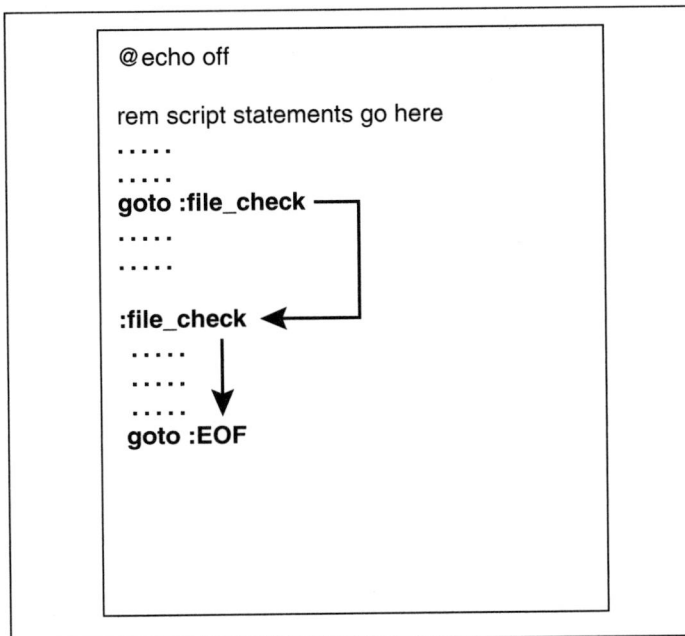

```
@echo off

rem script statements go here
.....
.....
goto :file_check
.....
.....

:file_check
  .....
  .....
  .....
goto :EOF
```

FIGURE 8.4

The GOTO *and* LABEL *statements can create subroutines that allow processing control to jump from one location to another within a script.*

The Windows shell has a built-in label named :EOF that terminates scripts. Its syntax is as follows:

```
goto :EOF
```

EOF represents the end of the file and, because Windows shell scripts terminate at the end of the file, this command is commonly used to end procedures and scripts in a controlled fashion. The following example demonstrates the use of this form of the GOTO statement.

```
@echo off

echo This is a little script that demonstrates
echo how the GOTO :EOF statement works

goto :EOF

echo Because the GOTO :EOF statement precedes the
echo ECHO statements that follow it, the ECHO
echo statements are never executed
```

As the following command output shows, the script terminates as soon as the GOTO :EOF statement is executed.

This is a little script that demonstrates
how the GOTO :EOF statement works

As a wrap-up of the discussion of GOTO statement, the following example demonstrates how you can incorporate all the various forms of the GOTO statements into your scripts.

```
@echo off

:check_loop
   dir accounting.xls>accounting.log 2>&1 && goto :file_found
   echo File ACCOUNTING.XLS was not found.
   choice Do you wish to check again?
   if errorlevel == 2 goto :exit
   if errorlevel == 1 goto :check_loop
   goto :EOF

:file_found
   echo File ACCOUNTING.XLS was found.
   echo Script terminating successfully!
   goto :EOF

:exit
   echo Please contact accounting manager and report missing file.
   goto :EOF
```

The script is organized into three sections, each of which is identified by a label. The first section is called :check_loop. It looks for a file named ACCOUNTING.XLS. If it finds the file, control is transferred to the :file_found label. All error and normal output is redirected to a file named ACCOUNTING.LOG. This keeps the display clear of unwanted messages.

If the user wants it to, the script will continue to check for the presence of the missing file. This is achieved using the CHOICE.EXE command. The CHOICE.EXE command is a Windows NT and Windows 2000 Resource Kit command that allows you to prompt the users for input. In its default format, it accepts a Y/N response as demonstrated in this script. If the users press the Y key, control is transferred to the :check_loop label and the script checks for the file again. If the users press N, control passes to the :exit label.

The `:file_found` label identifies a subroutine that displays a message stating that the file has been found. The subroutine ends with the GOTO `:EOF` statement, which prevents any additional statement from processing and terminates the script.

The `:exit` label displays a message advising the users to contact the accounting manager. It then executes the GOTO `:EOF` statement.

NOTE

Notice how the GOTO `:EOF` statement appears at the end of each subroutine. This statement defines the end of the subroutine. It also ensures that none of the statements following the subroutine are executed. Finally, it terminates the script.

The following output demonstrates what you see when the script finds the ACCOUNTING.XLS file when it first looks for it.

```
C:\>file_check
File ACCOUNTING.XLS was found.
Script terminating successfully!
```

The following output demonstrates what you see when the script cannot find the ACCOUNTING.XLS file and the user tries two additional times to look for it.

```
C:\>file_check
File ACCOUNTING.XLS was not found.
Do you wish to check again?[Y,N]?Y
File ACCOUNTING.XLS was not found.
Do you wish to check again?[Y,N]?Y
File ACCOUNTING.XLS was not found.
Do you wish to check again?[Y,N]?N
Please contact accounting manager and report missing file.
```

The following output demonstrates what you see when the script is unable to find the ACCOUNTING.XLS file when it first looks for it and when the user tries a second time and is successful.

```
C:\>file_check
File ACCOUNTING.XLS was not found.
Do you wish to check again?[Y,N]?Y
File ACCOUNTING.XLS was found.
Script terminating successfully!
```

Organizing Your Scripts with Procedures

The Windows shell also supports the establishments of procedures using the CALL statement and the LABEL statement. The CALL statement works in much the same way as the GOTO statement except the CALL statement ensures that when the called procedure terminates, control returns to the first statement that follows the script's CALL statement.

The Windows shell provides for the following two types of procedures:

- ◆ **Internal procedures**. The CALL statement transfers control to the designated label inside the script. The script continues processing from that point until either the end of file is reached or a GOTO :EOF statement is executed, at which time control returns to the first statement following the CALL statement.

- ◆ **External procedures**. The CALL statement starts another script and transfers control to it. The child script executes and, upon termination, control returns to the first statement following the CALL statement in the parent script.

Procedures resemble nested scripts in that both can call external scripts. However, there are several differences that make the procedures a better programming construct. The CALL command supports both internal and external procedures, whereas nested scripts can only execute external scripts. In addition, executing an external procedure does not require a new instance of the Windows shell because the called procedure runs in the current shell environment. Also, because procedures run in the current shell environment, they have the capability to interact with the current settings and variables.

Internal Procedures

Internal procedures are similar to subroutines except that control is eventually returned to the statement that follows the CALL statement. This process is depicted in Figure 8.5.

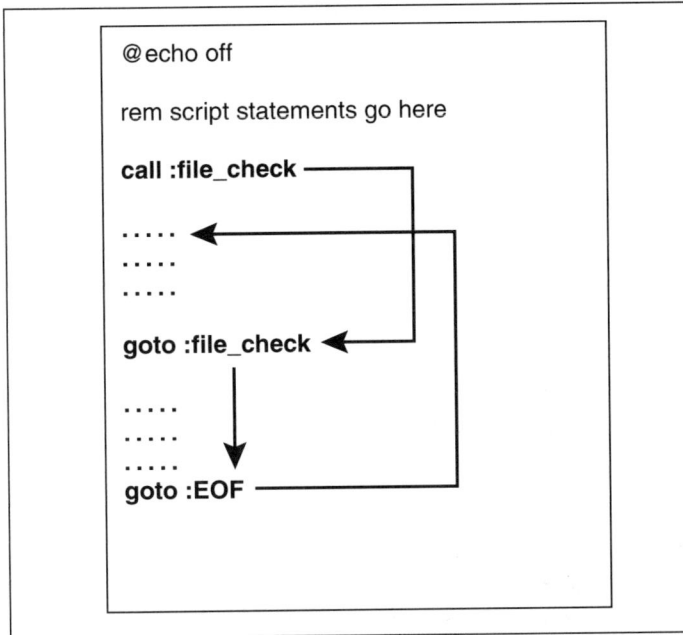

```
@echo off

rem script statements go here

call :file_check

.....
.....
.....

goto :file_check

.....
.....
.....
goto :EOF
```

FIGURE 8.5

The CALL and LABEL statements create procedures that allow processing control to jump from one location to another and then return.

There are several other differences between subroutines and CALL statements. These differences are outlined in Table 8.1.

Table 8.1 Windows Shell Subroutines Versus Procedures

Subroutines	Procedures
Work in conjunction with the LABEL statement.	Works in conjunction with the LABEL statement.
Executes using the GOTO command.	Executes using the CALL command.
Processing control jumps to the specified label and proceeds to the end of the file or the GOTO :EOF statement.	Processing control jumps to the specified label and then proceeds to the end of the file or the GOTO :EOF statement before returning.
Script arguments are available in the subroutine.	Script arguments are not available to the procedure.

The syntax for an internal procedure is as follows:

```
call :procedure_name
```

The CALL command is followed by a space, a colon, and then the name of the internal procedure. The format of a typical procedure generally adopts the following format:

```
:procedure_name
  One or more statements . . . .
  goto :EOF
```

The procedure name is identified by its label and is then followed by one or more statements. Procedures end with a GOTO :EOF statement.

NOTE

Be careful to always include the GOTO :EOF statement at the end of your procedures. Otherwise, the Windows shell will process any statements that follow the procedure until the next GOTO :EOF statement or until the end of file is reached, at which time control will return to the statement that followed the CALL statement.

The Windows shell expects each procedure to receive its own set of arguments. You can pass arguments to an internal procedure, as shown here:

```
call :procedure_name arg1 arg2 arg3 ……
```

Because procedures have their own set of arguments, they cannot, by default, access the list of arguments that have been passed to the script. One way around this is to pass individual scripts arguments to the procedure when it is called. Another way is to pass all script arguments using the following syntax:

```
call :procedure_name %*
```

TIP

Other ways of passing information to procedures include saving information in files that the procedure can then read or storing information in variables that the procedure can reference.

The following example demonstrates how you can improve the organization of your scripts using procedures. The script is organized into three procedures. The :main procedure controls the overall logic flow of the entire script and directs the execution of the other procedures. The :main procedure is called as soon as the script is started. In this simple script, the :main procedure then calls :procedure1, which executes and returns control to the :main procedure. The :main procedure then calls procedure2, which also executes and returns control to the :main procedure. The :main procedure then terminates itself by issuing the GOTO :EOF statement.

```
@echo off

echo Calling main procedure

call :main

goto :EOF

:main
  echo Processing main procedure

  echo Calling procedure1
  call :procedure1

  echo Calling procedure2
  call :procedure2

  goto :EOF

:procedure1
  echo Procedure1 has been processed!
  goto :EOF

:procedure2
  echo procedure2 has been processed!
  goto :EOF
```

The following output shows the results of executing the previous script. As the output shows, each procedure was executed under the control of the :main procedure.

```
Calling main procedure
Processing main procedure
Calling procedure1
Procedure1 has been processed!
Calling procedure2
Procedure2 has been processed!
```

External Procedures

External procedures are similar to nested scripts and are depicted in Figure 8.6. When a script starts an external procedure, it pauses until the external procedure completes, at which time it resumes its own execution. A script can make any number of external procedure calls, each of which shares the same execution environment as the calling script.

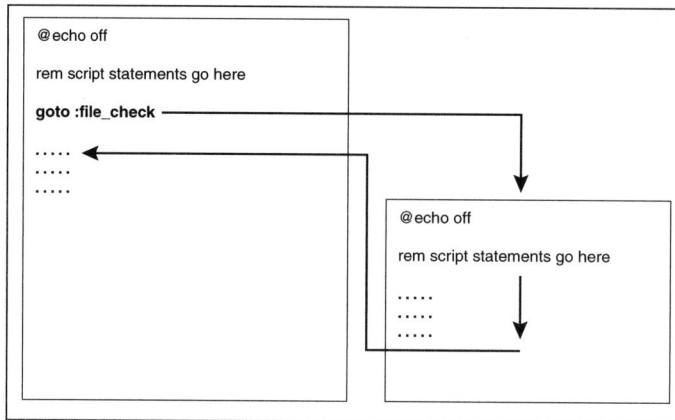

FIGURE 8.6

External procedures allow your scripts to call other scripts as procedures.

The syntax for an external procedure call is shown here:

```
call script_name
```

External procedure calls execute other scripts instead of internal statements. External procedure calls still use the CALL command but do not require or permit the use of the colon character before the procedure. Like internal procedure calls, external procedure calls expect to receive their own set of arguments. These arguments can be passed by adding them behind the script name, as shown in the following example:

```
call script1 arg1 arg2 arg3
```

The following example shows a script that makes two external procedure calls. The first script is named MAIN_SCRIPT.BAT. It consists of three procedures. The first procedure is called :main and it is executed as soon as the script begins execution. The :main procedure then executes two external procedures, named SCRIPT1.BAT and SCRIPT2.BAT, before executing a GOTO :EOF statement, which then returns control to the statement below the CALL statement that called :main. The script then terminates.

```
@echo off

echo Main_script executing!

call :main

echo Main_script.bat terminating!

Goto :EOF

:main
   echo Processing main procedure

   echo Calling procedure1
   call script1.bat

   echo Calling procedure2
   call script2.bat

   goto :EOF
```

SCRIPT1.BAT, which follows, simply displays a message letting you know when the script has been run.

```
@echo off
```

```
echo Script1.bat is executing
```

Like SCRIPT1.BAT, SCRIPT2.BAT displays a message before returning control to MAIN_SCRIPT.BAT.

```
@echo off

echo Script2.bat is executing
```

The following output shows what you see when you execute MAIN_SCRIPT.BAT.

```
C:\>main_script.bat
Main_script executing!
Processing main procedure
Calling procedure1
Script1.bat is executing
Calling procedure2
Script2.bat is executing
Main_script.bat terminating!
```

Limiting the Scope of Environment Settings and Variables

You were introduced to the topic of variable localization in Chapter 5, "Working with Variables," where you were shown how the SETLOCAL and ENDLOCAL commands can prevent changes in one part of a script from affecting the value of similarly named variables in another part of the script.

Because procedures execute within the current command shell, they can affect the local environment. This can be both a convenient and dangerous consequence, depending on how carefully you design your scripts. If you want procedures to have access to variables used by the rest of the script, you do not have to do anything other than reference them from within your procedures. However, if you want to prevent procedures from changing settings that affect other parts of the script, you can do so by placing the SETLOCAL and ENDLOCAL commands at the beginning and end of your procedures.

When you reference variables inside the SETLOCAL and ENDLOCAL statements, any changes that you make to them are discarded when the procedure ends. In addition to variables, you can also discard any changes made to drive and folder settings using the PUSHD and POPD commands. Both of these options are demonstrated in the following sections.

Limiting Variable Scope

By default, a variable's scope is global within the script. However, it can be localized using the SETLOCAL and ENDLOCAL commands. You can protect the rest of your script from changes made to variables in your procedures by using these commands, as demonstrated in the following example.

The script begins by initializing the values of two variables, x and y and then calls the :main procedure, which displays the values of these variables. The :main procedure then calls :procedure1. :procedure1 begins and ends with the SETLOCAL and ENDLOCAL commands. It then changes the value of its copy of x and y and displays their modified values. Control then returns to the :main procedure, which then returns control back to the statement below the CALL :main statement. The values of the two variables are again displayed, showing that they remain unchanged by the modifications that were made by :procedure1.

```
@echo off

rem Initialize variables
set /a x = 1
set /a Y = 2

call :main

echo In the main procedure x = %x%
echo In the main procedure y = %y%

Goto :EOF

:main
```

```
echo In the main procedure x = %x%
echo In the main procedure y = %y%

call :procedure1

goto :EOF

:procedure1

setlocal

set /a x += 1
set /a y += 1
echo In procedure1 x = %x%
echo In procedure2 y = %y%

endlocal

goto : EOF
```

The following output shows the results of running the previous script.

```
In the main procedure x = 1
In the main procedure y = 2
In procedure1 x = 2
In procedure2 y = 3
In the main procedure x = 1
In the main procedure y = 2
```

TIP

Be careful when limiting variable scope within your script procedures. Make sure you properly execute the ENDLOCAL command. For example, if you begin a procedure with SETLOCAL and end it with ENDLOCAL, but execute a GOTO statement in the middle of the procedure, the ENDLOCAL command will not be executed. You need to make sure that your scripts are prepared to handle this type of scenario. One way to handle this type of situation is with a compound command such as ENDLOCAL & GOTO :NEWPROCEDURE.

Drive and Folder Localization

Just as you can localize variable values within a procedure, you can also localize drive and folder settings. This is achieved using the PUSHD and POPD commands. This means that, for example, if the current drive and folder setting is c:\WINNT and a procedure was called that changed the settings to D:\TEMP, the settings will automatically be restored to c:\WINNT when the procedure ends.

The PUSHD command saves the current drive and folder setting and changes to the specified folder. Its syntax is as follows:

```
pushd path
```

Path specifies the new drive and folder settings.

The POPD command changes the current drive and folder settings back to the values saved by the PUSHD command. Its syntax is as follows:

```
popd
```

NOTE

If you specify a network path as the new setting, the PUSHD command automatically creates a temporary drive mapping using the first available drive letter. It then changes the current drive and folder settings as specified by the PUSHD command. The role of the POPD command is then to delete the temporary drive mapping and restore the previous settings.

The following example shows how you can limit the scope of drive and folder settings within procedures. After it's called, the :main procedure changes the drive and folder setting to c:\SMALL_DIR and displays its contents. It then calls :procedure1, which changes the settings to c:\BIG_DIR and displays the contents of that folder. When :procedure1 terminates, control returns to :main, which then issues the DIR command to verify that the original settings have been restored.

```
@echo off

call :main
```

```
Goto :EOF

:main

  cd c:\small_dir
  dir
  call :procedure1
  dir
  goto :EOF

:procedure1

  pushd c:\big_dir
  dir
  popd
  goto :EOF
```

When this example was executed, both the c:\SMALL_DIR and c:\BIG_DIR directories existed but did not contain any files or subfolders. The resulting output is shown here:

```
Volume in drive C has no label.
 Volume Serial Number is E45B-8CF4

 Directory of C:\small_dir

02/29/2000  02:31p       <DIR>          .
02/29/2000  02:31p       <DIR>          ..
02/29/2000  02:31p                    6 file1.txt
           1 File(s)              6 bytes
           2 Dir(s)     289,665,536 bytes free
 Volume in drive C has no label.
 Volume Serial Number is E45B-8CF4

 Directory of C:\big_dir

02/29/2000  02:33p       <DIR>          .
02/29/2000  02:33p       <DIR>          ..
02/29/2000  02:33p                    5 file2.txt
```

```
             1 File(s)              5 bytes
             2 Dir(s)      289,665,536 bytes free
  Volume in drive C has no label.
  Volume Serial Number is E45B-8CF4


  Directory of C:\small_dir


02/29/2000   02:31p       <DIR>            .
02/29/2000   02:31p       <DIR>            ..
02/29/2000   02:31p                    6 file1.txt
             1 File(s)              6 bytes
             2 Dir(s)      289,665,536 bytes free


C:\small_dir>
```

Tunneling Data Out of Your Procedures

One of the problems with limiting variable scope within procedures is that it makes it somewhat difficult to get any data back from the procedure that the rest of the script can process. However, by using a technique called *variable tunneling,* you can get around this.

Variable tunneling works by turning the ENDLOCAL command into a compound command using the following syntax:

```
endlocal & set ret=%ret%
```

This statement ends the local variable scope and returns the value of a variable named RET, which existed within the procedure. In order for this technique to work, you must always place ENDLOCAL before SET RET=%RET%, as demonstrated in the following examples.

The first example does not use this technique. As a result, when it executes, the value of RET is not available in the :main procedure.

```
@echo off


call :main
```

```
Goto :EOF

:main

  call :procedure1
  echo Procedure1 set RET = %RET%
  goto :EOF

:procedure1

  setlocal & pushd
  set /a RET = 5
  endlocal & popd
  goto :EOF
```

The following output was generated when the previous example was executed.

Procedure1 set RET =

However, in this second example, the value of RET is successfully passed from the procedure to the :main procedure. As you can see, the scope of the procedure is limited by both the SETLOCAL and PUSHD commands and the initial value of RET is deleted just in case it should have been already established at some other point in the script. The procedure ends with ENDLOCAL & POPD & SET RET=%RET%, which terminates the local variable scope and drive and folder settings while still tunneling out the value of RET.

```
@echo off

call :main

Goto :EOF

:main

  call :procedure1
  echo Procedure1 returned %RET%
  goto :EOF
```

```
:procedure1

  setlocal & pushd & set RET=
  set /a RET = 5
  endlocal & popd & set RET=%RET%
  goto :EOF
```

The following output verifies the success of the tunneling operation.

Procedure1 returned 5

Completing Your Windows Shell Script Template

The final step in the completion of your Windows shell script template requires that you add statements that incorporate procedures and procedure controls. The script template has been divided into three sections. The initialization section performs basic script-initialization processes such as variable declaration, debugging control, and an operating system check, in addition to other cosmetic commands, such as TITLE and CLS.

The main processing section controls the overall flow of the script, including the execution of its procedures. The procedure section is where all the procedures are organized. In addition, variables, drives, and folders have been limited in scope to the :main procedure.

```
@echo off
rem ******************************************
rem * Script Name: template.bat              *
rem * Author:   Jerry Ford                   *
rem * Address: Richmond Virginia             *
rem * Created: 04/07/01                      *
rem ******************************************

rem ************ Initialization section **************
```

```
if not "%OS%" == "Windows_NT" goto :exit
if /i "%debug%" == "on" (set trace=echo) else (set trace=rem)
%trace% Tracing on.
title "Insert script title message here"
cls


rem ************* Main processing section *************

call :main

rem Place calls to other procedures here

goto :EOF

rem *************    Procedure section    *************

:main
  setlocal & pushd & set ret=
  endlocal & popd & set ret=%ret%
  goto :EOF

:exit
  echo This script requires either Windows NT or 2000
```

You might want to use this shell script template as a starting point for all
your script development. You can modify it to suit your own programming style
and needs.

Chapter 9

Putting It All Together

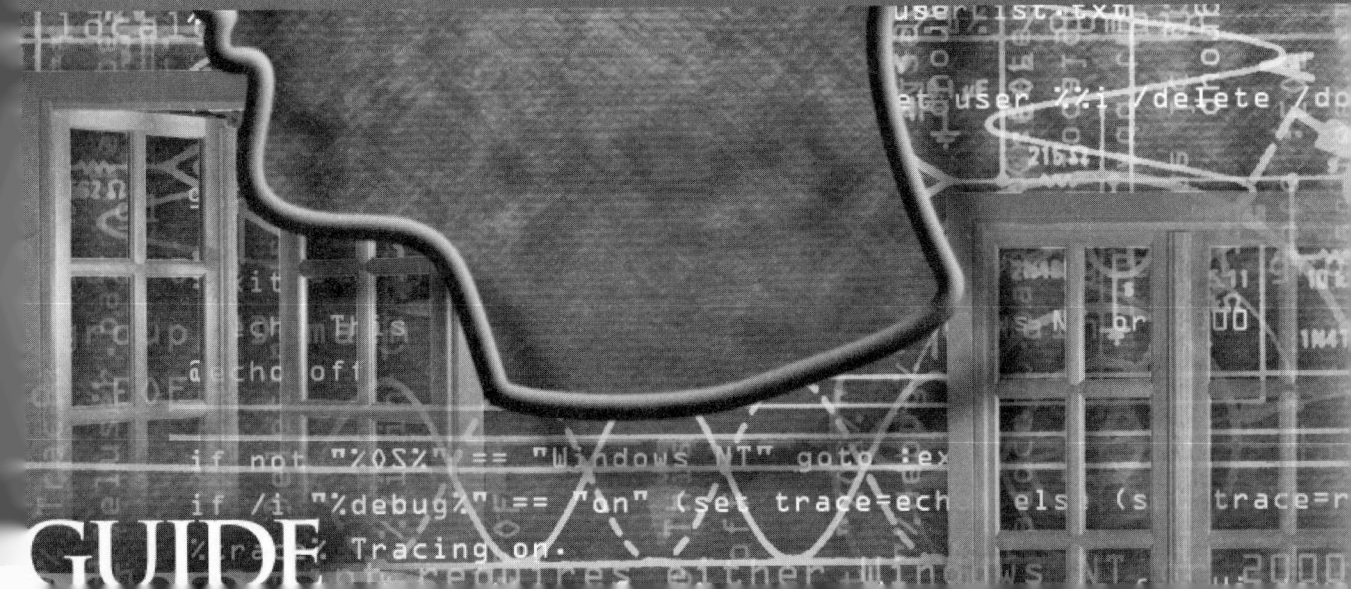

U p to this point, this book has focused on providing you with the background required to design and write your own shell scripts. The purpose of this chapter is to bring together all the things that you have learned about Windows shell scripting and to do so in the form of practical examples that you can use. Use these examples as a template for building your own Windows shell script library. In many cases, the scripts can be expanded to provide additional functionality. You can also copy the code from these examples to build entirely new solutions of your own.

Topics covered in this chapter include:

◆ Scheduling the execution of your scripts using Windows scheduling services

◆ Automating the creation of new user accounts

◆ Managing printers and services

◆ Mapping network drives

◆ Managing network resources

◆ Processing Windows event logs

Scheduling Script Execution

Windows NT 4 and Windows 2000 both support the automated scheduling of scripts. Windows NT 4 provides automated scheduling services via the Schedule service. To work with this service, you must use the AT command. This command allows you to view, add, and delete tasks. Before you can schedule the execution of your scripts on Windows NT 4, you must start and configure the Schedule service. This process is outlined in the next section.

Windows 2000 provides scheduling services via the Task Scheduler service. This service also requires some configuration before it is ready to provide scheduling support for your scripts. Configuration of this service is explained later in this chapter. Windows 2000 lets you schedule and manage scheduled tasks using the following options:

- **The AT command**. The same command interface provided by Windows NT 4.
- **The Scheduled Task Wizard**. A graphical interface that steps you through the process of setting up scheduled tasks.
- **The Scheduled Tasks Folder**. A folder that provides a view of the currently scheduled tasks and allows you to modify them.

Configuring the Windows NT 4 Schedule Service

By default, Windows NT 4's Schedule service runs using the LocalSystem account. Unfortunately, this account lacks a sufficient set of permissions to support the execution of most scripts. Therefore, you will probably need to create a new user account that has the appropriate set of permissions and then assign it to the Schedule service. The steps required to perform this process follow:

1. Select Start, Programs and User Manager for Domains. The User Manager for Domains dialog box appears.
2. Click User and then New User. The New User dialog box appears.
3. Type a name, such as Scheduler_acct, in the Username field. Then type a password in the Password and the Confirm Password fields.
4. Select the User Cannot Change Password option and the Password Never Expires option.
5. Click Groups and add the account to whatever groups are required so that you can execute the tasks that you plan to build into your scripts. Click OK.
6. Click Add to create the account. Click Close. Close the User Manager for Domains utility.

Now that an account has been created for the Scheduler server, you must set up the service to run using that account.

1. Click Start, Settings, and then Control Panel.
2. Double-click the Services icon.
3. Select the Scheduler service, as shown in Figure 9.1, and click Startup. The Service dialog box appears.

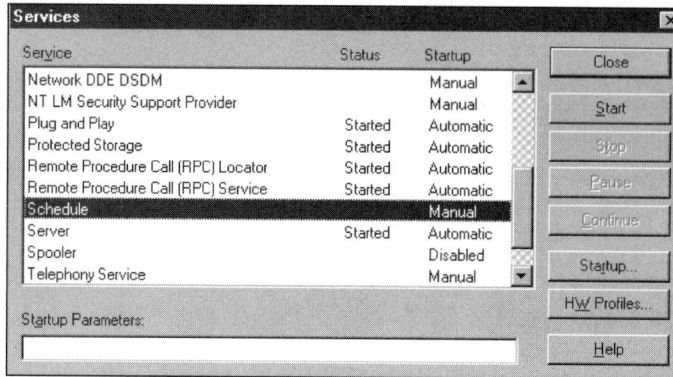

FIGURE 9.1

By default, the Windows NT 4 Schedule service is not started and must be configured before it is ready for use by your scripts.

4. Select Automatic from the Startup Type options and then click the This Account option and type the name of the account that you created for the scheduling server. See Figure 9.2.

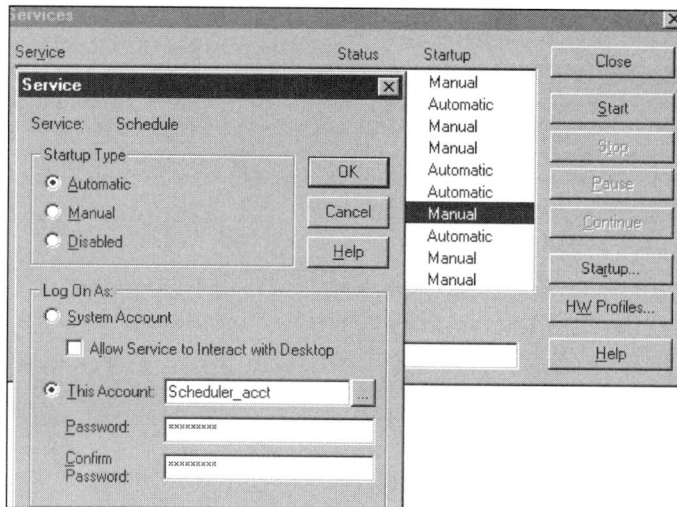

FIGURE 9.2

The Windows NT 4 Schedule service lacks sufficient permissions to perform many scripted activities and must be assigned a specific account with adequate permissions.

5. Type the account's password in the Password and Confirm Password fields and click OK.

6. On the Services dialog box, make sure that Schedule is still selected and that its Startup mode now says Automatic. Click Start. The Schedule services starts.

7. Close the Service dialog box.

The Scheduler service should now be ready to automatically start every time the server starts.

Working with the Windows NT 4 Schedule Service

The Windows NT 4 Schedule service can schedule the execution of tasks, including scripts, based on a schedule or on a specific date and time. This allows you to execute scripts even when you are not logged on to the computer. However, you need to remember that when you schedule the execution of scripts, you can only count on the availability of variables listed as system variables in the System utility's Environment Property sheet.

NOTE

Because only system variables are available to scripts executed by the scheduler, you need to take extra steps to make sure that your scripts that perform network management still work. Specifically, you cannot count on any network drive mappings being available, so you must add logic to your scripts to accommodate this shortcoming. You can do this by either mapping the network drives as part of the script or by using UNC names when referencing network resources. UNC stands for Universal Naming Conversion. The UNC name provides a standard means of addressing windows and network resources in the form of *Computer_name**Path**Resource_name*. For example, to reference a network drive named C on a computer named FileSvr, you would type **\\FileSvr\C.**

You can use the following statements as a model when mapping drives from within your scripts.

To map a drive:

```
net use driveletter: \\servername\sharename
```

To delete a drive mapping:

```
net use driveletter: /delete
```

To make the UNC name work with the network resource, use the following format:

```
del \\fileServer\myfolder\report.txt
```

where *fileServer* is the name of the server, *myfolder* is the name of the share, and *report.txt* is the name of the resource.

Windows NT 4 provides the AT command as the interface for working with the Schedule service. To view a list of the scheduled tasks, type **AT** and press Enter:

```
C:\>at
Status ID    Day                      Time              Command Line

         0   Each S                   8:00 PM           cmd /c
                                                         diskclean.bat
         1   Tomorrow                 10:00 AM          copy_reports.bat
```

In this example, two scripts have been scheduled for execution. The first is named DISKCLEAN.BAT and it has been scheduled to run every Saturday at 8pm. The second script is named COPY_REPORTS.BAT and it has been scheduled to run at 10am on the next day.

Using the AT command, you can add and delete new jobs. For example, the following command adds a script named CLEAR_TEMP.BAT every night of the week at 11pm:

```
at 23:00 /every:M,T,W,Th,F,S,Su cmd /c clear_temp.bat
```

Scheduled tasks can be deleted by referencing their schedule ID. For example, the following command removes the COPY_REPORTS.BAT script from the schedule:

```
at 1 /delete
```

Similarly, you can delete all tasks using the following command:

```
at /delete
```

NOTE

You must have administrative privileges to schedule tasks on Windows NT and Windows 2000.

You can also schedule jobs to run on remote servers by specifying two backslashes followed by the network server's name. This name must appear after the AT command and before any other parameters, as demonstrated:

```
at \\servername 23:00 /every:M,T,W,Th,F,S,Su cmd /c clear_temp.bat
```

Additional information, including the complete syntax of the AT command, is available in Appendix A, "A Windows Command Reference."

Configuring the Windows 2000 Task Scheduler Service

Like Windows NT 4's Schedule service, the Windows 2000 Task Scheduler service requires configuration before you can use it to schedule your scripts. The configuration process is outlined in the following steps:

1. Create a special account that will be used to provide the Task Scheduler Service with the appropriate level of permissions needed to execute your scripts.

2. Click Start, Settings, and then Control Panel.

3. Open the Administrative Tools folder and double-click Services.

4. Locate the Task Scheduler service, as shown in Figure 9.3. Double-click it. The Task Scheduler Properties dialog box appears.

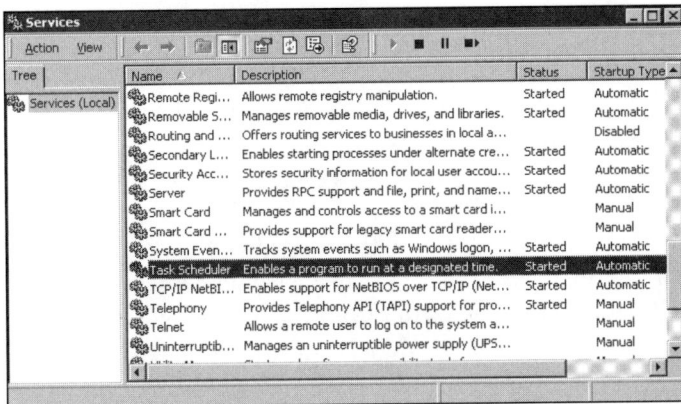

FIGURE 9.3

By default, the Windows 2000 Task Scheduler service is started automatically when Windows 2000 starts.

5. If the service is not already active, click Start.

6. Select Automatic from the Startup type options and then click the Log On property sheet.

7. Select the This Account option and type the name of the account that you created for the scheduling server, as demonstrated in Figure 9.4.

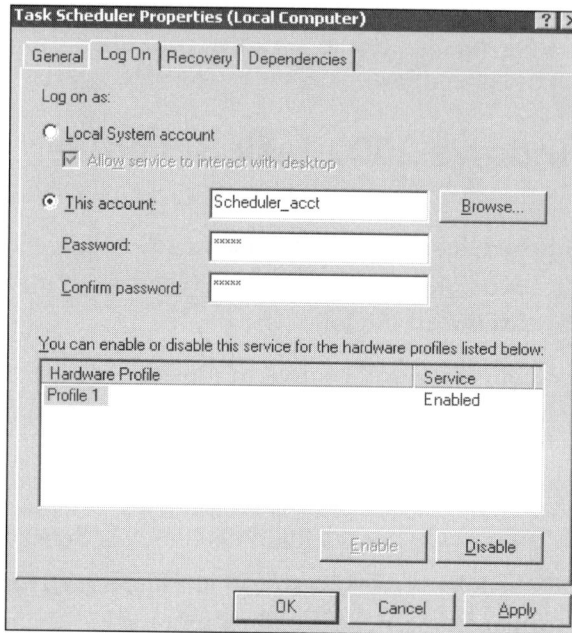

FIGURE 9.4

The Windows 2000 Task Scheduler service lacks an appropriate set of permissions to run most scripts.

8. Type the account's password in the Password and Confirm Password fields and click OK.

Working with the Windows 2000 Scheduled Tasks Folder and the Scheduled Task Wizard

You can interact with the Windows 2000 Task Scheduler by using the AT command at the command prompt or by using the Scheduled Tasks folder and Scheduled Task Wizard. When working from the command line you can use the same examples discussed previously for working with the Windows NT 4 AT command.

The Scheduled Tasks folder and Scheduled Task Wizard provide a GUI interface for managing scheduled tasks. To access the Scheduled Tasks folder, select Start, Programs, Accessories, System Tools, and then Scheduled Tasks. The Scheduled Tasks folder appears in Figure 9.5. In this example, two scripts are currently scheduled for execution.

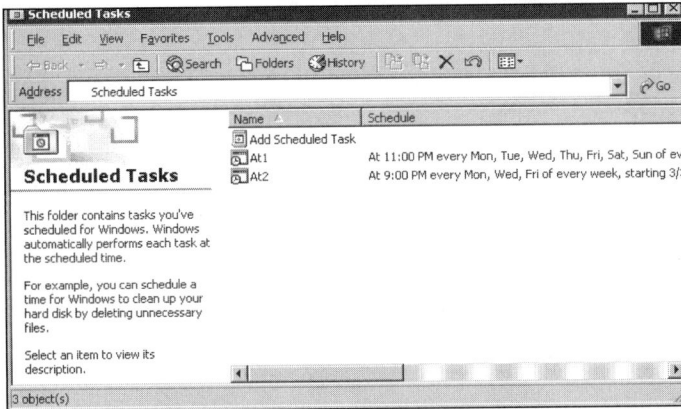

FIGURE 9.5

The Windows 2000 Scheduled Tasks folder lists all scheduled tasks and provides access to the Scheduled Task Wizard.

You can delete a scheduled task by right-clicking it and selecting Delete. You can modify its schedule by right-clicking it, selecting Properties, and then clicking the Schedule property sheet, as shown in Figure 9.6.

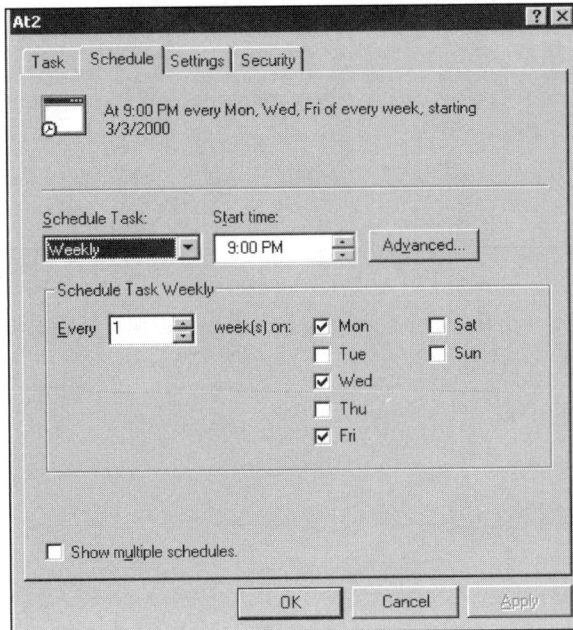

FIGURE 9.6

Each scheduled task has a properties sheet that allows you to change its schedule.

The following process outlines how to schedule the execution of a script using the Windows 2000 Scheduled Task Wizard:

1. Double-click the Add Scheduled Task icon. The Scheduled Task Wizard appears.

2. Click Next. You are presented with a list of Windows applications that you can schedule, as shown in Figure 9.7. Unfortunately, scripts do not show up in this list by default, so you have to click Browse and locate them yourself. After locating and selecting your script, click Next.

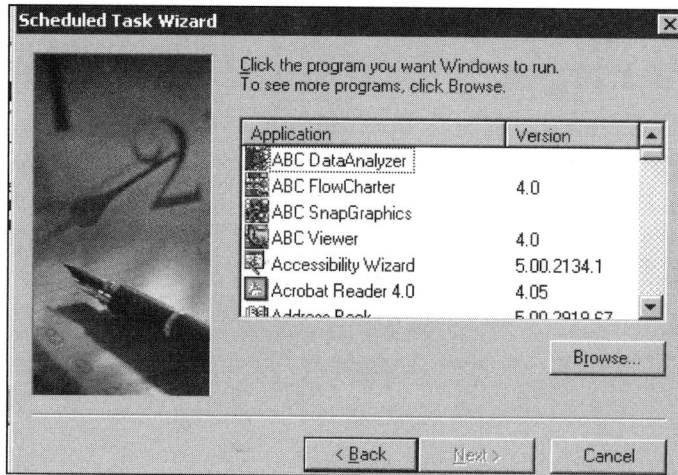

FIGURE 9.7

Click Browse to locate the script for which you are building a schedule.

3. Type a descriptive name for the task and then select one of the available scheduling options. Click Next as shown in Figure 9.8.

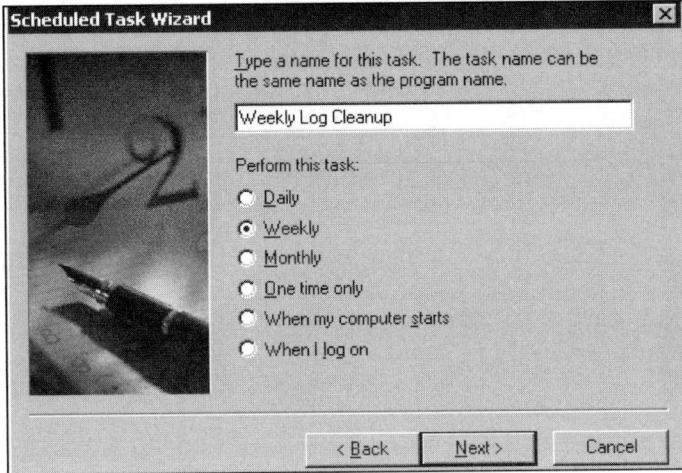

FIGURE 9.8

The Schedule Task Wizard provides a variety of scheduling options.

4. The dialog box that you see next depends on the scheduling option you choose. For example, Figure 9.9 shows the dialog box for the weekly schedule option. Select the appropriate scheduling options and click Next.

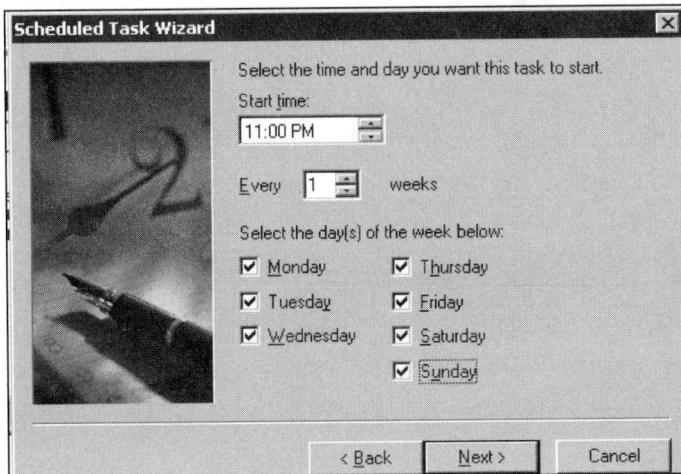

FIGURE 9.9

Each scheduling option can be further refined to create a detailed schedule for your scripts.

5. Next, type the name and password of a user account as demonstrated in Figure 9.10. The script will be executed using this user account's permissions.

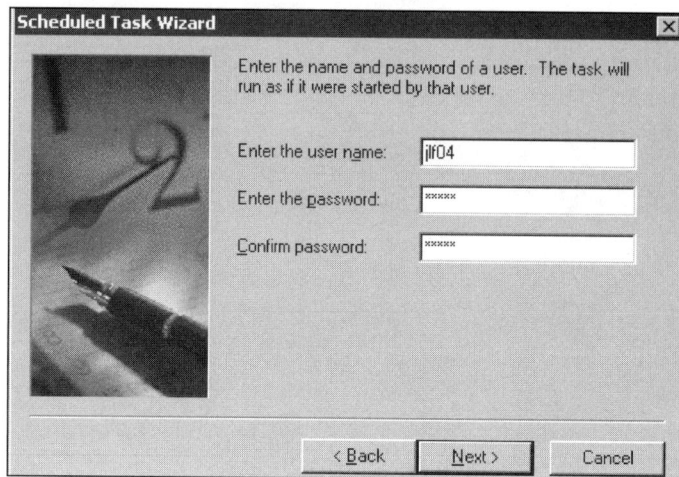

FIGURE 9.10

Each scheduled task created by the Scheduled Task Wizard requires a username and password that will be used to execute the task.

6. Windows 2000 displays summary information for the task. Verify that everything looks correct and then click OK.

Account Administration

Windows NT 4 and Windows 2000 provide the following commands for creating and managing user accounts:

- ◆ NET ACCOUNTS. Configures password policies.
- ◆ NET GROUP. Configures global group membership.
- ◆ NET LOCALGROUP. Configures local group membership.
- ◆ NET USER. Configures user accounts.

Using these commands, you can alter the policies that govern user passwords and create new user accounts. You can also add or remove user accounts for both local and global groups. Your scripts can manage accounts on both a local and domain level.

The following example demonstrates one way of scripting the creation of a new user account for a network administrator. The syntax for executing this script is as follows:

```
makeuser username
```

MAKEUSER is the name of the script and *username* is the name of the user account to be created. As the example shows, the script is divided into three sections. The initialization section verifies that the script has been started on a supported operating system and displays a message in the command console's title bar.

The main section controls the overall flow of the script by calling three procedures, which perform account creation and the administration of local group management and global group management.

The procedure sections contain the following procedures:

◆ :CREATE_ACCT. Uses the NET USER command to create a new user account in the current domain.

◆ :DEFINE_LC_GROUPS. Uses the NET LOCALGROUP command to add the new account to the Administrators group.

◆ :DEFINE_GL_GROUPS. Uses the NET GROUP command to add the account into the Domain Admins account.

```
@echo off
rem ******************************************
rem * Script Name: makeuser.bat              *
rem * Author:  Jerry Ford                    *
rem * Address: Richmond Virginia             *
rem * Created: 04/09/01                      *
rem ******************************************

rem **** Perform script initialization here ****

if not "%OS%" == "Windows_NT" goto :exit
if /i "%debug%" == "on" (set trace=echo) else (set trace=rem)
%trace% Tracing on.
title "Makeuser.bat - Creates and configures a new administrator's
account"
cls

rem ******** Main processing section *********

%trace% Creating Admin account for %1%
```

```
call :create_acct %1%
call :define_lc_groups %1%
call :define_gl_groups %1%

goto :EOF


rem ********** Procedures go here ************

:create_acct
  rem create the new domain account
  net user %1% * /add /domain
  goto :EOF

:define_lc_groups
  rem Add the account to the Administrators local group
  net localgroup Administrators /add %1% /domain
  goto :EOF

:define_gl_groups
  rem Add the account to the Domain Admins global group
  net group "Domain Admins" %1% /add /domain
  goto :EOF

:exit
  echo This script requires either Windows NT or 2000
```

NOTE

The Windows NT 4 and Windows 2000 Resource Kits both supply a command named ADDUSERS.EXE that you can use to create new accounts based on a list of entries in a comma-delimited file.

In this next example, a script named DELUSER.BAT deletes user accounts based on a list that it reads from a file named USER_LIST.TXT. The contents of USER_LIST.TXT are shown here:

```
markland
michael
nick
lee
```

The syntax for executing this script is as follows:

```
deluser filename
```

DELUSER.BAT is the name of the script and *filename* is the name of a file that contains a list of the accounts to be deleted. The script itself is shown next. The logic to process the input file and delete the user accounts from the domain is located in the main processing section. A FOR loop iterates throughout the file and executes the NET USER command with the /DELETE and /DOMAIN switches. The /DELETE switch deletes the account and the /DOMAIN switch makes sure that the deletion is performed in the domain and not on the local computer.

```
@echo off
rem *****************************************
rem * Script Name: deluser.bat              *
rem * Author:  Jerry Ford                   *
rem * Address: Richmond Virginia            *
rem * Created: 04/09/01                     *
rem *****************************************

rem **** Perform script initialization here ****

if not "%OS%" == "Windows_NT" goto :exit
if /i "%debug%" == "on" (set trace=echo) else (set trace=rem)
%trace% Tracing on.
title "Deluser.bat - Deletes user accounts stored in the specified
file"
cls

rem ******** Main processing section *********
```

```
%trace% Deleting users accounts in user_List.txt

for /f %%i in (user_list.txt) do (net user %%i /delete /domain)

goto :EOF

rem ********** Procedures go here *************

:exit
   echo This script requires either Windows NT or 2000
```

On Windows NT and Windows 2000 networks, every computer must have a registered account before it can be used to log in to the domain. The following example demonstrates how to automate the creation of computer accounts. It consists of two parts: a file named COMP_LIST.TXT, which contains a list of Windows NT 4 and Windows 2000 accounts to be established, and a script named ADDCOMP.BAT. The text of the COMP_LIST.TXT file appears here:

```
computer1
computer2
computer3
computer4
computer5
```

The syntax for executing this script is as follows:

```
addcomp filename
```

ADDCOMP.BAT is the name of the script and *filename* is the name of the file that contains a list of the computer accounts. The script uses a FOR statement in the main processing section to create a loop that iterates throughout the specified file (%1%). With each iteration, the NET COMPUTER command creates a new account for one of the computers. The only switch used is /ADD; it does exactly what its name implies.

```
@echo off
rem *****************************************
rem * Script Name: addcomp.bat             *
rem * Author:   Jerry Ford                 *
rem * Address: Richmond Virginia           *
rem * Created: 04/09/01                    *
rem *****************************************

rem **** Perform script initialization here ****

if not "%OS%" == "Windows_NT" goto :exit
if /i "%debug%" == "on" (set trace=echo) else (set trace=rem)
%trace% Tracing on.
title "addcomp.bat - Creates computer accounts for Windows NT and 2000

computers"
cls

rem ********* Main processing section **********

%trace% Deleting users accounts in comp_list.txt

for /f %%i in (%1) do (net computer \\%%i /add)

goto :EOF

rem *********** Procedures go here *************

:exit

   echo This script requires either Windows NT or 2000
```

Computer and Network Administration

The sections that follow present a list of computer and network tasks that can be automated using Windows shell scripts. Some of these examples make use of commands found in the Windows NT 4 and Windows 2000 Resource Kits. Use these examples as templates for creating your own automated solutions.

Managing Printer Services and Queues

You can use Windows shell scripts to view and manage print queues. You simply use the NET PRINT command and the following syntax:

```
net print \\computername\sharename
```

Computername is the name of the computer that has shared the printer and *sharename* is the name by which it is managed. Like other NET commands, you can use the NET PRINT command to manage both local and network print queues.

The following example demonstrates how the NET PRINT command can be used to view and manage printer queues.

```
First, you can use NET PRINT to view the status of print jobs for a
given print queue:
C:\>net print \\Celeron-400\color_printer


Printers at \\Celeron-400
```

Name	Job #	Size	Status
──────────────────────────			
color_printer Queue Active*	2 jobs		*Printer
Administrator	9	162308	Printing
Administrator	10	112164	Waiting

Two print jobs are currently in the printer queue. The first print job has been assigned a job number of 9 and the second print job's job number is 10. You can use the following form of the NET PRINT command to suspend a print job:

```
net print \\Celeron-400 12 /hold
```

If you display the printer queue again, it will show the print job's new status, as shown:

```
C:\>net print \\Celeron-400\color_printer
```

```
Printers at \\Celeron-400


Name                        Job #      Size           Status


_____
color_printer Queue          2 jobs                  *Printer
Active*
     Administrator             11     159972          Printing

     Administrator             12     163192          Held in
queue
```

You can then release the held job as shown:

```
C:\>net print \\Celeron-400 11 /release
```

You can also delete a print job by referencing its job ID, as demonstrated:

```
C:\>net print \\Celeron-400 12 /delete
```

As the following example shows, you can view information about an individual job by typing **NET PRINT JOB#:**

```
net print 12
Job #              12
Status             Waiting
Size               1024
Remark
Submitting user    Administrator
Notify             Administrator
Job data type
Job parameters

Additional info
```

Another facet of printer management involves stopping and starting the spooling service. This is done with the NET START and NET STOP commands.

Use these commands to start and stop the spooler service on Windows NT 4:

```
net start Print Spooler
```

```
net stop Print Spooler
```

Use these commands to start and stop the spooler services on Windows 2000:

```
net start Spooler
```

```
net stop Spooler
```

The following example shows a script named PTRMAINT.BAT that can be used to stop and start the spooler services on Windows NT 4 and Windows 2000 systems. The syntax for executing this script is as follows:

```
ptrmaint [pause | resume]
```

The main processing section first checks to determine which version of the command shell is executing the script. A CMDEXTVERSION of 2 indicates Windows 2000, whereas a value of 1 means Windows NT 4. A variable named %SERVICE% is then assigned a value of either Print Spooler for Windows 2000 or Spooler for Windows NT 4.

The rest of the main procedure is included in one of two IF statements. The first IF statement determines whether the script was passed an argument of PAUSE, whereas the second IF statement looks for a value of RESUME. When the argument is PAUSE, the NET SEND command sends a message to any users currently connected to the server and informs them that the printer is about to be taken out of commission. Then a NET STOP %SERVICE% command is issued. The value of %SERVICE% is substituted before the command executes, which ensures that the appropriate name is used to stop the service.

When the argument is RESUME, the NET SEND command sends a message to all currently connected users that informs them that the printer is coming back online. The spooling service is then started.

```
@echo off
rem ******************************************
rem * Script Name: ptrmaint.bat              *
rem * Author:   Jerry Ford                   *
rem * Address: Richmond Virginia             *
rem * Created: 04/10/01                      *
rem ******************************************

rem **** Perform script initialization here ****
```

```
if not "%OS%" == "Windows_NT" goto :exit
if /i "%debug%" == "on" (set trace=echo) else (set trace=rem)
%trace% Tracing on.
title "Ptrmaint.bat - Pauses printer output in preparation for mainte-
nance work"
cls

rem ********* Main processing section **********

if cmdextversion 2 (
  set service="Print Spooler"
) else (
  set service="Spooler"
)

if /i "%1%" == "pause" (
  echo Notifying all users that the %2% will be unavailable for a
while.

  net send /users Printer %2% is down for system maintenance.

  echo Pausing printer output. Wait for the printer to stop before
starting!

  net stop %service%

  goto :EOF
)

if /i "%1%" == "resume" (
  echo Notifying all users that %2% is available again

  net send /users Printer %2% is ready for use again.

  echo starting Printer Spooler.

  net start %service%
```

```
   goto :EOF
)

goto :EOF

rem ********** Procedures go here ************

:exit

   echo This script requires either Windows NT or 2000
```

> **NOTE**
>
> The NET SEND command sends messages to users currently connected to the computer on which the command was issued. This command can send messages to all users, including those connected using Windows 95, 98, or Me as long as the WINPOPUP.EXE application is active on those systems. The /USERS switch directs the message to all connected users. You can also send the message to a specific user by replacing /USERS with a username or send the message to everyone in the current domain by specifying *.

The following output shows what you see when the script is executing using the PAUSE argument.

```
ptrmaint.bat pause color_printer
Notifying all users that the color_printer will be unavailable for a
while.
The message was successfully sent to all users of this server.


Pausing printer output. Wait for the printer to stop before starting!
The Print Spooler service is stopping.

The Print Spooler service was stopped successfully.
```

The following output shows what you see when the script is executing using the RESUME argument.

```
Notifying all users that color_printer is available again
No users have sessions with this server.
```

```
starting Printer Spooler.
The Print Spooler service is starting.

The Print Spooler service was started successfully.
```

Creating and Deleting Shares

You can use the NET SHARE command in your scripts to view, add, and delete shared resources on a Windows network. Shared resources include printers, drives, and folders. Typing **NET SHARE** and pressing Enter lists all shared resources on a computer, including hidden shares, as shown here:

```
C:\>net share


Share name     Resource                            Remark

_____

D$             D:\                                 Default share
print$         C:\WINNT\System32\spool\drivers     Printer Drivers
ADMIN$         C:\WINNT                            Remote Admin
IPC$                                               Remote IPC
C$             C:\                                 Default share
A              A:\
c              C:\
E              E:\
color_printer  LPT1:                               Spooled Marketing
                                                   Color Printer
```

You can create a new share by specifying the new share name, an equal sign, and then the path of the resource to be shared. For example, you can crate a new share named MKT_FOLDER for a folder located on the C:\MARKETING folder with a comment of "Marketing department shared folder" as shown:

```
net share MKT_FOLDER=c:\marketing /remark:"Marketing department
shared folder"
```

You can later terminate the sharing of the C:\MARKETING folder by specifying the following command in your script:

```
net share MKT_FOLDER /delete
```

Managing Network Connections

The NET SESSION command provides your scripts with a command for listing and disconnecting network sessions on the local computer. Type **NET SESSION** and press Enter to view all active network sessions on the computer, as shown:

```
C:\>net session
```

Computer Idle time	Username	Client Type	Opens
\\OEMCOMPUTER 00:00:00	ADMINISTRATOR	OEMWORKGROUP	2
\\OEMCOMPUTER 00:00:09		OEMWORKGROUP	0

The NET SESSION command provides the following information:

◆ **Computer**. Name of the connected computer.

◆ **Username**. Name of the connected user.

◆ **Client type**. The type of operating system used by the connected computer.

◆ **Opens**. The number of opened resources.

◆ **Idle time**. The length of time that the session has been idle.

To display session information for a client named LAPTOP, type:

```
net session \\laptop
```

To disconnect all active sessions with the server, type:

```
net session /delete
```

Working with Event Logs

One of the most important resources provided by Windows NT 4 and Windows 2000 are their event logs. Unfortunately, the Windows shell does not have a means of interacting directly with these logs. However, the Resource Kits for these two operating systems provide commands that allow your scripts both read and write access to these logs.

Processing Event Logs

The DUMPEL.EXE command lets you copy the contents of event logs into tab-delimited text files. It also allows your scripts to filter events in order to limit the amount of data that must be processed. For example, to copy the local application log to a file named APPLOG.TXT on a network server named FILESERVER, type:

```
dumpel -f applog.txt -s fileserver -l application
```

The following command performs the same copy operation but adds a filter so that only two specified events are included in the output file.

```
dumpel -f applog.txt -s fileserver -l application -e 4126 4124
```

The next example modifies the previous one by adding a -r switch behind the -e switch. This command then creates the output file, but this time it includes all events except for the two specified types of events.

```
dumpel -f applog.txt -s fileserver -l application -e 4126 4124 -r
```

Using Scripts to Write Messages to Event Logs

LOGEVENT.EXE allows you to write events to one of the Windows Event Viewer logs on both local and network computers. The command allows you to specify severity, category number, source, event ID, timeout, and the event message. Valid severities include Error, Failure, Information, Success, and Warning. For example, the following command places an event into the System event log with a severity of Error, a category number of 999, and a message:

```
logevent -s E -c 999 "This message was written by a batch script!"
```

This first entry at the top of Figure 9.11 is the event log entry created by the previous command.

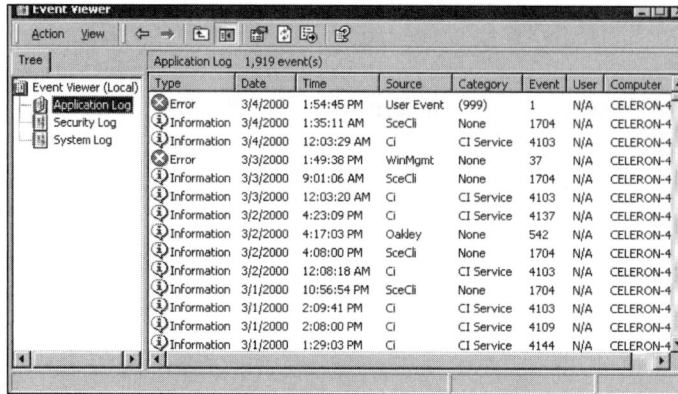

FIGURE 9.11

The Windows NT 4 and Windows 2000 Resource Kits' LOGEVENT.EXE command lets you write messages to event logs directly from within your scripts.

Managing Services

You can start and stop services on Windows NT 4 or Windows 2000 by any of the following means:

◆ Using the Service utility on Windows NT 4

◆ From the MMC Services console on Windows 2000

◆ From the command line using NET commands

Windows NT 4 and Windows 2000 provide the following commands for working with services:

◆ NET CONTINUE. Activates a suspended service, making it available to users.

◆ NET PAUSE. Suspends a service. Pausing a service allows users currently accessing the service to complete their work but denies access to other users.

◆ NET START. Starts a stopped service, making it available to users.

◆ NET STOP. Stops an active service. This immediately terminates any existing user activity and prevents any new activity until the service is started.

Windows NT 4 and Windows 2000 both provide a range of services, although not all may be active. To view a list of all active services, type NET START at the command prompt and press Enter as shown:

```
C:\>net start
These Windows 2000 services are started:
```

```
COM+ Event System
Computer Browser
DHCP Client
Distributed Link Tracking Client
DNS Client
Event Log
Indexing Service
IPSEC Policy Agent
Logical Disk Manager
Messenger
Network Connections
Plug and Play
Print Spooler
Protected Storage
Remote Procedure Call (RPC)
Remote Registry Service
Removable Storage
Secondary Logon Service
Security Accounts Manager
Server
System Event Notification
Task Scheduler
TCP/IP NetBIOS Helper Service
Telephony
Windows Management Instrumentation Driver Extensions
Workstation
```

Any of these services can be managed from the command line or from your scripts.

TIP

The Windows NT 4 and Windows 2000 Resource Kits provide additional commands for managing services. The NETSVC.EXE command starts and stops services across the network. SCLIST.EXE lists the services and views their status. The SVCMON.EXE command monitors services and alerts administrators when their status changes and the DELSRV.EXE removes a service.

NOTE

As you have seen throughout this chapter, there are many helpful commands available in the Windows NT 4 and Windows 2000 Resource Kits that you can incorporate into your shell scripts. This chapter has only touched on a few of the Resource Kits' commands. They also include commands that work with the Registry; perform advanced services administration; provide information on disk, memory, and processor usage; compress and uncompress files; manage remote access services; and much more. Windows Resource Kits are an indispensable part of any administrator's bag of tricks and it is highly recommended that you spend some time working with them. As of the writing of this book, more information can be found at `http://www.microsoft.com/Windows`.

What's Next?

This marks the end of the first half of this book. You have been presented with a through review of Windows shell scripting and seen many examples that you can use as templates for creating your own scripts. Appendix A provides a command reference to assist you with syntax issues when developing new scripts.

As you begin to develop your own library of Windows shell scripts, you might want to spend a little time on the Internet, where tons of additional information and free scripts await you. The next half of this book focuses on Microsoft's Windows Script Host, or WSH. The WSH is a complete scripting environment that allows you to create scripts based on popular scripting languages, such as VBScript and JScript. Mastery of one or both of these scripting languages will provide you with a very powerful foundation upon which to begin or continue a career as a Windows system administrator.

W S H

PART III

Working with the Windows Script Host

Chapter 10

Introducing the
Windows Script Host

This is the first chapter dealing with the Windows Script Host (WSH) and therefore provides the foundation upon which the remaining chapters build. It provides an overview of the components of the WSH and explains how they all fit and work together. This includes both the WScript and CScript script engines as well as the WSH object model.

By the time you finish this chapter, you will be ready to begin tackling JScript or VBScript and other advanced WSH topics. This chapter also explains how to use XML to combine the best of JScript and VBScript in a single Windows Script file.

Topics covered in this chapter include:

◆ Understanding the WSH object model
◆ Configuring the WScript and CScript execution environments
◆ Understanding XML and its role in creating Windows scripts
◆ Creating Windows Script Files

Understanding How the WSH Works

The WSH is an advanced scripting environment for creating and executing scripts on Windows operating systems. WSH scripts can be written using any WSH-compatible scripting language and can run on multiple platforms, including Windows 98, Windows Me, Windows NT 4, Windows 2000, and Windows XP. The WSH is made up of three key components:

◆ **WScript.exe.** A scripting host designed to support interactive scripting.
◆ **CScript.exe.** A scripting host designed to support command-line and background scripting.
◆ **WSH.OCX.** The WSH Core Object Model, which provides access to a collection of objects that can be used to interact with the operating system.

NOTE

Both WScript and CScript provide the same level of functionality and you can usually execute your scripts using either execution host with little if any impact on the way the script executes.

You create and store WSH scripts as plain text files that contain either JScript or VBScript statements. Once created, these scripts can then be submitted to the appropriate scripting host. Typically, the WScript host processes scripts that interact with users and requires a graphic dialog box, whereas CScript processes command-line scripts that run as background programs.

In addition to stand-alone JScripts and VBScripts, WSH 2.0 supports the capability to combine scripting languages into a single executable file known as a Windows script file or .wsf file. Windows script files allow you to leverage the strengths of different languages to solve problems. Table 10.1 lists the various file types supported by the WSH. As you can see, there is a fourth file type known as a *Windows script host properties file*. When present, this file allows you to customize many attributes associated with your scripts and is explained later in this chapter.

Table 10.1 WSH Scripting Engine File Extensions

Extension	Description
.js	Specifies a JScript file.
.vbs	Specifies a VBScript file.
.wsf	Specifies a Windows script file.
.wsh	Specifies a Windows script host properties file.

Regardless of whether you place your scripts inside of Windows script files or run them as JScript or VBScript files, all scripts must be processed by either the WScript or CScript execution hosts.

Configuring the Scripting Hosts

Before you begin writing and executing WSH scripts, you should understand their execution environment and how to configure it. Both WScript and CScript have their own configuration settings.

You can establish a default WScript configuration that governs the execution of all script processed by the WScript execution host. In addition, you can create .wsh files for individual scripts that override the default configuration settings. Configuration settings for the CScript host are established from the command line and apply to all scripts processed by that host. However, like the WScript host, the default CScript configuration settings can be overridden by command-line options. These configuration options are explained in the following sections.

Configuring the WScript Execution Host

As already stated, you can establish a default configuration that is applied anytime the WScript execution host processes a script that does not have its own individual configuration. Configuration options include limiting the total execution time that a script can run and determining whether the WSH logo is displayed when the WScript execution host is called from the command line.

The CScript execution host is configured from the command line. A specific configuration can be saved and applied to all scripts processed by that host. However, you cannot save individual script's configurations. Individual scripts can, however, be configured for CScript execution from the command line before being executed.

Specifying a Default WScript Configuration

The following instructions explain how to configure a default configuration for scripts processed by the WScript execution host. This configuration applies to all script processed by the WScript.exe execution host that do not already have their own configuration settings.

1. Click Start, Run and then type **WScript.exe** and click OK.
2. The Windows Script Host Settings dialog box appears, as shown in Figure 10.1.

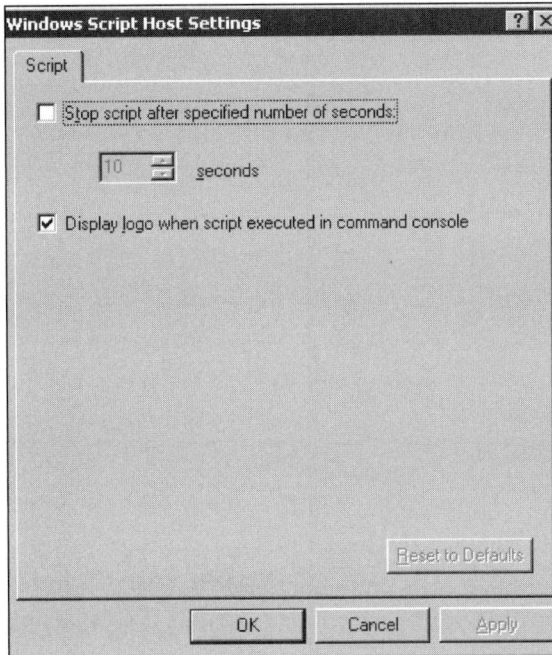

FIGURE 10.1

Configuring execution settings for the WScript execution host.

3. By default, there is no execution time limit. To change this default, click "Stop script after specified number of seconds" and type a new setting in the Seconds field.

4. To enable or disable the display of the logo message before script execution, set or clear the "Display logo when script executed in command console" option.

5. Click OK.

Configuring a WScript Configuration for an Individual Script

You can override the default parameters that you set for the WScript execution host for individual scripts by using the following procedure.

1. Locate the script that you want to configure, right-click it, and select Properties. The properties dialog box for the script appears.

2. Select the Script property sheet, as shown in Figure 10.2.

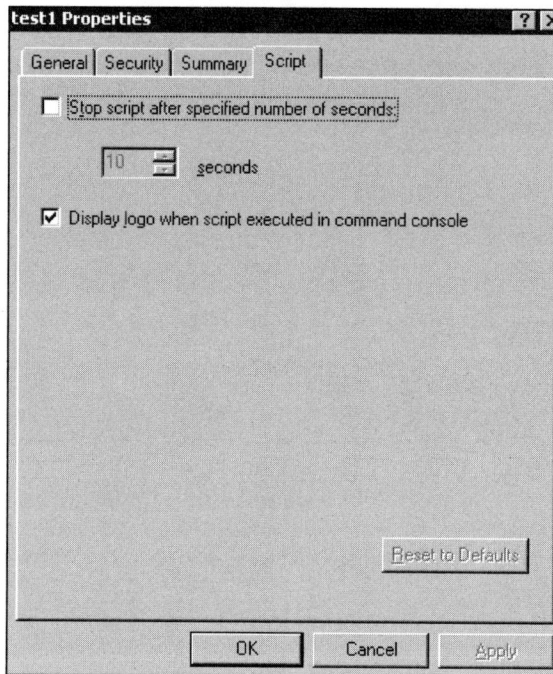

FIGURE 10.2

Configuring execution settings for an individual script.

3. To change the execution time limit for the script, make sure that the "Stop script after specified number of seconds" option is enabled and type a new setting in the Seconds field.

4. To enable or disable the display of the logo message during script execution, set or clear the "Display logo when script executed in command console" option.

5. Click OK.

> **NOTE**
>
> For each script that you create customized settings for, a `.wsh` file of the same name is automatically created that stores the script's customized settings. This file has a format very similar to old-style `.ini` files and is stored in the same folder as the script. An example of a `.wsh` file follows:
>
> ```
> [ScriptFile]
> Path=C:\MYTEST.js
> [Options]
> Timeout=6
> DisplayLogo=0
> ```
>
> PATH identifies the location of the script. TIMEOUT and DISPLAYLOGO correspond to the options on the script's property sheet.
>
> You can run a script by executing its `.wsh` file or by running the original script, in which case the execution host automatically looks for a corresponding `.wsh` file and, if it finds one, it uses its specified setting to run the script. Otherwise, the default execution host settings are used to execute the script.

Configuring the CScript Execution Host

You can specify execution options for scripts when running them from the command line. The CScript.exe and WScript.exe execution hosts share the same set of command-line options. The syntax for running a script from the command line is:

```
cscript scriptname [//options] [arguments]
wscript scriptname [//options] [arguments]
```

WSCRIPT and CSCRIPT specify the appropriate scripting execution host. *SCRIPTNAME* is the name of the script to execute. *//OPTIONS* are optional specifications that govern the execution of the script. *ARGUMENTS* are optional arguments that are passed to the script for processing.

> **NOTE**
>
> You can view all of the available *//OPTIONS* by typing **cscript** and pressing Enter at the command prompt.

Table 10.2 describes the available command-line options.

Table 10.2   CScript and WScript Command-Line Options

Option	Description
//?	Displays command syntax.
//b	Runs the script in batch mode, suppressing all message output and errors (opposite of interactive mode).
//d	Starts the script debugger.
//e:jscript | e:vbscript	Specifies the script engine that processes the script.
//h:wscript | h:script	Specifies the WSH executable that executes the script.
//i	Runs the script in interactive mode (opposite of batch mode). This is the default option.
//job:*id*	Executes a job stored in a .wsf file.
//logo	Displays the CScript logo.
//nologo	Disables the display of the CScript logo.
//s	Stores the specified options as the default options for current and future use.
//t:*nn*	Establishes a timeout setting that limits the amount of time a script can execute. The default is no time limit.
//x	Starts the script in the script debugger.

Executing Scripts from the Command Line

The following example shows how you format a command to execute a script named myscript.js using the CScript execution host with an option that specifies a 15-second execution limit.

```
cscript myscript.js //T:15
```

You can add as many options as are required by prefixing each additional option with the // characters, as shown:

```
cscript myscript.js //T:15 //nologo
```

Here, the same script is called but this time, in addition to a 15-second execution limit, the `//NOLOGO` option turns off the display of the WSH logo before script execution.

Establishing Default Command-Line Execution Settings

You can establish default command-line execution settings for the CScript execution host by typing **CScript** followed by the list of options and the `//s` option, as shown.

```
cscript //i //nologo //s
```

After this statement is processed, any command-line script that the current user runs via the CScript execution host will execute in interactive mode without displaying the WSH logo. These settings remain in effect until the user changes them by re-executing the command with a different set of options. Note that the default CScript settings established in this manner affect only the user that set them and are in effect only as long as that user is logged on to the system. This means that if you schedule the execution of a script when you are not logged on, these settings will not be in effect.

NOTE

CScript default execution settings are stored on a per-user basis in the `HKEY_CURRENT_USER` key in the Registry.

Setting a Default Execution Host

By default, the WSH sets WScript as the execution host for all scripts. You can change the default execution host to CScript by typing the following at the command prompt:

```
cscript //H:cscript
```

Likewise, you can change back to the WScript execution host by typing the following:

```
wscript //H:wscript
```

212 | *Part III*   **WORKING WITH THE WINDOWS SCRIPT HOST**

Combining JScript and VBScript

JScript's roots go back to Netscape's implementation of the JavaScript Web scripting language. VBScript, on the other hand, has evolved from the Microsoft Visual Basic programming language. Both have strong Web programming features. Over the last several years, Microsoft has worked hard to evolve both scripting languages into state of the art scripting languages. At the same time, many of the differences between the two languages have disappeared. The primary difference between the two languages now is more a matter of syntax than of raw capabilities.

Despite Microsoft's efforts to enrich both languages, there are still situations when one language is better suited than another. For example, JScript has a superior collection of methods for performing mathematical calculations, whereas VBScript has far more capabilities when it comes to working with arrays.

A new feature that Microsoft introduced with WSH 2.0 is the capability to combine both JScripts and VBScripts into a single file known as a Windows script file, or `.wsf`. Microsoft manages this feature through the integration of the XML language and its traditional scripting languages.

Using XML

The *Extensible Markup Language* or *XML* is a markup language used to create structured documents. Like HTML, which is also a markup language, XML makes use of tags to identify the various structured components that make up documents. XML was introduced in 1996. XML 1.0 was released in 1998 and is still the current standard.

At one point, XML was thought to be the replacement for HTML but instead has become a close partner in the form of XHTML. In addition, companies such as Oracle and Microsoft have embraced XML and are working to integrate it into their applications. One example of such integration is the introduction of Windows script files in WSH 2.0. Windows script files are plain text files that combine multiple scripts written in different scripting languages into a singe file. The role of XML is to provide a format that identifies and manages this integration.

NOTE

To learn more about XML, check out `http://www.xml.com`. You will find information on current and proposed XML standards as well as tons of tips and advice.

WSH's XML implementation uses a limited set of XML tags to format Windows script files. These files are saved using a `.wsf` file extension. You can create such files using any plain text editor or XML editor.

NOTE

Examples of XML editors include XMLwriter (`http://xmlwriter.net`), the Athens XML Editor (`http://www.swiftinc.co.jp`), and XMLEdit (`http://www.turbopower.com`).

Table 10.3 provides a quick reference of the XML tags supported by WSH. Each of these tags is explained in greater detail in the sections that follow.

Table 10.3   WSH-Supported XML Elements

Element	Description
`<?job ?>`	Controls error handling and debugging.
`<?XML ?>`	Specifies the XML level used in the `.wsf` file.
`<job>`	Identifies a specific job within a `.wsf` file.
`<object>`	Specifies an object for reference within the `.wsf` file.
`<package>`	Allows you to include more than one job within a `.wsf` file.
`<reference>`	Provides references to external libraries.
`<resource>`	Specifies static data that can be referenced by scripts within a `.wsf` file.
`<script>`	Identifies a specific script within a `.wsf` file.

Note: XML elements are only supported in the form of `.wsf` files introduced by WSH version 2.0.

A Typical Windows Script File XML Layout

The following example demonstrates the XML layout of a typical Windows script file. It includes two automated tasks, each of which consists of a single script. Because more than one job is included in the Windows script file, the <PACKAGE></PACKAGE> tags must be used. Only one pair of <PACKAGE></PACKAGE> tags is permitted in a Windows script file. The first job consists of a one-line JScript script and the second job consists of a one-line VBScript script. An unlimited number of jobs can be included within the file, each of which can contain any number of scripts written in different script languages. Each of the statements shown in this example is explained in the sections that follow.

```
<?xml version="1.0"?>
<package>

  <job id="job_1">
  <?job error="true" debug="true"?>
   <script language="JScript">
     WScript.Echo ("This is my first Windows script file!")
   </script>
  </job>

  <job id="job_2">
  <?job error="true" debug="true"?>
    <script language="VBScript">
      WScript.Echo "This is my first Windows script file!"
    </script>
  </job>

</package>
```

The <?job ?> Tag

The <?job ?> tag provides XML error and debug instructions and is implemented using the following syntax:

```
<?job error="flag" debug="flag" ?>
```

Both ERROR and DEBUG options represent Boolean values of true or false. For example, the following XML statement displays run-time and other error messages while enabling debugging:

```
<?job error="true" debug="true" ?>
```

NOTE

If you set debug="false", you cannot start the Windows script debugger for the Windows script file.

The <?XML ?> Tag

The <?XML ?> tag specifies the XML version that the file was written for. This statement enforces a stricter interpretation of code syntax. It is implemented using the following syntax:

```
<?XML version="version" [standalone="DTDflag"] ?>
```

VERSION represents the XML version of the file and is specified in the form of x.x. The current XML version supported by WSH is 1.0. *DTDFLAG* references an external Document Type Definition. However, this option is currently unsupported, so the value is always set to yes.

For example, the following XML statement specifies XML version 1.0:

```
<?XML version="1.0" standalone="yes" ?>
```

If present, this statement must be the first tag in the Windows script file.

The <job> Tag

The <job></job> tags identify individual jobs within a Windows script file and are implemented using the following syntax:

```
<job [id=JobID]>
. . .
</job>
```

JOBID identifies a specific job by name. JOBID is required only when two or more jobs are present. Jobs consist of one or more instances of scripts that are written using different scripting languages.

For example, the following XML statement defines a job that consists of two separate scripts. The first script is written in JScript and the second is written in VBScript.

```
<job id="job_1">
<?job error="true" debug="true"?>
 <script language="JScript">
   WScript.Echo ("This is my first Windows script file!")
 </script>
 <script language="VBScript">
   WScript.Echo "This is my first Windows script file!"
 </script>
</job>
```

> **NOTE**
>
> When two or more jobs are included within a Windows script file, they must be enclosed within the `<package></package>` tags.

The `<object>` Tag

The `<object>` tag specifies objects that can be referenced by scripts within the Windows script file. It is implemented using the following syntax:

```
<object id="objID" [classid="clsid:GUID" | progid="progID"] />
```

OBJID is the name that references the object. *CLASSID* is the class ID of the registered object and *PROGID* is the program ID. Either *CLASSID* or *PROGID* must be specified.

The `<package>` Tag

The `<package></package>` tags are used when a Windows script contains more than one job. They can be included in Windows script files that contain a single job, but are not required. They are implemented using the following syntax:

```
<package>
 . . .
</package>
```

The following example demonstrates the use of the `<package></package>` tags. In this case, two jobs are defined:

```
<package>
  <job id="job_a">
   <script language="JScript">
     WScript.Echo ("This is a JScript!")
   </script>
  </job>
  <job id="job_b">
    <script language="VBScript">
      WScript.Echo "This is a VBScript."
    </script>
  </job>
</package>
```

The <reference> Tag

The `<reference>` tag provides for the inclusion of external libraries made available by external objects from other applications installed on the computer. WSH allows you to instantiate new objects based on these external objects and provides the capability to access relevant properties and methods of the object. However, your scripts cannot reference any constant values that are stored in the object external library. The `<reference>` tag is designed to remedy this dilemma. It is implemented using the following syntax:

```
<reference [object="progID" | guid="typelibGUID"] [version="version"]
/>
```

You can reference an external library by either its *PROGID* or *GUID*. *VERSION* is an optional parameter that refers to the version number of the library. The external library is usually located in the owning object's executable (`.exe`) or in an accompanying `.dll` file. Sometimes you find them in `.tlb` files.

NOTE

A reference to external libraries is an advanced programming concept best addressed in other books. It is mentioned here to round out the discussion of WSH-supported XML tags and to provide you with a high-level view of its capability.

The <resource> Tag

The <resource> tag allows you to establish a constant value for a piece of data that can be referenced from other scripts. This eliminates the need to duplicate the resource within all scripts. It is implemented using the following syntax:

```
<resource id="resourceID">
 . . .
</resource>
```

RESOURCEID identifies a specific resource and must be unique within the Windows script file. For example, the following XML statement defines a resource that consists of a text message that serves as a standardized message for all scripts.

```
<resource id="unknownErrorType">
 . . . Error: The script encountered an unknown error
</resource>
```

The message stored in the previous example can then be referenced from within a script as demonstrated in the following example:

```
<?xml version="1.0"?>

<job id="job_1">
<?job error="true" debug="true"?>
<resource id="unknownErrorType">
   Error: The script encountered an unknown error
</resource>
 <script language="VBScript">
   MsgBox getResource("unknownErrorType")

 </script>
</job>
```

Figure 10.3 shows the results of running the previous example.

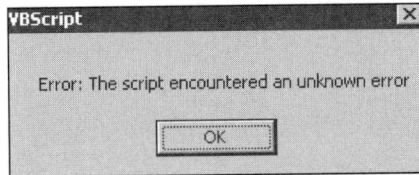

FIGURE 10.3

You can create standard messages that can be accessed by any script within the Windows script file.

NOTE

The `<resource>` tag must be placed within the `<job></job>` tags and its value is therefore limited to all scripts contained within the `<job></job>` tags.

The `<script>` Tag

The `<script></script>` tags identify individual scripts within jobs in a Windows script file and are implemented using the following syntax:

```
<script language="language" [src="script"]>

  ...

</script>
```

LANGUAGE identifies the script language that the script is written in and *SCRIPT* is an optional parameter that specifies the location of an external script. This external script can be called in placed of a script embedded directly into the file.

In the following example, two script files have been created. The first file contains a Windows script file with a single job that executes two JScripts. The first script is embedded in the file and the second script is called as an external reference. The source for the Windows script file follows:

```
<job id="job_1">
<?job error="true" debug="true"?>
 <script language="JScript">
   WScript.Echo ("This is my first Windows script file!")
 </script>
 <script language="JScript" src="script2.js" />
</job>
```

The source for the second script is shown here:

```
WScript.Echo ("This is my second Windows script file!")
```

When the Windows script file is executed, it first processes the embedded script that displays a test message. It then executes the external script that displays a message of its own.

Running Windows Script Files

Windows script files are executed just like other script files. You can double-click them and you can run them from the command line. The behavior of these scripts depends on their contents. Double-clicking a Windows script executes the script. If the script contains just one job, the job is executed. However, if the Windows script contains more than one job, only the first job executes.

You can run Windows scripts from the command line using either the WScript or CScript. If you type

```
wscript.exe test.wsf
```

or

```
cscript.exe test.wsf
```

the first job in the Windows script executes. To execute other jobs in the Windows script file, you must specify the job's name using the following syntax:

```
wscript.exe WindowsScript //job:jobname
```

For example, typing this

```
wscript.exe test.wsf //job:job_1
```

runs job_1 using the WScript host. If a second job was contained in the Windows script file, it can run using the CScript host, as follows:

```
cscript.exe test.wsf //job:job_2
```

Drag-and-Drop Script Execution

In addition to the traditional ways of executing scripts, WSH 2.0 introduces the drag-and-drop execution of scripts. In this case, drag-and-drop execution means that you can write scripts that allow you to drag and drop files on top of them. These files are automatically translated into arguments and passed onto the script as input parameters. This new feature enables the creation of scripts that can perform functions similar to the Windows Recycle Bin. Instead of deleting files that are dragged and dropped, you can archive files on a network server or send them as e-mail.

For example, consider the following two examples.

```
var objArgs = WScript.Arguments
for (i = 0; i <= WScript.Arguments.length - 1; i++) {
  WScript.Echo ("Filename = ", objArgs(i))
}

Set objArgs = WScript.Arguments
For i = 0 to objArgs.Count - 1
  WScript.Echo "Filename = " + objArgs(i)
Next
```

The first example is a JScript script that displays the names of any files that are dragged and dropped onto it. The second script is a VBScript script that performs the same task.

Understanding the WSH Object Model

The WSH provides access to a core object model that your scripts can use to access and automate many Windows resources. This model consists of nine objects. At the top of the model is the root object WScript. This object is automatically initialized at the beginning of script execution and is therefore always available. Two other objects, WshNetwork and WshShell, can be created using the `CreateObject()` method.

Together the WScript, WshNetwork, and WshShell objects are known as *exposed objects* because they can be created and referenced directly within scripts. The remaining objects are known as *non-exposed objects* because they can be created only by executing a method that belongs to one of the three exposed objects. Figure 10.4 presents a graphical depiction of the WSH Core Object Model and shows how the objects relate to one another.

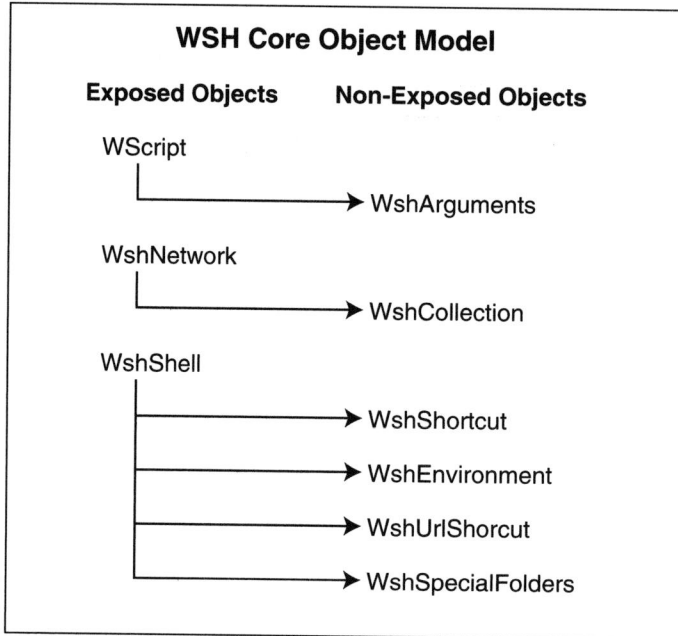

FIGURE 10.4

The WSH object model consists of exposed and non-exposed objects that provide access to a number of Windows resources.

As you can see, each of the exposed objects is the parent to one or more non-exposed objects. Therefore, a method of the parent object is required to instantiate a child object. Table 10.4 shows the methods required to create a non-exposed object.

Table 10.4   Instantiating Non-Exposed WSH Objects

Object	Method for Object Creation
WshArguments	WScript.Arguments
WshCollection	WshNetwork.EnumNetworkDrives
WshShortcut	WshShell.CreateShortcut
Wsh.Environment	WshShell.Environment
WshUrlShortcut	WshShell.CreatShortcut
WshSpecialFolders	WshShell.SpecialFolders

Each object in the WSH Core Object Model provides access to a different set of methods and properties that your scripts can use to automate the Windows environment. Table 10.5 provides a brief description of these objects. *Methods* are functions associated with objects that can be used to manipulate the object. *Properties* are attributes of objects that store information about some quality of the object. WSH Core Object methods and properties are defined in Tables 10.6 and 10.7.

TIP

Many WSH objects share the same methods or properties. So for the sake of efficiency, object methods and properties are listed once in Tables 10.6 and 10.7 and then referenced as necessary in Table 10.5.

Table 10.5   The WSH Object Model

Object	Description
WScript	The WSH root object. Provides access to script arguments and supports the creation of new objects.
	Properties: Application, Arguments, FullName, Name, Path, ScriptFullName, ScriptName, StdErr, StdIn, StdOut, and Version.
	Methods: ConnectObject, CreateObject, DisconnectObject, Echo, GetObject, Quit, and Sleep.
WshArguments	Provides access to command-line arguments.
	Properties: Count, Item, and Length.
	No methods.
WshEnvironment	Provides access to environment variables.
	Properties: Count, Item, and Length.
	Method: Remove.
WshNetwork	Provides access to network resources, including network printers and shared drives. Also provides other network-related information.
	Properties: ComputerName, UserDomain, and UserName.
	Methods: AddPrinterConnection, EnumNetworkDrives, EnumPrinterConnection, MapNetworkDrive, RemoveNetworkDrive, RemovePrinterConnection, and SetDefaultPrinter.

continues

Table 10.5   The WSH Object Model *(continued)*

Object	Description
WshShell	Provides access to environment variables and the Registry. Also supports messaging and shortcut access.
	Properties: `Environment` and `SpecialFolders`.
	Methods: `AppActivate`, `CreateShortcut`, `ExpandEnvironmentStrings`, `LogEvent`, `Popup`, `RegDelete`, `RegRead`, `RegWrite`, `Run`, and `SendKeys`.
WshShortcut	Provides the capability to create shortcuts.
	Properties: `Arguments`, `Description`, `FullName`, `Hotkey`, `conLocation`, `TargetPath`, `WindowStyle`, and `WorkingDirectory`.
	Method: `Save`.
WshSpecialFolders	Provides access to Windows folders and the Start menu folder.
	Properties: `Count`, `Item`, and `Length`.
	No methods.
WshUrlShortcut	Provides the capability to creates shortcuts of URLs.
	Properties: `FullName` and `TargetPath`.
	Method: Save.

Note: All WSH object model objects are supported by both WSH 1.0 and WSH 2.0.

Table 10.6   WSH Object Methods

Method	Supporting Version	Description
AddPrinterConnection	1	Maps network printers
AddWindowsPrinterConnection	2	Adds a printer connection
AppActivate	2	Activates the specified window
Close	2	Terminates an open stream
ConnectObject	2	Connects to an object
CreateObject	1	Creates an object
CreateShortcut	1	Establishes a shortcut
DisconnectObject	1	Disconnects an object

Table 10.6   WSH Object Methods

Method	Supporting Version	Description
Echo	1	Displays text messages
EnumNetworkDrives	1	Provides access to drive mappings
EnumPrinterConnections	1	Provides access to printer mappings
ExpandEnvironmentStrings	1	Returns the contents of the Process environmental variable as a string
GetObject	1	Retrieves an Automation object
getResource	2	Retrieves the value of a resource specified by the <resource> tag
LogEvent	2	Writes an event to the Windows event log
MapNetworkDrive	1	Maps a network drive
Popup	1	Displays a pop-up message box
Quit	1	Terminates the script
Read	2	Returns a string of characters from an input stream
ReadAll	2	Returns the s string consisting of all the characters in the input stream
ReadLine	2	Returns a string containing a line from the input stream
RegDelete	1	Deletes a specified key or value from the Registry
RegRead	1	Returns a specified key or value from the Registry
RegWrite	1	Writes a specified key or value to the Registry
Remove	1	Deletes an environmental variable
RemoveNetworkDrive	1	Removes a network drive mapping
RemovePrinterConnection	1	Removes a network printer
Run	1	Starts a new process

continues

Table 10.6   WSH Object Methods *(continued)*

Method	Supporting Version	Description
Save	1	Creates a shortcut in a specified location
SendKeys	2	Emulates keystrokes and sends them to a specified window
SetDefaultPrinter	1	Sets the default printer
Skip	2	Skips a specified number of characters when reading from an input stream
SkipLine	2	Skips a line when reading from the input stream
Sleep	2	Halts script execution for a specified number of seconds
Write	2	Sends a string to an output stream
WriteBlankLines	2	Sends a blank line in the form of newline character to an output stream
WriteLine	2	Sends a line in the form of a string followed by the newline character to an output stream

Table 10.7   WSH Object Properties

Method	Supporting Version	Description
Application	1	Retrieves the IDispatch interface for the WScript object
Arguments	1	Provides a pointer to the WshArguments collection
AtEndOfLine	2	Returns a value of true or false depending on whether the end-of-line marker is the next element in the stream
AtEndOfStream	2	Returns a value of true or false depending on whether the end of an input stream has been reached

Table 10.7 WSH Object Properties

Method	Supporting Version	Description
Column	2	Retrieves the column number of the current column position in an input stream
ComputerName	1	Returns a string containing a computer's name
Count	1	Returns an enumerator value
Description	1	Retrieves a shortcut's description
Environment	1	Returns WshEnvironment
FullName	1	Returns the path of a shortcut or executable program
HotKey	1	Retrieves a shortcut's hotkey
IconLocation	1	Returns the location of the specified icon
Item	1	Retrieves an item from the specified collection
Length	1	Returns an account of enumerated items
Line	2	Retrieves the line number of the current line in an input stream
Name	1	Returns a string specifying the name of the WScript object
Path	1	Returns a string specifying the location of the folder containing either CScript.exe or WScript.exe
ScriptFullName	1	Returns the path of the executing script
ScriptName	1	Returns the name of the executing script
SpecialFolders	1	Provides access to the Start menu and desktop folders
StdErr	2	Provides write access to a script's error output stream
StdIn	2	Provides read access to a script's input stream
StdOut	2	Provides write access to a script's output stream
TargetPath	1	Specifies a shortcut's path to the object it represents

continues

Table 10.7 WSH Object Properties *(continued)*

Method	Supporting Version	Description
UserDomain	1	Returns a string containing the domain name
UserName	1	Returns a string containing the user name
Version	1	Retrieves the version number of the WSH
WindowStyle	1	Retrieves a shortcut's window style
WorkingDirectory	1	Returns a shortcut object's working directory

JScript versus VBScript

Now that you have nearly finished this chapter and understand the WSH, its object model, and how to format .wsf files, it's time to consider which scripting language you will use to write your scripts.

JScript is the close cousin of JavaScript and will probably be the easier of the two languages to pick up, especially if you have done any Web page development in the past and have some level of familiarity with JavaScript. VBScript, on the other hand, is easier to learn if you have any experience with Microsoft's Visual Basic. You might also pick VBScript if you plan to one day work with Visual Basic.

Chapter 11, "Writing JScript Scripts," presents a review of the JScript scripting language. Chapter 12, "Writing VBScript Scripts," presents a VBScript review. Appendixes B and C provide references to these languages.

If you are new to both languages, I suggest that you pick one language and work through the book using it alone. You can then come back when you are comfortable with your first language and learn the second one. The material presented for each scripting language is formatted in a nearly identical fashion. This is so that, once you have worked your way through the book using one scripting language, you should be comfortable working on the other. Of course, if you prefer, you can always tackle both languages at the same time.

Chapter 11

Writing JScript Scripts

This chapter is designed to provide the non-JScript programmer with an introduction to the JScript language. It presents a quick review of the basic JScript programming constructs that you need to know in order to begin developing your own WSH scripts. Its purpose is to provide you with enough of an understanding of JScript so that you can work with the real-world WSH examples presented in Chapters 13 through 15.

Chapter 12, "Writing VBScript Scripts," provides a similar review of the VBScript scripting language. Depending on your programming background, you might want to examine that chapter before this one. If you have worked with JavaScript before, you will find JScript easy to master. However, if you have a Visual Basic programming background, VBScript will probably provide you with a better starting point.

Topics covered in this chapter include:

- ◆ Executing your JScript scripts
- ◆ Working with variables
- ◆ Mastering operations and expressions
- ◆ Performing conditional logic
- ◆ Creating JScript loops
- ◆ Organizing your scripts with functions
- ◆ Using arrays to manage and organize your data

Formatting Your Scripts

If you have ever done any JavaScript development on the Internet, you probably remember that JavaScript must be embedded inside HTML pages and enclosed inside special tags that identify it as JavaScript. Well, things are much simpler when writing JScript for the WSH. WSH JScripts consist of JScript statements and nothing more. The only thing that you need to be sure to do is save the script with a .js file extension. That way, the WSH knows which script execution host to submit the script to when executing it.

The exception to this rule is when you place JScript inside a Windows script file, in which case you do need to wrap your scripts within special tags. See Chapter 10, "Introducing the Windows Script Host," for more information on working with .wsf files.

The JScript Object Model

WSH includes a core object model that provides your scripts with access to Windows objects. The scripting engine that executes WSH scripts further supplements this model. JScript and VBScript have their own object models that provide access to system objects. Table 11.1 lists the object model provided by JScript.

Table 11.1   JScript Objects

Object	Description
ActiveXObject	Provides a reference to an automation object.
Array	Provides for the creation of arrays.
Boolean	Provides for the creation of a Boolean value.
Date	Provides access to dates and times methods.
Dictionary	Stores data key and item pairs.
Enumerator	Provides the capability to enumerate a collection of items.
Error	Provides access to script error information.
FileSystemObject	Provides access to filesystem resources.
Function	Provides the capability to create a function.
Global	Collects global methods into one object.
Math	Provides access to mathematical functions and constants.
Number	Provides access to a collection of numeric constants.
Object	Provides the capability to create an instance of any other object type.
RegExp	Saves information from regular expressions.
Regular Expression	Stores a regular expression pattern.
String	Provides the capability to manipulate strings.
VBArray	Provides the capability to use VBScript arrays.

Many of these JScript objects are demonstrated in the remaining chapters of this book. In addition to this collection of core objects, JScript also make available a collection of run-time objects that provide access to system resources. These objects are listed in Table 11.2 and demonstrated throughout the remainder of this book.

Table 11.2   JScript Run-Time Objects

Object	Description
Dictionary	Stores data key and item pairs.
Drive	Provides access to a disk drive's properties.
Drives Collection	Provides information about system drives.
File	Provides access to a file's properties.
Files Collection	Provides access to files contained in a folder.
FileSystemObject	Provides access to the entire filesystem.
Folder	Provides access to a folder's properties.
Folders Collection	Provides access to the folders contained within another folder.
TextStream	Provides for sequential file access.

Understanding JScript Syntax

JScript is an *interpreted* programming language. This means that instead of being precompiled the WSH WScript or CScript, execution host processes each statement within a JScript one at a time in the order presented.

Like VBScript files, JScript files are plain text files. JScript files are comprised of one or more JScript statements that perform a task. JScript files are saved with a .js file extension and can be created using any text editor. JScript provides a complete programming language implementation as is demonstrated throughout this chapter.

JScript is a flexible scripting language. It does not impose as strict a set of programming rules as in many other languages. For example, you can type JScript statements on one line or spread them out over many lines. JScript statements end with the ; (semicolon) character. However, if you want to, you can usually leave out the semicolon and JScript will still work just fine. It is strongly recommend that you terminate each JScript statement with a semicolon, because it makes your scripts easier to read.

> **TIP**
>
> You can even place multiple JScript statements on the same line by ending each with a semicolon.

> **NOTE**
>
> JScript is also supported as a scripting language by modern Web browsers. Its implementation when used in Web browsers is somewhat different. Specifically, it has access to a significantly different object model that's ideal for Web scripting, but prohibits access to local resources such as filesystems and local area network access.

Case Sensitivity

JScript is a case-sensitive scripting language. It requires that you type key JScript elements exactly as they have been defined. Therefore, it is important that you follow the spelling and structure that you see presented in this chapter in your own JScripts. This includes variables names, labels, methods, properties, and all other constructs. For example, if you create a JScript variable and name it `myfolder`, you must continue to reference it by this name using its exact spelling. In JScript, `MyFolder` and `myfolder` are interpreted as different variable names.

JScript Statement Syntax

Understanding JScript syntax is an important part of mastering JScript programming. Each JScript statement is implemented using a particular syntax and any failure to follow this syntax results in an error. For example, the following statement shows a one-line JScript script that displays a message using the `WScript.Echo` command.

```
WScript.Echo ("This is a JScript!");
```

NOTE

The `WScript.Echo("This is a JScript!")` statement in the preceding example demonstrates the use of the `ECHO` method of the `WScript` object to display a message. Its behavior depends on which scripting host is executing it. If the scripting host is `WScript.exe`, the message is displayed as a pop-up dialog box. However, if `CScript.exe` is executing the script, the message appears as text in the Windows command console.

JScript requires that the output message be placed within parentheses and quotes. If, for example, you forget to type one of the quotes, as shown here, you receive an error.

```
WScript.Echo (This is a JScript!");
```

Figure 11.1 shows the results of trying to execute the previous JScript statement.

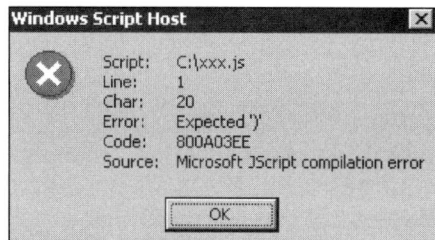

FIGURE 11.1

You receive a WSH error message indicating a syntax error in a JScript script.

TIP

Like most people, you will probably not be able to remember how to format every type of JScript language element. This means that you will refer to the examples in this chapter a lot. You should also check out Appendix B, which provides a JScript reference including additional programming examples and the proper spelling of many JScript elements. In addition, you can reference Microsoft's official JScript Language Reference at `http://msdn.microsoft.com/scripting`.

Understanding JScript Statements

As you have already seen, a JScript script consists of one or more JScript statements. Script statements make up the programming instructions that tell the script how to perform certain operations. There are many types of JScript statements. Often you can use more than one type of statement to perform the same task. This section organizes and presents the programming statements that comprise the JScript language using the following categories:

- ◆ Comments
- ◆ Variable declaration and assignment statements
- ◆ Conditional statements
- ◆ Looping statements
- ◆ Object-manipulation statements

Making Things Clear with Comments

JScript supports the addition of comment statements inside scripts so that you can document the internal programming logic of your scripts. Comment statements do not alter the processing flow of the script. They simply make it easier for someone else to read and understand your scripts.

You can add comments in your JScripts by placing them after a pair of forward slash characters, as demonstrated.

```
//The following statement displays a message in a pop-up dialog box
WScript.Echo ("This is a JScript!");
```

Using this same format, you can also add comments at the end of your JScript statements as shown here.

```
WScript.Echo ("This is a JScript!"); //The following statement displays a
message in a pop-up dialog
```

JScript also supports the inclusion of multi-line comments by placing comment text inside of /* and */, as demonstrated here.

```
/* This is a multi-line JScript comment. As you can see, it spans two
lines within the script. Like the other format of the comment, this
statement does not affect the script itself */
```

Add comments liberally and use them to provide an explanation of logic within the script. Not only do comments make your script easier for someone else to read but they also make it easier for you to follow your own programming logic should you need to modify a script months or years later.

The following example shows how you might effectively apply comments in a JScript.

```
// *******************************************
// * Script Name: example.js              *
// * Author:   Jerry Ford                   *
// * Address: Richmond Virginia            *
// * Created: 04/25/01                     *
// *******************************************


// **** Perform script initialization here ****


//Initialize a variable containing a user's name
var name = "Jerry Ford";


// ********* Main processing section *********


//Call a function that displays the user's name
DisplayName(name);


// ********** Procedures go here ************


//This function displays whatever name is passed to it
function DisplayName(name_arg)
{
   WScript.Echo ("Good morning " + name_arg);
}
```

The previous example also demonstrates the use of two other JScript programming elements, variables and functions, both of which are explained in detail later in this chapter.

Storing Information in Variables

Like Windows shell scripting, both JScript and VBScript support the use of variables to store and retrieve information. Variables can be referenced throughout the script and can be changed at any time.

Table 11.3 presents a list of JScript-supported data types that you can use to store variable data in your scripts.

Table 11.3   JScript Value Types

Value	Description
Boolean	A value indicating a `true` or `false` condition
Numbers	A numeric value such as 5 or 9.123
Strings	A text string such as `"JScript processing complete!"`

NOTE

In addition, JScript also supports two special data types. The `Null` data type contains an empty value and the `Undefined` data type is set when a variable has been initialized, but not yet assigned a value.

Declaring Variables

JScript provides the `VAR` keyword for declaring a variable. It is always best to declare a variable before using it. It makes your scripts easier to read and is considered better programming technique. The syntax for using the `VAR` keyword to declare a variable is as follows:

```
var variablename = value
```

VARIABLENAME is the name of the variable and *VALUE* is the value that you are assigning to it. For example, the following example

```
var primary_drive = "C";
```

creates a variable named `primary_drive` and assigns it the value of C. You can use the `VAR` keyword to create a variable but not assign any value to it by doing the following:

```
var primary_drive;
```

You can also declare a variable by simply referring to it, as shown.

```
primary_drive = "C";
```

If the `primary_drive` variable exists, this statement changes its value. If the variable does not exist, the statement creates it and assigns its value. However, this method of variable creation is generally discouraged in favor of using the more formal VAR statement.

Rules for Variable Names

JScript is a little picky when it comes to naming variables. The following list outlines JScript's rules for naming variables:

- JScript only supports the following characters: a-z, A-Z, 0-9, and the underscore character (_).
- JScript is case-sensitive. For example, primary_drive and Primary_drive are considered two different variables.
- JScript does not support spaces in variable names.
- JScript does not allow you to use any *reserved words* as variable names. Refer to Appendix B for JScript's list of reserved words.

> **TIP**
>
> Try creating variable names that describe their purpose or contents. For example, `primary_drive` is a much more descriptive variable name than `pd`. Descriptive variable names will make your scripts easier to read and maintain.

Understanding a Variable's Scope

JScript allows you to define variables so that they can be referenced throughout a script or only within a portion of the script, known as a *function*. A variable that's available throughout a script has a global scope, whereas a variable available only within a function is said to have a local scope. This capability to limit a variable's scope allows you to better organize and control script logic.

Local Variables

Local variables are created using the VAR keyword within a function. Functions are groups of statements that can be called upon throughout the script and allow you to better organize your scripts while also creating reusable code. Functions are covered in greater detail later in this chapter.

The following example demonstrates how to create a local variable. A function named DisplayMsg() is created that defines a local variable and then displays its value using a WScript.Echo statement. The function is designed to be called from another location in the script and, once executed, returns processing control back to the statement that follows the statement that called the function. Because the variable has a local scope, its value cannot be referenced from other parts of the script.

```
function DisplayMsg()
{
  var msg_text = "In a function the var statement creates local vari-
ables.";
  WScript.Echo(msg_text);
}
```

Global Variables

Global variables are variables that have been declared outside of a function. Therefore, global variables can be referenced from any location within the script. Global variables can be created with or without the use of the VAR keyword.

For example, either of the following statements creates a global variable that can be referenced anywhere within the script, including within the script's functions.

```
var computer_name = "SQL_Server";
computer_description = "Primary SQL server for Inventory Systems";
```

Manipulating Numeric Variables Using Expressions

The most common way to assign a value to a variable is to use the = assignment operator, as demonstrated here:

```
var total_count = "5";
```

Once you have declared a variable, you can use JScript expressions to manipulate numeric variable values. JScript provides a robust collection of operators that can be used within expressions to alter the values of numeric variables. These operators are listed in Table 11.4.

Table 11.4 JScript Operators

Operator	Description
+	Adds two values
–	Subtracts one value from another
*	Multiplies two values
/	Divides one value into another
–x	Reverses the sign of x
x++	Returns x, and then increments x by one
++x	Increments x by one, and then returns x
x– –	Returns x, and then decrements x by one
– –x	Decrements x by one, and then returns x

For example, the following expression changes the value of a variable named count by adding 5 to its current value.

```
count = count + 5;
```

Subtraction, multiplication, and division operators work in similar fashion. Placing a – character in front of a number reverses its sign. The next four operators in Table 11.4 require explanation. The x++ and ++x operators increment the value of a variable by 1. One common use for variables is as counters for tabulating the number of times that a loop has processed. The x++ and ++x operators are well suited for this purpose. Likewise, the x– – and – –x operators decrement a variable value by one. For example, the following statement declares a variable and sets its value equal to 1:

```
var count = 1;
```

The next statement increments the value of count by 1:

```
count = ++count;
```

The ++x and x++ operators are similar. Both increment a value of x by one. The only difference between them is the timing of the increment. With ++x, the value of x changes before the value of assignment operation occurs. With x++, the value of x occurs after the assignment operation has occurred. For example,

```
x = 1
count = ++x
WScript.Echo(count)
WScript.Echo(x)
x = 1
count = x++
WScript.Echo(count)
WScript.Echo(x)
```

The following output is generated when this script is executed.

```
2
2
1
2
```

The first line of the script sets the value of x equal to 1. The second line increments the value of x by 1 and then adds the results to a variable named count. The value of both variables is then displayed. Both count and x are set equal to 2.

The second half of the script resets the value of x and starts over. This time, the x is incremented after the assignment of count, therefore the value of count remains 1 when displayed.

Shortcuts for Assigning Values to Variables

The most common way to assign a value to a JScript variable is using the = assignment operator, as demonstrated here:

```
current_count = 0
```

JScript provides a collection of shortcut operators that simplify the assignment of variable values. These operators are outlined in Table 11.5.

Table 11.5   Assignment Operators

Operator	Description
=	Sets a variable value equal to a value
+=	Shorthand for x = x + y
−=	Shorthand for x = x - y
*=	Shorthand for x = x * y
/=	Shorthand for x = x / y

For example, you can add the value of one variable to another as shown.

```
current_count = current_count + total_count
```

Or you can use the following shortcut.

```
current_count += total_count
```

Comparing JScript Values

One of the most common activities in any script is to compare one value against another and then perform a particular action based on that comparison. To assist you with these types of tasks, JScript provides you with a collection of comparison operators. These comparison operators are defined in Table 11.6.

Table 11.6   JScript Comparison Operators

Operator	Description
==	Equal to
!==	Not equal to
>	Greater than
<	Less than
>=	Greater than or equal to
<=	Less than or equal to
!x	False
&&	Both true
||	Either true

For example, you can compare two variables to determine whether they contain the same value, as shown.

```
if (your_count == my_count); {
  WScript.Echo("Both variables have the same value")
}
```

You can invert the comparison by adding the ! character in front of the == characters, as shown.

```
if (your_count !== my_count);
```

You can also determine whether one value is greater than or less than another. For example, you can determine whether the value of one variable is greater than or equal to another, as shown.

```
if (your_count >= my_count);
```

Establishing Alternative Logical Execution Paths

You can build logic into your scripts that performs different steps based on the condition of tested criteria. This is accomplished using *conditional statements*. JScript provides the following set of conditional statements.

◆ **if**. Tests a condition and then selects an execution path based on the result of that test.

◆ **switch**. Compares a value to a series of values and executes the logical path of the first matching condition.

The *if* Statement

The JScript `if` statement performs a Boolean test and executes either of two execution paths based on whether the results of the test are `true` or `false`. The syntax of the `if` statement is shown here:

```
if (condition)
  statement
```

For example, you can test the value of a variable and conditionally execute a statement as shown.

```
if (count = 1)
  count++;
```

Here, the value of the variable count is evaluated. If it is equal to 1, its value is incremented by 1. If its value it not equal to 1, it does not get incremented.

You can use an if statement to execute more than one conditional statement at a time. This is achieved by placing multiple statements within a pair of bracket characters. For example, you can modify the previous example to execute multiple statements when the value of count equals 1, as shown.

```
if (count = 1) {
  count++;
  WScript.Echo("This Is JScript In action!");
}
```

A variation of the if statement provides an alternative execution flow when the tested condition proves false. This is done by adding an else keyword to the if statement, as demonstrated.

```
if (count = 1) {
  count++;
  WScript.Echo("This Is JScript In action!");
}

else {
  WScript.Echo("This Is the alternate execution flow ");
}
```

You can use the if statement to perform more complicated comparison operations by embedding or nesting one if statement within another, as demonstrated:

```
if (count > 1) {
  if (count = 2) {
    WScript.Echo("The count Is set to 2.");
  }
  else {
    WScript.Echo("The count Is greater than 1 but not equal to 2.");
  }
}
```

The `switch` Statement

The JScript `switch` statement evaluates a series of conditions and is more efficient than the `if` statement when more than a few conditions need to be tested. It also makes your script much easier to read and manage. The syntax of the `switch` statement follows.

```
switch (expression) {
  case label:
    statements;
  break;

    .

    .

    .

  case label:
    statements;
  break;
  default:
    statements;
}
```

The `switch` statement performs a series of comparisons in which it compares the value of EXPRESSION against the values of each `case` statement. The first true `case` statement is executed. You can place one or more JScript statements inside each `case` test for execution. If none of the `case` tests are true, an optional `default` statement can be executed.

Each conditional test begins with the `case` statement and ends with the `break` statement. If you choose to remove the `break` statements, every conditional test runs and all matching conditions are executed.

For example, the following test checks the value of a variable named `folder` against a series of folder names and displays a message based on the results of the comparison.

```
folder = "Winnt"
switch (folder) {
  case "System32":
    WScript.Echo("Folder equals System32");
    break;
  case "Myfolder":
```

```
        WScript.Echo ("Folder equals Myfolder");
        break;
    case "Winnt":
        WScript.Echo ("Folder equals Winnt");
        break;
    default:
        WScript.Echo ("All test failed");
}
```

The following output is generated when you run this example.

```
Folder equals Winnt
```

Adding Looping Logic to Your JScripts

You can add loops to your scripts that repeatedly execute a series of commands in an efficient manner. This allows you to build efficient and powerful code with just a few statements. JScript provides the following set of statements to support looping.

- ◆ **for**. Creates a loop that processes until a specified condition becomes false.

- ◆ **while**. Creates a loop that processes for as long as a condition remains true.

- ◆ **do...while**. Creates a loop that processes until a condition becomes false.

- ◆ **label**. Establishes a reference point within a script and can create loops.

- ◆ **break**. Terminates the execution of a loop, label, or switch.

- ◆ **continue**. Interrupts the current iteration of a loop without terminating the loop itself.

The for Statement

The JScript for statement allows you to set up loops that process until a specified condition becomes false. It uses a controlling variable to manage the number of times that the loop executes. For loops are made up of three components including a starting expression, a test condition, and an increment. The syntax of the for statement is shown.

```
for (expression; condition; increment) {
  statements
}
```

EXPRESSION sets up a starting value, *CONDITION* specifies the condition that will terminate the loop when it's met, and *INCREMENT* specifies the value that's added to the variable in the *EXPRESSION* upon each iteration of the loop. Also, notice that each component of the `for` statement must be separated by the comma character.

You can experiment with `for` loops using the following example.

```
for (i=0; i<5; i++) {
  WScript.Echo("Let's count: ",i,"\n");
}
```

You will see the following results when you execute the previous example.

```
Let's count:   0

Let's count:   1

Let's count:   2

Let's count:   3

Let's count:   4
```

NOTE

You might have noticed that I embedded the `/n` element inside the `WScript.Echo` statement. Doing so provides a means of managing line breaks in JScript. The `/n` represents a newline character and forces a linefeed in script output.

The `while` Statement

The JScript `while` statement is designed to execute a loop for as long as a condition remains `true`. Its syntax is shown here:

```
while (condition) {
  statements
}
```

Any number of JScript statements can be placed within the `while` loop's opening and closing brackets. For example, the following `while` loop has been set up to execute as long as the value of the `count` variable is greater than 0.

```
count = 5;
WScript.Echo("Counting: ");
while (count > 0) {
  count−;
  WScript.Echo(count);
}
```

The script produces the following output. Notice that the first number displayed is 4 and not 5. This is because the `count−` statement decremented the value of count before it was displayed.

```
Counting:
4
3
2
1
0
```

The `do...while` Statement

The JScript `do...while` statement executes a loop repeatedly until a condition becomes `false`. Its syntax is shown here:

```
do {
  statements
} while (condition)
```

Its functionality is similar to that of the `while` loop. The difference is that the `do...while` loop will always execute one time, whereas the `while` loop might never execute. The reason for this is because the `while` loop always checks the value of its condition before starting its execution and the `do...while` waits and checks the condition after the first execution. Because of their similar design, you can often use the two types of loops interchangeably to get the same results. For example, you can rewrite the previous example to work just as well with a do...while loop, as shown.

```
counter = 5;
WScript.Echo("Counting: ");
do {
  counter-;
  WScript.Echo(counter);
}
while (counter > 0)
```

The script produces the following output.

```
Counting:
4
3
2
1
0
```

The label Statement

The JScript label statement allows you to create reference points in your scripts. You normally user the label statement to create loops with JScripts. The continue and break statements, which are discussed in the next two sections, make references to label statements. Once referenced, the execution flow of a script jumps from its current location to the statement that follows the label. The label statement's syntax is shown here:

```
label:
  statements
```

The following example builds on the previous while loop example. In this case, a label and a continue statement have been added. The loop begins processing and starts counting down from 5. However, on its third iteration, processing stops and the program flow jumps back to the beginning of the loop because the value of count became 3. This example shows how you can skip a cycle within a loop but continue processing.

```
count = 5;
WScript.Echo("Counting: \n");
count_loop:
while (count > 0) {
  count--;
  if (count == 3 ) {
    continue count_loop;
  }
  WScript.Echo(count);
}
```

The script produces the following output.

```
Counting:


4
2
1
0
```

The break Statement

The JScript break statement provides for the termination of a loop, label, or switch. You have already seen it in action previously in this chapter when the switch statement was discussed. When a script comes across a break statement, it immediately jumps processing control to the first statement that follows the loop, label, or switch.

For example, you can use the break statement to prematurely terminate a while loop, as shown in the following examples.

```
count = 5;
WScript.Echo("Counting: \n");
count_loop:
while (count > 0) {
  count--;
  WScript.Echo(count);
```

```
  if (count == 3 ) {
    WScript.Echo("A break statement has been encountered!");
    break;
  }
}
```

As the following output shows, the processing of the while loop is terminated when, on the third iteration, the count variable becomes equal to 3. This causes the break statement to execute.

Counting:

4

3

A break statement has been encountered!

The continue Statement

Like the break statement, the JScript continue statement can interrupt the normal processing flow of a loop. However, rather than terminating the loop, the continue statement simply skips the current execution and allows the loop to continue with its next iteration.

The following example modifies the previous one by replacing the break statement with the continue statement. As you can see, the processing of the loops third iteration is interrupted, but the fourth and fifth iterations still proceed.

```
count = 5;
WScript.Echo("Counting: \n");
count_loop:
while (count > 0) {
  count-;
  WScript.Echo(count);
  if (count == 3 ) {
    WScript.Echo("*** A continue statement has been encountered!***");
    continue;
  }
}
```

As the following output shows, the `continue` statement terminates the current iteration but allows the loop to continue processing.

Counting:

4

3

*** A continue statement has been encountered!***

2

1

0

JScript Object Manipulation

JScript supports the development of scripts that can manipulate objects. Objects are similar to variables except that they can contain more than one value or property. Objects also contain methods, called *functions*, which provide a means of manipulating the object or its data. Additional information on objects is provided in the chapters that follow.

Object-manipulation statements allow you to process an object's properties. JScript provides the following set of object-manipulation statements.

◆ `for…in`. Iterates through an object's properties.

◆ `with`. Provides a convenient way to save keystrokes by associating a set of commands with a particular object.

The `for...in` Statement

The JScript `for...in` statement iterates through an object's properties. Its syntax is shown here:

```
for (variable in object) {
  statements
}
```

For example, the following `for` statements loop through an array object and display its contents. Information on working with arrays is provided later in this chapter.

```
for (i in Myfolders) {
   WScript.Echo(Myfolders[i]);
}
```

The `with` Statement

The JScript `with` statement allows you to associate a group of statements with an object. The `with` statement can save keystrokes when writing your scripts. Its syntax is shown here:

```
with (object) {
    statements
}
```

For example, you can use the `with` statement to specify the `WScript` object and then leave off the `WScript` word portion when using commands that execute `WScript` methods. In the following example, `Echo` statements were used in place of `WScript.Echo` statements.

```
with (WScript) {
   Echo("Saving keystrokes");
   Echo("Using the with statement");
}
Saving keystrokes
Using the with statement
```

Storing Large Numbers of Values

A JScript *array* is an indexed list of values that are processed as a unit. JScript arrays can store any type of value. The first step in working with an array is to declare it, as demonstrated by the following example.

```
Myarray = new Array(5);
Myarray[0] = floppy;
Myarray[1] = hard_disk;
Myarray[2] = CD;
```

```
Myarray[3] = Zip_drive;
Myarray[4] = CD-RW;
```

The preceding example creates an array named Myarray using the new keyword. The array contains five elements. The first element in a JScript array has an indexed value of 0 and can be referenced using its index position. For example, this code displays the first element in the array:

```
WScript.Echo(Myarray[0]);
```

Looping through Arrays

The for...in statement can create a loop that processes any JScript array. The following examples show how you can add a for..in loop to process and loop through the Myarray array.

```
Myarray = new Array(5);
Myarray[0] = "floppy";
Myarray[1] = "hard_disk";
Myarray[2] = "CD";
Myarray[3] = "Zip_drive";
Myarray[4] = "CD-RW";

for (i in Myarray) {
   WScript.Echo(Myarray[i]);
}
```

The for...in loop implicitly sets up a variable named i and uses it as a counter as it iterates though the contents of Myarray. Each array element is displayed by substituting the array index number for the value of i in the WScript.Echo statement. The output of the previous script is shown here:

```
floppy
hard_disk
CD
Zip_drive
CD-RW
```

JScript also supports the use of dense arrays. A *dense array* is an array that is populated during declaration, which provides an efficient means for creating small arrays. The following example shows what happens when you substitute a dense array in the previous example:

```
Myarray = new Array("floppy", "hard_disk", "CD", "Zip_drive", "CD-RW");
Myarray_length = Myarray.length;
for (var i = 0; i < Myarray_length;i++) {
  WScript.Echo(Myarray[i]);
}
```

After creating the array, the script displays its contents using a `for` loop, which processes the array based on the value obtained from using the `length` property for the array. The following output shows the results of running this example:

```
floppy
hard_disk
CD
Zip_drive
CD-RW
```

Sorting Arrays

Arrays can store all sorts of information. But this does not mean that the array will be organized in a manner that is especially suitable for processing. One technique for organizing the contents of an array before processing them is *sorting*. The following example demonstrates how you can sort and display the elements stored in the `Myarray` array.

As you can see, all that was required to sort and display the contents of the array was to execute the array's `sort()` method inside of an `WScript.Echo` statement.

```
Myarray = new Array("floppy", "hard_disk", "CD", "Zip_drive", "CD-RW");
WScript.Echo(Myarray.sort());
```

The following output shows the results of running this example.

```
CD, CD-RW, Zip_drive, floppy, hard_disk
```

Organizing Your JScripts with Functions

A *function* is a collection of statements that can be called from anywhere in the script to perform a given task. Functions allow you to organize your scripts by group-related statements into organized procedures that can be called repeatedly.

TIP

Most programmers group their functions in a common location within their scripts. This makes the functions easy to find and makes the script more readable.

Building Functions

JScript functions have the following syntax.

```
function FunctionName (p1, p2,....pn) {
   statements
return
}
```

The `function` statement defines a new function and assigns the function's name. Following the function's name is a pair of parentheses containing a list of optional arguments that the function can process as input. A comma separates each argument. All the statements that make up the function are placed inside a pair of brackets and are followed by a `return` statement.

For example, you can create a function named `DisplayMsg()` that accepts a single argument and uses it to display a message. After displaying the message, the `return` statement returns control back to the statement that called the function.

```
function DisplayMsg(message) {
   WScript.Echo("This Is your message: " + message);
return
}
```

Executing Your Functions

You can call a function using either of two techniques. The first option is to simply type the function name as a statement, as shown here:

```
DisplayMsg("This is how you can call a function and pass is an
argument");
```

This method of function execution does not provide for the return of any data back from the function. It expects, therefore, that the function will perform all parts of whatever task it has been designed to do and then return processing control back to the statement that follows the function call.

The following method of function execution allows the calling statement to receive a value back from the function. For example, if the function's job is to query the user for a name, the function should return the user's name. The user's name is then returned to the calling statement and is automatically assigned to the value of the name variable.

```
Name = RetrieveName();
```

You will learn a great deal more about how to create and execute functions in the chapters that follow.

Chapter 12

Writing VBScript Scripts

This chapter is designed to provide the non-VBScript programmer with an introduction to the VBScript language. It provides a review of basic VBScript programming constructs and teaches you everything that you need to know to start writing your own WSH scripts. The goal of this chapter is to provide you with enough of a VBScript background to prepare you to work with the real-world WSH examples presented in Chapters 13 through 15.

Chapter 11, "Writing JScript Scripts," provides similar coverage of the JScript scripting language. The choice between learning JScript or VBScript is a matter of personal preference and depends on your programming background. If you have any programming experience with Visual Basic, you will find VBScript easy to master. However, if you have a Web scripting background and have used JavaScript, JScript is probably going to provide you with a better starting point.

Topics covered in this chapter include:

◆ Running VBScript scripts
◆ Storing information in variables
◆ Working with operators and expressions
◆ Exploring conditional logic
◆ Creating VBScript loops
◆ Organizing your scripts with functions
◆ Managing data with arrays

Formatting Your Scripts

If you have done any VBScript Web page development, you know that for Internet browsers to process VBScripts, you must embed them inside HTML pages and enclose them inside <SCRIPT></SCRIPT> tags that identify the beginning and end of the scripts. Fortunately, things are much simpler when writing VBScripts to be executed by WSH. Like WSH JScript files, WSH VBScript files are made up of plain text statements. Therefore, the only thing that you must do to prepare your scripts for processing by WSH is to save them with a `.vbs` file extension. WSH uses the file extension to determine which script execution host should process the script.

The only exception to this rule occurs when you want to embed VBScript scripts inside of Windows script files. In this case, you have to enclose your VBScripts inside special tags that identify them as VBScript code. Refer to Chapter 10, "Introducing the Windows Script Host," for additional information regarding working with `.wsf` files.

The VBScript Object Model

WSH provides a core object model that provides both JScripts and VBScripts with access to Windows objects. In addition, both languages supplement this object model with an object model of their own. Table 12.1 describes the objects that comprise the VBScript core object model.

Table 12.1 VBScript Objects

Object	Description
Class	Provides access to class events.
Dictionary	Stores data key and item pairs.
Err	Provides details about run-time errors.
FileSystemObject	Provides access to the entire filesystem.
Match	Accesses the read-only properties of a regular expression match.
Matches Collection	A collection of regular expression Match objects.
RegExp	Supports regular expressions.
SubMatches Collection	Accesses read-only values of regular expression submatch strings.

Many of these objects are demonstrated in the remaining chapters of this book. In addition to its collection of core objects, VBScript also provides a collection of run-time objects. These objects provide access to various system resources and are described in Table 12.2.

Table 12.2   VBScript Run-Time Objects

Object	Description
Dictionary	Stores data key and item pairs.
Drive	Provides access to a disk drive's properties.
Drives Collection	Provides information about system drives.
File	Provides access to a file's properties.
Files Collection	Provides access to files contained in a folder.
FileSystemObject	Provides access to the entire filesystem.
Folder	Provides access to a folder's properties.
Folders Collection	Provides access to the folders contained within another folder.

Understanding VBScript Syntax

VBScript is an *interpreted* programming language, which means that, unlike other programming languages such as Visual Basic or C++, VBScripts are not precompiled before execution. Therefore when VBScripts execute, the script execution hosts processes each statement in the script one at a time in the order in which they are presented.

Like JScript files, VBScript files are composed of plain text statements. VBScript files are saved with a .vbs file extension and can be created using any text editor. As you learn throughout this chapter, Microsoft's implementation of VBScript represents a complete programming language with all the major constructs that you expect in any scripting language.

NOTE

Although it is a complete language implementation, VBScript, like JScript, does not represent a stand-alone programming language in that it requires an execution host to execute it. VBScripts and JScripts can execute within either the `WScript.exe` or `CScript.exe` execution hosts or within Active Server Pages or Web pages when embedded within HTML pages.

NOTE

VBScript's implementation, when used in Web browsers, is somewhat different. It is supplied with a modified object model that provides access to a different set of resources. This means that the VBScript browser-based object model does not provide access to local resources such as disk drives and filesystem. It instead provides access to other objects such as forms and frames.

VBScript Case Sensitivity

VBScript variable names are case-sensitive. This means that you must refer to a VBScript variable using the exact case used to define it or VBScript will interpret it as a different variable. For example, if you create a VBScript variable and named it `myfolder`, you must continue to reference it by this name using its exact spelling. In VBScript, `MyFolder` and `myfolder` are interpreted as different variables.

However, VBScript is more lenient when it comes to the naming of other constructs such as functions, methods, and references to objects. For example, VBScript accepts either of the following spellings of the `WScript.Echo` statement.

```
WScript.Echo "This Is acceptable VBScript syntax"
wscript.echo "This Is acceptable VBScript syntax"
```

VBScript Statement Syntax

Mastering VBScript syntax is an essential part of learning to program with VBScript. Every VBScript statement has its own set of syntax requirements that must be followed exactly. If you fail to use proper syntax, your scripts will have errors and will not work as expected. For example, the following statement shows a one-line VBScript script that displays a message using the `WScript.Echo` command.

```
WScript.Echo "This is acceptable VBScript syntax"
```

NOTE

The `WScript.Echo("This is acceptable VBScript syntax")` statement demonstrates how to access methods provided by the WSH `WScript` object. In this example, the `WScript` object's `ECHO` method displays a message. The scripting host that executes it governs the behavior of this small one-line script. If the WScript execution host executes the script, the message will appear as a graphical pop-up dialog box. But if the CScript execution host processes the script, the message will display as text in the Windows command console.

As the previous example shows, VBScript requires that the message be placed inside a pair of matching quotes. If you fail to follow this syntactical rule, you will get an error. For example, if you forget to type the first quote, as demonstrated here, you will receive an error.

```
WScript.Echo This is unacceptable VBScript syntax"
```

Figure 12.1 shows the error message that occurs when the script is executed.

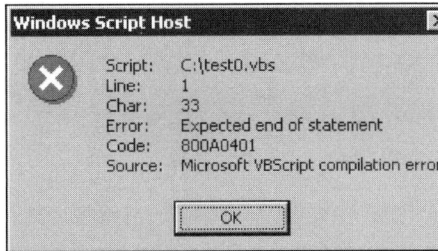

FIGURE 12.1

A WSH error message indicating a syntax error in a VBScript script.

> **TIP**
>
> Is it impossible to remember the proper syntax for every VBScript command. Therefore, you will probably spend a lot of time referencing this chapter when you first begin developing your own VBScripts. Don't forget to review Appendix C as well. It contains a VBScript reference that includes additional programming examples and the proper spelling of many VBScript elements. You can also check out Microsoft's official VBScript Language Reference at `http://msdn.microsoft.com/scripting`.

Creating VBScript Statements

VBScripts are composed of one or more VBScript statements. VBScript provides a rich collection of programming elements. This section reviews these statements using the following categories:

- ◆ Comments
- ◆ Variable declaration and assignment statements
- ◆ VBScript constants
- ◆ Conditional statements
- ◆ Looping statements
- ◆ Object-manipulation statements

Documenting Your VBScripts with Comments

VBScript allows you to insert comments inside your scripts so that you can document them. Comments have no impact on the performance of your scripts. They simply make your scripts easier for someone else to read and understand.

VBScript comments are added to your scripts by placing text after a single quotation mark, as demonstrated here.

```
'The following statement displays a message in a pop-up dialog box

WScript.Echo "This is a VBScript!"
```

You can also add comments at the end of your VBScript statements as shown here:

```
WScript.Echo "This is a VBScript!"     'The following statement displays a message in a pop-up dialog
```

Add comments to your VBScript liberally to define the purpose of every variable and to outline particularly complicated sections of code. This way, if you have to come back and make changes to a piece of code that you wrote months or years earlier, you will have a good starting point.

For example, you might want to add comments to all your VBScript using a template similar to the one presented here:

```
' *********************************************
' * Script Name: example.js                *
' * Author:   Jerry Ford                    *
' * Address: Richmond Virginia              *
' * Created: 04/25/01                       *
' *********************************************


' **** Perform script initialization here ****


' Initialize a variable containing a user's name

Dim name
name = "Jerry Ford"


' ******** Main processing section *********


' Call a function that displays the user's name


DisplayName(name)


' ********** Procedures go here ************
```

```
' This function displays whatever name is passed to it

Function DisplayName(name_arg)

  WScript.Echo "Good morning " & name_arg

End Function
```

This example includes a demonstration of two other VBScript programming constructs—variables and functions—both of which are explained in the sections that follow.

Storing Information in Variables

Like Windows shell scripting and JScript, VBScript supports the temporary storage of data in variables. Depending on the manner in which a variable is created, it can be referenced throughout a script or only in a localized section.

VBScript supports only one type of variable, known as a *variant*. A *variant* is a data type that can hold a number of different types of data. VBScript variants are flexible. They automatically behave like a string when they contain string information and like a number when they store a numeric value.

> **TIP**
>
> You can exercise a degree of control over the behavior of numeric data by adding and removing quotation marks. For example, a value of 10 is saved as a variant and treated as a numeric value, whereas a value of "10" is stored and treated as a string.

VBScript also supports a number of variant subtypes that allow you to further define the type of data stored in a variable. Table 12.3 presents a list of VBScript variant subtypes.

Table 12.3   VBScript Variant Subtypes

Subtype	Description
Empty	An uninitialized variant.
Null	A variant with a null value.
Boolean	A value of true or false.
Byte	An integer between 0 and −255.
Integer	An integer between −32,768 and 32,767.
Currency	A currency value.
Long	An integer value between −2,147,483,648 and 2,147,483,647.
Single	A single-precision floating-point number.
Double	A double-precision floating-point number.
Date	A number representing a date.
String	A text string.
Object	An object.
Error	An error number.

VBScript provides a number of conversion functions that enable you to convert from one variable subtype to another. This list includes the Asc, Cbool, Cbyte, Ccur, Cdate, CVbl, Chr, Cint, CLng, CSng, CStr, Hex and Oct functions.

Conversion functions allow you to specify a variant subtype. For example, you can create a variable named today and assign it a date, as shown here:

```
today = "May 14, 2001"
```

You can then display the value of this variable:

```
WScript.Echo today
May 14,2001
```

To convert this value to a date subtype, you can specify the following:

```
Mydate = Cdate(today)
```

Finally, you can display the results as shown here.

```
WScript.Echo Mydate
5/14/2001
```

More information about these functions is available in Appendix C.

Declaring Variables

VBScript provides the DIM keyword for declaring a variable. Although VBScript allows you to create variables by simply referencing them, it is better to declare a variable before using it. In addition to making your scripts easier to follow, it is considered good programming.

The syntax for using DIM to declare a variable is as follows:

```
Dim variablename
```

VARIABLENAME is the name of the variable. For example, the following statement creates a variable named primary_drive:

```
Dim primary_drive
```

You can then assign a value to the variable, as follows:

```
primary_drive = "C"
```

To create a variable without first declaring it, you only need to reference it, as shown here:

```
secondary_drive = "D"
```

However, this form of variable creation is discouraged because it increases the likelihood of typographical errors. Therefore, VBScript provides the Option Explicit statement as a means of forcing you to declare all variables. To use this option, simply type it as the first line in your VBScripts:

```
Option Explicit
Dim primary_drive
Dim secondary_drive
primary_drive = "C"
secondary_drive = "D"
```

When implemented, Option Explicit generates an error when an attempt is made by your script to create a variable without first explicitly declaring it.

As a convenience, VBScript allows you to declare more than one variable at a time:

```
Dim primary_drive, secondary_drive
```

The only requirement when declaring multiple variables using a single DIM statement is that a comma must separate each variable.

Rules for Variable Names

VBScript imposes a few rules when naming your variables. These rules for variable names are outlined here:

- ◆ They must begin with an alphabetic character.
- ◆ They cannot include the period (.) character.
- ◆ They are limited to a length of 255 characters.
- ◆ They are case-sensitive.

> **TIP**
>
> Give your variables descriptive names that provide information about their contents. For example, `primary_drive` is a much better name than `pd`. Descriptive variable names improve script readability and will make your life easier.

Understanding a Variable's Scope

VBScript supports two variable scopes. A *script level* scope is established whenever you declare a variable outside of a procedure. This makes the variable's value accessible throughout the script. A *local scope* is established any time a variable is declared inside a procedure, which means that the variable's value can only be accessed from within the procedure.

Local Variable Scope

Local variables are created anytime a variable is declared inside a procedure. A VBScript procedure is a subroutine or function consisting of a group of statements that can be called for execution from any point in the script. Procedures improve script organization and allow for the creation of reusable code within scripts. Procedures are covered in more detail later in this chapter.

The following example demonstrates how to create a VBScript local variable. A procedure named `DisplayMsg()` is created that defines the local variable and then uses it to display a message. Procedures are designed to be called from anywhere in a script. After execution, control is returned back to the calling statement.

```
function DisplayMsg()
  Dim msg_text
  msg_text = "This is an example of creating a local variable inside a
VBScript procedure."
  WScript.Echo msg_text
End Function
```

Script Level Variables

Script level variables are variables that are declared outside of a procedure. They can be referenced from any location within the script, including from within procedures. The following example creates an explicit global variable.

```
Dim computer_name
```

Manipulating Numeric Variables Using Expressions

You assign a value to a VBScript variable using the = assignment operator, as shown here:

```
total_count = 5
```

Once you declare a variable, you can assign it a value. VBScript provides a collection of arithmetic operators that you can use in expressions to change the value of numeric variables. These operators are listed in Table 12.4.

Table 12.4   VBScript Arithmetic Operators

Operator	Description
+	Add
−	Subtract
*	Multiply
/	Divide
Mod	Modulus
−x	Reverses the sign of x
^	Exponentiation

For example, the following expression changes the value of a variable named count by adding 5 to its current value:

```
count = count + 5
```

Subtraction, multiplication, and division operators work in similar fashion. Placing a – character in front of a number reverses its sign. The Mod operator retrieves the remainder of a division operation, as demonstrated here:

```
Dim x
Dim y
x = 9
y = 2
z = x Mod y
WScript.Echo z
```

When you execute the previous script, you will see a message displaying 1 as the result of the modulus operation.

Comparing VBScript Values

Throughout your VBScripts, you will find yourself performing comparisons of one condition against another and then following alternative logical paths depending on the results of these tests. VBScript provides a number of comparison operators to assist you in performing these operations, as outlined in Table 12.5.

Table 12.5   VBScript Comparison Operators

Operator	Description
=	Equal
<>	Not equal
>	Greater than
<	Less than
>=	Greater than or equal to
<=	Less than or equal to

For example, the following statements test the value of two variables and display a message if their values match.

```
if your_count == my_count Then
   WScript.Echo "Both variables have the same value"
End If
```

You can invert the comparison by replacing the = character with the <> characters, as demonstrated here:

```
if your_count <> my_count
```

Finally, you can also make greater than and less than comparisons between two variables. For example, to test whether one variable is greater than or equal to another, you can modify the previous example as shown here:

```
if your_count >= my_count
```

Working with VBScript Constants

VBScript supports the use of constants. *Constants* contain static values that never change. VBScript supplies a collection of built-in constants that you can reference in Appendix C. In addition, you can define your own constants as demonstrated here:

```
Const myfolder = "C:\user\jford\Myfolder"
```

This example establishes a constant name `myfolder` and assigns it a string value as denoted by its enclosure within quotation marks. The following example creates two more constants that store numeric and date values:

```
Const MyAge = 36
Const MyBirthday = #11-20-64#
```

Numeric constants are defined without the use of quotations, whereas date constants are created by enclosing the value inside a pair of # characters.

TIP

Consider developing a standard naming convention that differentiates between variables and constants. This will allow you to easily differentiate between the two when reading your code.

Creating Multiple Logical Execution Paths

You can incorporate logic into your scripts that allows you to develop alternative logic flows based on the condition of tested criteria. This is achieved by using *conditional statements*. VBScript provides the following pair of conditional statements.

◆ `If`. Selects from one of two execution paths based on the result of a tested condition.

◆ `Select Case`. Compares a value against a series of values and executes a logical path based on a matching condition.

The `If` Statement

The VBScript `If` statement compares two conditions and executes either of two logical processes depending on the results of the comparison. The syntax of the `If` statement is outlined here.

```
If condition Then
   statements
End If
```

For example, you can test the value of two variables and conditionally execute a statement as shown here.

```
if my_count = your_count Then
   WScript.Echo "The counts are equal to one another!"
End If
```

TIP

If your `If` statement is not too lengthy, you can place it on a single line as shown in the following example.

```
If x > y then WScript.Echo "x is greater than y."
```

Just be careful that the statement isn't too long, because it can make your code more difficult to read.

You can execute as many statements as required in your If statements by simply placing them in between the THEN and the End If keywords, as shown here:

```
if my_count = your_count Then
   WScript.Echo "The counts are equal to one another!"
   WScript.Echo "Maybe next time they will be different!"
End If
```

You can add an alternative execution path to your If statements by including the Else keyword, as demonstrated here:

```
if my_count = your_count Then
WScript.Echo "The counts are equal to one another!"
   WScript.Echo "Maybe next time they will be different!"
Else
   WScript.Echo "The counts are not equal to one another!"
   WScript.Echo "Maybe next time they will be the same!"
End If
```

Finally, you can modify your If statements to test multiple conditions by adding the ElseIf keyword. The following example demonstrates how to test for three separate conditions:

```
Option Explicit

Dim my_count
Dim your_count

my_count = 1
your_count = 2

if my_count = your_count Then
   WScript.Echo "The counts are equal to one another!"
   WScript.Echo "Maybe next time they will be different!"
ElseIf my_count > your_count Then
   WScript.Echo "my_count is greater than your_count!"
ElseIf my_count < your_count Then
   WScript.Echo "my_count is less than your_count!"
End If
```

You will see the following output when you run this script.

```
my_count is less than your_count!
```

The `Select Case` Statement

Although you can use the `If..Then..ElseIf` statement to process an unlimited number of conditions, the `Select Case` statement is more efficient for processing a large number of comparisons as long as the same condition is being tested each time.

The syntax of the `Select Case` statement is shown here.

```
Select Case value
  Case expression
    statements
      .
      .
      .
  Case expression
    statements
  Case Else
    statements;
End Select
```

The `Select Case` statement evaluates a condition one time and then performs a series of comparative tests. The following example demonstrates how to use the `Select Case` statement to test the value of a variable named `folder` against a series of folder names.

```
Option Explicit

Dim folder

folder = "Winnt"
```

```
Select Case folder
  Case "System32"
    WScript.Echo("Folder equals System32")
  Case "Myfolder"
    WScript.Echo ("Folder equals Myfolder")
  Case "Winnt"
    WScript.Echo ("Folder equals Winnt")
  Case Else
    WScript.Echo ("All test failed")
End Select
```

The following output is generated when you run this example.

```
Folder equals Winnt
```

Adding Looping Logic to Your VBScripts

Loops allow you to create scripts that can process large amounts of data by repeatedly executing a block of statements in an efficient manner. This allows you to create efficient and powerful scripts with just a few statements. VBScript supports the following collection of loop statements.

- ◆ **For...Next**. Creates and executes a loop a specified number of times.
- ◆ **Do While**. Creates a loop that processes while a specified condition is true.
- ◆ **Do Until**. Creates a loop that processes until a specified condition becomes true.
- ◆ **While...Wend**. Creates a loop that processes while a condition remains true.

The For...Next Statement

The VBScript `For...Next` statement allows you to set up a loop that processes a specific number of times. `For...Next` loops use a variable to control their execution. The syntax of the `For...Next` statement is shown here:

```
For counter = begin To end [Step step]
    statements
Next
```

COUNTER is the controlling variable, BEGIN specifies the starting value of COUNTER and END specifies the value COUNTER that terminates the loop. STEP is an optional parameter that specifies the value to increase the value of COUNTER.

For example, the following example is a For...Next loop that iterates five times:

```
For i = 1 To 5 Step 1
   WScript.Echo "Let's count " & i
Next
```

You will see the following output when you execute this example:

```
Let's count 1
Let's count 2
Let's count 3
Let's count 4
Let's count 5
```

The Do While Statement

The VBScript Do While statement can create a loop that executes as long as a condition remains true. It supports two types of syntax:

```
Do While condition
   statements
Loop
```

or

```
Do
   statements
Loop While condition
```

You can place as many VBScript statements as are required in between the Do While statement and the Loop statement. In this example, a loop is created that processes as long as the value of count is greater than 0. The value of count is initially equal to 5 and is decremented by 1 upon each iteration.

```
count = 5
```

```
WScript.Echo "Counting: "
Do While count > 0
  count = count - 1
  WScript.Echo(count)
Loop
```

The script produces the following output. Notice that the first number displayed is 4 and not 5. This is because the count = count - 1 statement decremented the value of count before it was displayed.

```
Counting:
4
3
2
1
0
```

In the case of the previous example, the Do While loop tested the condition before the loop processed for the first time. Therefore, if the condition were false, the loop would never have been processed. You can restructure this example to ensure that at least one iteration of the loop always occurs by moving the test condition from the beginning to the end of the loop, as shown in the following example:

```
count = 5

WScript.Echo "Counting: "
Do
  count = count - 1
  WScript.Echo(count)
Loop While count > 0
```

If you run this example, you will see that it still yields the same results. However, if you change the value of count to 0 and rerun both of the previous examples you will see that the first example never processes the loop while the second example processes one iteration of the loop.

The *Do Until* Statement

The VBScript Do Until statement executes a loop repeatedly until a condition becomes true. Its syntax is shown here:

```
Do Until condition statements
Loop
```

Or

```
Do
   statements
Loop Until condition
```

The Do Until loop is similar to the Do While loop except that it executes while a condition is false rather than while it is true. It can be configured to test its condition both before and after the loop executes as the following examples show.

The first example tests the specified condition before executing the loop:

```
count = 0
WScript.Echo "Counting: "
Do
   count = count + 1
   WScript.Echo(count)
Loop Until count > 4
```

The second example tests the specified condition after executing the loop:

```
count = 0
WScript.Echo "Counting: "
Do
   count = count + 1
   WScript.Echo(count)
Loop Until count > 4
```

As they are written, both examples produce the same output, shown here:

```
Counting:
1
2
3
4
```

The `While...Wend` *Statement*

The VBScript `While...Wend` statement executes a loop repeatedly as long as a condition is true. This statement is generally neglected in favor of the `Do While` or `Do Until` loops, which are more flexible and powerful. Its syntax is shown here:

```
While condition
  statements
Wend
```

The following example demonstrates the use of the `While...Wend` statement:

```
Dim x

x = 0
While x < 5
  WScript.Echo x
  x = x + 1
Wend
```

You'll see the following output when you run this example.

0

1

2

3

4

VBScript Object Manipulation

VBScript allows you to write scripts that can manipulate objects. Objects are like variables except that they can hold multiple values or properties. Objects also store methods. Methods are functions that can be executed for the purpose of manipulating an object or its data. You learn more about objects and object manipulation throughout the remainder of the book.

An object manipulation statement provides the means for processing an object's properties. The VBScript programming construct that provides this capability is the `For Each...Next` statement, which iterates through an object's properties.

The `For Each...Next` Statement

The VBScript `For Each...Next` statement iterates through an object's properties. Its syntax is shown here:

```
For Each element In collection
   statements
Next [element]
```

ELEMENT is a member of the specified *COLLECTION*. One type of collection that you might work with often is an array. Arrays are objects that can store large amounts of related data.

The following example shows how you might use the `For Each...Next` statement to process the contents of an array.

```
For Each i IN Myarray
   WScript.Echo i
Next
```

This example displays every element in an array called `Myarray`. You will find additional information about arrays in the following section.

Storing a Large Number of Values

An *array* is an indexed collection of values that can be processed as a unit. VBScript provides strong support for working with arrays. In fact, support for arrays is one of the areas where VBScripts is noticeably stronger than JScript. VBScript supports the creation of single and multidimensional arrays.

The following example shows you how to create a VBScript array. First you have to declare the array using the DIM statement followed by a name and a pair of parentheses that contains a value defining the length of the array. You can then populate the array, as shown here.

```
Dim Myarray(5)
Myarray(0) = "floppy"
Myarray(1) = "hard_disk"
Myarray(2) = "CD"
Myarray(3) = "Zip_drive"
Myarray(4) = "CD-RW"
```

In this case a single-dimensional array is created named Myarray. It is then populated with five elements. The first element in the array has an index value of 0. You can reference the value of any element in the array by specifying its index position, as demonstrated here:

```
WScript.Echo Myarray(0)
```

Looping through VBScript Arrays

The For Each...Next loop can process the elements in a VBScript array. The following example demonstrates how to display the contents of the previous array:

```
Dim Myarray(5)
Myarray(0) = "floppy"
Myarray(1) = "hard_disk"
Myarray(2) = "CD"
Myarray(3) = "Zip_drive"
Myarray(4) = "CD-RW"

For Each i IN Myarray
  WScript.Echo i
Next
```

A variable named i controls the processing of the loop. It is automatically incremented after each iteration. Each array element is displayed by substituting its index value for the value of i in the WScript.Echo statement. The output of the previous script is shown here:

```
floppy
hard_disk
CD
Zip_drive
CD-RW
```

Resizing Arrays

VBScript enables you to create dynamic arrays that you can then resize as necessary using the ReDim statement. For example,

```
ReDim Myarray(5)
Myarray(0) = "floppy"
Myarray(1) = "hard_disk"
Myarray(2) = "CD"
Myarray(3) = "Zip_drive"
Myarray(4) = "CD-RW"
```

This code creates a dynamic array and populates it with five elements. You can then resize the array to hold additional elements as shown here.

```
ReDim Myarray(10)
```

Changing the size of an array in this manner results in the loss of all its contents. If you want to preserve the array's contents and simply make the array larger, you can add the Preserve keyword to the ReDim statement, as shown here:

```
ReDim Preserve Myarray(10)
```

You can then add additional elements to the array as shown here.

```
Myarray(5) = "Monitor"
Myarray(6) = "Printer"
Myarray(7) = "Scanner"
Myarray(8) = "Touch_Pad"
Myarray(9) = "Speakers"
```

You can then use the following For loop to display the contents of the now expanded array:

```
For Each i IN Myarray
   WScript.Echo i
Next
```

The output of the new 10-element array appears as shown here:

```
floppy
hard_disk
CD
Zip_drive
CD-RW
Monitor
```

```
Printer
Scanner
Touch_Pad
Speakers
```

Multi-Dimensional Arrays

VBScript supports the creation of multi-dimensional arrays. In fact, VBScript can support arrays with up to 60 dimensions. The following statement demonstrates how to create a two-dimension array that consists of five rows by six columns.

```
Dim Myarray (4,5)
```

Because an array begins with an index of 0, the length of any dimension is then equal to the specified length of the dimension, plus 1. Additional dimensions can be defined by specifying additional comma-separated values.

Organizing Your VBScripts into Procedures

VBScript allows you to organize groups of statements into procedures that can be executed from any point within your scripts. Grouping statements into procedures makes your scripts easier to read and maintain. VBScript supports two types of procedures as listed here:

- ◆ **Sub**. A procedure that executes a set of statements but does not return any results.
- ◆ **Function**. A procedure that executes a set of statements and can return a result to the statement that called it.

TIP

Most programmers group their procedures in a common location within their scripts, which makes them easy to find and improves the overall organization of their scripts.

Working with *Sub* Procedures

The VBScript `Sub` procedure or subroutine is a collection of related statements that are executed as a group and return no value to the caller. Its syntax is outlined here:

```
[Public | Private] Sub name [(arglist)]
   statements
End Sub
```

Any number of optional arguments can be passed to the `Sub` routine. The `Sub` routine can be created with an optional `Public` or `Private` keyword. The `Private` keyword indicates that the `Sub` routine can only be accessed by other procedures in the script that defines it. The `Public` keyword indicates that the `Sub` routine can be called by any procedure in any script.

For example, you can create a `Sub` routine named `DisplayMsg()` that accepts a single argument and uses it to display a message. After displaying, the message control returns to the statement that called the `Sub` routine.

```
Sub DisplayMsg(message)
   WScript.Echo "This is your message: " & message
End Sub
```

You can call this `Sub` routine from anywhere in your script as demonstrated in the following example.

```
DisplayMsg("HI")
```

The following output is displayed when this example is executed.

```
This is your message: HI
```

Working with *Function* Procedures

The VBScript `Function` procedure or function is a collection of related statements that are executed as a group and can return a value to the caller. Its syntax is outlined here.

```
[Public | Private] Function name [(arglist)]
   statements
End Function
```

Any number of optional arguments can be passed to `Function`. Like the `Sub` routine, `Function` can be created using the optional `Public` or `Private` key-words. To return a value to the statement that executes the procedure, you must specify a variable of the same name as the function and set its value to the value that you want to pass back. For example, the following function returns a name to any statement that executes it:

```
Function AuthorName()
  AuthorName = "jerry Ford"
End Function
```

Executing VBScript Procedures

The following statement shows how you might execute a typical function from somewhere in your script. In this example, the variable named `myname` would then be equal to the name returned by the function:

```
myname = AuthorName()
```

Alternatively, you can also execute the function as follows:

```
WScript.Echo "My name is " & AuthorName()
```

In this example, the name returned by the function is automatically substituted in place of `AuthorName()`.

Chapter 13

Working with Files and Folders

One of the most basic tasks that you will need to master is how to programmatically work with the Windows file system. This includes working with files and folders. The techniques that you will learn in this chapter provide you with the building blocks that you need to write scripts that can read, process, and create files and logs and perform scripted file and folder administration.

Topics covered in this chapter include:

◆ Reviewing the WSH `FileSystemObject` model
◆ Checking for the existence of files and folders
◆ Copying, moving, creating, and deleting folders
◆ Copying, moving, creating, modifying, and deleting text files
◆ Reading and writing to files

The `FileSystemObject`

The WSH object model does not provide a means for interacting with Windows operating system drives, folders, and files. Instead, this functionality is provided by the scripting run-time library in the form of a single `.dll` file called `scrrun.dll` that is located in the `%windir%\system32` folder. Microsoft packages the scripting run-time library with both the JScript and VBScript distributions.

The primary object in the scripting run-time library is the `FileSystemObject`. This is the object that your scripts use to expose and work with the Windows file system. You may have noticed in Chapters 11 and 12 that the `FileSystemObject` is listed as being part of the JScript and VBScript Core Object Models. It is from this object that both scripting engines derive their run-time objects, as listed in Table 13.1.

Table 13.1 Run-time Objects and Collections Exposed via the `FileSystemObject`

Object	Description
Dictionary	Stores data key, item pairs.
Drive	Provides access to a disk drive's properties.
Drives Collection	Provides information about system drives.
File	Provides access to a file's properties.
Files Collection	Provides access to files contained in a folder.
Folder	Provides access to a folder's properties.
Folders Collection	Provides access to the folders contained within another folder.

Note: Unlike all the other run-time objects, the dictionary object can be used without requiring the FileSystemObject.

> **NOTE**
>
> After reading Chapters 11 and 12 you may have noticed that both the JScript and VBScript run-time object models were the same. This is because they originate from the same source, which is the scripting run-time library.

The scripting run-time library's `FileSystemObject` is referenced as `Scripting.FileSystemObject`. Your scripts must contain one instance of the `FileSystemObject` before they can work with the Windows file system.

You can create an instance of the `FileSystemObject` in JScript as shown here.

```
var x = new ActiveXObject ("Scripting.FileSystemObject");
```

Similarly, you can create an instance of the `FileSystemObject` in VBScript as shown here.

```
Set x = new WScript.CreateObject ("Scripting.FileSystemObject")
```

> **NOTE**
>
> You instantiate an instance of the `FileSystemObject` in VBScript using the familiar `WScript.CreateObject` method but for JScript you must use the `ActiveXObject` method.

After you have created an instance of the `FileSystemObject`, you can use it throughout your scripts to access and manipulate the Windows file system.

NOTE

One important thing to remember about file and folder administration is that on Windows NT, 2000, and XP, system files and folders are governed by the NTFS permissions, so you might have to take additional steps in order for your scripts to work as expected. However, Windows 95, 98, and Me operating systems use the less secure versions of the FAT file system and do not impose these security restrictions.

Performing File Administration

Windows file administration includes a number of tasks. These include such things as creating, deleting, copying, and moving files. You can perform these tasks using `FileSystemObject` methods. In addition, you can perform file administration using methods belonging to the file object.

Administering Files Using the `FileSystemObject`

The `FileSystemObject` provides a number of methods that allow you to work directly with files. These methods provide the capability to determine whether a file already exists, to create new files, and to copy, move, and delete files. Table 13.2 defines these methods.

Table 13.2   File-Related Methods of the `FileSystemObject` Object

Method	Description
BuildPath	Adds a name to the path.
CopyFile	Copies one or more files to a different location.
CreateTextFile	Creates a file and a `TextStream` object to be used when reading and writing to the file.
DeleteFile	Removes the specified file.
FileExists	Returns a `True` or `False` value depending on whether the specified file exists.
GetAbsolutePathName	Retrieves the complete path name.
GetBaseName	Retrieves the base file name without its file extension.
GetExtensionName	Retrieves a string that contains the file's extension as specified by its path.
GetFile	Retrieves a file object based on the files specified in the path.
GetFileName	Retrieves the last file name or folder of the specified path.
GetTempName	Retrieves a temporary file or folder name.
MoveFile	Moves one or more files to the specified location.
OpenTextFile	Opens a file and returns a `TextStream` object to use when referencing the file.

Determining if a File Exists

Before you try to perform a file copy, move, or deletion or even try to open a file, it's usually prudent to verify that the file actually exists. You can perform this check using the `FileSystemObject`'s `FileExists` method. This method returns the Boolean value of `True` if the file exists and `False` if it does not.

The following example demonstrates how you can check for the presence of a file named `myfile.txt` in the root directory located on the C: drive (using JScript).

```
var fso_obj = new ActiveXObject("Scripting.FileSystemObject");

if (fso_obj.FileExists("c:\\myfile.txt")) {

  WScript.Echo("File found.");
```

```
}

else {

  WScript.Echo("Unable to locate file.");

}
```

> **NOTE**
>
> Take note of the double slashes used in the previous JScript example when denoting folders. This is because the \ character has a special meaning in JScript and to use it you must first escape it.

The next example demonstrates how to perform the same file check using VBScript.

```
Dim fso_obj
Set fso_obj = CreateObject("Scripting.FileSystemObject")
If (fso_obj.FileExists("c:\myfile.txt")) Then
  WScript.Echo("File found.")
Else
  WScript.Echo("Unable to locate file.")
End If
```

Creating a New File

If you want to create a new file you can do so using the `FileSystemObject`'s `CreateTextFile` method. The following example demonstrates how to create a new file called `myfile.txt` in the `temp` directory of the C: drive (using JScript).

```
var fso_obj = new ActiveXObject("Scripting.FileSystemObject");
fso_obj.CreateTextFile("c:\\temp\\myfile.txt");
```

The next example demonstrates how to create the same file using VBScript.

```
Set fso_obj = CreateObject("Scripting.FileSystemObject")
fso_obj.CreateTextFile("c:\\temp\\myfile.txt")
```

Copying One or More Files

If you want to copy one or more files from one location to another you can use the `FileSystemObject`'s `CopyFile` method. Alternatively if you want to move an individual file you can also use the file object's `Copy` method.

The following example demonstrates how to copy a file called `myfile.txt` located in the `temp` directory of the C: drive to a folder called `mydir`, also located on the C: drive (using JScript):

```
var fso_obj = new ActiveXObject("Scripting.FileSystemObject");
fso_obj.CopyFile("c:\\temp\\myfile.txt", "c:\\mydir\\myfile.txt");
```

The next example demonstrates how to copy the same file using VBScript.

```
Set fso_obj = CreateObject("Scripting.FileSystemObject")
fso_obj.CopyFile "c:\temp\myfile.txt", "c:\mydir\myfile.txt"
```

You can use wild-card characters to copy more than one file at a time. For example, to copy all text files in `c:\temp` to `c:\mydir` using JScript, try the following.

```
var fso_obj = new ActiveXObject("Scripting.FileSystemObject");
fso_obj.CopyFile("c:\\temp\\*.txt", "c:\\mydir");
```

This same task can be performed using VBScript as shown here.

```
Set fso_obj = CreateObject("Scripting.FileSystemObject")
fso_obj.CopyFile "c:\temp\*.txt", "c:\mydir"
```

The `CopyFile` method has a third optional parameter that allows you to determine what happens when a file of the same name already exists in the destination folder. When set to `True` any matching files are overridden. When set to `False` they are not.

For example, you can force the overwriting of existing files using JScript as shown here.

```
var fso_obj = new ActiveXObject("Scripting.FileSystemObject");
fso_obj.CopyFile("c:\\temp\\*.txt", "c:\\mydir", "True");
```

But if you change the value of the third parameter from `True` to `False` the script will stop copying files the first time that it finds an existing duplicate file name in the destination directory and display a message similar to the following.

Microsoft JScript runtime error: File already exists

The following VBScript does not allow any files with the same name to be over-written.

```
Set fso_obj = CreateObject("Scripting.FileSystemObject")
fso_obj.CopyFile "c:\temp\*.txt", "c:\mydir", "False"
```

But this next script does.

```
Set fso_obj = CreateObject("Scripting.FileSystemObject")
fso_obj.CopyFile "c:\temp\*.txt", "c:\mydir", "True"
```

There are a couple of other issues that you need to be aware of when using the `CopyFile` method. These are:

- If the destination that you are trying to copy a file to has a read-only attribute, the copy operation will always fail.
- The `CopyFile` method stops at the first error that occurs. It's up to you to complete or undo any partially completed operation.
- An error occurs when a wild-card match does not match any files in the source folder.

Moving One or More Files

If you want to move one or more files from one location to another you can use the `FileSystemObject`'s `MoveFile` method. Alternatively if you want to move an individual file you can also use the file object's `Copy` method. Moving a file or group of files is very similar to copying them except that a copy of the file or files no longer resides in the original location.

The following example demonstrates how to move a file called `myfile.txt` located in the `temp` directory of the C: drive to a folder called `mydir`, also located on the C: drive (using JScript):

```
var fso_obj = new ActiveXObject("Scripting.FileSystemObject");
fso_obj.MoveFile("c:\\temp\\myfile.txt", "c:\\mydir\\myfile.txt");
```

The next example demonstrates how to copy the same file using VBScript.

```
Set fso_obj = CreateObject("Scripting.FileSystemObject")
fso_obj.MoveFile "c:\temp\myfile.txt", "c:\mydir\myfile.txt"
```

As with the `CopyFile` methods, you can move multiple files using wild cards. For example, the second statement in the JScript example can be rewritten to copy all `.txt` files as shown here.

```
fso_obj.MoveFile("c:\\temp\\*.txt", "c:\\mydir");
```

Likewise the second statement in the VBScript example can be written as this:

```
fso_obj.MoveFile "c:\temp\*.txt", "c:\mydir"
```

There are several issues that you should be aware of when moving files. These include:

◆ If the destination that you are trying to move a file to has a read-only attribute, the move operation will always fail.

◆ The MoveFile method stops at the first error that occurs. It's up to you to complete or undo any partially completed operations.

◆ An error occurs when a wild-card match does not match any files in the source folder.

Deleting One or More Files

To delete one or more files you can use the FileSystemObject's DeleteFile method. Alternatively if you want to move an individual file you can also use the file object's Delete method.

The following example demonstrates how to delete a file called myfile.txt located in the root of the C: drive (using JScript).

```
var fso_obj = new ActiveXObject("Scripting.FileSystemObject");
fso_obj.DeleteFile("c:\\myfile.txt");
```

The next example demonstrates how to delete the same file using VBScript.

```
Set fso_obj = CreateObject("Scripting.FileSystemObject")
fso_obj.DeleteFile "c:\myfile.txt"
```

If the specified destination file is a read-only file, the delete option will fail unless you specify an optional third parameter on the command. This parameter is a Boolean value. When set to True a matching file is deleted and when set to False it is not. For example, you can modify the last statement in the previous JScript example as follows to force the deletion of a read-only file.

```
fso_obj.DeleteFile("c:\\myfile.txt", "True");
```

In the same way you can modify the last line of the VBScript example as shown here.

```
fso_obj.DeleteFile "c:\myfile.txt", True
```

Finally, like the `CopyFile` methods you can use wild-card characters with the `DeleteFile` method to move more than one file at a time.

There are several issues that you should be aware of when deleting files. These include:

◆ The `DeleteFile` method stops at the first error that occurs. It's up to you to complete or undo any partially completed operations.

◆ You will receive an error if your script cannot find a file that matches the specified naming criteria.

Administering Files Using the File Object

The File object provides a number of methods that allow you to work directly with individual files. These methods provide the capability to copy, move, and delete files. Table 13.3 defines these methods.

Table 13.3   File-Related Methods of the File Object

Method	Description
Copy	Copies a file or folder to the specified location.
Delete	Removes the specified file or folder.
Move	Moves a file or folder to the specified location.
OpenAsTextStream	Opens a file and returns a `TextStream` object to use when referencing the file.

Using the File object's `Copy`, `Move`, or `Delete` methods is a three-step process. First you must establish an instance of the `FileSystemObject` in order to be able to work with the Windows file system. Then you need to use the `FileSystemObject`'s `GetFile` method to retrieve a file object representing the file that you want to work with. Finally you can specify the appropriate copy, move, or delete operation. Each of these types of file administrations is demonstrated in the following sections.

> **NOTE**
>
> The `Copy`, `Move`, and `Delete` methods can be used to delete folders as well as files so be careful when using it to specify the correct file name. Otherwise, if you have a similarly named folder you could accidentally delete it.

Copying an Individual File

You can use the file object's `Copy` method to copy a file when you only need to work with one file at a time. The following example demonstrates how to copy a file called `myfile.txt` located in the `temp` directory of the C: drive to a folder called `mydir`, also located on the C: drive (using JScript).

```
var fso_obj = new ActiveXObject("Scripting.FileSystemObject");
var file_name = fso_obj.GetFile("c:\\temp\\myfile.txt");
file_name.Copy("c:\\mydir\\myfile.txt");
```

The next example demonstrates how to copy the same file using VBScript.

```
Set fso_obj = CreateObject("Scripting.FileSystemObject")
Set file_name = fso_obj.GetFile("c:\temp\myfile.txt")
File_name.Copy "c:\mydir\myfile.txt"
```

Because the file object's `Copy` method only works with one file at a time, you cannot use the wild-card characters supported by the `FileSystemObject`'s `CopyFile` method. You can, however, use an optional third parameter to force the overwriting of a read-only file by specifying a Boolean value of `True` to overwrite the destination file or `False` to cancel the copy operation.

Moving an Individual File

You can use the file object's `Move` method to move a file when you only need to work with one file at a time. The following example demonstrates how to move a file called `myfile.txt` located in the `temp` directory of the C: drive to a folder called `mydir`, also located on the C: drive (using JScript):

```
var fso_obj = new ActiveXObject("Scripting.FileSystemObject");
var file_name = fso_obj.GetFile("c:\\temp\\myfile.txt");
file_name.Move("c:\\mydir\\myfile.txt");
```

The next example demonstrates how to copy the same file using VBScript.

```
Set fso_obj = CreateObject("Scripting.FileSystemObject")
Set file_name = fso_obj.GetFile("c:\temp\myfile.txt")
File_name.Move "c:\mydir\myfile.txt"
```

Because the file object's `Move` method only works with one file at a time, you cannot use the wild-card characters. However, unlike the `Copy` method, you cannot use the `Move` method to overwrite a file with the same name on the destination.

Deleting an Individual File

You can use the file object's `Delete` method to delete a file when you only need to work with one file at a time. The following example demonstrates how to delete a file called `myfile.txt` located in the root directory of the C: drive (using JScript).

```
var fso_obj = new ActiveXObject("Scripting.FileSystemObject");
var file_name = fso_obj.GetFile("c:\\myfile.txt");
file_name.Delete();
```

The next example demonstrates how to delete the same file using VBScript.

```
Set fso_obj = CreateObject("Scripting.FileSystemObject")
Set file_name = fso_obj.GetFile("c:\myfile.txt")
File_name.Delete
```

Because the File object's `Delete` method only works with one file at a time, you cannot use wild-card characters. You can, however, use an optional third parameter to force the deletion of a read-only file by specifying a Boolean value of `True`.

Performing Folder Administration

Windows folder administration includes a number of tasks that include creating, deleting, and copying, and moving folders. You can perform these tasks by using the `FileSystemObject` methods or the methods supplied by the file object.

Administering Folders Using the `FileSystemObject`

The `FileSystemObject` provides a number of methods that allow you to work directly with Windows folders. These methods include the capability to determine whether a folder already exists, to create new folders, and to copy, move, and delete folders from one location to another. Table 13.4 defines folder-related methods of the `FileSystemObject`.

Table 13.4 `FileSystemObject` Methods

Method	Description
`BuildPath`	Adds a name to the path.
`CopyFolder`	Performs a recursive copy of a folder to a different location.
`CreateFolder`	Creates the specified folder.
`DeleteFolder`	Removes the contents of the specified folder.
`FolderExists`	Returns a `True` or `False` value depending on whether the specified folder exists.
`GetAbsolutePathName`	Retrieves the complete path name.
`GetBaseName`	Retrieves the base file name without its file extension.
`GetFolder`	Retrieves the `Folder` object of the folder in the specified path.
`GetParentFolderName`	Retrieves a string representing the name of the parent folder.
`GetSpecialFolder`	Retrieves the name of the specified special folder.
`GetTempName`	Retrieves a temporary file or folder name.
`MoveFolder`	Moves one or more folders to the specified location.

Determining if a Folder Already Exists

Before you try to access a folder's contents or try to create a new folder, you should first determine whether that file exists. You can perform this task using the `FileSystemObject`'s `FolderExists` method. This method returns a Boolean value of `True` if the file exists and `False` if it does not.

The following example demonstrates how you can verify whether a folder named `myfolder` exists in the root directory located on the C: drive using JScript.

```
var fso_obj = new ActiveXObject("Scripting.FileSystemObject");
if (fso_obj.FolderExists("c:\\myfolder")) {
  WScript.Echo("Folder found.");
}
else {
  WScript.Echo("Unable to locate folder.");
}
```

NOTE

Folder names must be preceded by double slashes or escaped in JScript (such as when you're denoting folders), because the \ character is a special character.

The next example demonstrates how to perform the same file check using VBScript.

```
Dim fso_obj
Set fso_obj = CreateObject("Scripting.FileSystemObject")
If (fso_obj.FolderExists("c:\myfolder")) Then
  WScript.Echo("Folder found.")
Else
  WScript.Echo("Unable to locate folder.")
End If
```

Creating a New Folder

If, after determining that a folder that you want to work with does not exist, you want to create it, you can do so using the FileSystemObject's CreateFolder method. The method accepts a single argument, the name of the new folder. If the folder that you try to create already exists, your script will receive an error. You cannot overwrite an existing folder using the CreateFolder method.

The following example demonstrates how to create a new folder called myfolder in the root directory of the C: drive (using JScript).

```
var fso_obj = new ActiveXObject("Scripting.FileSystemObject");
var win_folder = fso_obj.CreateFolder("c:\\myfolder");
```

The next example demonstrates how to create the same file using VBScript.

```
Set fso_obj = CreateObject("Scripting.FileSystemObject")
Set win_folder = fso_obj.CreateFolder("c:myfolder")
```

Copying One or More Folders

If you want to copy one or more folders from one location to another you can use the FileSystemObject's CopyFolder method. Alternatively if you want to move an individual folder you can use the Copy method of the File object. The CopyFolder method recursively copies the folder and all its contents to the destination including any subfolders that the folder contains. The CopyFolder method requires two arguments: the source and destination. An optional third argument can be used to force the overwriting of the destination folder.

The following example demonstrates how to copy a folder called myfolder located in the root directory of the C: drive to a new folder called temp, which also exists on the C: drive (using JScript).

```
var fso_obj = new ActiveXObject("Scripting.FileSystemObject");
fso_obj.CopyFolder("c:\\myfolder", "c:\\temp");
```

The next example demonstrates how to copy the same folder using VBScript.

```
Set fso_obj = CreateObject("Scripting.FileSystemObject")
fso_obj.CopyFolder "c:\myfolder", "c:\temp"
```

These two examples assumed that the temp folder did not already exist and that as a result it was created and a copy of myfolder and its contents was then copied into it. Had the temp folder already existed, only the contents of myfolder would have been copied and not the folder itself.

Like the FileSystemObject's CopyFile method, you can specify wild-card characters to copy more than one folder at a time. Using an optional third argument you can specify what happens when the destination folder contains files or folders of the same name as those in the source folder. When set to True, any matching entries are overridden; when set to False they are not.

For example, you can force the overwriting of existing entries (using JScript) as shown here.

```
var fso_obj = new ActiveXObject("Scripting.FileSystemObject");
fso_obj.CopyFolder("c:\\myfolder", "c:\\temp", "True");
```

The following VBScript performs the same operation.

```
Set fso_obj = CreateObject("Scripting.FileSystemObject")
fso_obj.CopyFolder "c:\myfolder", "c:\temp", "True"
```

There are a couple of other issues that you need to be aware of when using the `CopyFolder` method. These are:

◆ If the destination that you are trying to copy a file to has a read-only attribute, the copy operation will always fail.

◆ The `CopyFolder` method stops at the first error that occurs. It's up to you to complete or undo any partially completed operations.

◆ An error occurs if a wild-card match does not match any files in the source folder.

Moving One or More Folders

If you want to move one or more folders from one location to another you can use the `FileSystemObject`'s `MoveFolder` method. Alternatively if you want to move an individual folder you can use the `Move` method of the file object. The `MoveFolder` method recursively copies the folder and all its contents to the destination including any subfolders that the folder contains. The `MoveFolder` method requires two arguments. These are the source and destination.

The following example demonstrates how to move a folder called `myfolder` located in the root directory of the C: drive and to a new folder called `temp`, which also exists on the C: drive (using JScript).

```
var fso_obj = new ActiveXObject("Scripting.FileSystemObject");
fso_obj. MoveFolder("c:\\myfolder", "c:\\temp");
```

The next example demonstrates how to copy the same folder using VBScript.

```
Set fso_obj = CreateObject("Scripting.FileSystemObject")
fso_obj. MoveFolder "c:\myfolder", "c:\temp"
```

If both the source and destination folders already exist then only the contents of the source folder will be copied to the destination folder. Wild-card characters can be used to specify multiple source folders. However, the `MoveFolder` method does not support an overwrite option.

There are several issues that you should be aware of when moving folders. These include:

◆ The `MoveFolder` method stops at the first error that occurs. It's up to you to complete or undo any partially completed operations.

◆ An error occurs if a wild-card match does not match any files in the source folder.

Deleting One or More Folders

You can use the `FileSystemObject`'s `DeleteFolder` method to delete one or more folders. Alternatively, if you only need to delete an individual file you can use the File object's `Delete` method. The `DeleteFolder` method recursively deletes the contents of a folder, including any subfolders. The `DeleteFolder` method requires just one argument, the name of the folder to be deleted. An optional second argument can be used to force the deletion of a read-only folder.

The following example demonstrates how to delete a folder called `myfolder` located in the root directory of the C: drive (using JScript).

```
var fso_obj = new ActiveXObject("Scripting.FileSystemObject");
fso_obj.DeleteFolder("c:\\myfolder");
```

The next example demonstrates how to delete the same folder using VBScript.

```
Set fso_obj = CreateObject("Scripting.FileSystemObject")
fso_obj.DeleteFolder "c:\myfolder"
```

You can use wild-card characters to specify more than one folder to delete. But be careful with the command because it can very easily be used to delete the wrong folder.

There are several issues that you should be aware of when deleting folders. These include:

◆ The DeleteFolder method deletes folders regardless of whether they contain other subfolders or files.

◆ The DeleteFolder method stops at the first error that occurs. It's up to you to complete or undo any partially completed operations.

◆ An error occurs if a wild-card match does not match any files in the source folder.

Administering Folders Using the Folder Object

The Folder object provides a number of methods that allow you to administer individual folders. These methods provide the capability to copy, move, and delete files. Table 13.5 defines these methods.

Table 13.5   Methods of the Folder Object

Method	Description
Copy	Copies a folder to the specified location.
Delete	Removes or deletes the specified folder.
Move	Moves a folder to the specified location.

Using the Folder object's Copy, Move, and Delete methods is a three-step process. First you must establish an instance of the FileSystemObject in order to be able to work with the Windows file system. Then you need to use the FileSystemObject's GetFile method to retrieve a folder object representing the folder that you will be working with. Finally you specify the appropriate copy, move, or delete operation.

Copying an Individual Folder

If you want to copy an individual folder, you can use the Copy method of the file object. However, if you need to copy multiple folders you should use the FileSystemObject's CopyFolder method. The Folder object's Copy method is the same method used by the file object to copy individual files as demonstrated earlier in this chapter.

The Copy method recursively copies the specified folder and all its contents to the destination including any subfolders that the folder contains. The following example demonstrates how to copy a folder called myfolder located in the root directory of the C: drive to a new folder called temp, which also exists on the C: drive (using JScript).

```
var fso_obj = new ActiveXObject("Scripting.FileSystemObject");
var folder_name = fso_obj.GetFolder("c:\\myfolder");
folder_name.Copy("c:\\temp");
```

The next example demonstrates how to copy the same folder using VBScript.

```
Set fso_obj = CreateObject("Scripting.FileSystemObject")
Set folder_name = fso_obj.GetFolder("c:\\myfolder")
folder_name.Copy "c:\\temp"
```

Because the Folder object's Copy method only works with one file at a time, you cannot use the wild-card characters supported by the FileSystemObject's CopyFile method. You can, however, use an optional parameter to force the overwriting of a read-only folder by specifying a Boolean value of True to over-write the destination file or False to cancel the copy operation. For example, you can modify the third line of the previous JScript example as shown here to force the replacement of an existing folder.

```
folder_name.Copy("c:\\temp", "True");
```

Likewise, the third statement in the previous VBScript can be modified as shown here.

```
folder_name.Copy "c:\\temp", "True"
```

Moving an Individual Folder

You can move an individual folder using the Folder object's Move method. However, to move multiple folders, you'll need to use the FileSystemObject's MoveFolder method. The Folder object's Move method is the same method used by the file object to move individual files as demonstrated earlier in this chapter.

The `Move` method recursively copies a folder and all its contents to the specified destination. This includes any subfolders that reside in the folder. The following example demonstrates how to move a folder called `myfolder` located in the root directory of the C: drive to a new folder called `temp`, which also exists on the C: drive (using JScript).

```
var fso_obj = new ActiveXObject("Scripting.FileSystemObject");
var folder_name = fso_obj.GetFolder("c:\\myfolder");
folder_name.Move("c:\\temp");
```

The next example demonstrates how to move the same folder using VBScript.

```
Set fso_obj = CreateObject("Scripting.FileSystemObject")
Set folder_name = fso_obj.GetFolder("c:\\myfolder")
folder_name.Move "c:\\temp"
```

Because the `Folder` object's `Move` method only works with one folder at a time, you cannot use the wild-card characters. In addition, you cannot use the `Move` method to overwrite an existing folder.

Deleting an Individual Folder

Use the `Folder` object's `Delete` method to delete a folder when you only need to work with one folder at a time. To delete multiple folders in one operation, you'll need to use the `FileSystemObject`'s `DeleteFolder` method. The `Folder` object's `Delete` method is the same method used by the file object to delete individual files.

The `Delete` method recursively removes a folder and all its contents to the specified destination including any subfolders that it contains. The following example demonstrates how to delete a folder called `myfolder` located in the root directory of the C: drive (using JScript).

```
var fso_obj = new ActiveXObject("Scripting.FileSystemObject");
var folder_name = fso_obj.GetFolder("c:\\myfolder");
folder_name.Delete();
```

The next example shows how to delete the same folder using VBScript.

```
Set fso_obj = CreateObject("Scripting.FileSystemObject")
Set folder_name = fso_obj.GetFolder("c:\myfolder")
folder_name.Delete
```

Because the `Folder` object's `Delete` method is limited to working with one folder at a time, you cannot use wild-card characters with it. You can, however, use an optional parameter to force the overwriting of a read-only folder by specifying a Boolean value of `True` to overwrite the destination folder or `False` to cancel the `delete` operation. For example, you might modify the previous JScript example as shown here to force the deletion of a read-only folder.

```
folder_name.Delete("True");
```

Likewise, you can modify the previous VBScript as shown here.

```
folder_name.Delete "True"
```

Reading and Writing to Files

Manipulating the contents of individual files is surprisingly easy and involves a handful of programming techniques. At the most basic level, files must be opened before you can do anything to them. You can use the `OpenTextObject` of the `FileSystemObject` to perform this operation.

NOTE

The file object provides the `OpenAsTextStream` method, which also allows you to open and work with file contents.

When you open a file you will also need to specify the kind of operation that you will be performing on it. The three basic file-manipulation operations are outlined in Table 13.6.

Table 13.6   File-Manipulation Operations

Constant	Operation	Numeric Representation
ForWriting	Opens a file for writing (start of file).	2
ForAppending	Opens a file for appending (end of file).	8
ForReading	Opens a file for reading.	1

To work with a file you must open it. If the file does not exist, you must create it. You do this by specifying a Boolean value of True or False. The affects of both of these options are outlined in Table 13.7.

Table 13.7   File-Creation Options

Boolean	Description
True	If the file exists, open it; if it does not exist, create and open it.
False	If the file exists, open it; if it does not exist, do not create it.

In addition to determining how and when to create files, you also need to specify the format of the file when creating it. There are three available format options as listed in Table 13.8.

Table 13.8   File-Formation Options

Format	Numeric Representation
Default	-2
ASCII	0
UNICODE	-1

Note: Default is set to ASCII on Windows 95, 98, and Me. On Windows NT, 2000, and XP, default is set to UNICODE.

Now that you are armed with the information provided in Tables 13.6 – 13.8, you are ready to begin manipulating the contents of files.

Writing to a File

There are four basic techniques you need to master in order to write to files. These are:

◆ Verifying that a file exists before trying to write to it

◆ Writing a specified number of characters to a file

◆ Writing to a file a line at a time

◆ Formatting a file with blank lines

Each of these techniques is explained in the sections that follow.

Verifying a File's Existence

You can use the `FileExists` method of the `FileSystemObject` to determine whether a file already exists before attempting to open it. If the file does exist, you can open it. If it does not exist, you can create and then open it.

Before you open the file you will need to decide how you plan to write to it. Your options are to either write to it or append to it. If you choose the write option, the file is reinitialized, meaning that its contents are lost, and the file pointer is placed in the first row and column of the file. If you choose to append to the end of the file, its contents are preserved and the file pointer is placed at the end of the file.

NOTE

The file pointer is a very important concept to understand. The file pointer indicates the current pointer position, which is where the next character will be written in a file. In a new file, the pointer begins in column 0, row 0. If one character is added to the file, the pointer shifts to column 2, row 1. If a carriage return is added, the pointer is moved to column 1, row 2. Understanding file pointer location becomes especially important when you find yourself trying to read or write files that have very specific formats where records and their individual fields have known fixed positions.

The following example shows you how to open a file name `mylog.txt` located in the `myfolder` directory of the C: drive (using JScript). If the file does not exist, it is created. The file is opened using the `ForWriting` constant so that it can be written to.

```
var fso_obj = new ActiveXObject("Scripting.FileSystemObject");
if (fso_obj.FileExists("c:\\myfolder\\mylog.txt"))
  var working_file = fso_obj.OpenTextFile("c:\\myfolder\\mylog.txt",
2);
else
  var working_file = fso_obj.OpenTextFile("c:\\myfolder\\mylog.txt", 2,
"True")
working_file.WriteLine("Hello World!");
working_file.Close();
```

The first thing that the script does is create an instance of the `FileSystemObject`. Next, it determines whether the file already exists. If it does exist, the script opens the file in writing mode as designed by the final parameter value of 2 (refer to Table 13.7). If the file does not exist, it is created and then opened. Notice that a variable was used to establish a means of referencing the file. The script then writes a single line of text to the file by appending the `WriteLine` method to the variable. Finally, the file is closed. If you open the `mylog.txt` file, you will see the results shown in Figure 13.1.

FIGURE 13.1

An example of a text file created by a script.

The following example shows how the script was rewritten to work as a VBScript.

```
set fso_obj = CreateObject("Scripting.FileSystemObject")
if (fso_obj.FileExists("c:\myfolder\mylog.txt")) Then
  Set working_file = fso_obj.OpenTextFile ("c:\\myfolder\\mylog.txt",
8)
Else
```

```
Set working_file = fso_obj.OpenTextFile ("c:\myfolder\mylog.txt", 2,
"True")
End If
working_file.WriteLine "Hello World!"
working_file.Close
```

Closing a File

It is very important that you close a file when you are done writing to it. If you fail to do so you run the risk of creating errors the next time the file is opened because the end-of-file marker will not have been created. In addition, in order to open a file to perform one operation you must have closed it after performing the previous operation. In order words, if you open a file and append to it you must close it before your script can read from it.

As you saw in the previous examples, closing a file is very straightforward. Just type the name of the variable associated with the file, a period, and the `Close` method. In JScript this looks something like this:

```
x.Close();
```

and in VBScript it looks like this:

```
x.Close
```

Writing a Number of Characters to a File

To write a given number of characters to a file you can use the `Write` method of the `FileSystemObject`. For example, the following JScript opens a file in append mode and adds the characters `Hello World` to it.

```
var fso_obj = new ActiveXObject("Scripting.FileSystemObject");
var working_file = fso_obj.OpenTextFile("c:\\myfolder\\mylog.txt", 8);
working_file.Write("Hello ");
working_file.Write("World!");
working_file.Close();
```

Because this script writes characters to the file, a carriage return is not executed at the end of each write operation. Therefore, the words `Hello` and `World!` appear on the same line in the file.

Writing One Line at a Time in a File

To write an entire line of text to a file you use the `WriteLine` method of the `FileSystemObject`. This method writes the specified line of text to the file and then adds a carriage return to the end. For example, the following JScript opens a file in append mode and adds two lines of text to it.

```
var fso_obj = new ActiveXObject("Scripting.FileSystemObject");
var working_file = fso_obj.OpenTextFile("c:\\myfolder\\mylog.txt", 8);
working_file.WriteLine("Hello World!");
working_file.WriteLine("This is the end");
working_file.Close();
```

When you open the file, you will see that both lines of text were written on a separate line in the file.

```
Set fso_obj = CreateObject("Scripting.FileSystemObject")
Set working_file = fso_obj.OpenTextFile("c:\myfolder\mylog.txt", 8)
working_file.WriteLine("Hello World!")
working_file.WriteLine("This is the end")
working_file.Close()
```

Adding Blank Lines to a File

Sometimes you want to add blank lines to files to improve their readability. This is especially true when you are creating a report. To write a blank line in a file you use the `WriteBlankLines` method of the `FileSystemObject`. The following example demonstrates how you can write a JScript script that provides a report formatted with blank lines.

```
var fso_obj = new ActiveXObject("Scripting.FileSystemObject");
var working_file = fso_obj.OpenTextFile("c:\\myfolder\\mylog.txt", 8);

var local_disk_c = fso_obj.GetDrive("c:")
var local_disk_d = fso_obj.GetDrive("d:")

working_file.WriteLine("*****************************************");
working_file.WriteLine("            Disk Statistics Report");
working_file.WriteLine("*****************************************");

working_file.WriteBlankLines(1)
```

```
working_file.WriteLine("Drive C:    Serial No. " +
local_disk_c.SerialNumber);
working_file.WriteBlankLines(1);
working_file.WriteLine("File System = " + local_disk_c.FileSystem);
working_file.WriteLine("Total Size  = " + local_disk_c.TotalSize);
working_file.WriteLine("Free Space  = " + local_disk_c.AvailableSpace);


working_file.WriteBlankLines(1)


working_file.WriteLine("Drive D:    Serial No. " +
local_disk_d.SerialNumber);
working_file.WriteBlankLines(1);
working_file.WriteLine("File System = " + local_disk_d.FileSystem);
working_file.WriteLine("Total Size  = " + local_disk_d.TotalSize);
working_file.WriteLine("Free Space  = " + local_disk_d.AvailableSpace);


working_file.Close();
```

In addition to using the `WriteLine` and `WriteBlankLines` methods of the `FileSystemObject`, this script also used the `GetDrive` method. If you open the `mylog.txt` file, you will see that the report shown in Figure 13.2 was generated.

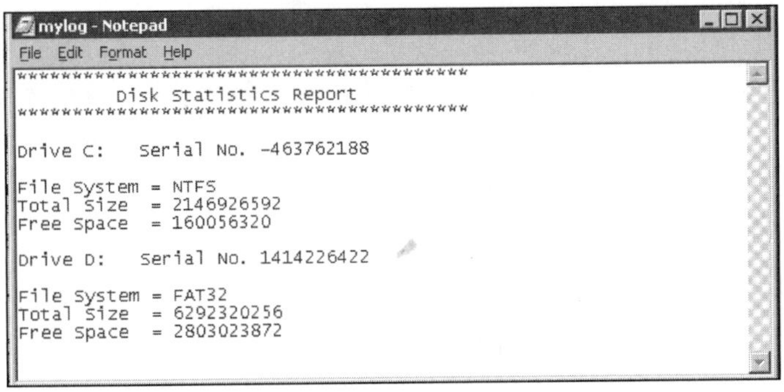

FIGURE 13.2

An example of a formatted report created by a script.

The following example shows how the script can be rewritten using VBScript.

```
Set fso_obj = CreateObject("Scripting.FileSystemObject")
Set working_file = fso_obj.OpenTextFile("c:\\myfolder\\mylog.txt", 8)
```

```
Set local_disk_c = fso_obj.GetDrive("c:")
Set local_disk_d = fso_obj.GetDrive("d:")

working_file.WriteLine("*****************************************")
working_file.WriteLine("            Disk Statistics Report")
working_file.WriteLine("*****************************************")

working_file.WriteBlankLines(1)

working_file.WriteLine("Drive C:    Serial No. " & _
local_disk_c.SerialNumber)
working_file.WriteBlankLines(1)
working_file.WriteLine("File System = " & local_disk_c.FileSystem)
working_file.WriteLine("Total Size  = " & local_disk_c.TotalSize)
working_file.WriteLine("Free Space  = " & local_disk_c.AvailableSpace)

working_file.WriteBlankLines(1)

working_file.WriteLine("Drive D:    Serial No. " & _
local_disk_d.SerialNumber)
working_file.WriteBlankLines(1)
working_file.WriteLine("File System = " & local_disk_d.FileSystem)
working_file.WriteLine("Total Size  = " & local_disk_d.TotalSize)
working_file.WriteLine("Free Space  = " & local_disk_d.AvailableSpace)

working_file.Close()
```

Reading File Contents

There are five basic techniques you need to master in order to read from files. These are:

◆ Verifying that a file contains text before attempting to read it
◆ Reading a specified number of characters from a file
◆ Reading a file one line at a time
◆ Skipping lines when reading a file
◆ Reading an entire file at one time

Each of these techniques is explained in the remaining sections of this chapter.

Verifying That a File Contains Data

You can use the AtEndOfStream property of the TextStream object to determine whether a file has data to process before trying to read it. You should also use this property each time you plan to read a line or specific number of characters from a file just to make sure that you have not reached the end of file marker.

For example, the following script opens a file for reading and uses a While loop to read it one line at a time until the AtEndOfStream property indicates the end of the file has been reached.

```
var fso_obj = new ActiveXObject("Scripting.FileSystemObject");
var working_file = fso_obj.OpenTextFile("c:\\myfolder\\mylog.txt", 1,
"True");


while (!working_file.AtEndOfStream) {
  read_rpt = working_file.ReadLine();
  WScript.Echo(read_rpt);
}
working_file.Close();
```

The following output is displayed when the script is executed.

```
*****************************************
          Disk Statistics Report
*****************************************


Drive C:    Serial No. -463762188


File System = NTFS
Total Size  = 2146926592
Free Space  = 160056320


Drive D:    Serial No. 1414226422


File System = FAT32
Total Size  = 6292320256
Free Space  = 2803023872
```

The following example shows how the JScript can be written as a VBScript.

```
Set fso_obj = CreateObject("Scripting.FileSystemObject")
Set working_file = fso_obj.OpenTextFile("c:\\myfolder\\mylog.txt", 1,
"True")

Do while False = working_file.AtEndOfStream
  read_rpt = working_file.ReadLine()
  WScript.Echo(read_rpt)
Loop
working_file.Close
```

Reading Characters from a File

To read a given number of characters from a file, you can use the Read method of the FileSystemObject. For example, the following JScript opens a file, skips the first four lines, reads the next 10 characters starting in column 2, and then stores the text in a variable named read_rpt. The value of read_rpt is then displayed. In this case, it displays the serial number of the C: drive.

```
var fso_obj = new ActiveXObject("Scripting.FileSystemObject");
var working_file = fso_obj.OpenTextFile("c:\\myfolder\\mylog.txt", 1,
"True");

for (i=0; i<4; i++) {
  working_file.skipLine()
}

working_file.skip(22)
read_rpt = working_file.Read(10);

WScript.Echo(read_rpt);
```

This script can be rewritten in VBScript, as shown here.

```
Set fso_obj = CreateObject("Scripting.FileSystemObject")
Set working_file = fso_obj.OpenTextFile("c:\\myfolder\\mylog.txt", 1,
"True")
```

```
For i = 1 to 4
  working_file.skipLine()
Next

working_file.skip(22)
read_rpt = working_file.Read(10)

WScript.Echo(read_rpt)
```

Reading a File One Line at a Time

Reading files one line at a time is a good approach to use when each line in the file represents a different record. To read one line from a file, you can use the ReadLine method of the FileSystemObject. For example, the following JScript statements read the current line in a file.

```
var fso_obj = new ActiveXObject("Scripting.FileSystemObject");
read_rpt = working_file.ReadLine();
```

If you wrap this statement inside a loop, you can spin through the entire file. Just remember to check for the end of file marker as demonstrated here.

```
while (!working_file.AtEndOfStream) {
  read_rpt = working_file.ReadLine();
  WScript.Echo(read_rpt);
}
```

The following VBScript statements duplicate the previous examples.

```
Set fso_obj = CreateObject("Scripting.FileSystemObject")
Set working_file = fso_obj.OpenTextFile("c:\\myfolder\\mylog.txt", 1,
"True")

Do while False = working_file.AtEndOfStream
  read_rpt = working_file.ReadLine()
  WScript.Echo(read_rpt)
Loop
```

Skipping Lines in a File

Sometimes files contain a fixed number of headers that you want to skip before beginning to read a file. Two `FileSystemObject` methods can help accomplish this task, as listed here.

◆ `Skip()`—Skips a specified number of characters.

◆ `SkipLine`—Skips an entire line in a file.

The `Skip()` method takes a simple argument, which is the number of characters to skip. For example, `working_file.skip(10)` skips the first 10 characters in a file referenced as `working_file`.

The `SkipLine` method skips just one line at a time but can be wrapped inside a loop to skip as many lines as required. The following JScript demonstrates this.

```
for (i=0; i<10; i++) {
  working_file.skipLine()
}
```

In this case the next 10 lines in the referenced file will be skipped. This same technique can be implemented in VBScript, as shown here.

```
For i = 1 to 10
  working_file.skipLine()
Next
```

Reading an Entire File

The last technique for reading a file involves reading the entire file all at once. This can be done using the `ReadAll` method of the `FileSystemObject`. For example, the following JScript uses the `ReadAll` method to process the entire file. It then displays the contents of the file using the WScript object's `Popup` method.

```
var NoTimeOut = 0

var ForReading = 1

var fso_obj = new ActiveXObject("Scripting.FileSystemObject");

var                         working_file                    =
fso_obj.OpenTextFile("c:\\myfolder\\mylog.txt",    ForReading,
"True");
```

```
var msg = WScript.CreateObject ("WScript.Shell");


read_rpt = working_file.ReadAll();


working_file.Close();


display_msg = msg.Popup(read_rpt, NoTimeOut,"Disk Statistics")
```

If you run this script, you should see output similar to that shown in Figure 13.3.

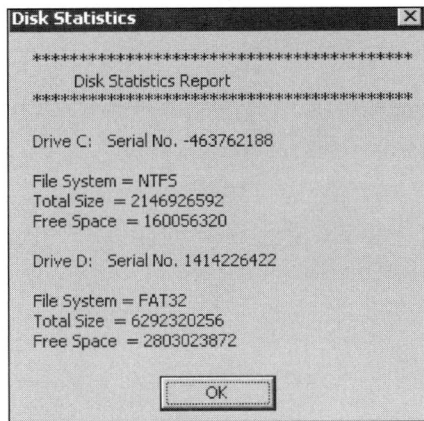

```
Disk Statistics
***************************************
        Disk Statistics Report
***************************************

Drive C:  Serial No. -463762188

File System = NTFS
Total Size  = 2146926592
Free Space  = 160056320

Drive D:  Serial No. 1414226422

File System = FAT32
Total Size  = 6292320256
Free Space  = 2803023872

            [ OK ]
```

FIGURE 13.3

Displaying the contents of an entire file.

The example can be rewritten in VBScript as shown here.

```
Dim NoTimeOut
Dim ForReading


NoTimeOut = 0
ForReading = 1


Set fso_obj = CreateObject("Scripting.FileSystemObject")
Set working_file = fso_obj.OpenTextFile("c:\\myfolder\\mylog.txt",
ForReading, "True")
Set msg = WScript.CreateObject ("WScript.Shell")
```

```
read_rpt = working_file.ReadAll()

working_file.Close()

display_msg = msg.Popup(read_rpt, NoTimeOut,"Disk Statistics")
```

You may have noticed a change in the presentation of the previous JScript and VBScript examples. To make the scripts a little more readable, variables were declared and assigned numeric values. The numeric values were then used in place of numeric settings when working with the `OpenTextFile` and `Popup` methods.

ADMINISTRATOR'S

Chapter 14

Managing the
Windows Desktop

GUIDE

This chapter explores the different ways that WSH can be used to configure and work with the Windows desktop and its applications. Configuration of desktop settings such as the Start menu items and shortcuts is not a very complicated process to perform manually. However, if you work on a number of computers at work and at home, reconfiguring the same desktop settings can become a bit of a chore. You can write scripts that automate this process, which allows you to quickly configure and later reconfigure desktop settings as you need.

This chapter also shows you how to use WSH to work directly with other applications such as Microsoft Word and Excel by writing data collected by scripts to these applications, which are known for their ability to attractively present information. Topics covered in this chapter include:

◆ Creating, modifying, and deleting Windows shortcuts

◆ Creating, deleting, and modifying URL shortcuts

◆ Customizing the Windows Start menu

◆ Customizing the Quick Launch bar

◆ Specifying the Automatic startup of Windows applications

◆ Writing scripts that integrate with Windows applications

Creating Shortcuts

A Windows shortcut is a link to another Windows object. You can use shortcuts to access Windows resources located anywhere on your computer, network, and even Web pages on the Internet. At a minimum, a shortcut contains the name of the target resource and its path. The kinds of resources that you can create a shortcut for include:

- ◆ Applications
- ◆ Files
- ◆ Folders
- ◆ Drives
- ◆ URLs

Shortcuts are really just small files stored inside folders. As such you can store a shortcut in any Windows folder. For example, Figure 14.1 shows a listing of the shortcuts stored on a computer running Windows 2000 Professional computer in the `\Winnt\Documents and Settings\Administrator\Start Menu` folder.

FIGURE 14.1

Viewing application shortcuts stored in the Start menu folder.

TIP

You can always tell a shortcut from other file types because its icon includes a small arrow in the lower-left corner, as demonstrated in Figure 14.2.

FIGURE 14.2

Shortcut icons always distinguish themselves with a small arrow in the lower-left corner.

Internet Explorer

Creating a shortcut is a multi-step process as outlined here:

1. Decide what resource you want to link to and where you want to store the shortcut.
2. Create a reference to the folder where the shortcut will be stored.
3. Create an instance of the shortcut object.
4. Establish link properties.
5. Save the link.

In the next several sections you will learn how to create, modify, and delete shortcuts on the Windows desktop and in other Windows folders.

Saving Shortcuts in a Windows Folder

Although it is common to create shortcuts to applications and folders that you use a lot on your desktop, it's not always a good idea. It does not take much to clutter up the desktop to the point where it becomes difficult to work with. One alternative is to create shortcuts in another folder and then to create a shortcut to that folder on the desktop. This way, your desktop remains clear but your shortcuts are easy enough to get to. For example, assuming that you already have a shortcut link on your desktop to a folder name myshortcuts on your local C: drive, you could add new shortcuts inside that folder.

Suppose that you wanted to place a shortcut to Notepad in the folder. The first step in writing a script to do this is to get a reference to the myshortcuts folder that your script can work with. To do this you'll need to first instantiate an instance of the FileSystemObject and then use its GetFolder method as shown here.

```
var fso_obj = new ActiveXObject("Scripting.FileSystemObject");
var trgt_folder = fso_obj.GetFolder("c:\\myshortcuts");
```

The `GetFolder` method returns a reference to the specified folder that you can then use throughout your script to work with the folder. Next you need to create an instance of the WScript Shell object and then use its `CreateShortcut` method to establish the shortcut.

```
var ws_obj = WScript.CreateObject("WScript.Shell");
var shortcut = ws_obj.CreateShortcut(trgt_folder + "\\Notepad.lnk");
```

Notice that the `CreateShortcut` method requires both the path and the name of the shortcut as its arguments. The `.lnk` portion of the shortcut name specifies a regular shortcut as opposed to a URL shortcut, which is covered later in this chapter.

To finish things up and save the shortcut, you need to specify the location of the Notepad executable and then save the shortcut, as shown here.

```
shortcut.TargetPath = "%windir%\\notepad.exe";
shortcut.Save();
```

`TargetPath` is a shortcut property that identifies the name and location of the Windows resource. `Save` is the only method that the `WshShortcut` object exposes. Its function is to save the shortcut in the destination folder. In this example the `c:\myshortcuts` folder is the destination.

The complete JScript example is shown here.

```
var fso_obj = new ActiveXObject("Scripting.FileSystemObject");
var trgt_folder = fso_obj.GetFolder("c:\\myshortcuts");
var ws_obj = WScript.CreateObject("WScript.Shell");
var shortcut = ws_obj.CreateShortcut(trgt_folder + "\\Notepad.lnk");
shortcut.TargetPath = "%windir%\\notepad.exe";
shortcut.Save();
```

This example can be rewritten using VBScript as shown here.

```
Set fso_obj = CreateObject("Scripting.FileSystemObject")
Set trgt_folder = fso_obj.GetFolder("c:\myshortcuts")
Set ws_obj = WScript.CreateObject("WScript.Shell")
Set shortcut = ws_obj.CreateShortcut(trgt_folder & "\\Notepad.lnk")
shortcut.TargetPath = "%windir%\notepad.exe"
shortcut.Save()
```

Saving Shortcuts on the Windows Desktop

When most people think about creating a shortcut, they tend to think of placing it on the Windows desktop. The process of creating a shortcut on the Windows desktop is not very different from creating it in a regular folder.

In order to create a shortcut and store it on the desktop, you must first establish a variable that you can programmatically use to reference the Windows desktop. Instead of creating am instance of the `FileSystemObject` and using its `GetFolder` method to get a reference to the target folder, you use the `SpecialFolders` method of the WScript Shell object to reference the `Desktop` special folder. This process is shown in the following JScript.

```
var ws_obj = WScript.CreateObject("WScript.Shell");
var trgt_folder = ws_obj.SpecialFolders("Desktop");
var shortcut = ws_obj.CreateShortcut(trgt_folder + "\\notepad.lnk");
shortcut.TargetPath = "%windir%\\notepad.exe";
shortcut.Save();
```

You can rewrite this script in VBScript as shown here.

```
Set ws_obj = WScript.CreateObject("WScript.Shell")
trgt_folder = ws_obj.SpecialFolders("Desktop")
Set shortcut = ws_obj.CreateShortcut(trgt_folder & "\\notepad.lnk")
shortcut.TargetPath = "%windir%\notepad.exe"
shortcut.Save
```

The `Desktop` is considered a special folder in Windows. When working with it from within your script, you do not access it using the methods of the `FileSystemObject`. Instead, you should establish the reference using the `SpecialFolders` method of the WScript object.

In addition to the Desktop, Windows supports a number of other special folders, many of which you probably recognize. Some of them are listed here.

- ◆ `AllUsersDesktop`
- ◆ `AllUsersStartMenu`
- ◆ `AllUsersPrograms`
- ◆ `AllUsersStartup`
- ◆ `Desktop`
- ◆ `Favorites`

- ◆ Programs
- ◆ SendTo
- ◆ StartMenu
- ◆ Startup

NOTE

The list of special folders varies by operating system. For example Windows 98, Me, and 2000 provide the My Pictures folder, whereas Windows 95 and NT do not. It is up to you to ensure that the special folder that you intend to work with exists on the system where your shortcut will reside.

NOTE

The locations of some special folders have changed from one version of Windows to another. Using the Special Folders method instead of the GetFolder method will help ensure that your scripts will be able to find your special folders no matter which version of Windows your scripts are running on.

Changes made to most folders affects only the currently logged on user. However the first four folders in the previous list affect all users. In other words, if you add a link to the Desktop special folder, it only affects the currently active user, but if you add that same link to the AllUsersDesktop folder, it affects every user of that computer.

You probably do not recognize the AllUsersDesktop special folder. This is because it does not exist as a regular folder with that name in Windows. To find it, you have to derive its existence from two folders. Figure 14.3 demonstrates how you can derive the location of this special folder.

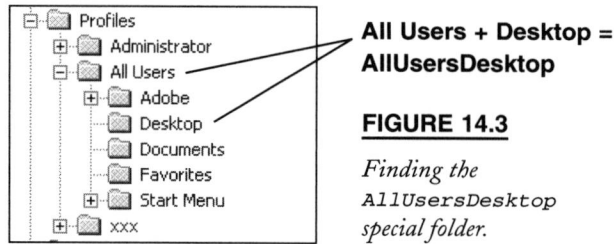

All Users + Desktop = AllUsersDesktop

FIGURE 14.3

Finding the `AllUsersDesktop` *special folder.*

As the callouts in Figure 14.3 show, you can derive the `AllUsersDesktop` special folder by combining the All Users folder name with its Desktop subfolder. Both of these folders are located within the profiles folders on Windows NT and 2000 systems.

Deleting Shortcuts

To delete a shortcut, you only need to delete the file that contains it. If the shortcut is stored in a regular Windows file you can delete it by first creating an instance of the `FileSystemObject` and then executing the `DeleteFile` method while specifying the path of the shortcut. For example, the following JScript deletes a shortcut called `notepad.lnk` stored in `c:\myshortcuts`.

```
var fso_obj = new ActiveXObject("Scripting.FileSystemObject");

fso_obj.DeleteFile("c:\\myshortcuts\\notepad.lnk");
```

In VBScript this example would be written as follows.

```
Set fso_obj = CreateObject("Scripting.FileSystemObject")
fso_obj.DeleteFile("c:\myshortcuts\notepad.lnk")
```

If the same shortcut had been created in the `Desktop` special folder, you could delete using a JScript as follows.

```
var ws_obj = WScript.CreateObject("WScript.Shell");
trgt_folder = ws_obj.SpecialFolders("Desktop");
var fso_obj = new ActiveXObject("Scripting.FileSystemObject");
var shortcut = fso_obj.GetFile(trgt_folder + "\\notepad.lnk");
shortcut.Delete();
```

Or, if you are working with VBScript, you might delete the shortcut as shown here.

```
Set ws_obj = WScript.CreateObject("WScript.Shell")
trgt_folder = ws_obj.SpecialFolders("Desktop")
Set fso_obj = CreateObject("Scripting.FileSystemObject")
Set shortcut = fso_obj.GetFile(trgt_folder & "\\notepad.lnk")
shortcut.Delete
```

Setting Shortcut Properties

Regular shortcuts, or shortcuts created with the `WshShortcut` object, have a number of configurable properties. For example, Figure 14.4 shows the properties of an Excel shortcut in Windows 2000.

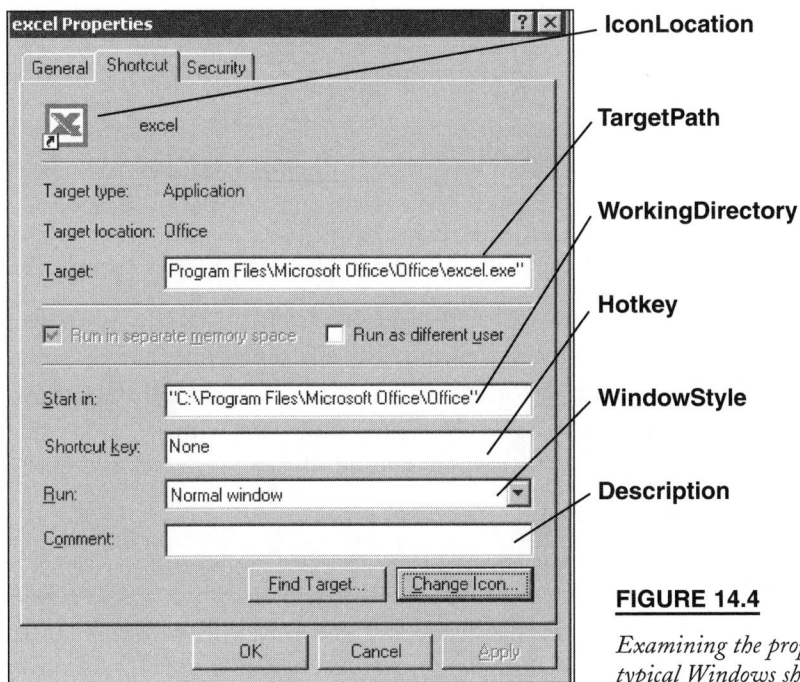

FIGURE 14.4

Examining the properties of a typical Windows shortcut.

Any shortcut that you create (except for those that refer to URL resources) will use the `WshShortcut` object. Each of the labeled properties in Figure 14.4 corresponds to a property of the `WshShortcut` object. This object provides a set of properties that you can use to specify the behavior of the shortcut. Only the `TargetPath` property is required. These properties are listed in Table 14.1.

Table 14.1 `WshShortcut` **Properties**

Property	Description
Arguments	Specifies arguments passed to the application when it starts.
Description	An optional description that's used to add a comment to the shortcut.
Hotkey	Defines a special keystroke sequence that can be used to launch a shortcut created on the Start menu and Windows desktop.
IconLocation	Specifies the icon to be used when displaying the shortcut.
TargetPath	Specifies the complete path, including file name, of the target resource.
WindowStyle	Specifies the initial Windows style to be used by the application when it starts.
WorkingDirectory	Specifies the default folder where the application will suggest saving files that it creates.

When you create a reference to a shortcut with an `.lnk` extension, the `CreateShortcut` method automatically returns a reference to the `WshShortcut` object. When you create a shortcut with an `.url` extension, the `WshUrlShortcut` object is returned instead. You configure shortcuts with a `.lnk` extension by creating the reference to the `WshShortcut` object and then configuring their properties.

URL shortcuts are much simpler than other shortcuts. They are created using the `WshUrlShortcut` object, which supports only a single property. The `WshUrlShortcut`'s `TargetPath` property specifies the complete URL represented by the shortcut.

Both the `WshShortcut` and the `WshUrlShortcut` objects provide a single method. You will use the `Save` method in your scripts to save the shortcut.

Passing Shortcut Arguments

The `Arguments` property defines arguments that will be passed to an application via the shortcut. For example, if one of your daily tasks is to update an Excel spreadsheet, you could create a shortcut on the Windows desktop that automatically starts Excel and opens the spreadsheet, as demonstrated in the following JScript.

```
var ws_obj = WScript.CreateObject("WScript.Shell");
var trgt_folder = ws_obj.SpecialFolders("Desktop");
var shortcut = ws_obj.CreateShortcut(trgt_folder +
"\\Time_Rpting.lnk");
shortcut.TargetPath = "c:\\Program Files\\Microsoft
Office\\Office\\excel.exe";
shortcut.Arguments = "c:\\Time_rpting.xls";
shortcut.Save();
```

When double-clicked, the shortcut opens Excel and loads a spreadsheet named `Time_rpting.xls` located in the root directory. The previous example works just as well when rewritten using VBScript, as shown here.

```
Set ws_obj = WScript.CreateObject("WScript.Shell")
trgt_folder = ws_obj.SpecialFolders("Desktop")
Set shortcut = ws_obj.CreateShortcut(trgt_folder + "\\Time_Rpting.lnk")
shortcut.TargetPath = "c:\Program Files\Microsoft
Office\Office\excel.exe"
shortcut.Arguments = "c:\Time_rpting.xls"
shortcut.Save
```

Adding a Shortcut Description

You can add a brief description that provides additional information about the shortcut using the `WshShortcut`'s `Description` property. For example, the following JScript statement can be used to add a comment to a shortcut.

```
shortcut.Description = "Departmental Time Reporting Spreadsheet";
```

As the following statement shows, the equivalent VBScript statement is very similar.

```
shortcut.Description = "Departmental Time Reporting Spreadsheet"
```

Setting Up a Keyboard Keystroke Combination

The `WshShortcut` `Hotkey` property allows you to specify a series of keystrokes that can be used to activate the shortcut when it is saved on the Start menu or on the Windows desktop. A `Hotkey` keystroke sequence is made up of at least two keystrokes, consisting of one or more modifier keys and a keyname key.

A modifier key can be any of the following:

- **Alt**. The Alternate key
- **Ctrl**. The Control key
- **Shift**. The Shift key
- **Ext**. The Windows key

Keyname keys can be any of the following:

- A–Z
- 0–9
- Back
- Tab
- Clear
- Return
- Escape
- Space
- Prior

For example, you can add a `Hotkey` keystroke sequence of CTRL + ALT + P to the Excel shortcut using JScript as shown here.

```
shortcut.Hotkey = "CTRL+Alt+P";
```

The VBScript version of this statement is shown here.

```
shortcut.Hotkey = "CTRL+Alt+P"
```

Changing a Shortcut's Icon

The syntax for the `IconLocation` property requires two parameters. The first parameter is the complete path of the icon and the second is its index location. By default, Windows uses the application's default icon when creating a shortcut. However, if you prefer you can specify an alternative icon using the `Icon`

`Location` property. Some Windows applications contain more than one icon. The first icon is the default and has an index value of 0. Its second icon, if present, has an index of 1. One way to determine which icons are available is to manually create a shortcut for the application. Then, right-click the shortcut, click Properties, select the Shortcut property sheet, and then click the Change icon. This opens the Change Icon dialog box, as demonstrated in Figure 14.5.

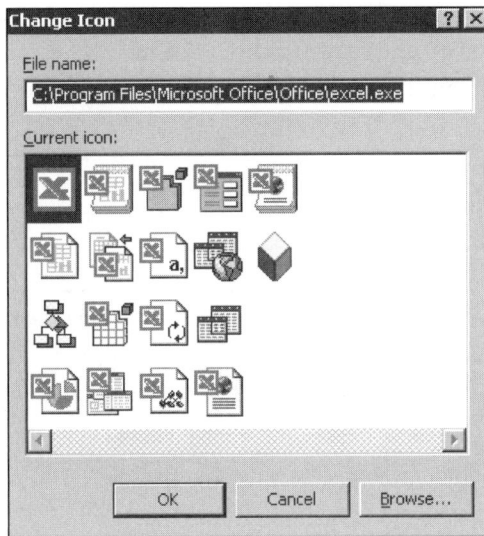

FIGURE 14.5

Examining alternative application icons.

TIP

Another way to determine whether an application provides more than one icon is from the Folder Options dialog box. To view an application's available list of icons on Windows NT and 98, start Windows Explorer, select Folder Options from the View menu, select the File Type property sheet, pick an application, and then click Edit followed by the Change Icon. On Windows 2000, click the Tools menu, select Folder Options, click the File Types property sheet, select an application, and then click Advanced followed by Change Icon.

For example, the following JScript statement sets the icon for a Microsoft Excel shortcut to an Excel icon represented by an index of one.

```
shortcut.IconLocation = "c:\\Program Files\\Microsoft
Office\\Office\\excel.exe, 1";
```

The VBScript equivalent of this statement is shown here.

```
shortcut.IconLocation = "c:\\Program Files\\Microsoft
Office\\Office\\excel.exe, 1"
```

Controlling How an Application Is First Displayed

The WindowsStyle property allows you to specify how an application is displayed after being activated by a shortcut. For example, you can specify whether the application should start in a maximized or minimized Window or whether it should receive focus or run in the background. Table 14.2 outlines the various options.

Table 14.2   Windows Style

Windows Style	Description
0	Runs in the background mode by hiding the window.
1	Restores a minimized or maximized window or activates and displays a new window.
2	Activates and minimizes the window.
3	Activates and maximizes the window.
4	Displays a window using its current location and size without affecting the currently active window.
5	Activates and displays a window using its location and size settings.
6	Minimizes a window and activates the most recently used window.
7	Displays a minimized window without affecting the currently active window.
8	Displays the window using its current settings without affecting the currently active window.
9	Restores a minimized or maximized window or activates and displays a new window.
10	Uses the state of the calling program to set the display state of the window.

Note: A window is said to have focus when it is selected. Having focus means that the window will by default receive keyboard input.

For example, the following JScript statement specifies that a shortcut should start the application and maximize its window.

```
shortcut.WindowStyle = 3;
```

Likewise, the following VBScript statement specifies the same setting.

```
shortcut.WindowStyle = 3
```

Setting a Shortcut's Working Directory

The WshShortcut's WorkingDirectory property specifies the application's default folder. The application will default to this location when saving or opening files. For example, the following JScript statement causes an application to suggest saving your work in a folder named c:\myfolder when you start the application from the shortcut.

```
shortcut.WorkingDirectory = "c:\\myfolder";
```

The following VBScript statement also determines an application's default folder.

```
shortcut.WorkingDirectory = "c:\\myfolder"
```

Working with URL Shortcuts

The process of creating a URL shortcut is very similar to that of creating a regular short. Instead of specifying .lnk at the end of the shortcut's name, you type .url. The WshUrlShortcut object only supports one property. In a URL shortcut, the TargetPath property is used to specify the URL that the link represents.

The following JScript example shows how to create a URL shortcut on the Windows desktop to **http://www.primapublishing.com**.

```
var ws_obj = WScript.CreateObject("WScript.Shell");
var trgt_folder = ws_obj.SpecialFolders("Desktop");
var shortcut = ws_obj.CreateShortcut(trgt_folder + "\\Prima Tech
Publishing.url");
shortcut.TargetPath = "www.primapublishing.com";
shortcut.Save();
```

Figure 14.6 shows the URL shortcut as it appears on the Windows desktop after the script is run.

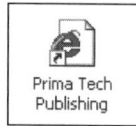

FIGURE 14.6

Creating a URL shortcut on the Windows desktop.

The following example shows how to create the same URL shortcut in VBScript.

```
Set ws_obj = WScript.CreateObject("WScript.Shell")
trgt_folder = ws_obj.SpecialFolders("Desktop")
Set shortcut = ws_obj.CreateShortcut(trgt_folder + "\\Prima Tech
Publishing.url")
shortcut.TargetPath = "www.primapublishing.com"
shortcut.Save
```

Managing Other Windows Features with Shortcuts

Saving shortcuts on the Windows desktop or within regular Windows folders is quite common and can make your life a lot easier. You may not realize it but many of the features that you use every day in Windows are managed as folders as well. For example, the Windows desktop and Start menu can both be managed as folders. By adding shortcuts within these folders you add items to the Windows desktop and Start menu. Another Windows feature, the Quick Launch bar shown in Figure 14.7, is also managed as a folder.

FIGURE 14.7

The Quick Launch bar is used to provide single-click access to commonly used resources from the Windows desktop.

You can use the WshSpecialFolders object to retrieve object references to these and other special folders. You can then use these references to configure the Windows Start menu, Quick Launch bar, and the Startup folder.

Customizing the Start Menu

The Start menu can be configured using the `Startmenu` special folder. This allows you to add and remove menu items to and from it using shortcuts. Likewise, you can add an entry under the Programs menu by referencing the `Programs` special folder. Both of these special folders let you configure menus for individual users. If instead you want to add the menu entry to every user's Start menu or Programs menu you can reference the `AllUsersStartMenu` and `AllUsersPrograms` special folders respectively.

For example, the following JScript creates a new menu entry on the local user's Start menu for the Notepad application.

```
var ws_obj = WScript.CreateObject("WScript.Shell");
var trgt_folder = ws_obj.SpecialFolders("Startmenu");
var shortcut = ws_obj.CreateShortcut(trgt_folder + "\\notepad.lnk");
shortcut.TargetPath = "%windir%\\notepad.exe";
shortcut.Save();
```

Figure 14.8 shows how the new Notepad menu item will appear on the Windows Start menu.

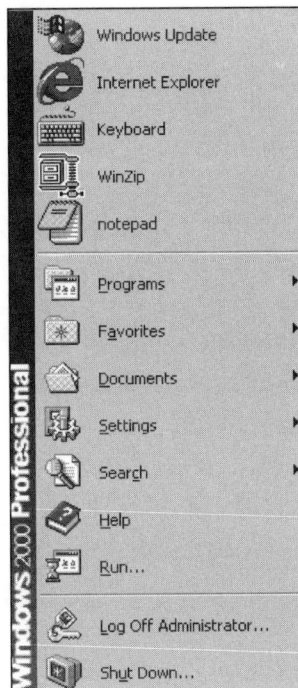

FIGURE 14.8

Adding shortcuts to the Windows Start menu.

The following example shows how to add a Notepad shortcut to the Start menu using VBScript.

```
Set ws_obj = WScript.CreateObject("WScript.Shell")
trgt_folder = ws_obj.SpecialFolders("Startmenu")
Set shortcut = ws_obj.CreateShortcut(trgt_folder & "\\notepad.lnk")
shortcut.TargetPath = "%windir%\notepad.exe"
shortcut.Save
```

If you no longer need the shortcut, you can remove it as shown by the following JScript.

```
var ws_obj = WScript.CreateObject("WScript.Shell");
trgt_folder = ws_obj.SpecialFolders("Startmenu");
var fso_obj = new ActiveXObject("Scripting.FileSystemObject");
var shortcut = fso_obj.GetFile(trgt_folder + "\\notepad.lnk");
shortcut.Delete();
```

Alternatively, you can delete the notepad menu entry using VBScript as shown here.

```
Set ws_obj = WScript.CreateObject("WScript.Shell")
trgt_folder = ws_obj.SpecialFolders("Startmenu")
Set fso_obj = CreateObject("Scripting.FileSystemObject")
Set shortcut = fso_obj.GetFile(trgt_folder & "\\notepad.lnk")
shortcut.Delete
```

Automatically Starting Windows Applications

The Windows Startup folder is represented in JScripts and VBScripts as the Startup special folder. By placing a shortcut into this folder, you cause the application associated with the shortcut to be automatically started when a user first logs on to the computer. If you use the AllUsersStartup special folder in place of the Startup special folder you can set up the application so that it starts up for all users of the computer.

For example, the following JScript places a shortcut for Microsoft Excel in the user's Startup folder, which will automatically open a spreadsheet called Time_rpting when the user logs on.

```
var ws_obj = WScript.CreateObject("WScript.Shell");
var trgt_folder = ws_obj.SpecialFolders("Startup");
var shortcut = ws_obj.CreateShortcut(trgt_folder +
"\\Time_Rpting.lnk");
shortcut.TargetPath = "c:\\Program Files\\Microsoft
Office\\Office\\excel.exe";
shortcut.Arguments = "c:\\Time_rpting.xls";
shortcut.Save();
```

If you prefer you can rewrite this script in VBScript as shown here.

```
Set ws_obj = WScript.CreateObject("WScript.Shell")
trgt_folder = ws_obj.SpecialFolders("Startup")
Set shortcut = ws_obj.CreateShortcut(trgt_folder + "\\Time_Rpting.lnk")
shortcut.TargetPath = "c:\Program Files\Microsoft
Office\Office\excel.exe"
shortcut.Arguments = "c:\Time_rpting.xls"
shortcut.Save
```

Configuring the Quick Launch Bar

The *Quick Launch bar* provides single-click access to any Windows resource that is added to it. It is available as part of the Windows active desktop and is included with Windows 98, 2000, and XP. Windows 95 and NT users can get it by installing Internet Explorer 4.0.

NOTE

For some reason, Microsoft did not include the Quick Launch bar with Internet Explorer 5.0. So to get it you need to install Internet Explorer 4 first and then upgrade to version 5.

By default, Windows adds the shortcuts for the Desktop, Internet Explorer, and Outlook Express to the Quick Launch bar. Most users add and remove shortcuts to the Quick Launch bar using Windows drag and drop. Programmatically, you can add an icon using JScript as shown here.

```
var ws_obj = new ActiveXObject("WScript.Shell");
var quick_lb = ws_obj.SpecialFolders("AppData");
```

```
var appdata_path = quick_lb + "\\Microsoft\\Internet Explorer\\Quick
Launch";
var shortcut = ws_obj.CreateShortcut(appdata_path + "\\calc.lnk");
shortcut.TargetPath = "%windir%\\system32\\calc.exe";
shortcut.Save();
```

Note that this shortcut is constructed slightly differently from other shortcuts that you have seen so far. It concatenates the `appdata` special folder with the location of the Quick Launch bar that resides within the `appdata` special folder.

Figure 14.9 shows how the Quick Launch bar appears after adding the new shortcut.

FIGURE 14.9

Viewing the results of adding an application shortcut to the Windows Quick Launch bar.

You can view the modified contents of the `appdata` special folder by looking in the `Profiles` folder. For example, on Windows 2000 systems the `appdata` special folder is typically located in `C:\Document and Settings\userid\Application Data\Microsoft\Internet Explorer\Quick Launch`, as demonstrated in Figure 14.10.

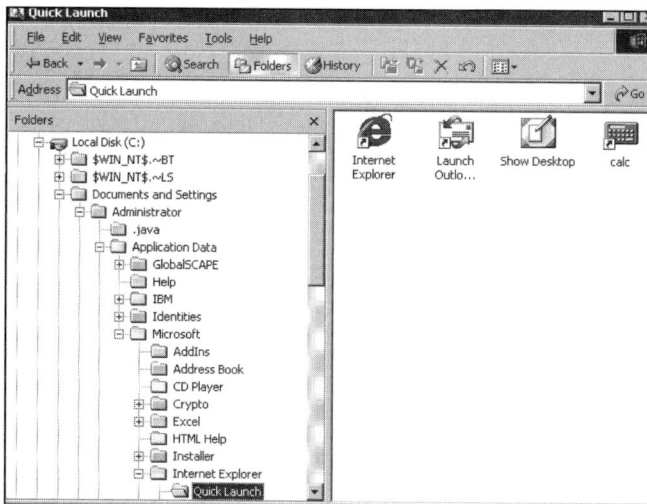

FIGURE 14.10

Viewing the contents of the Quick Launch bar special folder.

The following VBScript demonstrates how to add the same shortcut to the Quick Launch bar.

```
Set ws_obj = WScript.CreateObject("WScript.Shell")
quick_lb = ws_obj.SpecialFolders("AppData")
appdata_path = quick_lb + "\Microsoft\Internet

Explorer\Quick Launch"
Set shortcut = ws_obj.CreateShortcut(appdata_path +

"\\calc.lnk")

shortcut.TargetPath = "%windir%\system32\calc.exe"

shortcut.Save
```

Integrating WSH with Other Windows Applications

This section provides a demonstration of how you can use both JScripts and VBScripts to start and manipulate other Windows applications. In order to integrate WSH into a Windows application, the application must expose its object model so that your scripts can access the application's objects, methods, and properties.

For example, you can write a JScript and have it access the Microsoft Windows Excel's object model using the following statement.

```
var obj_xls = WScript.CreateObject("Excel.Application");
```

You can then use the obj_xls variable to access Excel methods and properties. The following JScript example shows how to start Excel and automatically populate data into a new spreadsheet.

```
// ********************************************
// * Script Name: open_xls.js                 *
// * Author:   Jerry Ford                     *
// * Address: Richmond Virginia               *
// * Created: 06/08/01                         *
// ********************************************
```

```
// **** Perform script initialization here ****

var obj_xls = WScript.CreateObject("Excel.Application");

// ********* Main processing section **********

//Call a function that sets up the spreadsheet

BuildXls();

// *********** Procedures go here *************

//This function creates a new Microsoft Excel spreadsheet

function BuildXls()
{
  //Open an Excel workbook and display it
  obj_xls.Visible = "TRUE";
  obj_xls.WorkBooks.Add;

  //Set the column widths
  obj_xls.Columns(1).ColumnWidth = 15;
  obj_xls.Columns(2).ColumnWidth = 25;
  obj_xls.Columns(3).ColumnWidth = 5;

  //Configure the first row to display in a bold font
  obj_xls.Range("A1:C1").Select;
  obj_xls.Selection.Font.Bold = "True";

  //Write the column headings
  obj_xls.Cells(1, 1).Value = "Constant";
  obj_xls.Cells(1, 2).Value = "Operation";
  obj_xls.Cells(1, 3).Value = "Code";

  //Populate the second row with data
  obj_xls.Cells(2, 1).Value = "ForWriting";
  obj_xls.Cells(2, 2).Value = "Opens a file for writing ";
  obj_xls.Cells(2, 3).Value = "2";
```

```
//Populate the third row with data
obj_xls.Cells(3, 1).Value = "ForAppending";
obj_xls.Cells(3, 2).Value = "Opens a file for appending ";
obj_xls.Cells(3, 3).Value = "8";


//Populate the fourth row with data
obj_xls.Cells(4, 1).Value = "ForReading";
obj_xls.Cells(4, 2).Value = "Opens a file for reading";
obj_xls.Cells(4, 3).Value = "1";



}
```

Figure 14.11 shows the spreadsheet created by this script. As you can see, not only were default column widths modified but also values were inserted into individual cells and formatted.

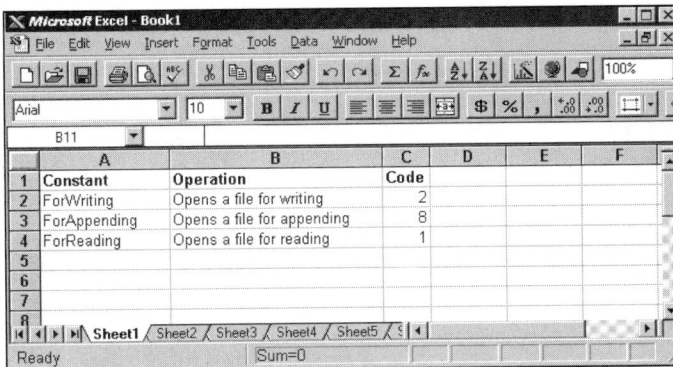

FIGURE 14.11

Creating and formatting an Excel spreadsheet from a script.

The following VBScript demonstrates how to build the same Excel spreadsheet using VBScript.

```
' *********************************************
' * Script Name: open_xls.vbs                 *
' * Author:   Jerry Ford                       *
' * Address: Richmond Virginia                 *
' * Created: 06/08/01                          *
' *********************************************


' **** Perform script initialization here ****
```

```
option Explicit
Dim obj_xls
Set obj_xls = WScript.CreateObject("Excel.Application")

' ********* Main processing section **********

'Call a function that sets up the spreadsheet

BuildXls

' ********** Procedures go here *************

'This function creates a new Microsoft Excel spreadsheet

Function BuildXls()

   'Open an Excel workbook and display it
   obj_xls.Visible = TRUE
   obj_xls.WorkBooks.Add

   'Set the column widths
   obj_xls.Columns(1).ColumnWidth = 15
   obj_xls.Columns(2).ColumnWidth = 25
   obj_xls.Columns(3).ColumnWidth = 5

   'Configure the first row to display in a bold font
   obj_xls.Range("A1:C1").Select
   obj_xls.Selection.Font.Bold = True

   'Write the column headings
   obj_xls.Cells(1, 1).Value = "Constant"
   obj_xls.Cells(1, 2).Value = "Operation"
   obj_xls.Cells(1, 3).Value = "Code"

   'Populate the second row with data
   obj_xls.Cells(2, 1).Value = "ForWriting"
   obj_xls.Cells(2, 2).Value = "Opens a file for writing "
   obj_xls.Cells(2, 3).Value = "2"
```

```
'Populate the third row with data
obj_xls.Cells(3, 1).Value = "ForAppending"
obj_xls.Cells(3, 2).Value = "Opens a file for appending "
obj_xls.Cells(3, 3).Value = "8"

'Populate the fourth row with data
obj_xls.Cells(4, 1).Value = "ForReading"
obj_xls.Cells(4, 2).Value = "Opens a file for reading"
obj_xls.Cells(4, 3).Value = "1"


End Function
```

Chapter 15

Computer and Network Administration

In this chapter, you learn to write Windows scripts that manage network drives and printers. You will see how to write messages to the Windows event logs as well as how to add and remove keys and values in the Windows Registry. The chapter concludes with a discussion on how to integrate WSH and the Windows shell. Topics covered in this chapter include:

◆ Managing network drives and printers
◆ Reading and writing to Windows event logs
◆ Reading and writing to the Windows Registry
◆ Creating users accounts
◆ Managing services, shares, and network connections
◆ Scheduling your scripts

Gathering Network Information

The WshNetwork object exposes resources on Microsoft Windows networks thus allowing your scripts to view network information. The WshNetwork object's properties provide access to several pieces of network information, as outlined in the following list.

◆ **ComputerName**—Returns a string containing a computer's name.
◆ **UserDomain**—Returns a string containing the domain name where the user is logged in.
◆ **UserName**—Returns a string containing the user's username.

In addition, the WshNetwork object's methods provide the capability to view network resources, connect and disconnect to network printers and drivers, and set a user's default printer. The WshNetwork object's methods are listed here.

◆ **AddPrinterConnection**—Connects to a network printer.
◆ **EnumNetworkDrives**—Provides access to drive mappings.
◆ **EnumPrinterConnection**—Provides access to printer connections.

- ◆ **MapNetworkDrive**—Maps a network drive.
- ◆ **RemoveNetworkDrive**—Removes a network drive mapping.
- ◆ **RemovePrinterConnection**—Removes a connection to a network printer.
- ◆ **SetDefaultPrinter**—Sets the default printer.

The following JScript demonstrates how to use the WshNetwork object's properties and its **EnumNetworkDrives** method to gather and display network information. The script begins by initializing the variables that will be used by the script. Next, it creates instances of the WshShell and WshNetwork objects. The script then displays each of the WshNetwork object's property values in a pop-up dialog box, as demonstrated in Figure 15.1.

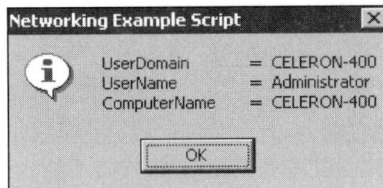

FIGURE 15.1

Executing a script that displays the properties of the WshNetwork object.

Next, the script asks the users whether they want to see a listing of all mapped network drives on the computer. If the user responds with a No, the script ends. If the user responds with Yes, the script uses the WshNetwork object's **EnumNetworkDrives** method to populate a variable with a listing of all the network drive connections on the computer. A FOR loop then displays the network drives in a pop-up dialog box, as demonstrated in Figure 15.2.

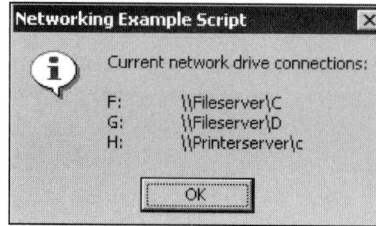

FIGURE 15.2

Executing a script that displays properties of the WshNetwork object.

For a detailed explanation of the activities performed at each step, examine the comments embedded within the script. The script is designed so that its comments provide its own internal documentation.

```
// *********************************************
// * Script Name: Network_chk.js            *
// * Author:   Jerry Ford                     *
// * Address: Richmond Virginia              *
// * Created: 06/09/01                        *
// *********************************************


// This JScript displays network properties and
// network drive mappings

// **** Perform script initialization here ****

//Define popup dialog button values
var ok_button = 0;
var ok_cancel_button = 1;
var yes_no_button = 4;
var question_icon = 32;
var info_icon = 64;

//Define the return value for the Yes and No
//popup dialog
var yes_popup_response = 6;
var no_popup_response = 7;

//Specify popup dialog title bar message
var popup_title   = "Networking Example Script";
```

```
//Define a variable to hold the list of mapped drives
var drive_collection;

//Instantiate the WScript Shell and Network objects
var ws_obj = WScript.CreateObject("WScript.Shell");
var ws_net = WScript.CreateObject("WScript.Network")

// ********* Main processing section **********

//Display Network properties in popup dialog
// /t = tab and /r = return
ws_obj.Popup("UserDomain \t= " + ws_net.UserDomain + "\r" +
             "UserName   \t= " + ws_net.UserName   + "\r" +
             "ComputerName \t= " + ws_net.ComputerName,
                0, popup_title, info_icon + ok_button );

//Call the Query_User function. If nothing is returned
//the scripts ends, otherwise enumerate mapped drives
if (Query_User("View a list of network drives?")) {

  //Place list of drives into a variable for examination
  var drive_collection = ws_net.EnumNetworkDrives();

  //Show enumeration results to the user
  if (drive_collection.length == 0) {
    ws_obj.Popup("There are no drives to enumerate.", 0,
    popup_title, info_icon + ok_button );
  } else {
      title_msg = "Current network drive connections: \r\n";
      for (i = 0; i < drive_collection.length; i += 2) {
        title_msg = title_msg + "\r\n" + drive_collection(i)
                    + "\t" + drive_collection(i + 1);
      }
      ws_obj.Popup(title_msg, 0, popup_title,
                    info_icon + ok_button );
  }
}
```

```
// ********** Procedures go here ************

//This function asks the user whether or not to
//enumerate mapped drives. Only return a Yes response
function Query_User(msg_arg){
  var response;
  response = ws_obj.Popup(msg_arg, 0, popup_title,
            question_icon + yes_no_button );
  return response == yes_popup_response;
}
```

A VBScript implementation of the previous example follows.

```
' ********************************************
' * Script Name: Network_chk.vbs       *
' * Author:   Jerry Ford                    *
' * Address: Richmond Virginia            *
' * Created: 06/09/01                      *
' ********************************************

' This JScript displays network properties and
' network drive mappings

' **** Perform script initialization here ****

'Force the explicit declaration of all variables
Option Explicit

'Declare popup dialog values
Dim ok_button, ok_cancel_button, Yes_no_button
Dim question_icon, info_icon
Dim popup_title, strMsg, i
Dim ws_net, ws_obj, drive_collection, CRLF
Dim yes_popup_response, no_popup_response

'Define popup dialog button values
ok_button = 0
ok_cancel_button = 1
```

```
yes_no_button = 4
question_icon = 32
info_icon = 64

'Specify popup dialog title bar message
popup_title     = "Windows Scripting Host Sample"

'Define return value for the Yes and No
'popup dialog
yes_popup_response = 6
no_popup_response = 7

'This variable will be used to force a carriage return Chr(13) and
'a line feed Chr(10)
CRLF = Chr(13) & Chr(10)

'Instantiate the WScript Shell and Network objects
Set ws_obj = WScript.CreateObject("WScript.Shell")
Set ws_net = WScript.CreateObject("WScript.Network")

' ********* Main processing section **********

'Display Network properties in popup dialog
'chr(9) = tab
ws_obj.Popup _
   "UserDomain" & Chr(9) & "= " & ws_net.UserDomain & CRLF & _
   "UserName"   & Chr(9) & "= " & ws_net.UserName   & CRLF & _
   "ComputerName" & Chr(9) & "= " & ws_net.ComputerName,     _
   0, popup_title, info_icon + ok_button

'Call the Query_User function. If nothing is returned
'the scripts ends, otherwise enumerate mapped drives
If Query_User("View a list of network drives?") Then
   'Place list of drives into a variable for examination
   Set drive_collection = ws_net.EnumNetworkDrives
```

```
'Show enumeration results to the user
If drive_collection.Count = 0 Then
  ws_obj.Popup "There are no drives to enumerate.", _
                0, popup_title, info_icon + ok_button
Else
  strMsg = "Current network drive connections: " & CRLF
  For i = 0 To drive_collection.Count - 1 Step 2
    strMsg = strMsg & CRLF & drive_collection(i) & _
            Chr(9) & drive_collection(i + 1)
  Next
  ws_obj.Popup strMsg, 0, info_icon + ok_button
  End If
End If


' *********** Procedures go here *************


'This function asks the user whether or not to
'enumerate mapped drives. Only return a Yes response
Function Query_User(msg_arg)
  Dim response
  response = ws_obj.Popup(msg_arg, 0, popup_title, _
            question_icon + yes_no_button)
  Query_User = response = yes_popup_response
End Function
```

Managing Network Drives

Network drives are shared network drives that have a logical connection on the local computer. Once your script is connected to a network drive it can access its contents just as if it were directly attached to the local computer. You can use the WshNetwork object's MapNetworkDrive method to programmatically work with network drives. The syntax of the MapNetworkDrive method is shown here.

```
WshNetwork.MapNetworkDrive drive_letter, network_name, [persistent],
[username], [password]
```

`Drive letter` specifies the available drive letter assignment on the local computer. *Network_name* provides the path to the network drive. `Persistent` is an optional parameter that determines whether the mapping lasts across user sessions and *username* and *password* optionally allow you to pass a username and password that are required to establish the mapping.

Mapping a Network Drive

Your scripts can create mappings to network drives using the `MapNetworkDrive` method of the WshNetwork object. The following JScript example demonstrates how to do this.

```
var ws_net = WScript.CreateObject("WScript.Network");
ws_net.MapNetworkDrive("z:", "\\\\FileServer\\c");
```

In this example, the script first creates an instance of the WshNetwork object and then creates the mapped drive by assigned a `z:` drive letter to the shared `c:` drive on network server called `FileServer`. Take note of the four backslashes used to specify the name of the network computer. The normal command-line syntax used to connect to a network computer is `\\name\resource`. However, because each backslash in JScript must be escaped, you end up with the somewhat peculiar syntax used in the previous example.

You can adapt this example to work in a VBScript, as shown here.

```
Set ws_net = WScript.CreateObject("WScript.Network")
ws_net.MapNetworkDrive "z:", "\\FileServer\c"
```

The drive mapping created in the previous examples is temporary and will be automatically disconnected when the user logs off. However, you can make the mappings permanent by specifying a Boolean value of `True` after the network drive path. Likewise, you can pass a username and password if they are required to make the connection to the network drive.

NOTE

Embedding a username and password in a script is a questionable thing to do because anyone with access to the script can read them.

> **TIP**
>
> If you execute your scripts via the Windows scheduling service, you cannot count on your personal drive mappings being available when your scripts execute. In this case you should incorporate code that handles the mapping of networking drives into your scripts.

Disconnecting a Network Drive

Once you no longer require access to a network drive, you should disconnect the drive mapping. You can do this using the `RemoveNetworkDrive` method of the WshNetwork object. The syntax of the `RemoveNetworkDrive` method is shown here.

```
WshNetwork.RemoveNetworkDrive drive_letter, [kill], [persistent]
```

Drive_letter is the driver letter currently assigned to the mapped network drive. `Kill` is an optional Boolean value that allows you to terminate a drive mapping even if it is currently being used and `persistent` is an optional Boolean value that allows you to disconnect persistent drive mappings. For example, the following JScript disconnects the network drive created earlier in this chapter.

```
var ws_net = WScript.CreateObject("WScript.Network");
ws_net.RemoveNetworkDrive("z:");
```

The following VBScript performs the same task.

```
Set ws_net = WScript.CreateObject("WScript.Network")
ws_RemoveNetworkDrive "z:"
```

Managing Network Printers

Connecting to network printers is very similar to connecting to network drives, except instead of using the WshNetwork object's `MapNetworkDrive` method, you use its `AddPrinterConnection` method. The syntax of the `AddPrinterConnection` method is shown here.

```
WshNetwork.AddPrinterConnection resource network_name, [persistent],
[username], [password]
```

Resource is the name of a local resource such as LPT1 or LPT2. *Network_name* provides the path to the network printer. Persistent is an optional parameter that determines whether the printer connection is persistent across user sessions. The *username* and *password* parameters optionally allow you to pass a user-name and password that are required to establish the connection.

Connecting to a Network Printer

The following JScript establishes a persistent printer connection to a network printer named Mrkting_ptr.

```
var ws_net = WScript.CreateObject("WScript.Network");
ws_net.AddPrinterConnection("LPT1", "\\\\Print_server\\HPDJ712c",
"True");
```

The example can be rewritten in VBScript, as shown here.

```
Set ws_net = WScript.CreateObject("WScript.Network")
Ws_net.AddPrinterConnection "LPT1", "\\Print_server\HPDJ712c", "True"
```

Disconnecting a Network Printer

Once you no longer need to use a network printer you should disconnect it. You can do this using the RemovePrinterConnection method of the WshNetwork object. The syntax of the RemovePrinterConnection method is shown here.

```
WshNetwork.RemovePrinterConnection resource, [kill], [persistent]
```

Resource is the name of a local resource such as LPT1 or LPT2. Kill is an optional Boolean that allows you to terminate a printer connection even if it is currently being used and persistent is an optional Boolean value that allows you to disconnect a persistent printer connection.

For example, the following JScript disconnects the previously established printer connection.

```
var ws_net = WScript.CreateObject("WScript.Network");
ws_net.RemovePrinterConnection "LPT1:";
```

Likewise, the following VBScript performs the same operation.

```
Set ws_net = WScript.CreateObject("WScript.Network")
Ws_net.RemovePrinterConnection "LPT1:"
```

Setting the Default Printer

You can specify a user's default printer using the Network object's `SetDefault-Printer` method. Its syntax is shown here.

```
WshNetwork.SetDefaultPrinter printer_name
```

Printer_name specifies the name of the printer to set as the default and is specified in the form of `\\Sever_name\Printer_name`. For example, the following JScript connects to a network server named `Print_server` and connects to its `HPDJ712c` printer. The script then sets the printer as the default printer.

```
var ws_net = WScript.CreateObject("WScript.Network");
ws_net.AddPrinterConnection("LPT1", "\\\\Print_server\\HPDJ712c",
"True");
ws_net.SetDefaultPrinter("\\\\Print_server\\HPDJ712c");
```

The following VBScript performs the same printer-management task.

```
Set ws_net = WScript.CreateObject("WScript.Network")
ws_net.AddPrinterConnection "LPT1:", "\\Print_server\HPDJ712c"
ws_net.SetDefaultPrinter "\\Print_server\HPDJ712c"
```

Working with Event Logs

Windows NT-based operating systems provide event logs that store information that can be used to review system status and look for problems. The three types of event logs are as follows.

- ◆ **Application**—Contains message events generated by compatible Windows applications.
- ◆ **System**—Contains message events logged by the operating system.
- ◆ **Security**—Contains message events related to system security and audit events.

You can use the built-in event viewer to browse event logs and examine event messages. Figure 15.3 shows the Event Viewer Management Console provided by Windows 2000.

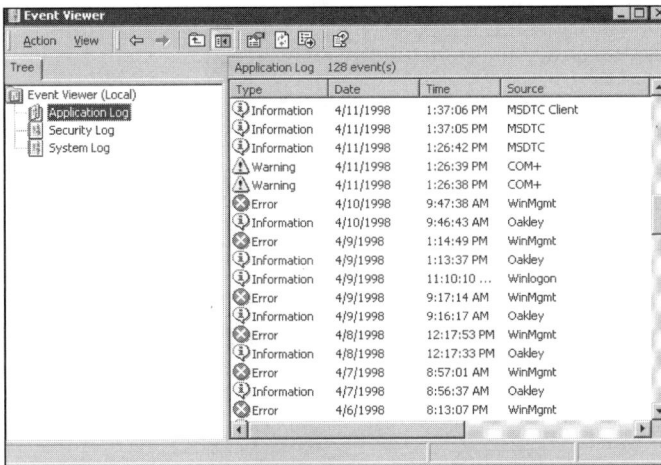

FIGURE 15.3

Viewing application events using the Windows Event Viewer.

Writing Event Messages to the Application Event Log

You can integrate logic into your scripts that allow them to write messages to the Windows NT, 2000, and XP application event log. This provides you with a standard means of reporting and tracking the success or failure of your script.

You write events to the event log using the WshShell object's LogEvent method. The syntax of the LogEvent method is shown here.

```
WshShell.LogEvent(event_type, msg_text, [trgt_svr])
```

Event_type represents the type of event to record. Table 15.1 lists the various event types that you can use in your scripts. *Msg_text* is the message text to be recorded and *trgt_svr* is an optional parameter that allows you to specify a remote server where the event should be logged. If you do not specify a *trgt_svr*, the event will be recorded on the local computer.

Table 15.1   Event Log Event Types

Type	Description
0	Successful operation
1	Error occurred
2	Warning message
4	Information message
8	Successful audit
16	Failed audit

For example, you can add a statement similar to the one shown here in JScript to write an informational event to the application log.

```
var ws_obj = WScript.CreateObject("WScript.Shell");
ws_obj.LogEvent(0, "Notepad startup complete.");
```

When executed, the previous JScript statement creates an event in the application event log. Figure 15.4 shows how the event appears when viewed on Windows 2000.

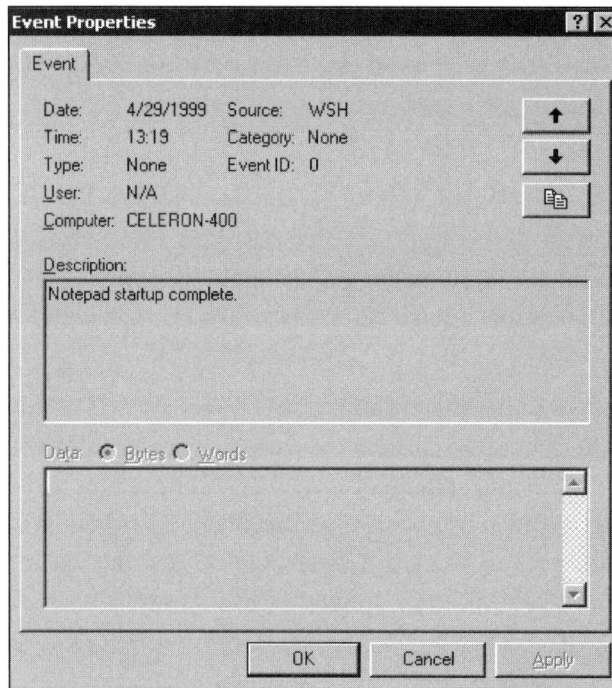

FIGURE 15.4

Viewing an application event log message created by a script.

The following VBScript example writes the same information event to the application log.

```
Set ws_obj = WScript.CreateObject("WScript.Shell")
ws_obj.LogEvent 0, "Notepad startup complete."
```

Reading Event Logs

Unfortunately, there is no method provided by any of the WSH objects that enables you to read event logs. Microsoft's solution to this dilemma is the DUMPEL utility. It's provided as part of the Windows NT and Windows 2000 Resource Kits.

The `dumpel.exe` command-line utility dumps the contents of a specified event log into a tab-delaminated text file. By specifying optional parameter settings, you can filter the event information that is written to the text file.

For example, to copy the local application log into a file named `app_log.txt` on a network server called `File_server`, you would execute the following command from the Windows command prompt.

```
dumpel -f app_log.txt -s File_server -l application
```

To execute the DUMPEL command-line utility from within a JScript or VBScript, you need to use the WshShell object's Run method. For example, the following JScript performs this same operation.

```
var ws_obj = WScript.CreateObject("WScript.Shell");
ws_obj.Run("dumpel -f app_log.txt -s File_server -l application ", 0,
"True");
```

The second parameter in the Run statement is 0, which controls the appearance of the Windows that runs the script. The third parameter determines whether the script waits for the command to complete processing before continuing. More information on the Run method is provided later in this chapter.

Once you have dumped the contents of the event log into a text file, you can use the methods of the FileSystemObject as explained in Chapter 13, "Working with Files and Folders," to read and process the event log information. Refer to Chapter 9, "Putting it All Together," to learn more about the DUMPEL command-line utility.

Working with the Windows Registry

The Windows Registry is an internal Windows database in which operating system, application, hardware, and user settings are stored. The Windows Registry is composed of five root keys, listed in Table 15.2.

Table 15.2   **Windows Registry Route Keys**

Registry Key	Shortcut	Description
HKEY_CLASSES_ROOT	HKCR	Maintains Windows file associations
HKEY_CURRENT_USER	HKCU	Stores information about the current user
HKEY_LOCAL_MACHINE	HKLM	Stores global computer settings
HKEY_USERS	-	Stores information regarding all users
HKEY_CURRENT_CONFIG	-	Stores current configuration information

You can manually work with the Windows Registry using the `Regedit` utility provided with Windows. Figure 15.5 shows the Windows 2000 `Regedit` utility as it is being used to examine the five root keys.

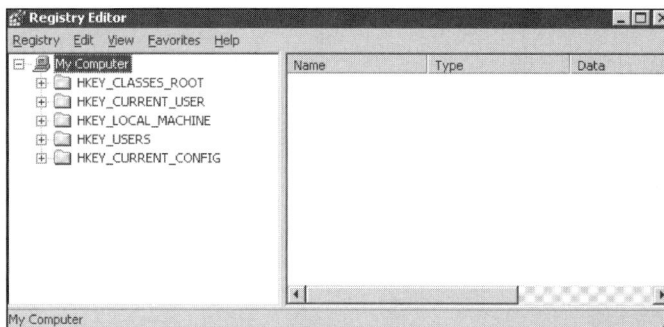

FIGURE 15.5

The `Regedit` utility supplied with Windows operating systems allows you to view and manipulate Registry keys and values.

Understanding the Registry's Structure

The Registry organizes its contents in a tree-like format under the five root keys. All data is stored in individual keys that have the following format.

Key : key_type : value

Key is a Registry key such as `HKEY_CLASSES_ROOT\.JS\Content Type`. `Key_type` identifies the types of data stored in the key. Valid types are listed here.

- ◆ **REG_BINARY**—Stores a binary value.
- ◆ **REG_SZ**—Stores a text string value.
- ◆ **REG_DWORD**—Stores a hexadecimal DWORD value.
- ◆ **REG_MULTI_SZ**—Stores a multiple string value.
- ◆ **REG_EXPAND_SZ**—Stores a string, such as `%ComSpec%`, that can be expanded.

`Value` is the actual value stored in the key. For example, the `HKEY_CLASSES_ROOT\.JS\Content Type` key is shown next. This key contains data in the form of `REG-SZ` and has a value of `application/x-javascript`.

```
HKEY_CLASSES_ROOT\.JS\Content Type       REG_SZ    application/x-
javascript
```

Manipulating Registry Contents

You can use three methods provided by the WshShell object to manipulate the Registry, as outlined here.

- ◆ `RegRead`—Retrieves a Registry key or value.
- ◆ `RegWrite`—Writes a Registry key or value.
- ◆ `RegDelete`—Deletes a Registry key or value.

Each of these WshShell methods is demonstrated in the sections that follow.

NOTE

The Registry is a key Windows component. Any mistake in working with the Registry can have devastating effects on your computer. Never make a change to the Registry without backing up the Registry and without having a solid understanding of the effects of the change.

Creating a Registry Key or Value

You can create new Registry keys or modify existing ones using the WshShell object's `RegWrite` method. For example, the following JScript statement creates a value named `MyName` under a key named `HKEY_CURRENT_USER\MyKey\` and assigns it a string of `Jerry Ford`. If the `MyKey` key under `HKEY_CURRENT_USER\MyKey\` does not exist, it is automatically created.

```
var WshShell = WScript.CreateObject("WScript.Shell");
WshShell.RegWrite("HKCU\\MyKey\\MyName", "Jerry Ford");
```

The following VBScript creates the same value in a VBScript.

```
Set WshShell = WScript.CreateObject("WScript.Shell")
WshShell.RegWrite "HKCU\MyKey\MyName", "Jerry Ford"
```

If you specify a path that ends with a backslash, the script creates a key instead of a value.

Reading a Registry Key or Value

You can read the Registry value created in the previous example using the WshShell object's `RegRead` method, as shown in the following JScript.

```
var WshShell = WScript.CreateObject("WScript.Shell");
results = WshShell.RegRead("HKCU\\MyKey\\Myname");
WScript.Echo(results);
```

If you are working with VBScript, you can read the value as demonstrated here.

```
Set WshShell = WScript.CreateObject("WScript.Shell")
results = WshShell.RegRead("HKCU\MyKey\Myname")
WScript.Echo results
```

Deleting a Registry Key or Value

If you no longer need to keep a Registry key or value, you can delete it using the WshShell object's `RegDelete` method. For example, the following JScript shows how you can delete the value created in the earlier example.

```
Set WshShell = WScript.CreateObject("WScript.Shell");
WshShell.RegDelete("HKCU\MyKey\MyName")
```

This example can be rewritten in VBScript as shown here.

```
Set WshShell = WScript.CreateObject("WScript.Shell")
WshShell.RegDelete "HKCU\MyKey\MyName"
```

Integrating WSH and the Windows Shell

The WshShell object's Run method allows you to execute command-line commands and utilities from within your JScripts and VBScripts. Using the Run method, you can start Windows applications and execute any command-line utility or command. The syntax of the Run method follows.

```
WScript.Run(command, [WindowStyle], [WaitonReturn])
```

Command specifies the application, utility, or command-line command to be executed. WindowStyle is an optional parameter that allows you to specify the style of the window that will hold the command, utility, or application. A listing of WindowStyle values is provided in Chapter 14, "Managing the Windows Desktop." WaitonReturn is a Boolean value of True or False that determines whether the script waits or continues its execution after executing the Run method. The default is to continue script execution.

In order to use the Run method in your script, you must create an instance of the WScript.Shell object, as demonstrated in the following JScript.

```
var ws_obj = WScript.CreateObject("WScript.Shell");
ws_obj.Run("notepad");
```

The VBScript equivalent is shown here.

```
Set ws_obj = WScript.CreateObject("WScript.Shell")
ws_obj.Run("notepad")
```

The Run method lets you pass arguments to the called command, utility, or application. For example, the following JScript starts Notepad and passes it the name of a file to load.

```
var ws_obj = WScript.CreateObject("WScript.Shell");
ws_obj.Run("notepad c:\\myreport.txt");
```

The equivalent VBScript is shown here.

```
Set ws_obj = WScript.CreateObject("WScript.Shell")
ws_obj.Run("notepad c:\myreport.txt")
```

Creating User Accounts

The Windows NT line of operating systems provides a number of commands that you can use to script the administration of local and domain user accounts. The commands include:

- **net user**—Configures user accounts.
- **net group**—Configures global group membership.
- **net localgroup**—Configures local group membership.

You can use the net user command to create or delete a user account. Then, you can use the net group and net localgroup commands to configure group membership for the account.

The following JScript example demonstrates one way of scripting the creation of a new user account for a network administrator. In this example, the JScript creates new administrator accounts based on a list of account names read from an external file. Each line in the external file contains a single new account name on each line in the file.

```
// ********************************************
// * Script Name: creat_accts.js              *
// * Author:   Jerry Ford                      *
// * Address: Richmond Virginia                *
// * Created: 06/09/01                          *
// ********************************************


// **** Perform script initialization here ****

//Instantiate the FileSystemObject so that the script can work with
//the Windows file system
var fso_obj = new ActiveXObject("Scripting.FileSystemObject");
```

```
//Instantiate the WshShell object so that the script can work with the
//WshShell's Run method
var ws_obj = WScript.CreateObject("WScript.Shell");

//Specify the path to the external file where the new account names
//are stored
var working_file = fso_obj.OpenTextFile("c:\\userlist.txt", 1, "True");

// ********* Main processing section **********

//Call the function that processes the new user accounts
CreateAccts();

// ********** Procedures go here *************

//This function performs the actual account creation and configuration
function CreateAccts()
{
  //Loop through and read the file a line at a time
  while (!working_file.AtEndOfStream) {
    new_acct = working_file.ReadLine();

    //Create the new domain account
    ws_obj.Run("net user " + new_acct + " newpasswd /add /domain", 0);

    //Add the account to the Administrators local group
    ws_obj.Run("net localgroup Administrators /add " + new_acct + "
/domain", 0);

  }
  //Close the file when done working with it
  working_file.Close();
}
```

The following VBScript performs the same operation as the previous JScript example.

```
' **********************************************
' * Script Name: creat_accts.vbs              *
' * Author:  Jerry Ford                        *
' * Address: Richmond Virginia                 *
' * Created: 06/09/01                          *
' **********************************************


' **** Perform script initialization here ****

'Instantiate the FileSystemObject so that the script can work with
'the Windows file system
Set fso_obj = CreateObject("Scripting.FileSystemObject")

'Instantiate the WshShell object so that the script can work with the
'WshShell's Run method
Set ws_obj = WScript.CreateObject("WScript.Shell")

'Specify the path to the external file where the new account names
'are stored
Set working_file = fso_obj.OpenTextFile("c:\\userlist.txt", 1, "True")

' ********* Main processing section **********

'Call the function that processes the new user accounts
CreateAccts()

' *********** Procedures go here ************

'This function performs the actual account creation and configuration
Function CreateAccts()
  'Loop through and read the file a line at a time
  Do while False = working_file.AtEndOfStream
    new_acct = working_file.ReadLine()
```

```
'Create the new domain account
ws_obj.Run("net user " + new_acct + " newpasswd /add /domain", 0)

'Add the account to the Administrators local group
ws_obj.Run("net localgroup Administrators /add " + new_acct + "
/domain", 0)

Loop

'Close the file when done working with it
working_file.Close

End Function
```

Refer to Chapter 9, "Putting It All Together," and Appendix A, "A Windows Command Reference," to learn more about working with the net user, net group, and net localgroup commands.

Managing Services

Windows NT, 2000, and XP systems provide a collection of services that can be managed completely from the command line and therefore by scripts. You can view a listing of the installed services on any Windows NT, 2000, or XP computer by typing **net start** at the command prompt and pressing Enter.

In addition to the net start command, you can manage Windows services using any of the commands outlined here.

- **net pause**—Pauses a running service but does not stop it.
- **net continue**—Resumes a paused service.
- **net start**—Starts a stopped service.
- **net stop**—Stops an active service.

Using the WshShell object's Run method, your scripts can execute these commands in any combination required to control the activity of the services. For example, the following JScript demonstrates how to start the Windows Task Scheduling service.

```
var ws_obj = WScript.CreateObject("WScript.Shell");
ws_obj.Run("net start schedule", 0, "True");
```

The service can be started just as easily from a VBScript as shown here.

```
Set ws_obj = WScript.CreateObject("WScript.Shell")
ws_obj.Run "net start schedule", 0, "True"
```

The syntax for pausing, continuing, and stopping services is the same as for starting them, as the following JScript statements show.

To start a service, use:

```
ws_obj.Run("net start schedule", 0, "True");
```

To pause a service, use:

```
ws_obj.Run("net pause schedule", 0, "True");
```

To continue a service, use:

```
ws_obj.Run("net continue schedule", 0, "True");
```

To stop a service, use:

```
ws_obj.Run("net stop schedule", 0, "True");
```

The following VBScript statements show you how to perform the same set of service-administration commands from a VBScript.

To start a service, use:

```
ws_obj.Run "net start schedule", 0, "True"
```

To pause a service, use:

```
ws_obj.Run "net pause schedule", 0, "True"
```

To continue a service, use:

```
ws_obj.Run "net continue schedule", 0, "True"
```

To stop a service, use:

```
ws_obj.Run "net stop schedule", 0, "True"
```

Refer to Chapter 9 and Appendix A to learn more about working with the `net start`, `net pause`, `net continue`, and `net stop` commands.

Scheduling Script Execution

You can schedule your Windows file scripts, JScripts, and VBScripts for automatic execution using a number of techniques. One option is to use the Windows Scheduled Task Wizard. The Windows Scheduled Task Wizard creates schedules for your scripts by stepping you through a series of Windows dialog boxes and asking you questions. Refer to Chapter 9 for more information on using the Scheduled Task Wizard.

On Windows NT, 2000, and XP, you can also schedule script execution from the command line using the AT command. Alternatively, you can write Windows shell scripts that use the AT command to schedule your Windows File scripts, JScripts, and VBScripts. To learn more about using the AT command from within Windows shell scripts, refer to Chapter 9.

To view a list of all the scheduled tasks on a given computer, you can type the AT command at the Windows command line and press Enter as shown here.

```
C:\>at
Status ID    Day             Time          Command Line
_____

         0   Each S          8:00 PM       cmd /c diskclean.bat
         1   Tomorrow        10:00 AM      copy_reports.bat
```

A listing of all the scheduled jobs is displayed. Each job is assigned a unique ID number that can be used to delete the job if necessary. You also see the time that the task is set to execute and the name of the task that will be executed.

You can use the WshShell object's Run command to execute the AT command directly from within your Windows file scripts, JScripts, and VBScripts. For example, when executed, the following JScript schedules the execution of another JScript called copy_files.js every Monday, Wednesday, and Friday night at 23:30.

```
var ws_obj = WScript.CreateObject("WScript.Shell");

ws_obj.Run("at 23:30 /every:M,W,F cmd /c copy_files.js ", 0, "True");
```

Assuming that this is the only currently scheduled job, typing **AT** and pressing Enter at the command line will return the following results.

```
C:\>at
Status ID   Day                Time            Command Line
------------------------------------------------------------------
          1   Each M W F         11:30 PM        cmd /c copy_files.js
```

To remove the execution of the script from the schedule, use its unique scheduling ID number assignment as shown in the following JScript.

```
var ws_obj = WScript.CreateObject("WScript.Shell");
ws_obj.Run("at 1 /delete", 0, "True");
```

If you are working with VBScript, you can schedule the execution of one VBScript from within another as shown here.

```
Set ws_obj = WScript.CreateObject("WScript.Shell")
ws_obj.Run "at 23:30 /every:M,W,F cmd /c copy_files.vbs", 0, "True"
```

Assuming that the scheduled VBScript was assigned a schedule ID of 2, you can remove it from the schedule as shown here.

```
Set ws_obj = WScript.CreateObject("WScript.Shell")
ws_obj.Run "at 2 /delete", 0, "True"
```

Other Management Tasks

By now you should have a good understanding of how to use the WshShell object's Run method to execute any Windows command-line utility or command. Other commands that you might want to investigate include:

- **net accounts**—Modifies the user accounts database and changes logon and password requirements.
- **net computer**—Adds or deletes computer accounts in the domain database.
- **net config**—Displays and changes configurable active services.
- **net file**—Displays a list of all open shared files on a server and the number of file locks on each file.
- **net name**—Displays the list of computer names that will accept messages or adds or removes a messaging name.

◆ **net print**—Lists or manages print jobs and printer queues.

◆ **net send**—Sends messages to users, computers, and messaging names.

◆ **net session**—Lists or terminates sessions with clients connected to the computer.

◆ **net share**—Creates, deletes, and displays shared resources.

◆ **net time**—Synchronizes the computer's internal clock with another computer's clock.

◆ **net use**—Displays information about network connections and connects a computer to network resources.

◆ **net view**—Displays a list of domains, computers, or resources being shared by a specified computer.

Refer to Appendix A to learn more about these commands.

W H
S

PART IV

Appendixes

Appendix A

A Windows Command Reference

T his appendix provides an alphabetical command reference of Windows 2000 shell commands. Each command includes a brief explanation of its purpose, its syntax, and a complete explanation of its parameters.

Although this appendix covers Windows 2000 shell commands, it can be used for Windows NT 4 in most cases. Two notable exceptions are the Windows NT 4 backup and restore commands, which are not supported by Windows 2000. For additional information regarding the commands covered in this appendix, consult the Windows Help system.

append

Enables programs to open files located in different folders as if they were stored in the current folder.

Syntax

append [;] [[drive:]path[;...]] [/x:{on | off}][/path:{on | off}] [/e]

Parameters

Parameter	Purpose
;	Clears the list of appended folders.
[drive:]path	Sets the drive, path, and folder to be appended.
/x:{on | off}	Determines whether the MS-DOS subsystem searches appended folders when running programs. With /x:on the program performs the search and with /x:off the program does not.
/path:{on | off}	Determines whether a program should search appended folders even when a path is provided along with the name of the file the program is looking for. /path:on is the default.
/e	Creates an environment variable named APPEND and sets its value equal to the list of appended folders. The /e switch can only be used once after each time you restart your system.

arp

A TCP/IP protocol command that displays and modifies the IP-to-MAC address translation tables used by the Address Resolution Protocol (ARP).

Syntax

```
arp -a [inet_addr] [-N [if_addr]]
arp -d inet_addr [if_addr]
arp -s inet_addr ether_addr [if_addr]
```

Parameters

Parameter	Purpose
-a	Lists ARP entries.
-g	Lists ARP entries in the same manner as -a.
[inet_addr]	Identifies an IP address.
-N	Lists ARP entries for the network interface specified by if_addr.
[if_addr]	Identifies the IP address of the network interface whose address translation table should be modified. Otherwise, the first applicable interface will be used.
-d	Removes the entry specified by inet_addr.
-s	Adds a permanent entry in the ARP cache which associates the inet_addr IP address with the ether_addr MAC address.
ether_addr	Specifies a MAC address.

assoc

Lists or changes file extension associations.

Syntax

```
assoc [.ext[=[filetype]]]
```

Parameters

Parameter	Purpose
None	Lists current file associations.
.ext	Specifies a specific file extension to list or modify.
[filetype]	Identifies a file type to be associated with the specified file extension.

at

Displays a listing of scheduled tasks (command, script, or program) and schedules the execution of new tasks.

Syntax

```
at [\\computername] [[id] [/delete] | /delete [/yes]]
at [\\computername] time [/interactive] [/every:date[,...] |
/next:date[,...]] command
```

Parameters

Parameter	Purpose
None	Displays a listing of all scheduled tasks.
[\\computername]	Specifies a remote computer where the task is to be executed. If omitted the command is scheduled locally.
id	Identifies the ID number assigned to a scheduled command.
[/delete]	Terminates a scheduled command. If id is not present, all scheduled tasks are terminated.
[/yes]	Requires a confirmation before terminating a scheduled task.
time	Identifies the time to execute the task expressed as hh:mm on a 24-hour clock.
[/interactive]	Permits interaction with the desktop and the logged on user.
/every:date[,...]	Establishes a schedule for task execution based on specified days of the week or month. The date is specified as M, T, W, Th, F, S, Su or 1 – 31. Multiple dates are separated by commas. If omitted, the schedule is set to the current day.
/next:date[,...]	Runs the task on the next occurrence of the day (M, T, W, Th, F, S, Su) or date (1 - 31). Multiple dates are separated by commas. If omitted the schedule is set to the current day.
command	Specifies the task to execute.

atmadm

Monitors connections and addresses and displays statistics for asynchronous transfer mode (ATM) networks.

Syntax

```
atmadm [-c][-a] [-s]
```

Parameters

Parameter	Purpose
[-c]	Lists information about the computer's established connections to the ATM network.
[-a]	Displays the registered ATM network service access point address for each ATM network interface on the computer.
[-s]	Provides statistical data for active ATM connections.

attrib

Lists or modifies file attributes.

Syntax

```
attrib [+r|-r] [+a|-a] [+s|-s] [+h|-h] [[drive:][path] filename]
[/s[/d]]
```

Parameters

Parameter	Purpose
[+r]	Specifies the read-only attribute.
[-r]	Clears the read-only attribute.
[+a]	Specifies the archive attribute.
[-a]	Clears the archive attribute.
[+s]	Identifies the file as a system file.
[-s]	Clears the system file attribute.
[+h]	Specifies the hidden file attribute.
[-h]	Clears the hidden file attribute.

continues

Parameters *(continued)*

Parameter	Purpose
[[*drive:*][*path*] *filename*]	Sets the drive, path, and file name to be processed.
[/s]	Applies changes to matching files in the current directory and all subdirectories.
[/d]	Processes directories.

cacls

Displays or changes file access control lists (ACLs).

Syntax

cacls *filename* [/t] [/e] [/c] [/g *user:perm*] [/r *user* [...]] [/p
user:perm [...]] [/d *user* [...]]

Parameters

Parameter	Purpose
filename	Displays a specified file's ACLs.
[/t]	Modifies the ACLs of specified files in the directory and its subdirectories.
[/e]	Edits an ACL rather than replacing it.
[/c]	Makes changes regardless of errors.
[/g *user:perm*]	Sets specified user access rights including: n - None r - Read c - Change f - Full Control
[/r *user*]	Removes user access rights.
[/p *user:perm*]	Replaces user access rights, including: n - None r - Read c - Change f - Full Control
[/d *user*]	Denies user access.

call

Calls a label or another script for execution as a procedure.

Syntax

```
call [drive:][path] filename [batch-parameters]
call :label [arguments]
```

Parameters

Parameter	Purpose
[drive:][path] filename	Sets the location and name of the script.
[batch-parameters]	Identifies the command-line information to be passed to the script.
label	Specifies a label within the script to jump.

chcp

Displays or modifies the active console code page number.

Syntax

```
chcp [nnn]
```

Parameters

Parameter	Purpose
None	Displays the active console code page number.
[nnn]	Specifies one of the following code pages:

437	United States
850	Multilingual (Latin I)
852	Slavic (Latin II)
855	Cyrillic (Russian)
857	Turkish
860	Portuguese
861	Icelandic
863	Canadian-French
865	Nordic
866	Russian
869	Modern Greek

chdir (cd)

Displays the current directory name or changes the current directory.

Syntax

```
chdir [/d] [drive:][path] [..]
cd [/d] [drive:][path] [..]
```

Parameters

Parameter	Purpose
None	Displays the names of the current drive and directory.
[/d]	Changes the current drive and directory.
[drive:][path]	Changes to a specified drive and directory.
[..]	Changes the current directory to the parent directory.

chkdsk

Displays disk status and corrects errors found on the specified disk.

Syntax

```
chkdsk [drive:][[path] filename] [/f] [/v] [/r] [/l[:size]] [/x]
```

Parameters

Parameter	Purpose
None	Displays disk status for the current drive.
[drive:]	Specifies the drive to be checked.
[path] filename	Specifies files(s) to be checked for fragmentation.
[/f]	Repairs disk errors.
[/v]	Displays the name of each file that is processed.
[/r]	Finds bad sectors and attempts to recover lost data.
/l[:size]	NTFS only. Displays or changes log file size on NTFS volumes.
[/x]	NTFS only. Forces the volume dismount on NTFS volumes.

Parameters

Parameter	Purpose
[/i]	NTFS only. Speeds up chkdsk by performing a less extensive check on NTFS volumes.
[/c]	NTFS only. Eliminates checking of cycles inside folders on NTFS volumes.

chkntfs

Displays or schedules the automatic system checking on a FAT, FAT32, or NTFS volumes during system initialization.

Syntax

```
chkntfs [/t[:time]] [/x] [/c] volume: [...]
chkntfs /d
```

Parameters

Parameter	Purpose
volume:	Displays file system type of the specified volume.
/d	Restores default settings.
[/t]	Displays or modifies remaining time for automatic file checking.
[/x]	Prevents a specified volume from being checked during system initialization.
[/c]	Specifies that the volume be checked during system initialization.

cipher

Displays or modifies folder and file encryption on NTFS volumes.

Syntax

```
cipher [/e| /d] [/s:dir] [/a][/i] [/f] [/q] [/h] [pathname [...]]
```

Parameters

Parameter	Purpose
None	Displays the current encryption status of the current folder and its contents.
[/e]	Encrypts the specified folders and turns on encryption for any files that may later be added to the folder.
[/d]	Decrypts the specified folders and turns off encryption for any files that may later be added to the folder.
[/s: *dir*]	Performs the specified operation on all folders and subfolders in the specified folder.
[/a]	Performs the specified operation on all specified files.
[/i]	Performs the specified operation even if errors occur.
[/f]	Encrypts or decrypts all specified objects regardless of their current encryption status.
[/q]	Limits reporting to essential information only.
[/h]	Displays files with hidden or system attributes.
[*pathname*]	Sets a folder, file, or pattern.

cls

Clears the command console screen and displays the command prompt and cursor.

Syntax

```
cls
```

cmd

Starts a new instance of the Windows shell.

Syntax

```
cmd [ [/c | /k] [/q] [/a | /u] [/t:fg] [/x | /y] string]
```

Parameters

Parameter	Purpose
[/c]	Exits the shell after executing the specified command.
[/k]	Executes the specified command and continues.
[/q]	Disables echoing.
[/a]	Formats output as ANSI characters.
[/u]	Formats output as Unicode characters.
[/t:*fg*]	Specifies foreground and background colors.
[/x]	Enables extensions to CMD.EXE that are used by assoc, call, cd, chdir, color, del, endlocal, erase, for, ftype, goto, if, md, mdir, popd, prompt, pushd, set, setlocal, shift, and start.
[/y]	Disables extensions to CMD.EXE for backward compatibility.
[*string*]	Sets the command to be executed.

color

Sets console foreground and background colors. Returns ERRORLEVEL 1 if you try to set the foreground and background colors to the same value.

Syntax

color *bf*

Parameters

Parameter	Purpose
none	Restores default colors.
B	Sets the background color based on a hexadecimal value.
f	Sets the foreground color based on a hexadecimal value.
	Hexadecimal color assignments include:
	0 Black
	1 Blue
	2 Green
	3 Aqua

continues

Parameters *(continued)*

Parameter	Purpose
4	Red
5	Purple
6	Yellow
7	White
8	Gray
9	Light blue
A	Light green
B	Light aqua
C	Light red
D	Light purple
E	Light yellow
F	Bright white

comp

Performs a comparison of two files or two sets of files on a byte-by-byte basis.

Syntax

comp [data1] [data2] [/d] [/a] [/l] [/n=number] [/c]

Parameters

Parameter	Purpose
[data1]	Sets the path and file name of the first file or set of files.
[data2]	Sets the path and file name of the second file or set of files.
[/d]	Displays any differences using a decimal format.
[/a]	Displays any differences in character format.
[/l]	Displays line numbers where differences occur.
[/n=number]	Compares the specified number of lines in both files.
[/c]	Performs a case-insensitive comparison.

compact

Displays and changes compression settings for files and folders on NTFS partitions.

Syntax

compact [/c|/u] [/s[:*dir*]] [/a] [/q] [/i] [/f] [*filename*[...]]

Parameters

Parameter	Purpose
None	Displays information of the compression state for the current folder.
[/c]	Compresses the folder or file.
[/u]	Uncompresses the folder or file.
[/s:*dir*]	Specifies that all subfolders should be processed.
[/a]	Displays hidden or system files.
[/q]	Limits reporting to essential information only.
[/i]	Specifies that errors should be ignored.
[/f]	Forces the compression or uncompression of the folder or file.
[*filename*]	Sets the file or directory.

convert

Converts FAT and FAT32 volumes to NTFS volumes.

Syntax

convert [*drive:*] /fs:ntfs [/v]

Parameters

Parameter	Purpose
[drive:]	Sets the drive to be converted.
/fs:ntfs	Sets that the volume be converted.
[/v]	Turns on verbose messaging.

copy

Copies one or more files.

Syntax

```
copy [/a | /b] source [/a | /b] [[/a | /b] + source [/a | /b] [+ ...]]
[/v] [/n] [/y | /-y] [/z] [/a | /b] [destination [/a | /b]]
```

Parameters

Parameter	Purpose
source	Specifies the file name of a file or set of files to be copied.
[destination]	Specifies the name and destination where the file is to be copied.
[/a]	Identifies the file as an ASCII text file.
[/b]	Identifies the file as a binary file.
[/v]	Verifies the success of the copy operation.
[/n]	Uses a short file name as the destination file's new file name.
[/y]	Suppresses any confirmation prompts.
[/-y]	Displays confirmation prompts.
[/z]	Turns on a restartable mode before copying network files so that if network connectivity is lost, the copy operation will resume when connectivity is re-established.

country

Configures the MS-DOS subsystem so that it can use international dates, time, currency, case conversions, and decimal separators.

Syntax

```
country=xxx[,[yyy][,[drive:][path] filename]]
```

Parameters

Parameter	Purpose
xxx	Identifies the Country/Region code.
[*yyy*]	Identifies Country/Region code page.
[*drive:*][*path*] *filename*	Sets the drive, path, and file name of the file that contains the Country/Region information.

date

Displays or changes the current date.

Syntax

```
date [mm-dd-yy]
date [/t]
```

Parameters

Parameter	Purpose
[*mm-dd-yy*]	Specifies the date.
	mm must be 1 -12
	dd must be 1 - 31
	yy must be 80 - 99 or 1980 - 2099
[/t]	Displays the date without prompting for a date change.

debug

Starts the Debug program used to test MS-DOS executables.

Syntax

```
debug [[drive:][path] filename [parameters]]
```

Parameters

Parameter	Purpose
[*drive:*][*path*] *filename*	Specifies the drive, path, and file name of the executable file to text.
[*parameters*]	Command-line parameters required by the executable file.

del (erase)

Deletes a file.

Syntax

```
del [drive:][path] filename [ ...] [/p] [/f] [/s] [/q]
[/a[:attributes]]
erase [drive:][path] filename [ ...] [/p] [/f] [/s] [/q]
[/a[:attributes]]
```

Parameters

Parameter	Purpose
[*drive:*][*path*] *filename*	Specifies the drive, path, and file name of the file(s) to delete.
[/p]	Prompts for confirmation.
[/f]	Deletes read-only files.
[/s]	Deletes files in the current folder and its subfolders.
[/q]	Suppresses the confirmation prompts.
[/a]	Deletes files based on file attributes.

device

Loads a device driver into memory.

Syntax

```
device=[drive:][path] filename [dd-parameters]
```

Parameters

Parameter	Purpose
[*drive:*][*path*] *filename*	Specifies the drive, path, and file name of the device driver.
[*dd-parameters*]	Command-line parameters required by the device driver.

devicehigh

Loads a device driver into the upper memory.

Syntax

devicehigh=[*drive:*][*path*] *filename* [*dd-parameters*]

Parameters

Parameter	Purpose
[*drive:*][*path*] *filename*	Specifies the drive, path, and file name of the device driver.
[*dd-parameters*]	Command-line parameters required by the device driver.

dir

Displays a directory file listing.

Syntax

dir [*drive:*][*path*][*filename*] [...] [/p] [/w] [/d] [/a[[:]*attribut-es*]][/o[[:]*sortorder*]] [/t[[:]*timefield*]] [/s] [/b] [/l] [/n] [/x] [/c]

Parameters

Parameter	Purpose
None	Displays the disk's volume label, serial number, and a listing of its contents.
[`drive:`] [`path`]	Specifies the drive and path for the folder to be displayed.
[`filename`]	Specifies a particular file(s) to be displayed.
[`/p`]	Displays data a screen at a time.
[`/w`]	Displays the folder listing in multiple columns.
[`/d`]	Same as `/w` but sorts files by column.
`/a` [[`:`] `attributes`]	Limits the displays to directories and files that match supplied attributes. The following attributes can be used:
	`h` Hidden files
	`s` System files
	`d` Directories
	`a` Files ready to be archived
	`r` Read-only files
	`-h` Non-hidden files
	`-s` Non-system files
	`-d` Only display files
	`-a` Files without changes since the last backup
	`-r` Non-read-only files
`/o` [[`:`] `sortorder`]	Specifies the sort order used to display directory and file names. The following options can be used:
	`n` Alphabetically by name
	`e` Alphabetically by extension
	`d` By date and time
	`s` By size
	`g` Show folders before files
	`-n` Reverse alphabetical order by name
	`-e` Reverse alphabetical order by extension
	`-d` By reverse date and time
	`-s` By reverse size

Parameters

Parameter	Purpose
`-g`	Show folders after files
`/t [[:]timefield]`	Determines the time field used to display or sort the listing. Valid options:
	c Creation time
	a Last access time
	w Last written time
`[/s]`	Lists every occurrence of the specified file name
`[/b]`	Lists each directory or file name
`[/l]`	Displays unsorted lowercase folder and file names
`[/n]`	`Displays a long list format`
`[/x]`	Displays the short names
`[/c]`	Displays the thousand separator (comma) when showing file sizes

`diskcomp`

Compares the contents of two floppy disks.

Syntax

```
diskcomp [drive1: [drive2:]]
```

Parameters

Parameter	Purpose
`[drive1]`	Identifies the location of the first disk.
`[drive2]`	Identifies the location of the second disk.

`diskcopy`

Copies the contents of a source disk to a destination disk.

Syntax

```
diskcopy [drive1: [drive2:]] [/v]
```

Parameters

Parameter	Purpose
[drive1]	Identifies the location of the source disk.
[drive2]	Identifies the location of the destination disk.
[/v]	Verifies a successful copy operation.

diskperf

Specifies the types of counters that can be used with the System Monitor.

Syntax

```
diskperf [-y[d|v]|-n[d|v] [\\computername]
```

Parameters

Parameter	Purpose
None	Displays the status of performance counters.
[-y]	Specifies that the physical and logical disk performance counters should be started at system initialization.
[-yd]	Enables disk performance counters for physical drives at system initialization.
[-yv]	Enables disk performance counters for logical drives at system initialization.
[-n]	Prevents disk performance counters from start at system initialization.
[-nd]	Disables physical drive disk performance counters at system initialization.
[-nv]	Disables logical drive disk performance counters at system initialization.
[\\computername]	Allows you to specify a network computer for viewing.

dos

Allows the MS-DOS subsystem to maintain a link with the upper memory area (UMA) or to load part of itself into high memory area (HMA).

A WINDOWS COMMAND REFERENCE   *Appendix A*   **399**

Syntax

```
dos=high|low[,umb|,noumb]
dos=[high,|low,]umb|noumb
```

Parameters

Parameter	Purpose
high|low	Specifies where the MS-DOS subsystem should load itself.
[umb|noumb]	Sets the MS-DOS subsystem link with conventional memory and UMA.

doskey

Executes the Doskey program, which recalls commands and creates macros.

Syntax

```
doskey [/reinstall] [/listsize=size] [/macros:[all | exename]] [/history] [/insert|/overstrike] [/exename=exename] [/macrofile=filename]
[macroname=[text]]
```

Parameters

Parameter	Purpose
[/reinstall]	Installs a new copy of Doskey.
[/listsize=size]	Sets the maximum number of commands contained in the history buffer.
[/macros]	Displays macros.
[all]	Displays macros for all executables.
[exename]	Displays the specified executable's macro.
[/history]	Displays commands currently stored in memory.
[/insert | /overstrike]	Specifies the insert mode.
[/exename=exename]	Identifies the program that will run the macro.
[/macrofile=filename]	Identifies the file that contains macros to be installed.
[macroname=[text]]	Creates a macro and assigns the commands set by text.

dosonly

Prevents non-MS-DOS applications from being executed at COMMAND.COM.

Syntax

```
dosonly
```

echo

Displays a message or enables and disables command echoing.

Syntax

```
echo [on | off] [message]
```

Parameters

Parameter	Purpose
None	Displays the current echo setting.
on | off	Turns command echoing on or off.
[message]	Specifies text to be displayed.

echoconfig

Displays messages when processing the MS-DOS subsystem CONFIG.NT and AUTOEXEC.NT files during the initialization of the MS-DOS subsystem.

Syntax

```
echoconfig
```

edit

Starts the MS-DOS editor.

Syntax

```
edit [[drive:][path] filename] [/b] [/g] [/h] [/nohi]
```

Parameters

Parameter	Purpose
[*drive:*][*path*] *filename*	Specifies the drive, path, and file name of a text file and creates it if it does not exist.
[/b]	Displays the MS-DOS editor with a black background and white foreground.
[/g]	Speeds up screen updating on a CGA monitor.
[/h]	Displays the number of lines that can be displayed for your monitor.
[/nohi]	Changes from a 16-color to an 8-color scheme.

edlin

Starts a line-oriented ASCII text editor.

Syntax

```
edlin [drive:][path] filename [/b]
```

Parameters

Parameter	Purpose
[*drive:*][*path*] *filename*	Specifies the drive, path, and file name of an ASCII file.
[/b]	Instructs edlin to ignore the end-of-file characters.

endlocal

Ends localization of environment changes in a scripts and restores environment variables to their previous values.

Syntax

```
endlocal
```

evntcmd

Displays SNMP events.

Syntax

```
evntcmd [/?|/h] [/s sysname][/v number][/n]
```

Parameters

Parameter	Purpose
[/?|/h]	Displays help.
[/s sysname]	Sets the target system name.
[/v number]	Sets the level of messaging: 0=none; 10=detailed.
[/n]	Prevents the restart the SNMP service when trap changes are received.

exit

Terminates a Windows shell session.

Syntax

```
exit
```

expand

Uncompresses compressed files from distribution disks.

Syntax

```
expand [-r] source [destination]
expand -d source.cab [-f:files]
expand source.cab -f:files destination
```

Parameters

Parameter	Purpose
[-r]	Renames files as it expands them.
-d	Displays the list of files at the specified source location.
[-f:*files*]	Specifies the files in a .CAB that are to be expanded.
source	Specifies the location of the files to expand.
[*destination*]	Specifies the location where files are to be expanded.

fc

Compares two files and reports on their differences.

Syntax

```
fc [/a] [/b] [/c] [/l] [/lbn] [/n] [/t] [/u] [/w] [/nnnn]
[drive1:][path1]filename1 [drive2:][path2]filename2
fc /b [drive1:][path1]filename1 [drive2:][path2]filename2
```

Parameters

Parameter	Purpose
[/a]	Displays the first and last line for each set of differences.
[/b]	Performs a comparison of the files in binary mode.
[/c]	Ignores differences in case.
[/l]	Performs a comparison of the files in ASCII mode.
[/lbn]	Specifies the number of lines used by the internal line buffer. This value must be greater than or equal to the number of differing lines in the files being compared.
[/n]	Displays the line numbers.
[/t]	Prevents the expansion of tabs into spaces.
[/u]	Performs a comparison of the files as Unicode text files.

continues

Parameters *(continued)*

Parameter	Purpose
[/w]	Compresses white space during the comparison.
[/*nnnn*]	Sets the number of consecutive lines that must be matched before the two files are identified as resynchronized.
[*drive1*:][*path1*]*filename1*	Sets the drive, path, and file name of the first file.
[*drive2*:][*path2*]*filename2*	Sets the drive, path, and file name of the second file.

fcbs

Sets a limit on the number of file control blocks (FCBs) that the MS-DOS subsystem access simultaneously.

Syntax

```
fcbs=x
```

Parameters

Parameter	Purpose
x	Sets the number of FCBs with a maximum setting of 255.

files

Limits the number of files that the MS-DOS subsystem can open at one time.

Syntax

```
files=x
```

Parameters

Parameter	Purpose
x	Sets the number of files with a maximum setting of 255.

find

Searches for a string of text in a file(s) and displays any matches.

Syntax

```
find [/v] [/c] [/n] [/i] "string" [[drive:][path]filename[...]]
```

Parameters

Parameter	Purpose
[/v]	Displays lines that do not match the string.
[/c]	Displays a count of matching lines.
[/n]	Displays a line before each line.
[/i]	Performs a case-insensitive search.
"string"	Specifies the string to search for.
[drive:][path] filename	Specifies the drive, path, and file name of the file to be searched.

findstr

Searches for strings in files using regular expressions.

Syntax

```
findstr [/b] [/e] [/l] [/c:string] [/r] [/s] [/i] [/x] [/v] [/n] [/m]
[/o] [/g:file] [/f:file] [/d:dirlist] [/a:color attribute] [strings]
[[drive:][path] filename [...]]
```

Parameters

Parameter	Purpose
[/b]	Specifies that the match must occur at the beginning of a line.
[/e]	Specifies that the match must occur at the end of a line.
[/l]	Performs a literal search using the search string.
[/c: string]	Uses the specified string as a literal search string.
[/r]	Uses search strings as regular expressions.

continues

Parameters *(continued)*

Parameter	Purpose
[/s]	Searches for matches in the current folder and all subdirectories.
[/I]	Specifies a case-insensitive search.
[/x]	Prints lines that contain a match.
[/v]	Prints lines that do not contain a match.
[/n]	Prints the line number.
[/m]	Prints the file name where a match is found.
[/o]	Prints the seek offset before each match.
[/g *file*]	Specifies a file that contains the search strings.
[/f *file*]	Specifies a file that contains a file list.
[/d *dirlist*]	Searches a comma-delimited list of folders.
[/a *color attribute*]	Specifies two character hexadecimal color attributes.

finger

Displays user information on a specified system running the Finger service.

Syntax

```
finger [-l] [user]@computer [...]
```

Parameters

Parameter	Purpose
[-l]	Provides information using a long list format.
[*User*]	Specifies a user. If omitted, information about all users is displayed.
@*computer*	Specifies the computer where the information is to be collected.

for

Executes a command for each file in a set of files.

Syntax

```
for %%variable in (set) do command [command-parameters]
```

Parameters

Parameter	Purpose
%%variable	Specifies a parameter that the for command replaces with each text string in the specified set until all files have been processed.
(set)	Specifies a file(s) or text string(s) to process.
command	Specifies the command to be executed in each file in the set.
[command-parameters]	Provides parameters to be used by the specified command.

forcedos

Starts a program using the MS-DOS subsystem.

Syntax

```
forcedos [/d directory] filename [parameters]
```

Parameters

Parameter	Purpose
[/d directory]	Sets the directory to be used by the specified program.
filename	Identifies the program to be started.
[parameters]	Provides parameters to be used by the specified program.

format

Formats a disk.

Syntax

```
format volume [/fs:file-system] [/v:label] [/q] [/a:unitsize] [/f:size]
[/t:tracks /n:sectors] [/c] [/x] [/1] [/4] [/8]
```

Parameters

Parameter	Purpose
`volume:`	Sets the mount point, volume, or drive to be formatted.
`[/fs:file-system]`	Specifies one of the following file systems: FAT, FAT32, or NTFS.
`[/v:label]`	Sets the volume label.
`[/a:unitsize]`	Sets the allocation unit size to use on FAT, FAT32, or NTFS volumes.
`[/q]`	Performs a quick format.
`[/f:size]`	Specifies the size of the floppy disk.
`[/t:tracks]`	Specifies the number of tracks on the disk.
`[/n:sectors]`	Specifies the number of sectors per track.
`[/c]`	Specifies that files created on the new volume should automatically compress.
`[/x]`	Automatically dismount a volume if required before formatting it.
`[/1]`	Formats one side of a floppy disk.
`[/4]`	Formats 5.25-inch, 360KB, double-sided, double-density floppy disks on a 1.2-MB disk drive.
`[/8]`	Formats a 5.25-inch disk with eight sectors per track as required by MS-DOS version 2 and earlier.

ftp

Transfers files to and from a computer running an FTP service.

Syntax

```
ftp [-v] [-n] [-i] [-d] [-g] [-s:filename] [-a] [-w:windowsize] [com-
puter]
```

Parameters

Parameter	Purpose
[-v]	Prevents the display of remote server messages.
[-n]	Suppresses autologin upon the initial connection.
[-i]	Prevents interactive prompting for multiple file transfers.
[-d]	Enables debugging.
[-g]	Permits the use of wildcard characters in local file and path names.
[-s:*filename*]	Identifies a text file that contains FTP commands that should be automatically executed when the FTP session starts.
[-a]	Uses any local interface to bind data connection.
[-w:*windowsize*]	Changes the default transfer buffer size from 4096 to a new value.
[*computer*]	Specifies a remote computer to connect to.

ftype

Displays or modifies file types used to associate file name extensions.

Syntax

```
Ftype [filetype[=[command]]]
```

Parameters

Parameter	Purpose
[*filetype*]	Specifies the file type you want to work with.
[*command*]	Specifies the open command that is used to open files of this type.

goto

Instructs the shell to jump to a label in a script and begins processing commands starting with the next line.

Syntax

```
goto label
```

Parameter

Parameter	Purpose
label	Identifies the line in a script where the shell should jump to.

graftabl

Instructs Windows to display the extended characters from a specified code page in full screen mode.

Syntax

```
graftabl [xxx] [/status]
```

Parameters

Parameter	Purpose
[*xxx*]	Specifies the code page. Valid options are:
	437 United States
	850 Multilingual (Latin I)
	852 Slavic (Latin II)
	855 Cyrillic (Russian)
	857 Turkish
	860 Portuguese
	861 Icelandic
	863 Canadian-French
	865 Nordic
	866 Russian
	869 Modern Greek
[/status]	Identifies the currently selected code page.

graphics

Allows you to print the contents of the command shell Window to a printer.

Syntax

```
graphics [type] [[drive:][path] filename] [/r] [/b] [/lcd]
[/printbox:std | /printbox:lcd]
```

Parameters

Parameter	Purpose	
[*type*]	Specifies printer type.	Valid options are:
	color1	IBM PC color printer with black ribbon
	color4	IBM PC color printer with RGB ribbon
	color8	IBM PC color printer with CMY ribbon
	hpdefault	Any Hewlett-Packard PCL printer
	deskjet	Hewlett-Packard DeskJet printer
	graphics	IBM personal graphics printer, IBM Proprinter, or IBM Quietwriter printer
	graphicswide	IBM personal graphics printer with an 11-inch wide carriage
	laserjet	Hewlett-Packard LaserJet printer
	laserjetii	Hewlett-Packard LaserJet II printer
	paintjet	Hewlett-Packard PaintJet printer
	quietjet	Hewlett-Packard QuietJet printer
	quietjetplu	Hewlett-Packard QuietJet Plus printer
	ruggedwriter	Hewlett-Packard RuggedWriter printer
	ruggedwriterwide	Hewlett-Packard RuggedWriterwide printer
	thermal	IBM PC convertible Thermal printer
	thinkjet	Hewlett-Packard ThinkJet printer
[*drive:*] [*path*] *filename*	Specifies the drive, path, and file name of the printer profile.	
[/r]	Prints the image as displayed on the screen.	
[/b]	Prints the background in color.	
[/lcd]	Prints an image using the LCD aspect ratio.	
[/printbox:std | /printbox:lcd]	Selects the printbox size.	

help

Provides online information about commands.

Syntax

```
help [command]
```

Parameter

Parameter	Purpose
[command]	Specifies the command.

hostname

Displays the TCP/IP name of the computer.

Syntax

```
hostname
```

if

Supports conditional logic in scripts.

Syntax

```
if [not] errorlevel number command [else expression]
if [not] string1==string2 command [else expression]
if [not] exist filename command [else expression]
if [/i] string1 compare-op string2 command [else expression]
if cmdextversion number command [else expression]
if defined variable command [else expression]
```

Parameters

Parameter	Purpose
[not]	Reverses the test condition.
errorlevel number	Sets a true condition if the previous program returned an exit code equal to or greater than number.
command	Identifies a command that the shell is to execute if the preceding condition is satisfied.

Parameters

Parameter	Purpose
string1==string2	Specifies a true condition when *string1* and *string2* are the same.
exist *filename*	Specifies a true condition when a *filename* exists.
compare-op	Can be any of the following operators:
	EQU equal to
	NEQ not equal to
	LSS less than
	LEQ less than or equal to
	GTR greater than
	GEQ greater than or equal to
[/i]	Forces case-insensitive string comparisons.
cmdextversion *number*	Compares the internal version number associated with CMD.EXE to the specified number.
defined *variable*	Returns true if the environment variable is defined.
[*else expression*]	Specifies the command and any parameters that need to be passed to the command.

install

Loads memory-resident programs into memory.

Syntax

```
install=[drive:][path] filename [command-parameters]
```

Parameters

Parameter	Purpose
[*drive:*][*path*] *filename*	Specifies the drive, path, and file name of the memory-resident program.
[*command-parameters*]	Specifies parameters to be passed to the program.

ipconfig

A diagnostic command that displays current TCP/IP network configuration settings.

Syntax

```
ipconfig [/all | /renew [adapter] | /release [adapter]]
```

Parameters

Parameter	Purpose
None	Displays the IP address, subnet mask, and default gateway for each network interface.
[/all]	Produces all available configuration information.
/renew [adapter]	Submits a request to renew the DHCP configuration parameters.
/release [adapter]	Discards the current DHCP configuration.

ipxroute

Displays and changes information about IPX routing tables.

Syntax

```
ipxroute servers [/type=x]
ipxroute stats [/show] [/clear]
ipxroute table
```

Parameters

Parameter	Purpose
servers [/type=x]	Displays the Service Access Point (SAP) table.
stats [/show] [/clear]	Displays or clears IPX router interface statistics.
table	Displays the IPX routing table.

irftp

Sends and receives data over an infrared link.

Syntax

```
irftp [/h] [[drive:][path]filename [morefiles]]
irftp /s
```

Parameters

Parameter	Purpose
/h	Specifies hidden mode, which prevents the display of the Wireless Link dialog box.
[[drive:][path]filename [morefiles]	The drive, path, and file names you want to transmit.
/s	Opens Wireless link properties.

label

Creates, deletes, or modifies a disk's volume label.

Syntax

```
label [drive:][label]
```

Parameters

Parameter	Purpose
none	Instructs the shell to prompt you to change or delete the current label.
[drive:]	Specifies a disk.
[label]	Specifies a new volume label.

loadfix

Loads a program above the first 64KB of conventional memory and executes it.

Syntax

```
loadfix [drive:][path] filename
```

Parameters

Parameter	Purpose
[drive:][path]	Specifies the drive and path of the program.
filename	Specifies the program name.

lpq

A diagnostic utility that provides status information about a print queue on a computer running the LPD server.

Syntax

lpq -SServer -PPrinter [-1]

Parameters

Parameter	Purpose
-SServer	Specifies computer name.
-PPrinter	Specifies the printer name.
[-1]	Provides for a detailed status.

lpr

A utility used to submit a print file to a computer running an LPD server.

Syntax

lpr -SServer -PPrinter [-CClass] [-JJobname] [-O option] filename

Parameters

Parameter	Purpose
-SServer	Specifies the computer name or IP address of the computer where the printer is located.
-PPrinter	Specifies the printer name.
[-CClass]	Specifies banner page content for the class.
[-JJobname]	Specifies the print job name.

Parameters

Parameter	Purpose
[-O *option*]	Specifies the file type. Text is the default.
filename	Specifies the file to be printed.

mem

Displays information about memory usage of programs loaded into memory in the MS-DOS subsystem.

Syntax

```
mem [/program|/debug|/classify]
```

Parameters

Parameter	Purpose
None	Displays the MS-DOS subsystem memory status.
/program	Displays the status of programs loaded into memory. This switch is mutually exclusive with the other switches.
/debug	Displays the status currently loaded programs and internal drivers. This switch is mutually exclusive with the other switches.
/classify	Displays the status of programs loaded into conventional memory and the upper memory area. This switch is mutually exclusive with the other switches.

mkdir (md)

Creates a directory or subdirectory.

Syntax

```
mkdir [drive:]path
md [drive:]path
```

Parameters

Parameter	Purpose
[*drive:*]	Specifies the drive where the new folder is to be created.
path	Specifies the folder's name and path.

more

Displays output one screen at a time.

Syntax

```
command name | more [/c] [/p] [/s] [/tn] [+n]
more [[/c] [/p] [/s] [/tn] [+n]] < [drive:] [path] filename
more [/c] [/p] [/s] [/tn] [+n] [files]
```

Parameters

Parameter	Purpose
[*drive:*] [*path*] *filename*	Specifies a file to display.
command name	Specifies a command to execute and display its output.
[/c]	Clears the screen.
[/p]	Expands form-feed characters.
[/s]	Removes multiple blank lines from the display.
[/t*n*]	Changes tabs to the specified number of spaces.
[+*n*]	Displays the file beginning on line *n*.
[*files*]	Specifies a collection of files to display.

mountvol

Creates, deletes, or displays a volume mount point.

Syntax

```
mountvol [drive:]path VolumeName
mountvol [drive:]path /d
mountvol [drive:]path /l
```

Parameters

Parameter	Purpose
`[drive:]path`	Specifies an NTFS folder to contain the mount point.
`VolumeName`	Identifies the volume name that is the target of the mount point.
`/d`	Removes a volume mount point in the specified folder.
`/l`	Displays the mounted volume name in the specified folder.

move

Moves one or more files from one location to another.

Syntax

```
move [/y | /-y] [source] [target]
```

Parameters

Parameter	Purpose
`[/y]`	Suppresses confirmation prompts.
`[/-y]`	Enables confirmation prompting.
`[source]`	Specifies the location of the source file(s) to be moved.
`[target]`	Specifies the destination location of the file(s).

nbtstat

Displays current TCP/IP connections and statistics using NetBIOS over TCP/IP.

Syntax

```
nbtstat [-a remotename] [-A IP address] [-c] [-n] [-R] [-r] [-S] [-s]
[interval]
```

Parameters

Parameter	Purpose
[-a *remotename1*]	Displays a remote computer's name table using its name.
[-A *IP address*]	Displays a remote computer's name table using its IP address.
[-c]	Displays the contents of the NetBIOS name cache.
[-n]	Displays local NetBIOS names.
[-R]	Purges all names from the NetBIOS name cache and reloads the Lmhosts file.
[-r]	Displays name-resolution statistics.
[-S]	Displays client and server sessions in the form of IP addresses.
[-s]	Attempts to display client and server sessions using host names.
[*interval*]	Displays statistics at the specified *interval* (in seconds).

net accounts

Modifies the user accounts database and changes logon and password requirements.

Syntax

```
net accounts [/forcelogoff:{minutes | no}] [/minpwlen:length] [/maxp-
wage:{days | unlimited}] [/minpwage:days] [/uniquepw:number] [/domain]
net accounts [/sync] [/domain]
```

Parameters

Parameter	Purpose
None	Displays current domain, logon, and password settings.
[/forcelogoff:{*minutes*	no}]	Specifies a number of minutes to wait before terminating a user session with a server when the user's logon time expires. No prevents a forced logoff.
[/minpwlen:*length*]	Sets the minimum password length.
[/maxpwage:{*days*	unlimited}]	Sets a password expiration period.
[/minpwage:*days*]	Specifies a minimum number of days that must pass before a user can change passwords.

Parameters

Parameter	Purpose
[/uniquepw:*number*]	Establishes a password history requirement that prevents users from reusing a password for the specified number of times.
[/*domain*]	Specifies that the operation should occur on a domain controller instead of locally.
[/sync]	Causes the primary domain controller to synchronize with all the backup domain controllers.

net computer

Adds or deletes computer accounts in the domain database.

Syntax

```
net computer \\computername {/add | /del}
```

Parameters

Parameter	Purpose
computername	Specifies the computer to be added or deleted.
/add	Adds the computer.
/del	Deletes the computer.

net config

Displays and changes configurable active services.

Syntax

```
net config [service [options]]
```

Parameters

Parameter	Purpose
None	Displays a list of configurable services.
[service]	Specifies the service to be configured.
[options]	Sets options specific to the service.

net continue

Reactivates a suspended service.

Syntax

```
net continue service
```

Parameters

Parameter	Purpose
service	Sets the server to reactivate.

net file

Displays a list of all open shared files on a server and the number of file locks on each file.

Syntax

```
net file [id [/close]]
```

Parameters

Parameter	Purpose
None	Displays a list of the open files on a server.
id	Identifies the number of the file.
[/close]	Closes an open file and releases any locked records.

net group

Adds, displays, or changes global groups on Windows domains.

Syntax

```
net group [groupname [/comment:"text"]] [/domain]
net group groupname {/add [/comment:"text"] | /delete} [/domain]
net group groupname username[ ...] {/add | /delete} [/domain]
```

Parameters

Parameter	Purpose
None	Displays a list of groups on the server.
[groupname]	Specifies a group name to add, expand, or delete.
[/comment:"text"]	Adds a comment for a new or existing group.
[/domain]	Performs the operation on the primary domain controller instead of locally.
username[...]	Lists one or more user names to be added or removed from a group.
[/add]	Adds a group or a user name to a group.
[/delete]	Deletes a group or user name from a group.

net help

Lists network commands for which help is available and provides help for specified network commands.

Syntax

```
net help [command]
net command {/help | /?}
```

Parameters

Parameter	Purpose
None	Displays a list of network commands and topics for which help is available.
[command]	Specifies a command to retrieve help for.
{/help	/?}	Displays syntax for the command.

net helpmsg

Provides help with Windows error messages.

Syntax

```
net helpmsg message#
```

Parameter

Parameter	Purpose
message#	Specifies the four-digit number of the error message.

net localgroup

Adds, displays, or modifies local groups.

Syntax

```
net localgroup [groupname [/comment:"text"]] [/domain]
net localgroup groupname {/add [/comment:"text"] | /delete} [/domain]
net localgroup groupname name [ ...] {/add | /delete} [/domain]
```

Parameters

Parameter	Purpose
None	Displays the name of the server and local groups on the server.
[groupname]	Specifies the name of the local group.
[/comment:"text"]	Adds or changes a comment for a new or existing group.
[/domain]	Performs the operation on the primary domain controller instead of locally.
name [...]	Lists one or more user names or group names to be added or removed from a local group.
/add	Adds either a user name or a global group to a local group.
/delete	Removes a user name or group name from a local group.

net name

Displays the list of computer names that will accept messages or adds or removes a messaging name.

Syntax

```
net name [name [/add | /delete]]
```

Parameters

Parameter	Purpose
None	Displays a list of names already in use.
[name]	Specifies a name to a computer.
[/add]	Adds a name to the computer.
[/delete]	Removes a name from the computer.

net pause

Pauses active services.

Syntax

```
net pause service
```

Parameter

Parameter	Purpose
service	Name of the service.

net print

Lists or manages print jobs and printer queues.

Syntax

```
net print \\computername\sharename
net print [\\computername] job# [/hold | /release | /delete]
```

Parameters

Parameter	Purpose
computername	Specifies the name of the computer that manages the printer queue.
sharename	Specifies the name of the printer queue.
job#	Specifies the ID number assigned to a print job.
[/hold]	Places a print job on hold.
[/release]	Releases a print job from a hold status.
[/delete]	Deletes a print job.

net send

Sends messages to users, computers, and messaging names.

Syntax

```
net send {name | * | /domain[:name] | /users} message
```

Parameters

Parameter	Purpose
name	Specifies a user name, computer name, or messaging name.
*	Sends the message to all names in the domain or your workgroup.
/domain[:name]	If name is not specified it sends the message to all the names in the domain. If name is specified, the message is sent to all the names in the specified domain or workgroup.
/users	Sends message to all users currently connected to the server.
message	Specifies the message text.

net session

Lists or terminates sessions with clients connected to the computer.

Syntax

```
net session [\\computername] [/delete]
```

Parameters

Parameter	Purpose
None	Displays information about all active sessions.
[*computername*]	Identifies a specific network computer.
[/delete]	Terminates a session with *computername* and then closes all open files on the computer for the session.

net share

Creates, deletes, and displays shared resources.

Syntax

```
net share sharename
net share sharename=drive:path [/users:number | /unlimited]
[/remark:"text"]
net share sharename [/users:number | unlimited] [/remark:"text"]
net share {sharename | drive:path} /delete
```

Parameters

Parameter	Purpose
None	Displays information about all resources that are currently shared on the computer.
sharename	Specifies the name assigned to the shared resource.
drive:path	Specifies the absolute path of the folder to be shared.
/users:*number*	Limits the maximum number of users who can simultaneously access the share.
/unlimited	Allows unlimited simultaneous access to the share.
/remark:"*text*"	Adds a comment to the shared resource.
/delete	Terminates the sharing of a resource.

net start

Displays a list of started services. It is also used to start services.

Syntax

```
net start [service]
```

Parameters

Parameter	Purpose
None	Displays a list of active services.
[service]	Specifies the name of a service to start.

net statistics

Displays log statistics for the local workstation service or server service or any other services for which statistics are available.

Syntax

```
net statistics [workstation | server]
```

Parameters

Parameter	Purpose
None	Displays a list of the active services that provide statistics.
[workstation]	Displays local workstation service statistics.
[server]	Displays local server service statistics.

net stop

Terminates a network service.

Syntax

```
net stop service
```

Parameters

Parameter	Purpose
Service	Specifies any valid Windows NT or 2000 service.

net time

Synchronizes the computer's internal clock with another computer's clock.

Syntax

```
net time [\\computername | /domain[:domainname] | /rtsdomain[:domain-
name]] [/set]
net time [\\computername] [/querysntp] | [/setsntp[:ntp server list]]
```

Parameters

Parameter	Purpose
None	Displays the date and time as set on the computer designated as the network's time server.
\\computername	Specifies the name of a network server.
/domain[:domainname]	Specifies a domain to synchronize with.
/rtsdomain[:domainname]	Specifies a domain of the Reliable Time Server to synchronize with.
/set	Synchronizes the computer's internal clock with the specified computer or domain.
/querysntp	Displays the name of the Network Time Protocol server.
/setsntp[:ntp server list]	Specifies a list of Network Time Protocol servers to be used using host names of IP addresses.

net use

Displays information about network connections and connects a computer to network resources.

Syntax

```
net use [devicename | *] [\\computername\sharename[\volume]] [password
| *]] [/user:[domainname\]username] [[/delete] | [/persistent:{yes |
no}]]
net use devicename [/home[password | *]] [/delete:{yes | no}]
net use [/persistent:{yes | no}]
```

Parameters

Parameter	Purpose
None	Displays a list of network connections.
[*devicename*]	Assigns a name to a new connection or specifies a device that is to be disconnected. For disk drives, use the D: through Z: and for printers use LPT1: through LPT3:.
[*computername**sharename*]	Specifies the name of the network computer and its shared resource.
[*volume*]	Specifies a server with a NetWare volume.
[*password*]	Specifies a password required to access the resource.
[*]	Specifies that you want to be prompted for the password.
[/user]	Specifies a different user name to be used when making the connection.
[*domainname*]	Allows you to specify another domain.
[*username*]	Specifies the user name to use when logging on.
[/delete]	Terminates a network connection.
[/persistent]	Allows you to define persistent connections that span system restarts.
[yes]	Restores the connection at next logon.
[no]	Doesn't restore the connection at next logon.

net user

Displays user account information or adds and modifies user accounts.

Syntax

```
net user [username [password | *] [options]] [/domain]
net user username {password | *} /add [options] [/domain]
net user username [/delete] [/domain]
```

Parameters

Parameter	Purpose
`None`	Displays a list of user accounts on the local computer.
`[username]`	Specifies the account name to add, delete, change, or view.
`[password]`	Assigns a password to a new account or changes the password of an existing account.
`*`	Prompts for the password.
`[/domain]`	Performs the operation on the primary domain controller instead of locally.
`/add`	Adds a user account.
`[/delete]`	Deletes a user account.
`[options]`	Specifies any of the following options:
`/active:{no	yes}`	Enables or disables the account.
`/comment:"text"`	Adds comments to an account.
`/countrycode:nnn`	Specifies the Country/Region codes to be used for help and error messages.
`/expires:{date	never}`	Specifies the status of account expiration.
`/fullname:"name"`	Sets a user's full name rather than a user name.
`/homedir:path`	Establishes the user's home directory.
`/passwordchg:{yes	no}`	Determines whether the users can change their passwords.
`/passwordreq:{yes	no}`	Specifies a password requirement.
`/profilepath:[path]`	Establishes the user's logon profile.
`/scriptpath:path`	Establishes the path for the user's logon script.
`/times:{times	all}`	Defines time frames in which the user is permitted to use the computer. For example: W,8AM-5PM; F,8AM-1PM.
`/usercomment:"text"`	Determines whether an administrator can change or add to the user comment.
`/workstations: {computername[,...]	*}`	Specifies up to eight workstations where the user is permitted to log on.

net view

Displays a list of domains, computers, or resources being shared by a specified computer.

Syntax

```
net view [\\computername | /domain[:domainname]]
net view /network:nw [\\computername]
```

Parameters

Parameter	Purpose
None	Displays a list of computers in the domain.
[\\computername]	Specifies a computer so that its resources can be viewed.
/domain[:domainname]	Specifies the domain that is to be viewed.
/network:nw	Displays servers on a Novell NetWare network.

netstat

Displays statistics for current TCP/IP connections.

Syntax

```
netstat [-a] [-e] [-n] [-s] [-p protocol] [-r] [interval]
```

Parameters

Parameter	Purpose
[-a]	Displays all connections.
[-e]	Displays Ethernet-related statistics.
[-n]	Displays IP addresses and port numbers in numerical form.
[-s]	Displays per-protocol statistics for TCP, UDP, ICMP, and IP.
[-p protocol]	Shows connections for the specified TCP/IP protocol.
[-r]	Displays the routing table.
[interval]	Displays statistics at the specified interval (in seconds).

nslookup

Display information from Domain Name System name servers.

Syntax

```
nslookup [-option ...] [computer-to-find | - [server]]
```

Parameters

Parameter	Purpose
[-option ...]	Specifies nslookup commands to be used as command-line options.
[computer-to-find]	Displays information for computer-to-find using the default DNS server.
[server]	Specifies a different DNS server to query.

ntcmdprompt

Runs CMD.EXE instead of COMMAND.COM after starting a TSR.

Syntax

```
ntcmdprompt
```

path

Establishes a search path for executable files.

Syntax

```
path [[drive:]path[;...]] [%path%]
```

Parameters

Parameter	Purpose
None	Displays the current search path.
[drive:]path	Specifies a location to search.
;	If used as the only parameter, it clears all path settings.
[%path%]	Appends the current path to the new setting.

pathping

A route-tracing command that combines the functionality of the ping and tracert commands.

Syntax

pathping [-n] [-h maximum_hops] [-g host-list] [-p period] [-q num_queries [-w timeout] [-T] [-R] target_name

Parameters

Parameter	Purpose
-n	Specifies not to resolve addresses to host names.
-h maximum_hops	Specifies a maximum number of hops when trying to reach the target.
-g host-list	Allows computers to be separated by intermediate gateways along host-list.
-p period	Specifies the time to wait (in milliseconds) between pings.
-q num_queries	Specifies the number of queries allowed for servers along the route.
-w timeout	Specifies the length of time to wait for a reply (in milliseconds).
-T	Includes a layer-2 priority tag to each ping packet that is sent to network devices along the route.
-R	Determines whether each network device on the route supports the Resource Reservation Setup Protocol (RSVP).
target_name	Specifies the destination target using either its host name or its IP address.

pause

Suspends processing of a script and prompts the user to press any key to continue.

Syntax

```
pause
```

pentnt

Looks for the floating-point division error in the Pentium chip, disables floating-point hardware, and turns on floating-point emulation if found.

Syntax

```
pentnt [-c] [-f] [-o] [-?|-h]
```

Parameters

Parameter	Purpose
[-c]	Turns on conditional emulation.
[-f]	Turns on forced emulation.
[-o]	Turns off forced emulation and turns on floating-point hardware.
[-?|-h]	Displays command help.

ping

Tests connections with network devices on TCP/IP networks.

Syntax

```
ping [-t] [-a] [-n count] [-l length] [-f] [-i ttl] [-v tos] [-r count]
[-s count] [[-j computer-list] | [-k computer-list]] [-w timeout]
destination-list
```

Parameters

Parameter	Purpose
`[-t]`	Repeatedly pings the specified computer.
`[-a]`	Resolves IP addresses to computer names.
`[-n count]`	Sends the specified number of ECHO packets as defined by `count`.
`[-l length]`	Transmits ECHO packets of the specified `length`.
`[-f]`	Prevents packets from being fragmented by gateways.
`[-i ttl]`	Sets the TTL field to the specified `ttl` value.
`[-v tos]`	Sets the TOS field to the specified by `tos` value.
`[-r count]`	Stores the route taken by outgoing packets and returning packets in the Record Route field.
`[-s count]`	Sets a timestamp for the number of hops as set by `count`.
`[-j computer-list]`	Routes packets by way of the list of computers specified by `computer-list` and permits consecutive computers to be separated by intermediate gateways.
`[-k computer-list]`	Routes packets by way of the list of computers specified by `computer-list` and prevents consecutive computers from being separated by intermediate gateways.
`[-w timeout]`	Specifies the time-out interval (in milliseconds).
`destination-list`	Specifies a list of target computers.

popd

Changes to the directory stored by `pushd`.

Syntax

```
popd
```

print

Displays the contents of a print queue or prints a text file.

Syntax

```
print [/d:device] [[drive:][path] filename[ ...]]
```

Parameters

Parameter	Purpose
None	Displays the print queue contents.
[/d:*device*]	Specifies a print device. Use LPT1, LPT2, and LPT3 or *servername**print_share*.
[*drive:*][*path*] *filename*	Specifies the drive, path, and file name of the file to be printed.

prompt

Changes the command prompt.

Syntax

prompt [*text*]

Parameters

Parameter	Purpose
none	Resets the command prompt to its default setting.
[*text*]	Specifies the text to be displayed as the command prompt. In addition to text, you can also include the following:

$q	equals sign
$$	dollar sign
$t	time
$d	date
$p	drive and path
$v	Windows version number
$n	drive
$g	greater-than sign
$l	less-than sign
$b	pipe
$_	Enter-linefeed
$e	ANSI escape code (code 27)
$h	Backspace

continues

Parameters *(continued)*

Parameter	Purpose
$a &	ampersand
$c	left parenthesis
$f	right parenthesis
$s	space
$+	Zero or more plus sign (+) characters depending upon the depth of the pushd directory stack
$m	Remote name associated with the current drive letter

pushd

Records the name of the current directory for use by the popd command and then changes to the specified directory.

Syntax

```
pushd [path]
```

Parameters

Parameter	Purpose
[path]	Specifies a directory to set as the current directory.

qbasic

Starts Qbasic.

Syntax

```
qbasic [/b] [/editor] [/g] [/h] [/mbf] [/nohi] [[/run][drive:][path]
filename]
```

Parameters

Parameter	Purpose
/b	Displays QBasic with a black background and a white foreground.
/editor	Starts the MS-DOS editor.
/g	Provides the fastest update for a CGA display.
/h	Displays the maximum number of lines possible.
/mbf	Converts the built-in functions MKS\$, MKD\$, CVS, and CVD to MKSMBF\$, MKDMBF\$, CVSMBF, and CVDMBF.
/nohi	Permits the monitors that do not support high-intensity video.
/run	Runs a Basic program before displaying it.
[*drive:*][*path*] *filename*	Specifies the drive, path, and file name of a QBasic file to load when QBasic starts.

rcp

Copies files between a Windows computer and a UNIX system.

Syntax

```
rcp [-a | -b] [-h] [-r] source1 source2 ... sourceN destination
```

Parameters

Parameter	Purpose
[-a]	Specifies the use of the ASCII transfer mode.
[-b]	Specifies the use of the binary image transfer mode.
[-h]	Transfers files with hidden attributes on Windows computers.
[-r]	Copies the contents of all subdirectories to the destination server.
source and *destination*	Must be of the form [*computer*[.*user*]:]*filename*].

recover

Attempts to recover information from a damaged disk.

Syntax

```
recover [drive:][path] filename
```

Parameter

Parameter	Purpose
[drive:][path] filename	Identifies the drive, path, and file name of the file to be recovered.

rem

Used to place comments in scripts.

Syntax

```
rem [comment]
```

Parameter

Parameter	Purpose
[comment]	A string of descriptive text information.

rename (ren)

Renames a file or group of files.

Syntax

```
rename [drive:][path] filename1 filename2
ren [drive:][path] filename1 filename2
```

Parameters

Parameter	Purpose
`[drive:][path] filename1`	Specifies the drive, path, and file name of the file to be renamed.
`filename2`	Specifies the new name for the file.

`replace`

Replaces files in the destination directory with files that have the same name.

Syntax

```
replace [drive1:][path1] filename [drive2:][path2] [/a] [/p] [/r] [/w]

replace [drive1:][path1] filename [drive2:][path2] [/p] [/r] [/s] [/w]
[/u]
```

Parameters

Parameter	Purpose
`[drive1:][path1] filename`	Specifies the drive, path, and file name of the source file(s).
`[drive2:][path2]`	Specifies the drive and path of the destination file(s).
`[/a]`	Adds files to the destination folder.
`[/p]`	Prompts for confirmation before a replacement is allowed.
`[/r]`	Permits the replacement of read-only files.
`[/w]`	Waits for you to insert a disk before beginning to look for source file(s).
`[/s]`	Searches all subfolders in the destination folder and replaces matching files.
`[/u]`	Replaces files in the destination folder only if they are older than the files in the source folder.

rexec

Executes commands on remote computers that support the REXEC service.

Syntax

```
rexec computer [-l username] [-n] command
```

Parameters

Parameter	Purpose
computer	Specifies the remote computer.
[-l username]	Specifies a user name on the remote computer.
[-n]	Redirects the input of Rexec to NULL.
command	Specifies the command to be executed..

rmdir (rd)

Deletes a folder.

Syntax

```
rmdir [drive:]path [/s] [/q]
rd [drive:]path [/s] [/q]
```

Parameters

Parameter	Purpose
[drive:]path	Specifies the drive and path of the folder to be deleted.
[/s]	Deletes the folder and its subfolders and their contents.
[/q]	Deletes folders without requiring confirmation.

route

Configures routing tables.

Syntax

```
route [-f] [-p] [command [destination] [mask subnetmask] [gateway]
[metric costmetric]]
```

Parameters

Parameter	Purpose
[-f]	Clears the routing tables of gateway entries.
[-p]	Makes routes persistent across system restarts.
[command]	Prints, adds, deletes, or changes the destination.
[destination]	Specifies the computer where the command will be sent.
[mask subnetmask]	Specifies a subnet mask for the route entry.
[gateway]	Specifies a gateway.
[metric costmetric]	Assigns an integer cost metric.

rsh

Executes commands on remote computers that run the RSH service.

Syntax

rsh computer [-l username] [-n] command

Parameters

Parameter	Purpose
computer	Specifies the remote computer.
[-l username]	Specifies a user name to use at the remote computer.
[-n]	Redirects the input of Rsh to NULL.
command	Specifies the command.

runas

Permits the execution of specific tools and programs with different permissions than those provided by the user's current account.

Syntax

runas [/profile] [/env] [/netonly] /user:UserAccountName program

Parameters

Parameter	Purpose
/profile	Provides the name of the user's profile.
/env	Replaces the user's local environment with the current network environment.
/netonly	Specifies that the user information is to be used for remote access.
/user:*UserAccountName*	Specifies the account with which to execute the program in the form of *user@domain* or *domain\user*.
program	Specifies the program or command to be executed by specified account.

set

Displays, changes, and deletes environment variables.

Syntax

```
set [variable=[string]]
```

Parameters

Parameter	Purpose
None	Displays environment settings.
variable	Identifies the variable to set or modify.
string	Sets the value of the variable to *string*.

setlocal

Initiates the localization of environment variables in a script.

Syntax

```
setlocal option
```

Parameter

Parameter	Purpose
`option`	Either `enableextensions` or `disableextensions`. This enables or disables the command extensions.

setver

Modifies the version number that the MS-DOS subsystem reports to executing programs.

Syntax

```
setver [drive:path] [filename n.nn]
setver [drive:path] [filename [/delete [/quiet]]
setver [drive:path]
```

Parameters

Parameter	Purpose
None	Displays the current version table.
`[drive:path]`	Specifies drive and path to SETVER.EXE.
`[filename]`	Specifies a program name to be added to the version table.
`[n.nn]`	Specifies the MS-DOS version that is reported to the specified program file.
`[/delete]`	Removes the version table entry for the specified program file.
`[/quiet]`	Hides deletion messages.

shell

Specifies an alternative command interpreter to be used in place of the MS-DOS subsystem.

Syntax

```
shell=[[drive:]path] filename [parameters]
```

Parameters

Parameter	Purpose
`[[drive:]path] filename`	Specifies the drive, path, and file name of the alternative command interpreter.
`[parameters]`	Provides any command-line parameters required by the alternative command interpreter.

shift

Shifts (changes) the position of replaceable parameters in a script.

Syntax

```
Shift /n
```

Parameters

Parameter	Purpose
`/n`	Identifies the argument where shifting should begin, where *n* is a value from 0 – 8.

sort

Reads input and sorts it before writing it as output.

Syntax

```
sort [/r] [/+n] [/m kilobytes] [/l locale] [/rec characters]
[[drive1:][path1]filename1] [/t [drive2:][path2]] [/o
[drive3:][path3]filename3]
[command |] sort [/r] [/+n] [/m kilobytes] [/l locale] [/rec
characters] [[drive1:][path1]filename1] [/t [drive2:][path2]] [/o
[drive3:][path3]filename3]
```

Parameters

Parameter	Purpose
/r	Reverses the sort order.
/+n	Specifies the starting character position, *n*, where sort begins its comparison.
/m *kilobytes*	Specifies the allocation of memory for use by the sort command (in kilobytes).
/l *locale*	Changes the sort order of characters as defined by the default locale. The only available option is the "C" locale.
/rec *characters*	Sets the maximum number of characters that can be contained in a line on the input file (default is 4,096, maximum is 65,535).
[*drive1:*][*path1*]*filename1*	Specifies the location of the file to be sorted.
/t [*drive2:*][*path2*]	Specifies a path to a folder that the sort command can use for working storage when the data to be sorted cannot fit into memory.
/o [*drive3:*][*path3*]*filename3*	Specifies where a file's sorted input is to be stored.

subst

Establishes an association between a path and a drive letter.

Syntax

```
subst [drive1: [drive2:]path]
subst drive1: /d
```

Parameters

Parameter	Purpose
None	Displays the names of any virtual drives.
[*drive1:*]	Specifies the virtual drive.
[*drive2:*]	Specifies the physical drive containing the specified path.
[*path*]	Specifies the path to be assigned to the virtual drive.
/d	Removes a virtual drive.

tcmsetup

Configures the telephony client.

Syntax

```
tcmsetup [/q] [/x] /c server1 [server2 ... serverN]
tcmsetup [/q] /c /d
```

Parameters

Parameter	Purpose
[/q]	Prevents message box displays.
[/x]	Sets connection-oriented callbacks for heavy traffic networks with high pack-loss.
/c	Specifies client setup. Required parameter.
server1	Contains the remote server where the client will use TAPI service providers.
[server2 ... serverN]	Lists additional servers that are available to the client.
/d	Clears the list of remote servers and disables the telephony client.

tftp

Transfers files between the local computer and a remote computer running the TFTP service.

Syntax

```
tftp [-i] computer [get | put] source [destination]
```

Parameters

Parameter	Purpose
[-I]	Sets binary image transfer mode.
computer	Specifies the local or remote computer.
[put]	Uploads files to the file *source* on the remote computer.
[get]	Downloads the file on the remote computer to the file *source* on the local computer.

Parameters

Parameter	Purpose
source	Identifies the file to transfer.
[destination]	Identifies where to transfer the file.

time

Displays system time or changes the computer's internal clock.

Syntax

```
time [hours:[minutes[:seconds[.hundredths]]][A|P]]
```

Parameters

Parameter	Purpose
None	Displays the computer's clock time and prompts for the new time.
[hours]	Sets the hour.
[minutes]	Sets the minutes.
[seconds]	Sets the seconds.
[hundredths]	Sets hundredths of a second.
[A|P]	Sets A.M or P.M. for the 12-hour format.

title

Places a message on the command console's title bar.

Syntax

```
title [string]
```

Parameter

Parameter	Purpose
[string]	Specifies the message text.

tracert

A utility used to determine the route taken to a destination.

Syntax

```
tracert [-d] [-h maximum_hops] [-j computer-list] [-w timeout]
target_name
```

Parameters

Parameter	Purpose
[-d]	Prevents the resolution of IP addresses to host names.
[-h *maximum_hops*]	Sets a maximum number of hops.
[-j *computer-list*]	Specifies a loose source route along *computer-list*.
[-w *timeout*]	Waits the specified number of milliseconds for each reply.
target_name	Identifies the target computer.

tree

Provides a graphic view of the folder structure for the specified path or disk.

Syntax

```
tree [drive:][path] [/f] [/a]
```

Parameters

Parameter	Purpose
[*drive:*]	Identifies a drive that contains a disk whose directory structures should be displayed.
[*path*]	Identifies a folder whose directory structure is to be displayed.
[/f]	Displays the file names found in each directory.
[/a]	Sets the tree command to display text characters in place of graphic characters when identifying links to a subfolder.

type

Displays the contents of a text file.

Syntax

```
type [drive:][path] filename
```

Parameter

Parameter	Purpose
[drive:][path] filename	Specifies the drive, path, and file name that is to be viewed.

ver

Displays the Windows version number.

Syntax

```
ver
```

vol

Displays the serial number and disk volume label of the disk.

Syntax

```
vol [drive:]
```

Parameter

Parameter	Purpose
[drive:]	Specifies the drive whose information you want to display.

xcopy

Copies folders and the contents including files and subfolders.

Syntax

```
xcopy source [destination] [/w] [/p] [/c] [/v] [/q] [/f] [/l]

[/d[:date]] [/u] [/i] [/s [/e]] [/t] [/k] [/r] [/h] [/a|/m] [/n]
[/exclude:filename] [/y | /-y] [/z]
```

Parameters

Parameter	Purpose
source	Specifies location and name of the files to be copied.
[destination]	Specifies the destination of the copied files.
[/w]	Displays a confirmation message and waits for a reply.
[/p]	Prompts for confirmation before creating destination files.
[/c]	Ignores all errors.
[/v]	Verifies the success of each copy operation.
[/q]	Prevents the display of xcopy messages.
[/f]	Displays the file names being copied.
[/l]	Prevents command execution and displays a list of files that would have been copied.
/d[:date]	Copies source files that have been changed on or after date.
[/u]	Copies files from source if they also exist on destination.
[/I]	Creates the destination folder if it does not exist if source is a directory or contains wildcards.
[/s]	Copies directories and subdirectories as long as they contain files.
[/e]	Copies all subfolders.
[/t]	Copies the subdirectory structure and not the files.
[/k]	Copies read-only files to the destination where they will retain their read-only status.
[/r]	Overwrites read-only files.
[/h]	Copies files with the hidden and system file attributes.

Parameters

Parameter	Purpose
[/a]	Copies source files that have archive file attributes set.
[/m]	Copies source files that have archive file attributes set and then turns off archive file attributes.
[/n]	Copies files using their NTFS short names.
[/exclude:*filename*]	Excludes the files listed in *filename* from being copied.
[/y]	Suppresses confirmation prompts when overwriting existing destination files.
[/-y]	Requires confirmation prompts before overwriting existing destination files.
[/z]	Copies files to the network in restartable mode so that the copy operations will resume after failed connections are reestablished.

ADMINISTRATOR'S

Appendix B

**JScript Language
Reference**

JScript is one of the two scripting languages provided by Microsoft for the WSH. JScript provides a complete programming language including statements, operators, conditional flow control, looping, and a powerful object model that provides access to a full range of methods and properties.

This appendix is designed to supplement the JScript review presented in Chapter 11. It provides a JScript reference in the form of a collection of organized tables. Each table provides summary information about a particular aspect of JScript.

Topics covered in this appendix include:

- ◆ JScript reserved words
- ◆ JScript statements
- ◆ JScript special characters
- ◆ JScript objects
- ◆ JScript properties
- ◆ JScript methods
- ◆ JScript functions
- ◆ JScript operators
- ◆ JScript error messages

JScript Reserved Words

There are a number of words in JScript that you cannot use as variables, function labels, or labels. These words are known as *reserved words*. They make up key elements of the JScript language. In addition, there is a second grouping of reserved words known as future reserved words that have been set aside for later incorporation into JScript.

The following list defines the JScript collection of reserved words.

break	instanceof
case	new
catch	null
continue	return
debugger	switch
default	this
delete	throw
do	true
else	try
false	typeof
finally	var
for	void
function	while
if	with
in	

The following list defines the JScript collection of future reserved words.

abstract	int
boolean	interface
byte	long
char	native
class	package
const	private
double	protected
enum	public
export	short
extends	static
final	super
float	synchronized
goto	throws
implements	transient
import	volatile

JScript Statements

Like any programming language, JScript consists of a collection of predefined statements. These statements that comprise the JScript programming language are listed in Table B.1.

Table B.1 JScript Scripting Statements

Statement	Description
break	Terminates the processing of a loop.
catch	Supplies statements to be executed when a specified error occurs while allowing the script to continue processing.
//	Marks a single-line comment.
/*..*/	Marks a multi-line comment.
continue	Terminates the current iteration of a loop and begins another iteration.
do...while	Executes one or more statements and then checks to see if a condition is true. If the condition is not true it executes the statement(s) again, repeatedly testing the condition.
for	Executes a collection of one or more statements as long as a condition continues to prove true.
for...in	Executes one or more statements based on the number of occurrences of an element in an object or the number of entries in an array.
function	Defines a function within a script.
if	Executes one or more statements based on the value of an expression.
if...else	Executes one or more statements based on the value of an expression. Otherwise, provides an alternative set of statements that are executed when the condition proves false.
Label	An identifier used to mark a location in a script.
return	Forces the termination of a function and passes back a value to the caller of the function.
@set	Establishes a variable that will be used by conditional compilation statements.
switch	Establishes a set of conditional tests each of which can execute one or more statements based on the value of a tested expression.
this	A reference to the current object.
throw	Generates an error that can be managed by a try...catch statement.

Table B.1   JScript Scripting Statements

Statement	Description
try	Performs JScript error handling.
var	Defines a JScript variable.
while	Executes a statement or a collection of statements as long as the specified statement remains false.
with	Specifies a default object to be used with one or more statements.

Special Characters

There are a number of special characters in JScript that require special attention. These characters must be escaped (using the \ character) in order to use them as text within your scripts. Table B.2 identifies each of these special characters.

Table B.2   JScript Special Characters

Character	Description
$	Matches the position at the end of a string.
( )	Identifies the start and ending of a subexpression.
*	Matches a subexpression for zero or more occurrences.
+	Matches a subexpression for one or more occurrences.
.	Matches a single character.
[	Identifies the start of a bracketed expression.
?	Matches a subexpression for zero or one occurrence.
\	Identifies the character that follows as a special character.
^	Matches the position starting at the beginning of a string.
{	Identifies the start of a quantifier expression.
|	Specifies a choice condition.

JScript Core Objects

JScript provides its own object model. These objects provide access to a collection of properties and methods that your scripts can then access. The methods and properties provided by these core objects provide the capability to perform an assortment of tasks such as create and work with arrays, access error messages, access mathematical constants, and manipulate strings. Table B.3 provides a complete listing of JScript core objects.

Table B.3 JScript Objects

Object	Description
`ActiveXObject`	Provides a reference to an automation object.
	Properties: N/A.
	Methods: N/A.
`Array`	Provides for the creation and management of arrays.
	Properties: `constructor`, `length`, `prototype`.
	Methods: `concat`, `join`, `pop`, `push`, `reverse`, `shift`, `slice`, `sort`, `splice`, `toLocaleString`, `toString`, `unshift`, and `valueOf`.
`Boolean`	Provides for the creation of a Boolean value.
	Properties: `constructor`, `prototype`.
	Methods: `toString`, `valueOf`.
`Date`	Provides access to dates and times methods.
	Properties: `constructor`, `prototype`.
	Methods: `getDate`, `getDay`, `getFullYear`, `getHours`, `getMilliseconds`, `getMinutes`, `getMonth`, `getSeconds`, `getTime`, `getTimezoneOffset`, `getUTCDate`, `getUTCDay`, `getUTCFullYear`, `getUTCHours`, `getUTCMilliseconds`, `getUTCMinutes`, `getUTCMonth`, `getUTCSeconds`, `getVarDate`, `getYear`, `setDate`, `setFullYear`, `setHours`, `setMilliseconds`, `setMinutes`, `setMonth`, `setSeconds`, `setTime`, `setUTCDate`, `setUTCFullYear`, `setUTCHours`, `setUTCMilliseconds`, `setUTCMinutes`, `setUTCMonth`, `setUTCSeconds`, `setYear`, `toGMTString`, `toLocaleString`, `toUTCString`, `toString`, `valueOf`, `parse`, `UTC` method.

Table B.3 JScript Objects

Object	Description
Enumerator	Provides the capability to enumerate a collection of items. Properties: N/A. Methods: `atEnd`, `item`, `moveFirst`, `moveNext`.
Error	Provides access to script error information. Properties: `description`, `number`. Methods: N/A.
Function	Provides the capability to create a function. Properties: `arguments`, `caller`, `constructor`, `prototype`. Methods: `toString`, `valueOf`.
Global	Collects global methods into one object. Properties: `Infinity`, `NaN`. Methods: `escape`, `eval`, `isFinite`, `isNaN`, `nescape`, `parseFloat`, `parseInt`.
Math	Provides access to mathematical functions and constants. Properties: `E`, `LN2`, `LN10`, `LOG2E`, `LOG10E`, `PI`, `SQRT1_2`, `SQRT2`. Methods: `abs`, `acos`, `asin`, `atan`, `atan2`, `ceil`, `cos`, `exp`, `floor`, `log`, `max`, `min`, `pow`, `random`, `round`, `sin`, `sqrt`, `tan`.
Number	Provides access to a collection of numeric constants. Properties: `MAX_VALUE`, `MIN_VALUE`, `NaN`, `NEGATIVE_INFINITY`, `POSITIVE_INFINITY`, `constructor`, `prototype`. Methods: `toLocaleString`, `toString`, `valueOf`.
Object	Provides the capability to create an instance of any other object type. Properties: `prototype`, `constructor`. Methods: `toLocaleString`, `toString`, `valueOf`.
RegExp	Saves information from regular expressions. Properties: `$1...$9`, `index`, `input`, `lastIndex`, `lastMatch`, `lastParen`, `leftContext`, `rightContext`. Methods: N/A.
String	Provides the capability to manipulate strings. Properties: `constructor`, `length`, `prototype`.

continues

Table B.3   JScript Objects *(continued)*

Object	Description
	Methods: `anchor`, `big`, `blink`, `bold`, `charAt`, `charCodeAt`, `concat`, `fixed`, `fontcolor`, `fontsize`, `fromCharCode`, `indexOf`, `italics`, `lastIndexOf`, `link`, `match`, `replace`, `search`, `slice`, `small`, `split`, `strike`, `sub`, `substr`, `substring`, `sup`, `toLowerCase`, `toUpperCase`, `toString`, `valueOf`.
`VBArray`	Provides the capability to use VBScript arrays.
	Properties: N/A.
	Methods: `dimensions`, `getItem`, `lbound`, `toArray`, `ubound`.

JScript Object Properties

An object's properties are the attributes of the object and contain stored values that represent some quality of the object. Table B.4 defines the properties supported by JScript objects.

Table B.4   JScript Properties

Property	Description
`$1...$9`	Returns the last nine recorded elements found in a pattern match.
`arguments`	Returns an array that contains all the arguments passed to a function.
`caller`	Provides the current function with a reference to the calling function.
`constructor`	Identifies a function that creates an object.
`description`	Retrieves the text message associated with a specific error.
`E`	Returns Euler's constant (2.718).
`index`	Returns the position of the specified substring found in a string.
`Infinity`	Returns `POSITIVE_INFINITY`.
`input`	Returns the string that was the subject of a search operation.
`lastIndex`	Returns the last position of a specified substring in a string.
`length (Array)`	Returns a numeric value equal to the highest element in an array + 1.

Table B.4   JScript Properties

Property	Description
length (Function)	Returns the total number of arguments specified in a function.
length (String)	Returns the String object's length.
LN2	Returns the natural logarithm of 2 (2.302).
LN10	Returns the natural logarithm of 10 (.693).
LOG2E	Returns Euler's constant (2.718).
LOG10E	Returns the base-10 logarithm of Euler's constant.
MAX_VALUE	Returns the largest number that can be represented in JScript.
MIN_VALUE	Returns the smallest possible number that can be represented in JScript.
NaN	Returns a special NaN (not a number) value.
NEGATIVE_INFINITY	Returns a value that is bigger than the largest negative number supported by JScript (NEGATIVE INFINITY).
number	Returns the error number for the specified error.
PI	Returns the value of PI, which is approximately 3.141549.
POSITIVE_INFINITY	Returns a value larger than the largest number that can be represented in JScript (POSITIVE INFINITY).
prototype	Returns a reference to an object class's prototype.
source	Returns the text of the regular expression pattern.
SQRT1_2	Returns the square root of 1 (.707).
SQRT2	Returns the square root of 2 (1.414).

JScript Object Methods

An object's methods are the actions that objects can do. Methods can be used to control the object or its data. Table B.5 defines the methods supported by JScript objects.

Table B.5 JScript Methods

Method	Description
abs()	Returns the absolute value.
acos()	Inverse trigonometric function that returns the arccosine of the argument.
asin()	Inverse trigonometric function that returns the arcsine of the argument.
atan()	Inverse trigonometric function that returns the arctangent of the argument.
atan2()	Inverse trigonometric function that returns the angle from the x axis to point (y,x).
atEnd	Returns a True or False value depending on whether the enumerator is at the end of the collection.
ceil()	Returns the lowest integer greater than or equal to the argument.
charAt()	Returns the character at the specified position in the string where the index of the string object begins at zero.
charCodeAt	Retrieves the Unicode encoding for a character.
compile	Compiles the specified regular expression.
concat (Array)	Combines two arrays into a new array.
concat (String)	Combines two strings into one new string.
cos()	Trigonometric function that returns the cosine of the argument.
dimensions	Retrieves the number of dimensions currently in a VBArray.
escape	Encodes string objects.
eval	Evaluates and runs JScript code.
exec	Searches for a match within a string.
exp()	Exponential logarithm.
floor()	Returns the highest integer less than or equal to the argument.
fromCharCode()	Creates a string value based on the supplied code set.
getDate	Returns the current day of the month.
getDay	Returns the current day of the week.
getFullYear	Returns the current year.
getHours	Returns the current hour.
getItem	Returns the specified item.

Table B.5 JScript Methods

Method	Description
getMilliseconds	Returns the current time in milliseconds.
getMinutes	Returns the current time in minutes.
getMonth	Returns the current month.
getSeconds	Returns the current time in seconds.
getTime	Returns the current time.
getTimezoneOffset	Returns the difference between local time and Universal Coordinated Time.
getUTCDate	Returns the current date using Universal Coordinated Time.
getUTCDay	Returns the current day using Universal Coordinated Time.
getUTCFullYear	Returns the current year using Universal Coordinated Time.
getUTCHours	Returns the current hour using Universal Coordinated Time.
getUTCMilliseconds	Returns the current time in milliseconds using Universal Coordinated Time.
getUTCMinutes	Returns the current time in minutes using Universal Coordinated Time.
getUTCMonth	Returns the current month using Universal Coordinated Time.
getUTCSeconds	Returns the current time in seconds using Universal Coordinated Time.
getVarDate	Retrieves the VT_DATE value.
getYear	Returns the current year from the Date object.
indexOf()	Returns the position of a specified substring.
isFinite	Returns a value of True or False depending on whether the supplied number is finite.
isNaN	Returns a Boolean value that indicates whether a value has a reserved value of NaN.
item	Retrieves the current item from a collection.
join	Returns a String object that contains a all elements in an array.
lastIndexOf()	Return the last position of a specified substring.
lbound	Returns the lowest index value in a VBArray.

continues

Table B.5   JScript Methods *(continued)*

Method	Description
log()	Natural logarithm.
match	Creates an array with the results of a string search using a regular expression object.
max(x,y)	Returns either x or y depending on which is higher.
min(x,y)	Returns either x or y depending on which is lower.
moveFirst	Changes the current collection item to the first item in the collection.
moveNext	Changes the current collection item's position to the next position in the collection.
parse	Parses a date string returning the number of milliseconds between the date and midnight, January 1, 1970.
parseFloat	Retrieves a floating-point number converted from a string value.
parseInt	Returns an integer value from a string.
pow(x,y)	Returns the value of x^y.
random()	Returns a random number between 0 and 1.
replace	Retrieves a string after replacing text using a regular expression.
reverse	Reverses the elements in an array.
round()	Rounds the argument to the nearest integer.
search	Returns the index position of the first substring match in a search.
setDate	Changes the date in the Date object to local time.
setFullYear	Changes the year in the Date object to local time.
setHours	Changes the hour in the Date object to local time.
setMilliseconds	Changes the milliseconds in the Date object to local time.
setMinutes	Changes the minutes in the Date object to local time.
setMonth	Changes the month in the Date object to local time.
setSeconds	Changes the seconds value in the Date object to local time.
setTime	Changes the date and time value in the Date object.
setUTCDate	Changes the numeric date in the Date object to Universal Coordinated Time.
setUTCFullYear	Changes the year in the Date object to Universal Coordinated Time.

Table B.5 JScript Methods

Method	Description
setUTCHours	Changes the hours in the Date object to Universal Coordinated Time.
setUTCMilliseconds	Changes the milliseconds in the Date object to Universal Coordinated Time.
setUTCMinutes	Changes the minutes in the Date object to Universal Coordinated Time.
setUTCMonth	Changes the month in the Date object to Universal Coordinated Time.
setUTCSeconds	Changes the seconds in the Date object to Universal Coordinated Time.
setYear	Changes the year in the Date object.
sin()	Trigonometric function that returns the sine of the argument.
slice (Array)	Creates a new array from a portion of the current array.
slice (String)	Creates a new string using a portion of the current string.
sort	Sorts the elements in an array.
split()	Organizes a string into an array.
sqrt()	Returns the square of the argument.
substr	Returns a substring of a specified length beginning at a specified location.
substring()	Returns the specified portion of a string.
tan()	Trigonometric function that returns the tangent of the argument.
test	Returns a True or False value depending on whether a pattern can be located within a string.
toArray	Converts a VBArray into JScript array and returns the results.
toGMTString	Retrieves the current date using Greenwich Mean Time.
toLocalString	Retrieves a date string converted to the current locale.
toLowerCase()	Returns the string in all lowercase characters.
toString	Converts an object to a string and returns its value.
toUpperCase()	Returns the string in all uppercase characters.
toUTCString	Converts a date to Universal Coordinated Time and returns the results as a string.

continues

Table B.5   JScript Methods *(continued)*

Method	Description
ubound	Returns the top index value from a VBArray dimension.
unescape	Decodes `String` objects.
UTC	Returns the number of milliseconds between a date and midnight, January 1, 1970 Universal Time Coordinate.
valueOf	Returns the specified object's primitive value.

JScript Run-time Objects

In addition to JScript core objects JScript also provides a collection of run-time objects. These objects provide methods and properties that your scripts can use to access a computer's file system. Table B.6 provides a summary of JScript run-time objects.

Table B.6   JScript Run-time (`FileSystem`) Objects

Object	Description
Dictionary	Stores data key, item pairs. Properties: `Count`, `Item`, `Key`. Methods: `Add (Dictionary)`, `Exists`, `Items`, `Keys`, `Remove`, `RemoveAll`.
Drive	Provides access to a disk drive's properties. Properties: `AvailableSpace`, `DriveLetter`, `DriveType`, `FileSystem`, `FreeSpace`, `IsReady`, `Path`, `RootFolder`, `SerialNumber`, `ShareName`, `TotalSize`, `VolumeName`. Methods: N/A.
Drives Collection	Provides information about system drives. Properties: `Count`, `Item`. Methods: N/A.
File	Provides access to a file's properties. Properties: `Attributes`, `DateCreated`, `DateLastAccessed`, `DateLastModified`, `Drive`, `Name`, `ParentFolder`, `Path`, `ShortName`, `ShortPath`, `Size`, `Type`. Methods: `Copy`, `Delete`, `Move`, `OpenAsTextStream`.

Table B.6 JScript Run-time (FileSystem) Objects

Object	Description
Files Collection	Provides access to files contained in a folder.
	Properties: Count, Item.
	Methods: N/A
FileSystemObject	Provides access to the entire file system.
	Properties: Drives.
	Methods: BuildPath, CopyFile, CopyFolder, CreateFolder, CreateTextFile, DeleteFile, DeleteFolder, DriveExists, FileExists, FolderExists, GetAbsolutePathName, GetBaseName, GetDrive, GetDriveName, GetExtensionName, GetFile, GetFileName, GetFolder, GetParentFolderName, GetSpecialFolder, GetTempName, MoveFile, MoveFolder, OpenTextFile.
Folder	Provides access to a folder's properties.
	Properties: Attributes, DateCreated, DateLastAccessed, DateLastModified, Drive, Files, IsRootFolder, Name, ParentFolder, Path, ShortName, ShortPath, Size, SubFolders, Type.
	Methods: Copy, Delete, Move, OpenAsTextStream.
Folders Collection	Provides access to the folders contained within another folder.
	Properties: Count, Item.
	Methods: Add (Folders).
TextStream	Provides for sequential file access.
	Properties: AtEndOfLine, AtEndOfStream, Column, Line.
	Methods: Close, Read, ReadAll, ReadLine, Skip, SkipLine, Write, WriteBlankLines, WriteLine.

JScript Run-time Properties

Each of the JScript run-time objects has its own set of properties. These properties are the attributes of the object and contain stored values that represent some quality of the object. Your scripts can reference and change these properties. Table B.7 defines the properties supported by JScript's run-time objects.

Table B.7   JScript Run-time (`FileSystem`) Properties

Property	Description
AtEndOfLine	Returns a value of `True` or `False` depending on whether the file pointer immediately precedes the end-of-line marker in a `TextStream` file.
AtEndOfStream	Returns a value of `True` or `False` depending on whether the file pointer is at the end of a `TextStream` file.
Attributes	Gets or changes files and folders attributes.
AvailableSpace	Retrieves the amount of free space available on the specified local or network drive.
Column	Retrieves the column number or character position in a `TextStream` file.
CompareMode	Gets or changes the comparison mode that is used to compare a `Dictionary` object's string keys.
Count	Counts and returns the collection or `Dictionary` object items.
DateCreated	Retrieves the creation date and time of a file or folder.
DateLastAccessed	Retrieves the last access date and time of a file or folder.
DateLastModified	Retrieves the modification date and time of a file or folder.
Drive	Retrieves the drive letter where the specified file or folder resides.
DriveLetter	Retrieves the drive letter of a local or network drive.
Drives	Creates a `Drives` collection made up of all the `Drive` objects on the local machine.
DriveType	Retrieves a value that indicates the specified drive's type.
Files	Creates a `Files` collection made up of all `File` objects within the specified folder.
FileSystem	Retrieves the file system type on the specified drive.
FreeSpace	Retrieves the amount of free space available to the user for the specified local or network drive.
IsReady	Returns a value of `True` or `False` depending on whether the specified drive is ready.
IsRootFolder	Returns a value of `True` or `False` depending on whether the specified folder is the root folder.
Item	Gets or changes an item based on the specified `Dictionary` object key.

Table B.7 JScript Run-time (`FileSystem`) Properties

Property	Description
Key	Sets a `Dictionary` object key.
Line	Retrieves the current line number in the `TextStream` file.
Name	Gets or changes the name of a file or folder.
ParentFolder	Retrieves the parent folder object of the specified file or folder.
Path	Retrieves the specified file, folder, or drive's path.
RootFolder	Retrieves a `Folder` object that represents the root folder for the specified drive.
SerialNumber	Retrieves the decimal serial number that identifies a disk volume.
ShareName	Retrieves a drive's network share name.
ShortName	Retrieves the 8.3 character short name of a file or folder.
ShortPath	Retrieves the short path associated with the 8.3 character file name.
Size	Returns the byte size of the specified file or folder.
SubFolders	Creates a `Folders` collection made up of the folder within the specified folder.
TotalSize	Retrieves the number of bytes left on the specified local or network drive.
Type	Retrieves a file or folder's type.
VolumeName	Gets or changes a drive's volume name.

JScript Run-time Methods

Each of the JScript run-time objects has its own collection of run-time methods. These run-time methods can be used to control the object or its data. Table B.8 defines the run-time methods supported by JScript's run-time objects.

Table B.8 JScript Run-time (`FileSystem`) Methods

Method	Description
Add (Dictionary)	Adds a key and item pair to the specified `Dictionary` object.
Add (Folders)	Adds a `Folder` to the specified collection.
BuildPath	Adds a name to the path.
Close	Terminates an open `TextStream` file.
Copy	Copies a file or folder to the specified location.
CopyFile	Copies one or more files to a different location.
CopyFolder	Copies a folder recursively to a different location.
CreateFolder	Creates the specified folder.
CreateTextFile	Creates a file and a `TextStream` object to be used when reading and writing to the file.
Delete	Removes the specified file or folder.
DeleteFile	Removes the specified file.
DeleteFolder	Removes the contents of the specified folder.
DriveExists	Returns a `True` or `False` value depending on whether the specified drive exists.
Exists	Returns a `True` or `False` value depending on whether the specified key exists in the `Dictionary` object.
FileExists	Returns a `True` or `False` value depending on whether the specified file exists.
FolderExists	Returns a `True` or `False` value depending on whether the specified folder exists.
GetAbsolutePathName	Retrieves the complete path name.
GetBaseName	Retrieves the base file name without its file extension.
GetDrive	Retrieves the `Drive` object representing the drive in the specified path.
GetDriveName	Retrieves a string that contains the name of the drive for the specified path.
GetExtensionName	Retrieves a string that contains the file's extension as specified by its path.
GetFile	Retrieves a `File` object based on the files specified in the path.

Table B.8   JScript Run-time (`FileSystem`) Methods

Method	Description
GetFileName	Retrieves the last file name or folder of the specified path.
GetFileVersion	Retrieves the version number of the specified file.
GetFolder	Retrieves the `Folder` object of the folder in the specified path.
GetParentFolderName	Retrieves a string representing the name of the parent folder.
GetSpecialFolder	Retrieves the name of the specified special folder.
GetTempName	Retrieves a temporary file or folder name.
Items	Returns an array holding all items in a `Dictionary` object.
Keys	Returns an array holding all keys in a `Dictionary` object.
Move	Moves a file or folder to the specified location.
MoveFile	Moves one or more files to the specified location.
MoveFolder	Moves one or more folders to the specified location.
OpenAsTextStream	Opens a file and returns a `TextStream` object to use when referencing the file.
OpenTextFile	Opens a file and returns a `TextStream` object to use when referencing the file.
ReadAll	Reads the whole `TextStream` file and returns its contents as a string.
ReadLine	Reads a line in a `TextStream` file and returns it as a string.
Remove	Deletes a key, item pair in a `Dictionary` object.
RemoveAll	Deletes all key, item pairs in a `Dictionary` object.
Skip	Skips the specified number of characters positions when processing a `TextStream` file.
SkipLine	Skips the next line when processing a `TextStream` file.
Write	Writes a string in a `TextStream` file.
WriteBlankLines	Writes a number of newline characters in a `TextStream` file.
WriteLine	Writes a string and a newline character in a `TextStream` file.

JScript Functions

JScript functions allow you to organize your scripts into procedures. JScript provides a small collection of predefined scripts that you can execute, as specified in Table B.9.

Table B.9 Pre-Defined JScript Functions

Function	Description
GetObject	Provides a reference to an automation object.
ScriptEngine	Provides a string that specifies the currently executing scripting language.
ScriptEngineBuildVersion	Provides the build version number of the currently executing scripting engine.
ScriptEngineMajorVersion	Provides the major version number of the currently executing scripting engine.
ScriptEngineMinorVersion	Provides the minor version number of the currently executing scripting engine.

JScript Operators

Like VBScript, JScript supports a rich collection of operators that are used when working with and manipulating values. The next three sections outline the different categories of commonly used JScript operators.

Manipulating Numeric Values

Numeric operators allow you to alter a value in the form of a numeric equation. The numeric operators supported by JScript are listed in Table B.10.

Table B.10 JScript Numeric Operators

Operator	Description	Example
+	Add	i = 2 + 1
–	Subtract	i = 2 - 1
*	Multiply	i = x * 2
/	Divide	i = x / 2
%	Modulus	i = x % 2
-x	Reverses the sign of x	i = -i
x++	Returns x, then increments x by one	i = y++
++x	Increments x by one, then returns x	i = ++y
x--	Returns x, then decrements x by one	i = y--
--x	Decrements x by one, then returns x	i = --y

Assignment operators assign values to variables. In addition to the traditional = assignment, JScript supports a collection of shorthand operators that make your scripts more efficient and readable. Table B.11 lists JScript's assignment operators.

Table B.11 JScript Assignment Operators

Operator	Description	Examples
=	Sets a variable equal to a value	x = y + 1
+=	Shorthand for x = x + y	x += y
-=	Shorthand for x = x - y	x -= y
*=	Shorthand for x = x * y	x *= y
/=	Shorthand for x = x / y	x /= y
%=	Shorthand for x = x % y	x %= y

Comparison operators test the value of two variables. Comparison operators are used with compound command or IF statements to implement conditional logic within your scripts. Table B.12 lists the comparison operators supported by JScript.

Table B.12   JScript Comparison Operators

Operator	Description	Example
==	Equal	x == y
!=	Not equal	x != y
>	Greater than	x > y
<	Less than	x < y
>=	Greater than or equal to	x >= y
<=	Less than or equal to	x <= y
!x	False condition	!x
&&	Both are true	x && y
||	Either is true	x || y

Order of Precedence within Numeric Expressions

The order in which numeric data is manipulated in an expression is determined by a strict set of rules. Table B.13 lists the rules that define this order of precedence.

Table B.13   JScript Order of Precedence

Operators	Description
\	Escape
(), (?:), (?=), []	Parentheses and brackets
*, +, ?, {n}, {n,}, {n,m}	Quantifiers
^, $, \metacharacter	Anchors and sequences
|	Alternation

Note: All operations are evaluated from left to right.

JScript Error Messages

During script development, errors will occur. JScript errors are reported in the form of error messages. These error messages are displayed in pop-up dialog boxes, as demonstrated in Figure B.1.

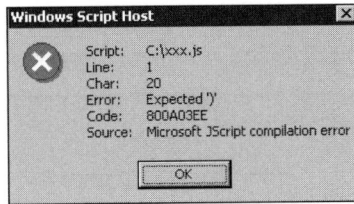

FIGURE B.1

A WSH error message indicating a JScript syntax error in a JScript script.

JScript errors include syntax and run-time errors. The next two sections provide a list of these messages.

Syntax Error Messages

JScript syntax errors occur when a JScript statement is improperly structured. These errors occur when the script is loading. The script never begins to execute. Table B.14 provides a review of JScript's syntax error messages.

Table B.14   JScript Syntax Errors

Error	Description
1019	Can't have break outside of loop
1020	Can't have continue outside of loop
1030	Conditional compilation is turned off
1027	default can only appear once in a switch statement
1005	Expected (
1006	Expected)
1012	Expected /
1003	Expected :
1004	Expected ;
1032	Expected @
1029	Expected @end
1007	Expected]
1008	Expected {
1009	Expected }
1011	Expected =
1033	Expected catch

continues

Table B.14   JScript Syntax Errors *(continued)*

Error	Description
1031	Expected constant
1023	Expected hexadecimal digit
1010	Expected identifier
1028	Expected identifier, string, or number
1024	Expected `while`
1014	Invalid character
1026	Label not found
1025	Label redefined
1018	`return` statement outside of function
1002	Syntax error
1035	Throw must be followed by an expression on the same source line
1016	Unterminated comment
1015	Unterminated string constant

Run-time Error Messages

JScript run-time errors occur after the script has loaded and begun its execution. JScript errors occur when the script attempts to perform an invalid action such as attempting to reference a resource that does not exist. Table B.15 provides a review of JScript's run-time error messages.

Table B.15   JScript Run-time Errors

Error	Description
5029	Array length must be a finite positive integer
5030	Array length must be assigned a finite positive number
5028	Array or arguments object expected
5010	Boolean expected
5003	Cannot assign to a function result
5000	Cannot assign to `this`

Table B.15   JScript Run-time Errors

Error	Description
5006	Date object expected
5015	Enumerator object expected
5022	Exception thrown and not caught
5020	Expected) in regular expression
5019	Expected] in regular expression
5023	Function does not have a valid prototype object
5002	Function expected
5008	Illegal assignment
5021	Invalid range in character set
5014	JScript object expected
5001	Number expected
5007	Object expected
5012	Object member expected
5016	Regular expression object expected
5005	String expected
5017	Syntax error in regular expression
5026	The number of fractional digits is out of range
5027	The precision is out of range
5025	The URI to be decoded is not a valid encoding
5024	The URI to be encoded contains an invalid character
5009	Undefined identifier
5018	Unexpected quantifier
5013	VBArray expected

TIP

Additional JScript reference materials can be found at
`http://msdn/Microsoft.com/scripting`.

Appendix C

VBScript Language Reference

VBScript is one of the two scripting languages provided by Microsoft for the WSH. Like JScript, VBScript provides a complete programming language including statements, operators, conditional flow control, looping, and a powerful object model that provides access to a full range of methods and properties.

This appendix is designed to supplement the VBScript overview presented in Chapter 12, "Writing VBScript Scripts." It provides a VBScript reference in the form of a collection of organized tables. Each table provides summary information about a particular aspect of VBScript.

Topics covered in this appendix include:

- ◆ VBScript data types
- ◆ VBScript statements
- ◆ VBScript special characters
- ◆ VBScript objects
- ◆ VBScript properties
- ◆ VBScript methods
- ◆ VBScript functions
- ◆ VBScript operators
- ◆ VBScript constants
- ◆ VBScript events
- ◆ VBScript error messages

VBScript Data Types

VBScript supports a single data type known as a variant. A variant can contain different kinds of data and VBScript treats it differently depending on how it is used. For example, a variant acts like a string when it contains a string value and a number when it contains a numeric value.

> **NOTE**
>
> You can control how VBScript interprets numeric characters by adding or removing quotation marks. For example, a value of 44 is treated as a numeric value, whereas a value of "44" is treated as a string.

A variant can be further classified into a number of subtypes, each of which represents a different type of value. Table C.1 lists all of the VBScript supported data types.

Table C.1   VBScript Data Subtypes

Subtype	Description
Empty	An uninitialized variant.
Null	A variant to a null value.
Boolean	A value of True or False.
Byte	An integer whose value is between 0 and 255.
Integer	An integer whose value is between -32,768 and 32,767.
Currency	A currency value between -922,337,203,685,477.5808 and 922,337,203,685,477.5807.
Long	An integer value whose range is between -2,147,483,648 and 2,147,483,647.
Single	A floating-point number whose range is between -3.402823E38 and -1.401298E-45 or 1.401298E-45 and 3.402823E38.
Double	A floating-point number whose range is between -4.94065645841247E-324 and -1.79769313486232E308 or 1.79769313486232E308 and 4.94065645841247E-324 .
Date	A number representing a date between January 1, 100 and December 31, 9999.
String	A string up to two billion characters long.
Object	An object.
Error	An error number.

VBScript Statements

Like any programming language, VBScript consists of a collection of predefined statements. The statements that comprise the VBScript programming language are listed in Table C.2.

Table C.2   VBScript Scripting Statements

Statement	Description
Call	Redirects flow control in the script to a procedure.
Class	Defines a class name.
Const	Defines a constant.
Dim	Defines a VBScript variable.
Do...Loop	Repeats a group of statements as long as a condition is True or until the condition becomes True.
Erase	Reinitializes the elements in an array.
Execute	Runs the specified statement.
ExecuteGlobal	Runs the specified statement in a script's global namespace.
Exit	Terminates a loop, sub, or function.
For...Next	Repeats a loop a specified number of times.
For Each...Next	Iteratively processes the contents of an array or collection.
Function	Defines a function name and its arguments.
If...Then...Else	Performs the execution of one or more statements based on the value of the tested expression.
On Error	Turns on error-handling.
Option Explicit	Explicitly declares all variables in your script.
Private	Defines a private variable.
Property Get	Defines a property name and its arguments and returns its value.
Property Let	Defines a property procedure's name and arguments.
Property Set	Defines a property procedure's name and arguments.
Public	Defines a public variable.
Randomize	Initializes the random-number generator.
ReDim	Defines or redefines dynamic-array variables.

Table C.2 VBScript Scripting Statements

Statement	Description
Rem	Used to place comments in scripts.
Select Case	Defines a collection of tests and executes only one based on the value of an expression.
Set	Assigns object references to variables.
Sub	Defines a Sub name and its arguments.
While...Wend	Performs the execution of one or more statements as long as the specified condition remains True.
With	Associates a series of statements that are to be executed for a specified object.

Special Characters

There are a number of characters in VBScript that require special attention. These characters must be escaped (using the \ character) in order to use them as text within your scripts. Table C.3 identifies each of these special characters.

Table C.3 VBScript Special Characters

Character	Description
$	Matches the position at the end of a string.
( )	Identifies the start and ending of a subexpression.
*	Matches a subexpression for zero or more occurrences.
+	Matches a subexpression for one or more occurrences.
.	Matches a single character.
[	Identifies the start of a bracketed expression.
?	Matches a subexpression for zero or one occurrence.
\	Identifies the character that follows as a special character.
^	Matches the position starting at the beginning of a string.
{	Identifies the start of a quantifier expression.
|	Specifies a choice condition.

VBScript Core Objects

VBScript provides its own object model. These objects provide access to a collection of properties and methods that your scripts can then access. The methods and properties provided by these core objects provide the capability to perform an assortment of tasks such as create and work with arrays, access error messages, access mathematical constants, and manipulate strings. Table C.4 provides a complete listing of VBScript's core objects.

Table C.4   **VBScript Objects**

Object	Description
`Class`	Provides access to the events.
	Properties: N/A.
	Methods: N/A.
	Events: `Initialize`, `Terminate`.
`Dictionary`	Stores data key, item pairs.
	Properties: `CompareMode`, `Count`, `Item`, `Key`.
	Methods: `Add`, `Exists`, `Items`, `Keys`, `Remove`, `RemoveAll`.
	Events: N/A.
`Err`	Provides details about run-time errors.
	Properties: `Description`, `HelpContext`, `HelpFile`, `Number`, `Source`.
	Methods: `Clear`, `Raise`.
	Events: N/A.
`FileSystemObject`	Provides access to the entire file system.
	Properties: `Drives`.
	Methods: `BuildPath`, `CopyFile`, `CopyFolder`, `CreateFolder`, `CreateTextFile`, `DeleteFile`, `DeleteFolder`, `DriveExists`, `FileExists`, `FolderExists`, `GetAbsolutePathName`, `GetBaseName`, `GetDrive`, `GetDriveName`, `GetExtensionName`, `GetFile`, `GetFileName`, `GetFolder`, `GetParentFolderName`, `GetSpecialFolder`, `GetTempName`, `MoveFile`, `MoveFolder`, `OpenTextFile`.
	Events: N/A.

Table C.4 **VBScript Objects**

Object	Description
Match	Accesses the read-only properties of a regular expression match.
	Properties: FirstIndex, Length, Value.
	Methods: N/A.
	Events: N/A.
Matches Collection	A collection of regular expression Match objects.
	Properties: Count, Item.
	Methods: N/A.
	Events: N/A.
RegExp	Supports regular expressions.
	Properties: Global, IgnoreCase, Pattern.
	Methods: Execute, Replace, Test.
	Events: N/A.
SubMatches Collection	Accesses read-only values of regular expression sub-match strings.
	Properties: Count, Item.
	Methods: N/A.
	Events: N/A.

VBScript Core Object Properties

An object's properties are the attributes of the object. They contain stored values that represent some quality of the object. Table C.5 defines the properties supported by VBScript objects.

Table C.5 **VBScript Properties**

Property	Description
Description	Retrieves an error message.
FirstIndex	Returns the first position of a specified substring in a string.
Global	Changes or retrieves a Boolean value.
HelpContext	Retrieves the context ID of Help file topic.

continues

Table C.5   VBScript Properties *(continued)*

Property	Description
HelpFile	Returns the path to a Help file.
IgnoreCase	Retrieves a Boolean value that indicates whether a pattern search is case-sensitive.
Length	Returns the length of a search string match.
Number	Returns the error number for the specified error.
Pattern	Retrieves the regular expression pattern in a search operation.
Source	Retrieves the name of the object that generates an error.
Value	Returns the value of a search string match.

VBScript Core Object Methods

An object's methods are the actions that objects can take. Methods can be used to control the object or its data. Table C.6 defines the methods supported by VBScript's objects.

Table C.6   VBScript Methods

Method	Description
Clear	Clears an `Err` object's property settings.
Execute	Performs a regular expression search against a string.
Raise	Used to simulate a run-time error.
Replace	Replaces text in a regular expression search.
Test	Performs a regular expression search against a string.

VBScript Run-time Objects

In addition to VBScript core objects, VBScript also provides a collection of run-time objects. These objects provide methods and properties that your scripts can use to access a computer's file system. Table C.7 provides a summary of VBScript's run-time objects.

Table C.7   VBScript Run-time (`FileSystem`) Objects

Object	Description
Dictionary	Stores data key, item pairs.
	Properties: CompareMode, Count, Item, Key.
	Methods: Add, Exists, Items, Keys, Remove, RemoveAll.
Drive	Provides access to a disk drive's properties.
	Properties: AvailableSpace, DriveLetter, DriveType, FileSystem, FreeSpace, IsReady, Path, RootFolder, SerialNumber, ShareName, TotalSize, VolumeName.
	Methods: N/A.
Drives Collection	Provides information about system drives.
	Properties: Count, Item.
	Methods: N/A.
File	Provides access to a file's properties.
	Properties: Attributes, DateCreated, DateLastAccessed, DateLastModified, Drive, Name, ParentFolder, Path, ShortName, ShortPath, Size, Type.
	Methods: Copy, Delete, Move, OpenAsTextStream.
Files Collection	Provides access to files contained in a folder.
	Properties: Count, Item.
	Methods: N/A.
FileSystemObject	Provides access to the entire file system.
	Properties: Drives.
	Methods: BuildPath, CopyFile, CopyFolder, CreateFolder, CreateTextFile, DeleteFile, DeleteFolder, DriveExists, FileExists, FolderExists, GetAbsolutePathName, GetBaseName, GetDrive, GetDriveName, GetExtensionName, GetFile, GetFileName, GetFolder, GetParentFolderName, GetSpecialFolder, GetTempName, MoveFile, MoveFolder, OpenTextFile.
Folder	Provides access to a folder's properties.
	Properties: Attributes, DateCreated, DateLastAccessed, DateLastModified, Drive, Files, IsRootFolder, Name, ParentFolder, Path, ShortName, ShortPath, Size, SubFolders, Type.

continues

Table C.7 VBScript Run-time (FileSystem) Objects *(continued)*

Object	Description
	Methods: Copy, Delete, Move, OpenAsTextStream.
Folders Collection	Provides access to the folders contained within another folder.
	Properties: Count, Item.
	Methods: Add.

VBScript Run-time Properties

Each of the VBScript run-time objects has its own set of properties. These properties are the attributes of the object and contain stored values that represent some quality of the object. Your scripts can reference and change the value of these properties. Table C.8 defines the properties supported by VBScript's run-time objects.

Table C.8 VBScript Run-time (FileSystem) Properties

Property	Description
AtEndOfLine	Returns a value of True or False depending on whether the file pointer immediately precedes the end-of-line marker in a TextStream file.
AtEndOfStream	Returns a value of True or False depending on whether the file pointer is at the end of a TextStream file.
Attributes	Gets or changes file and folder attributes.
AvailableSpace	Retrieves the amount of free space available on the specified local or network drive.
Column	Retrieves the column number of character position in a TextStream file.
CompareMode	Gets or changes the comparison mode that is used to compare a Dictionary object's string keys.
Count	Counts and returns the collection or Dictionary object items.
DateCreated	Retrieves the creation date and time of a file or folder.
DateLastAccessed	Retrieves the last access date and time of a file or folder.
DateLastModified	Retrieves the modification date and time of a file or folder.

Table C.8   VBScript Run-time `(FileSystem)` Properties

Property	Description
Drive	Retrieves the drive letter where the specified file or folder resides.
DriveLetter	Retrieves the drive letter of local or network drive.
Drives	Creates a `Drives` collection made up of all the `Drive` objects on the local machine.
DriveType	Retrieves a value that indicates the specified drive's type.
Files	Creates a `Files` collection made up of all `File` objects within the specified folder.
FileSystem	Retrieves the file system type on the specified drive.
FreeSpace	Retrieves the amount of free space available to the user for the specified local or network drive.
IsReady	Returns a value of `True` or `False` depending on whether the specified drive is ready.
IsRootFolder	Returns a value of `True` or `False` depending on whether the specified folder is the root folder.
Item	Gets or changes an item based on the specified `Dictionary` object key.
Key	Sets a `Dictionary` object key.
Line	Retrieves the current line number in the `TextStream` file.
Name	Gets or changes the name of a file or folder.
ParentFolder	Retrieves the parent folder object of the specified file or folder.
Path	Retrieves the specified file, folder, or drive's path.
RootFolder	Retrieves a `Folder` object that represents the root folder for the specified drive.
SerialNumber	Retrieves the decimal serial number that identifies a disk volume.
ShareName	Retrieves a drive's network share name.
ShortName	Retrieves the 8.3 character short name of a file or folder.
ShortPath	Retrieves the short path associated with the 8.3 character file name.
Size	Returns the byte size of the specified file or folder.
SubFolders	Creates a `Folders` collection made up of the folder within the specified folder.

continues

Table C.8   VBScript Run-time (`FileSystem`) Properties *(continued)*

Property	Description
TotalSize	Retrieves the number of bytes left on the specified local or network drive.
Type	Retrieves information about a file or folder's type.
VolumeName	Gets or changes a drive's volume name.

VBScript Run-time Methods

Each VBScript run-time object has its own collection of run-time methods. These run-time methods can be used to control the object and its data. Table C.9 defines the run-time methods supported by VBScript's run-time objects.

Table C.9   VBScript Run-time (`FileSystem`) Methods

Method	Description
Add (Dictionary)	Adds a key and item pair to the specified `Dictionary` object.
Add (Folders)	Adds a `Folder` to the specified collection.
BuildPath	Adds a name to the path.
Close	Terminates an open `TextStream` file.
Copy	Copies a file or folder to the specified location.
CopyFile	Copies one or more files to a different location.
CopyFolder	Recursively copies a folder to a different location.
CreateFolder	Creates the specified folder.
CreateTextFile	Creates a file and a `TextStream` object to be used when reading and writing to the file.
Delete	Removes the specified file or folder.
DeleteFile	Removes the specified file.
DeleteFolder	Removes the contents of the specified folder.
DriveExists	Returns a `True` or `False` value depending on whether the specified drive exists.
Exists	Returns a `True` or `False` value depending on whether the specified key exists in the `Dictionary` object.

Table C.9   VBScript Run-time (`FileSystem`) Methods

Method	Description
FileExists	Returns a `True` or `False` value depending on whether the specified file exists.
FolderExists	Returns a `True` or `False` value depending on whether the specified folder exists.
GetAbsolutePathName	Retrieves the complete path name.
GetBaseName	Retrieves the base file name without its file extension.
GetDrive	Retrieves the `Drive` object representing the drive in the specified path.
GetDriveName	Retrieves a string that contains the name of the drive for the specified path.
GetExtensionName	Retrieves a string that contains the file's extension as specified by its path.
GetFile	Retrieves a `File` object based on the files specified in the path.
GetFileName	Retrieves the last file name or folder of the specified path.
GetFileVersion	Retrieves the version number of the specified file.
GetFolder	Retrieves the `Folder` object of the folder in the specified path.
GetParentFolderName	Retrieves a string representing the name of the parent folder.
GetSpecialFolder	Retrieves the name of the specified folder.
GetTempName	Retrieves a temporary file or folder name.
Items	Returns an array holding all items in a `Dictionary` object.
Keys	Returns an array holding all keys in a `Dictionary` object.
Move	Moves a file or folder to the specified location.
MoveFile	Moves one or more files to the specified location.
MoveFolder	Moves one or more folders to the specified location.
OpenAsTextStream	Opens a file and returns a `TextStream` object to use when referencing the file.
OpenTextFile	Opens a file and returns a `TextStream` object to use when referencing the file.
Read	Returns a string based on a specified number of characters from a `TextStream` file.

continues

Table C.9   **VBScript Run-time (`FileSystem`) Methods** *(continued)*

Method	Description
ReadAll	Reads the whole `TextStream` file and returns its contents as a string.
ReadLine	Reads a line in a `TextStream` file and returns it as a string.
Remove	Deletes a key, item pair in a `Dictionary` object.
Skip	Skips the specified number of character positions when processing a `TextStream` file.
SkipLine	Skips the next line when processing a `TextStream` file.
Write	Writes a string in a `TextStream` file.
WriteBlankLines	Writes a number of newline characters in a `TextStream` file.
WriteLine	Writes a string and a newline character in a `TextStream` file.

VBScript Functions

VBScript functions allow you to organize your scripts into procedures. VBScript provides a large collection of predefined scripts that you can execute as specified in Table C.10.

Table C.10   **Pre-Defined VBScript Functions**

Function	Description
Abs	Returns a number's absolute value.
Array	Returns an array based on the supplied argument list.
Asc	Returns the ANSI code of the first letter in the supplied argument.
Atn	Inverse trigonometric function that returns the arctangent of the argument.
CBool	Converts an expression to a Boolean value and returns the result.
CByte	Converts an expression to a variant subtype of `Byte` and returns the result.

Table C.10 **Pre-Defined VBScript Functions**

Function	Description
CCur	Converts an expression to a variant subtype of Currency and returns the result.
Cdate	Converts an expression to a variant subtype of Date and returns the result.
CDbl	Converts an expression to a variant subtype of double and returns the result.
Chr	Returns a character based on the supplied ANSI code.
Cint	Converts an expression to a variant subtype of Integer and returns the result.
CLng	Converts an expression to a variant subtype of Long and returns the result.
Cos	Trigonometric function that returns the cosine of the argument.
CreateObject	Creates an Automation object and returns a reference to it.
CSng	Converts an expression to a variant subtype of Single and returns the result.
CStr	Converts an expression to a variant subtype of String and returns the result.
Date	Returns the current date.
DateAdd	Adds an additional time interval to the current date and returns the result.
DateDiff	Compares two dates and returns the number of intervals between them.
DatePart	Returns a portion of the specified date.
DateSerial	Returns a Variant (subtype Date) based on the supplied year, month, and day.
DateValue	Converts a string expression into a variant of type Date and returns the result.
Day	Converts an expression representing a date into a number between 1 and 31 and returns the result.
Eval	Returns the results of an evaluated expression.
Exp	Returns the value of an argument raised to a power.
Filter	Returns an array based on a filtered set of elements using supplied filter criteria.

continues

Table C.10   Pre-Defined VBScript Functions *(continued)*

Function	Description
FormatCurrency	Returns an expression that has been formatted as a currency value.
FormatDateTime	Returns an expression that has been formatted as a date or time value.
FormatNumber	Returns an expression that has been formatted as a numeric value.
FormatPercent	Returns an expression that has been formatted as a percentage (including the accompanying %).
GetLocale	Returns the locale ID.
GetObject	Returns a reference for an Automation object.
GetRef	Returns a reference for a procedure.
Hex	Returns a hexadecimal string that represents a number.
Hour	Returns a whole number representing an hour in a day (0 – 23).
InputBox	Returns user input from a dialog box.
InStr	Returns the starting location of the first occurrence of a substring within a string.
InStrRev	Returns the ending location of the first occurrence of a substring within a string.
Int	Returns the integer portion from the supplied number.
IsArray	Returns a value of True or False depending on whether a variable is an array.
IsDate	Returns a value of True or False depending on whether an expression is properly formatted for a data conversion.
IsEmpty	Returns a value of True or False depending on whether a variable is initialized.
IsNull	Returns a value of True or False depending on whether an expression is set to Null.
IsNumeric	Returns a value of True or False depending on whether an expression evaluates to a number.
IsObject	Returns a value of True or False depending on whether an expression has a valid reference for an Automation object.
Join	Returns a string that has been created by concatenating the contents of an array.
Lbound	Returns the smallest possible subscript for the specified array dimension.

Table C.10 Pre-Defined VBScript Functions

Function	Description
Lcase	Returns a lowercase string.
Left	Returns characters from the left side of a string.
Len	Returns a number or string's character length.
LoadPicture	Returns a picture object.
Log	Returns the natural log of the specified argument.
Ltrim	Trims any leading blank spaces from a string and returns the result.
Mid	Returns a number of characters from a string based on the supplied start and length arguments.
Minute	Returns a number representing a minute within an hour in range of 0 − 59.
Month	Returns a number representing a month within a year in the range of 1 − 12.
MonthName	Returns a string containing the name of the specified month.
MsgBox	Returns a value specifying the button a user clicks on in a dialog box.
Now	Returns the current date and time.
Oct	Returns a string containing an octal number representation.
Replace	Returns a string after replacing occurrences of one substring with another substring.
RGB	Returns a number that represents an RGB color.
Right	Returns characters from the right side of a string.
Rnd	Returns a randomly generated number.
Round	Returns a number after rounding it by a specified number of decimal positions.
Rtrim	Trims any trailing blank spaces from a string and returns the result.
ScriptEngine	Returns a string identifying the current scripting language.
ScriptEngineBuildVersion	Returns the scripting engine's build number.

continues

Table C.10   Pre-Defined VBScript Functions *(continued)*

Function	Description
ScriptEngineMajorVersion	Returns the scripting engine's major version number.
ScriptEngineMinorVersion	Returns the scripting engine's minor version number.
Second	Returns a number representing a second within a minute in range of 0 – 59.
Sgn	Returns the sign of the specified argument.
Sin	Trigonometric function that returns the sine of the argument.
Space	Returns a string consisting of a number of blank spaces.
Split	Organizes a string into an array.
Sqr	Returns a number's square root.
StrComp	Returns a value and specifies the results of a string comparison.
String	Returns a character string made up of a repeated sequence of characters.
StrReverse	Reverses the character order of a string and returns the result.
Tan	Trigonometric function that returns the tangent of the argument.
Time	Returns a Variant of subtype Date that has been set equal to the system's current time.
Timer	Returns a value representing the number of seconds that have passed since midnight.
TimeSerial	Returns a Variant of subtype Date that has been set equal to containing the specified hour, minute, and second.
TimeValue	Returns a Variant of subtype Date that has been set using the specified time.
Trim	Returns a string after removing any leading or trailing spaces.
TypeName	Returns a string that specified the Variant subtype information regarding the specified variable.
Ubound	Returns the largest subscript for the specified array dimension.

Table C.10 Pre-Defined VBScript Functions

Function	Description
Ucase	Returns an uppercase string.
VarType	Returns a string that specified the `Variant` subtype information regarding the specified variable.
Weekday	Returns a whole number in the form of 1 – 7, which represents a given day in a week.
WeekdayName	Returns a string identifying a particular day in the week.
Year	Returns a number specifying the year.

VBScript Operators

Like JScript, VBScript supports a rich collection of operators that you use when working with and manipulating values. The next two sections outline two categories of commonly used VBScript operators.

Manipulating Numeric Values

Arithmetic operators allow you to alter a value when using numeric equations. The numeric operators supported by VBScript are listed in Table C.11.

Table C.11 VBScript Arithmetic Operators

Operator	Description	Example
+	Add	i = 2 + 1
–	Subtract	i = 2 - 1
*	Multiply	i = x * 2
/	Divide	i = x / 2
Mod	Modulus	i = 7 Mod 2
–x	Reverses the sign of x	i = -3 * 3
^	Exponentiation	i = 5^5

Comparison operators test the value of two variables. Comparison operators are generally used in conjunction with the IF statement to implement conditional logic within your scripts. Table C.12 lists the comparison operators supported by VBScript.

Table C.12 VBScript Comparison Operators

Operator	Description	Example
=	Equal	x = y
<>	Not equal	x <> y
>	Greater than	x > y
<	Less than	x < y
>=	Greater than or equal to	x >= y
<=	Less than or equal to	x <= y

Order of Precedence within Numeric Expressions

The order in which numeric data is manipulated in an expression is determined by a strict set of rules. Table C.13 defines the rules that define this order of precedence.

Table C.13 VBScript Order of Precedence

Operators	Description
\	Escape
(), (?:), (?=), []	Parentheses and brackets
*, +, ?, {n}, {n,}, {n,m}	Quantifiers
^, $, \metacharacter	Anchors and sequences
		Alternation

Note: All operations are evaluated from left to right.

VBScript Constants

In VBScript, a constant is similar to a variable in that it can contain a string or number. However, unlike variables, the value of a constant never changes. Constants provide your scripts with values that you can count on without actually knowing them. VBScript constants are outlined in Table C.14.

Table C.14 VBScript Constants

Constant	Description
Color	Provides a list of color constants.
Comparison	Provides a list of constants that can be used in comparisons.
Date and Time	Provides a list of constants for the days of the week constants and a list of related date constants.
Date Format	Provides a list of constants that can be used to format date and time values.
Miscellaneous	Provides a list of constants that are not placed in other constant categories.
MsgBox	Provides a list of buttons and icons that make up a message box.
String	Provides a list of string-related constants.
Tristate	Provides a constant for use with regional computer settings and miscellaneous VBScript-related constants.
VarType	Provides a list of Variant subtypes.
VBScript	Provides a list of VBScript constant categories.

VBScript Run-time Constants

VBScript expands its available list of constants with a group of run-time constants outlined in Table C.15.

Table C.15 VBScript Run-time Constants

Constant	Description
DriveType	Provides a reference to the following constants:
	Unknown: An undetermined drive type.
	Removable: A drive that supports removable media.
	Fixed: Includes all fixed drives including hard drives.
	Remote: Shared network drives.
	CDROM: CD-ROM drives.
	RAMDisk: Logical drives created using a block of reserved memory.
File Attribute	Provides a reference to the following constants:
	Normal: A normal file without any set attributes.
	ReadOnly: A read-only file.
	Hidden: A hidden file.
	System: A system file.
	Directory: A folder.
	Archive: Identifies whether a file has changed since last backup.
	Alias: A shortcut.
	Compressed: A compressed file.
File Input/Output	Provides a reference to the following constants:
	ForReading: Opens a file in a read only state.
	ForWriting: Opens a file in a read/write state.
	ForAppending: Opens a file and writes to the end of the file without replacing any of its existing contents.
FileSystemObject	The following list describes the various categories of constants provided for the FileSystemObject, along with a brief description:
	DriveType: Identifies available drive types.
	File Attribute: Identifies types of file attributes.
	File Input/Output: Identifies constants that can be used in file input/output operations.
	SpecialFolder: Identifies special folders.

Table C.15   VBScript Run-time Constants

Constant	Description
SpecialFolder	Provides a reference to the following constants:
	WindowsFolder: The Windows folder that contains Windows operating system files.
	SystemFolder: The System folder that contains various device drivers and library files.
	TemporaryFolder: The Windows Temp folder.

VBScript Events

VBScript supports two types of events that occur when an instance of an associated class is either initialized or terminated. These events are defined in Table C.16.

Table C.16   VBScript Events

Event	Description
Initialize	Executes when an instance of an associated class is initialized.
Terminate	Executes when an instance of an associated class is terminated.

VBScript Error Messages

During script development errors will occur. VBScript errors are reported in the form of error messages. VBScript errors include syntax and run-time errors. The next two sections provide a list of these error messages.

Syntax Error Messages

VBScript syntax errors occur when a VBScript statement is improperly structured. These errors occur when the script is loading and before the script gets a chance to execute. Table C.17 provides a review of VBScript's syntax error messages.

Table C.17   VBScript Syntax Errors

Error	Description
1001	Out of Memory
1002	Syntax error
1005	Expected (
1006	Expected)
1010	Expected identifier
1011	Expected =
1012	Expected If
1013	Expected To
1013	Invalid number
1014	Expected End
1014	Invalid character
1015	Expected Function
1015	Unterminated string constant
1016	Expected Sub
1017	Expected Then
1018	Expected Wend
1019	Expected Loop
1020	Expected Next
1021	Expected Case
1022	Expected Select
1022	Expected expression
1024	Expected statement
1025	Expected end of statement
1026	Expected integer constant
1027	Expected While or Until
1028	Expected While, Until, or end of statement
1029	Expected With
1030	Identifier too long
1037	Invalid use of Me keyword

Table C.17   VBScript Syntax Errors

Error	Description
1038	`loop` without do
1039	Invalid `exit` statement
1040	Invalid `for` loop control variable
1041	Name redefined
1042	Must be first statement on the line
1044	Cannot use parentheses when calling a `Sub`
1045	Expected literal constant
1046	Expected `In`
1047	Expected `Class`
1048	Expected `Let` or `Set` or `Get` in property declaration
1048	Must be defined inside a class
1049	Expected `Property`
1051	Number of arguments must be consistent across properties specification
1052	Cannot have multiple default property/method in a class
1053	Class initialize or terminate do not have arguments
1054	Property `Set` or `Let` must have at least one argument
1055	Unexpected `Next`
1057	`Default` specification must also specify Public
1058	`Default` specification can only be on Property Get

Run-time Error Messages

VBScript run-time errors occur after the script has loaded and begun its execution. These types of errors occur when the script attempts to perform an invalid action such as attempting to reference a resource that does not exist. Table C.18 provides a review of VBScript's run-time error messages.

Table C.18 VBScript Run-time Errors

Error	Description
5	Invalid procedure call or argument `Overflow Out of Memory`
9	Subscript out of range
10	This array is fixed or temporarily locked Division by zero
13	Type mismatch
14	Out of string space
17	Can't perform requested operation
28	Out of stack space
35	Sub or function not defined
48	Error in loading DLL Internal error
91	Object variable not set
92	For loop not initialized
94	Invalid use of `Null`
424	Object required ActiveX component can't create object
430	Class doesn't support `Automation` file name or class name not found during `Automation` operation
438	Object doesn't support this property or method
445	Object doesn't support this action
447	Object doesn't support current locale setting
448	Named argument not found
451	Object not a collection
450	Wrong number of arguments or invalid property assignment
458	Variable uses an `Automation` type not supported in VBScript
462	The remote server machine does not exist or is unavailable
481	Invalid picture
500	Variable is undefined
502	Object not safe for scripting
503	Object not safe for initializing
504	Object not safe for creating
505	Invalid or unqualified reference

Table C.18   VBScript Run-time Errors

Error	Description
506	Class not defined
507	An exception occurred
5008	Illegal assignment
5017	Syntax error in regular expression
5018	Unexpected quantifier
5019	Expected] in regular expression
5020	Expected) in regular expression
5021	Invalid range in character set

TIP

Additional VBScript reference materials can be found at
http://msdn/Microsoft.com/scripting.

Glossary

@—A Windows shell script statement that allows you to turn off the display of a command.

ActivePerl—A complete stand-alone implementation of Perl that runs on Windows, Linux, and Solaris operating systems.

ActivePython—A Python scripting engine for WSH.

Argument—A piece of data passed to a script or function as input.

Array—An indexed list of values that can be processed as a unit.

Assoc—A Windows command that displays and changes file name extension associations.

At—A Windows command that allows you to schedule the automated execution of command, utilities, scripts, and applications.

Batch files—Plain-text files containing a sequential list of commands.

Batch mode—The mode that the Windows shell operates in when processing a shell script.

Boolean—A JScript value indicating a `true` or `false` condition.

Break—A JScript statement that terminates the execution of a loop, label, or switch.

Call—A shell scripting statement that works like the `goto` statement except that it ensures that when the called procedure terminates control, it returns to the first statement that follows the call statement.

cd (Chdir)—A Windows command that changes the current directory.

Chaining—Occurs when one script executes another script and terminates its own execution.

Cls—A Windows command that clears the screen and displays the command prompt.

Cmd—A command used to start a new Windows shell session.

Cmd switches—Optional parameters that affect the execution of a command.

Cmdextversion—An environment variable that specifies the current version of the command shell.

Color—A Windows command that sets the foreground and background colors for the Windows console.

Command console—A window that provides the interface for running and interacting with the Windows shell.

Command histroy—Text stored in command shell's history buffer that records every shell command that you type and makes them available for later recall.

Comments—Statements that are added to scripts that are ignored by the execution host but that provide valuable information to anyone editing or reading the script.

Compound command—A shell scripting command that allows you to chain together multiple commands on the same line by using a collection of reserved characters known as compound command symbols.

Comspec—An environment variable that identifies the location of the Windows shell.

Concatenation—The process of combining two or more strings into a single string.

Constants—VBScript elements that contain static values that never change.

Continue—A JScript statement that interrupts the current iteration of a loop without terminating the loop itself.

Copy—A Windows command that copies files from one location to another.

Core Object Model (COM)—An ActiveX control named WSH.ocx that provides access to Windows objects that JScripts and VBScripts use to interact with computer and network resources.

CScript—A WSH script execution host that provides support for text-based scripts.

Date—A Windows command that displays or changes the date.

Del—A Windows command that deletes one or more files.

Dense array—An array that is populated with data at the time of its creation.

Dictionary—A JScript or VBScript run-time object that stores data key, item pairs.

Dim—A VBScript statement used to define a variable.

Dir—A Windows command that displays a listing of the specified directory.

Do While—A JScript or VBScript statement that creates a loop that processes while a specified condition is true.

Do Until—A VBScript statement that creates a loop that processes until a specified condition becomes true.

Drive—A JScript or VBScript run-time object that provides access to a disk drive's properties.

Drives—A JScript or VBScript run-time collection that provides information about system drives.

Dumpel—A Windows NT or 2000 Resource Kit command-line utility that lets you copy the contents of event logs into tab-delaminated text files.

Echo—A Windows command that enables or disables command echoing.

Endlocal—Terminates a local scope, therefore causing any changes made to variables within the temporary scope to be discarded.

Erase—A Windows command that deletes one or more files.

Escaping—A programming technique used by JScripts that allows reserved characters to be used in script statements by placing a carat ^ character in front of the reserved character.

Exit—A Windows command that terminates the Windows Console and closes the command shell.

Expression—A statement that evaluates the value of variables and constants.

External commands—Commands that exist as executable files somewhere on your computer's hard drive.

File—A JScript or VBScript run-time object that provides access to a file's properties.

Files collection—A JScript or VBScript run-time collection that provides access to files contained in a folder.

FileSystemObject—The primary object in the Microsoft scripting run-time library that scripts can use to expose and work with the Windows file system.

Folder—A JScript or VBScript run-time object that provides access to a folder's properties.

Folders collection—A JScript or VBScript run-time collection that provides access to the folders contained within another folder.

For—A scripting command used to establish a loop that can be used to repeat the execution of one or more commands.

For Each..Next—A VBScript statement used to iterate through an object's properties.

For..Next—A VBScript statement that creates and executes a loop a specified number of times.

Function—A VBScript procedure that executes a set of statements and can return a result to the statement that called it.

Global variables—Variables that have been declared outside of a function and that can be referenced from any location within the script.

Goto—A shell script statement that changes processing flow in a script to a line marked with a label.

GUI (Graphical User Interface)—A point-and-click graphical interface used to interact with a computer operating system.

Hostname—An environment variable that contains the name of the current host.

If—A scripting statement that tests for a condition and executes a command when the condition is true.

Interactive mode—The mode that the Windows shell operates in when accepting user commands from the command prompt.

Internal commands—Commands built directly into the shell (cmd.exe).

Interpreted programming language—A scripting language that, instead of being precompiled, is processed one statement at a time at the moment of execution.

Ipconfig—A command that provides TCP/IP configuration information.

JavaScript—A programming language developed by Netscape that supports the development of client-side scripts that execute inside of Internet browsers.

<?job ?>—An XML tag that controls error handling and debugging.

<job>—An XML tag that identifies a specific job within a .wsf file.

.js—A JScript file extension.

JScript—Microsoft's implementation of Netscape's JavaScript Web scripting language, which can serve as a scripting engine for the WSH.

Label—An identifier that can be placed inside a Windows shell script to denote the beginning of a subroutine or procedure. Also a JScript statement that establishes a reference point within a script and can be used to create loops.

Local scope—A VBScript variable scope that is established whenever you declare a variable inside a procedure, thus making the variable inaccessible to other parts of the script.

Local variables—Variables created with a function and that cannot be reference outside of the function.

Logevent—A Windows NT or 2000 Resource Kit command-line utility that lets you write events to one of the Windows Event Viewer logs.

Loop—The process of repeating a set of instructions indefinitely.

Md (Mkdir)—A Windows command that creates a directory or subdirectory.

Method—A function associated with an object.

Modifiers—Arguments that modify the behavior of a switch.

Move—A Windows command that moves files from one location to another.

MsgBox—A VBScript function that displays a message and asks the user to click a response.

Multi-dimensional array—A VBScript array that supports up to 60 dimensions.

Nesting—Occurs when one script executes another script and then resumes its own execution when the called script terminates.

Net accounts—A Windows networking command that configures password policies.

Net continue—A Windows networking command that activates a suspended service making it available to users.

Net group—A Windows networking command that configures global group membership.

Net localgroup—A Windows networking command that configures local group membership.

Net pause—A Windows networking command that suspends a service. Pausing a service allows users currently using the service to complete their work but denies access to other users.

Net print—A Windows networking command that you can use to view and manage print queues.

Net start—A Windows networking command that starts a stopped service making it available to users.

Net stop—A Windows networking command that stops an active service. This immediately terminates any existing user activity with the service and prevents any new activity until the service is started.

Net user—A Windows networking command that configures user accounts.

Null—An empty value.

Number—A JScript numeric value.

Number_of_processors—An environment variable that specifies the number of processors or CPUs on the system.

<object>—An XML tag that specifies a object for reference within the .wsf file.

Object—A programming construct that contains its own properties and methods.

OS—An environment variable that identifies the version of Windows being run.

<package>—An XML tag that allows you to include more than one job within a .wsf file.

Parameters—Arguments that are passed to a command, utility, script, or application for processing.

Path—A Windows command that establishes a search path that Windows uses to locate executable files. Also an environment variable that contains a list of directories called the search path that the shell can use when looking for commands.

PATHEXT—An environment variable that lists all the file extensions that Windows associates with executable files (such as .com, .exe, .bat, and .cmd).

Pause—A Windows command that suspends script execution until the user presses a key to resume processing.

Perl (Practical Extraction and Reporting Language)—A scripting language with roots in the UNIX operating system.

PerlScript—A component of ActivePerl that provides a Perl scripting engine for the WSH.

Popd—Changes the current drive and folder settings back to the values saved by the `pushd` command.

Procedures—Occurs when a call statement executes an internal procedure or external script and then resumes execution when the called procedure or script terminates.

Program—A collection of stored programming statements that constitute a script or application.

Prompt—A Windows command that changes the Windows command prompt.

Property—A variable associated with an object.

Pushd—A shell script statement that changes to a specified directory and stores the previous directory for later reference by the `popd` command.

Python—A scripting language named after the comedic troupe Monty Python that is popular among the Linux community.

Rd—A Windows command that deletes a specified directory.

ReDim—A VBScript statement that lets you create dynamic arrays that can later be resized.

Redirection—A powerful programming technique that alters the flow of input or output to or from standard input, standard output, or standard error.

<reference>—An XML tag that provides references to external libraries.

Registry—An internal repository used by the Windows operating system to store configuration information including system, software, hardware, application, and user information.

Rem—A Windows shell script statement that allows comments to be added to scripts.

Ren—A Windows command that renames a file or folder.

Rename—A Windows command that renames a file or folder.

Reserved words—Words set aside by a programming language that cannot be used within scripts as variables, label, function, and procedure or subroutines names.

<resource>—An XML tag that specifies static data that can be referenced by scripts within the `.wsf` file.

REXX (Restructured Extended Extractor language)—A scripting language with a strong mainframe and OS/2 heritage.

Rmdir—A Windows command that deletes a specified directory.

Scheduled task folder—A folder that provides a view of all currently scheduled tasks and allows you to modify them.

Scheduled task wizard—A graphical interface that steps you through the process of setting up schedule tasks.

<script>—An XML tag that identifies a specific script within a `.wsf` file.

Script level scope—A VBScript variable scope established whenever you declare a variable outside of a procedure that makes the variable accessible throughout the script.

Scripting engines—Host-independent scripting engines, including JScript and VBScript, that snap into the WSH and allow you to write scripts.

Select Case—A VBScript statement that compares a value against a series of values and executes a logical path based on a matching condition.

Set—A Windows command that displays, creates, modifies, and deletes variables or a VBScript statement that allows you to declare a variable.

Setlocal—Records the value of environment variables in the Windows shell so that they can later be restored to their previous values by the endlocal command.

Shift—A Windows command that changes the position of parameters in a script.

Standard error—The default location where all shell error message output is sent that, by default, is set to the display.

Standard input—The default input source for all shell commands that, by default, is set to the keyboard.

Standard output—The default location where all shell output is sent that, by default, is set to the display.

Start—A command used to start a new Windows shell session in a new Windows Console.

Statement—A line of code in a script.

String—A JScript text string such as "JScript processing complete!".

Sub—A VBScript procedure that executes a set of statements but that does not return any results.

Subroutines—Occurs when a goto statement causes a jump the processing flow from one location in a script to another.

Switch—A JScript statement that compares a value to a series of values and executes the logical path of the first matching condition.

Switches—Arguments that alter the way in which the command is processed in the form of a forward slash followed by one or more characters.

SystemRoot—An environmental variable that specifies the location of the operating system; is usually C:\Winnt.

TextStream—A JScript or VBScript run-time object that provides for sequential file access.

Time—A Windows command that sets and displays the time.

Title—A command that specifies the text that is displayed in the Windows Console's title bar.

Type—A Windows command that displays the contents of a text file without opening it.

URL (Universal Resource Locator)—An address used to identify a site on the World Wide Web.

Username—An environment variable that contains the username of the currently logged on user.

Var—A JScript statement used to define a variable.

Variable tunneling—A Windows shell scripting technique that allows information to be returned from a procedure by turning the endlocal command into a compound command that includes the information to be returned.

Variant—A VBScript variable data type that can hold a number of different types of data.

.vbs—A VBScript file extension.

VBScript—A modified implementation of Microsoft's Visual Basic programming language that can serve as a scripting engine for WSH.

ver—A Windows command that displays the Windows version number.

While—A JScript statement that creates a loop that processes for as long as a condition remains true.

While..Wend—A VBScript statement that creates a loop that processes while a condition remains true.

Windir—An environment variable that specifies the location of the Windows folder.

Windows Shell—A command-line interface for executing Windows commands, Windows shell scripts, and WSH text-based scripts.

With—A JScript statement that provides a convenient way to save keystrokes by associating a set of commands with a particular object.

WScript—A WSH script execution host that supports the use of graphical pop-up dialog boxes. Also the WSH root object that provides access to script arguments and supports the creation of new objects.

WScript.Echo—Displays a message to the command line when executed by the CScript host and via the GUI dialog box when executed using the WScript host.

.wsf—A Windows Script file extension.

WSF (Windows Script File)—Allows you to combine JScript statements and VBScript statements into a single script that is saved using a .wsf file extension.

.wsh—A Windows Script Host file extension.

WSH (Windows Script Host)—A scripting technology that combines a core object model with different scripting engines to provide an advanced scripting environment for Microsoft Windows operating systems.

WshArguments—A WSH object that provides access to command-line arguments.

WshEnvironment—A WSH object that provides access to environment variables.

WshNetwork—A WSH object that provides access to network resources including network printers and shared drives. Also provides other network-related information.

WSH.ocx—An ActiveX control responsible for providing a core object model for all WSH scripts.

WshShell—A WSH object that provides access to environment variables and the Registry. Also supports messaging and shortcut access.

WshShell.Popup—Displays a pop-up message dialog box.

WshShortcut—A WSH object that provides the capability to create shortcuts.

WshSpecialFolders—A WSH object that provides access to Windows folders and the Start menu folder.

WshUrlShortcut—A WSH object that provides the capability to create shortcuts of URLs.

<?XML ?>—Specifies the XML level used in the .wsf file.

XML (Extensible Markup Language)—A language consisting of special markup tags to label Windows Script File elements.

Index